ANTHROPOLOGICAL PAPERS OF
THE UNIVERSITY OF ARIZONA
NUMBER 13

CULTURE CHANGE AND SHIFTING POPULATIONS IN CENTRAL NORTHERN MEXICO

WILLIAM B. GRIFFEN

THE UNIVERSITY OF ARIZONA PRESS
TUCSON 1969

THE UNIVERSITY OF ARIZONA PRESS

S. B. N. 8165-0140-8
L. C. No. 69-16327

CONTENTS

PREFACE v

ABSTRACT ix

1. INTRODUCTION 1

2. SPANISH-INDIAN CONTACT HISTORY: FROM THE FOUNDING OF PARRAS TO THE MID-EIGHTEENTH CENTURY 6

The Parras Missions and Early Bolsón History. 6

The 1644 Revolt 10

The 1650's 16

From 1660 to 1690 31

The 1690's 39

The Early Eighteenth Century 47

The Major Deportations 63

Extinction of the Aborigines and Arrival of the Apaches 70

3. TRIBAL AND BAND HISTORY AND GENERAL DISTRIBUTION 75

4. GENERAL ETHNOGRAPHY. 104

Material Culture 104

   Dress and Decoration 104

   Miscellaneous Material Items 106

   Dwellings 106

   Weapons. 107

   Stolen and Traded Goods 107

Subsistence. 109

   Gathering 110

   Agriculture 111

   Hunting 112

   Horses 114

General Social Organization. 114

   Bands 114

   Marriage 117

   Chieftains 118

Warfare 119

Religious and Ceremonial Life 122

   Dances. 122

   War Ceremonies 124

   Petroglyphs. 126

   Other Ceremonies 126

   Shamans, Curing, and Supernatural Power. 127

   Death and Burial 130

   Other Beliefs and Customs 132

   Games 132

   Counting 133

Language 133

5. SUMMARY OF BAND DISTRIBUTION AND HISTORY 138

6. GREATER BOLSÓN CULTURE CHANGE: ANALYSIS AND INTERPRETATION 143

7. SUMMARY AND CONCLUSIONS 152

APPENDIX 1

   Tribal and Band Groups 154

   Band and Group Names 155

APPENDIX 2

   Hints on Band Composition from the Parras Archives. 171

APPENDIX 3

   Ethnic Composition of the Cabeza "Nation" at Parras, 1693 - 1722 174

APPENDIX 4

   The Marin 1693 Report of Neuva Vizcaya Indians and Comparison with Retana's 1693 List 176

APPENDIX 5

   Chiefs' Names 178

BIBLIOGRAPHY. 180

MAPS

Figure 1.   Nueva Vizcaya   x

Figure 2.   Distribution of major tribal groups in Nueva Vizcaya. N. L., Nuevo
León; S. L. P.; San Luís Potosí.   xi

Figure 3.   Tentative distribution of some bands of the greater Bolsón de Mapiní   xii

PREFACE

The purpose of this paper is to consider the history and processes of culture contact of several now-extinct aboriginal groups who inhabited the area of central northern Mexico during part of the Spanish-Colonial period. Although the general region comprises roughly the area south of the Río Grande, east of the Florido River in Chihuahua, north of the town of Parras and the Laguna district (Torreón, Coahuila), and west of the modern highway that runs south from Piedras Negras to Saltillo, Coahuila, the study concentrates on the desert-dwelling Indians of the western half of this area — principally the eastern portion of the present-day Mexican state of Chihuahua. As a matter of convenience the entire region has been designated by several general terms, such as the "central desert" or the "Greater Bolsón de Mapimí," although it is recognized that some modern geographers object to such extensive use of "Bolsón de Mapimí" (Tamayo 1949: 479).

This region was inhabited by several major tribal groups, each of which consisted of a number of small, named bands. The names of some of these bands were often given a more general application by Spaniards to designate larger tribal groupings or clusters of bands. Therefore quotation marks have been employed in the text for the larger groups where necessary to distinguish between specific bands and the larger ethnic groupings. The term *band* is used for the small, named groups, although their specific characteristics are not yet known to any extent. The word *nation* has been retained here much as the Spaniards employed it — that is, for specific bands as well as for allied groups of bands.

The larger tribal associations are — moving across the area from south to north — the "Laguneros"; some "Coahuileños" (a Spanish appellation for people from Old Coahuila or the region around the city of Monclova which is conserved here), particularly what seem to have been the more southerly peoples such as "Cabezas" and "Salineros" and their associates; the "Tobosos," a more or less centrally located cluster of bands; and the Concho-speaking "Chisos" who inhabited the northern portion of the territory, along the Río Grande and into the Big Bend country of Texas. The period of study runs from about the time of Jesuit entrance and the beginning of missionization in the district of the towns of Parras and of San Pedro de la Laguna in the 1590's to the point of tribal extinction of the "Tobosos" and the "Chisos" during the second quarter of the eighteenth century.

A few of the peoples living in the eastern portion of the region, whom the Spaniards included in the term "Coahuileño," are touched upon. Inasmuch as relatively few data are available on these groups, current definition of the entire general eastern boundary remains quite vague. Such information as has come to light has been included either in the text or in the appendices in order to help complete the over-all picture, as well as for whatever value it may have for future investigators.

When the Spaniards first penetrated the Greater Bolsón de Mapimí country they found a large number of small bands of Indians who were basically nomadic food-gatherers and hunters. Eventually, under contact pressure and with the acceptance of certain foreign items such as the horse, the native societies underwent a number of

[v]

cultural modifications before they became extinct. One of the changes during the European contact period was the extinction and amalgamation of individual bands. This amalgamation has occasioned part of the terminological confusion in the documents as well as in the general literature. Some of the ethnic names were employed in a more or less generic sense; others refer only to a specific band; and a few, such as Toboso, Cocoyome, and Chiso, at one time or another were used to designate both a single band and a group of bands, or what for convenience may be called a tribe.

PURPOSE

The main purpose of this study has been to formulate some generalizations concerning culture contact processes that may be used to guide future research. Herein described are tribal distribution and culture for the early years of contact, the nature of Spanish contact and frontier conditions during this period of the Colony, and the impact that these had upon the native groups — an impact that caused a number of modifications in the aboriginal way of life and, ultimately, its disappearance. Not less important, although only touched upon here, are the changes that Spanish frontier society underwent because of the presence of the native groups.

Some of the culture change that occurred among the natives was directed by Spaniards at such institutions as missions, ranches, and mines. However, for the most part, this study presents a case of "nondirected" culture contact, where the natives themselves were the final authorities on what cultural items they would or would not accept. In broader theoretical terms, it is a case of "specific cultural evolution" (see Sahlins and Service 1960) where one society, in this instance the Spanish, becomes increasingly dominant and eventually causes the demise of the other(s), albeit not entirely by the processes conceived by the policymakers of the dominant society. On the other hand, this is a test case of the notion that human cultures are essentially conservative and modify in the face of "competition" only to the point where they will not have to change further, once the conditions that have instigated the changes have been met and adapted to (Harding 1960: 45-68). This notion seems to be a valid rule, by and large, only in those situations where the native cultural fabric is not rent to shreds by the agents of another society.

In a general sense this report is the history of a region and not of a specific group or groups of natives. The several chapters summarize historical events in order to bring out some of the details of Spanish-Indian contact interaction; they also present some general descriptive ethnography.

The generalizations herein are essentially conservative. For example, mutual identification on a linguistic or other basis of many native tribal and band names or speculations on a number of the ethnographic problems have not been attempted, because a number of untapped sources potentially afford considerably more information than now exists on the area. Likewise, a great number of geographical and place names exist for which the writer has been unable to determine locations, as the places no longer exist or the names have been changed since the Colonial period. Consequently, these names have been cited usually without comment, and the solution of the locations will have to rest on further research. The spellings of tribal and place names, often quite variable, have been left as they exist in the sources. No attempt has been made herein to plot cultural distributions.

difficulty in locating place names

The writer feels keenly the lack of sufficient information on tribal distribution and history in the early years, of adequate ethnographic and linguistic data on the cultural characteristics of the area that might also reveal closer tribal relationships, and, as already noted, of information on the eastern border of the region. However, the principal outlines of the cultural-historical processes of tribal extinction in the Greater Bolsón region can be determined.

The sources utilized are primarily documents originating from the city of Parral, the administrative capital of the Kingdom of Nueva Vizcaya during the Colonial period. Most of these documents are located in the Archives of the City of Parral (El Archivo del Hidalgo del Parral) and are now on microfilm, a copy of which is at the University of Arizona library.

In addition, a number of documents, emanating from Parral and elsewhere, have been consulted at the Bancroft Library, Berkeley, California; the University of Texas in the Latin American Collection and in the Documents Division; the Archivo General de la Nación, México, D.F.; and at the Centro de Documentación, Instituto Nacional de Historia, Castillo de Chapultepec, México, D.F. Further primary and secondary sources include records of parish archives, principally from the city of Parras de la Fuente, Coahuila. Records from the Cathedral of Parral and of the parish of Valle de Allende (called Valle de San Bartolomé during the Colonial Period) also have been consulted.

Of the primary sources, probably the most reliable for cultural information are the Spanish field reports of campaigns and the interrogations of Indians. Less reliable, although also primary, are the general administrative reports. Here, the Jesuit *Anuas* or annual reports are usually better than those of civil administrators. The general works of such Colonial writers as Alegre, Mota y Escobar, Pérez de Ribas, and Arlegui have, of course, also been used. Unfortunately these — particularly the last one — are often very general and lack adequate cultural detail, although they all contain much valuable information.

The writer has concerned himself primarily with the culture history of central northern Mexico and has not detailed the specific Spanish-Indian contact history. Much remains to be written and clarified with regard to battles, campaigns, haciendas as contact institutions, and the like. Documentary collections at Saltillo, Coahuila, Monterrey, Nuevo León, and other places in the eastern sections, as well as those at Guadalajara, Zacatecas, and Durango, should yield additional information that will significantly clarify many of the existing obscurities in the culture history of central northern Mexico.

The writer expresses his indebtedness to all the persons and institutions whose assistance made this study possible. Appreciation goes first to the National Science Foundation, which supported this work under their grant GS-5. Thanks are particularly in order to the people at the several libraries and documentary collections consulted, and to the Fathers at a number of churches in Mexico who permitted examination of their parish records from the seventeenth and eighteenth centuries.

Appreciation is given especially to Dr. Charles C. DiPeso of the Amerind Foundation, Dragoon, Arizona, who originally suggested a historical study concerning some of the extinct and little-known peoples of northern Mexico; to Dr. DiPeso and to Mr. and Mrs. George Chambers, of Tucson, Arizona, who made the microfilming of the Parral archives possible; to Dr. William C. Massey of Texas Christian University, Fort Worth, Texas, for permission to use microfilm copies of documents from the Mexican National Archives; and to Mr. John Q. Ressler, of the Museum of Northern Arizona, who prepared the maps.

It is not possible to list all the people who lent time and energies in one way or another — from general conversation and advice to specific suggestions — during the course of research. These include Dr. Wigberto Jiménez Moreno, Director of the Instituto Nacional de Historia, México, D.F., Dr. Philip W. Powell of the University of California at Santa Barbara, Dr. Woodrow Borah of the University of California at Berkeley, and Professor Eugenio del Hoyo of the Instituto Tecnológico de Monterrey, Monterrey, N.L., México, who gave valuable hints and suggestions. Included also are Dr. Nettie Lee Benson, Curator of the Latin American Collection at the University of Texas, Srta. Gloria

Grajales of the Universidad Nacional de México, and Mr. Basil Hedrick of Fullerton, California, who gave important bibliographical assistance during certain portions of the data collecting.

The writer is particularly grateful for assistance rendered by members of the office staff and faculty of the Department of Anthropology at the University of Arizona, especially by the members of his dissertation committee — Edward H. Spicer, Harry T. Getty, and Edward P. Dozier — who reviewed the manuscript.

Last, but foremost, the writer is indebted to his wife, Joyce, for her editorial help and for her understanding during the preparation of the manuscript.

ABSTRACT

The expansion of Spanish Colonial society into the central regions of northern Mexico set several different processes of change into motion. These modifications occurred on the social and cultural, as well as on the biological, level.

Before the period of European contact, the aborigines in the area lived in a number of almost identical social systems, which were ecologically quite stabilized within the environment of the region. The native social systems were largely independent of each other in a political and economic sense, although they were dependent on each other to some extent ceremonially and for the acquisition of marriage partners.

The bearers of the way of life of the Spanish Colonial society moved into this rather stable situation and disturbed the balance of ecological relationships in several fundamental ways. In the process of the "adaptive radiation" of Spanish society, Spaniards began to exploit the resources of the region in manners different from those employed by the aborigines, and with a different technology, creating a number of new conditions to which the natives were forced to adapt. As the aboriginal societies reoriented a number of their activities, their ties with neighboring societies — including the Spanish — were also modified, although the natives remained politically outside of Spanish domination. The processes of the adjustment of the native societies to the new environmental conditions included a decline in aboriginal population, an amalgamation of native bands or groupings, a greater geographical range of native exploitation of the natural habitat, and an over-all extension of peoples southward, before they disappeared from the scene.

The total process ultimately led to the extinction of the original native societies in the area, while their population was constantly replaced by newcomers from the north, the area of least Spanish concentration. The northern arrivals, however, ultimately vanished and were replaced by still others, a process that constantly involved peoples who lived farther and farther northward. Concurrently, while the native societies were adapting to the new conditions, Spanish frontier society was likewise forced to adjust to the changing native societies.

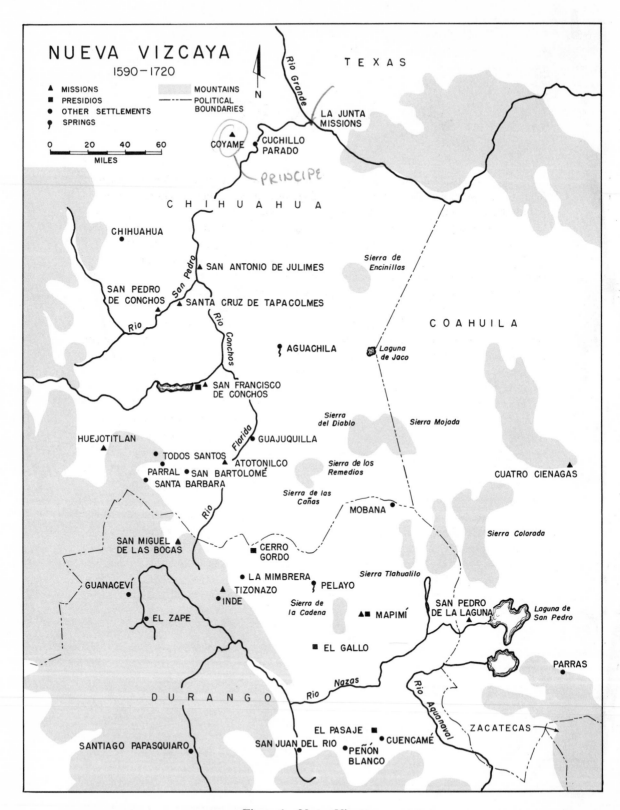

Figure 1. Nueva Vizcaya

Figure 2. Distribution of major tribal groups in Nueva Vizcaya. N. L., Nuevo León; S. L. P.; San Luís Potosí.

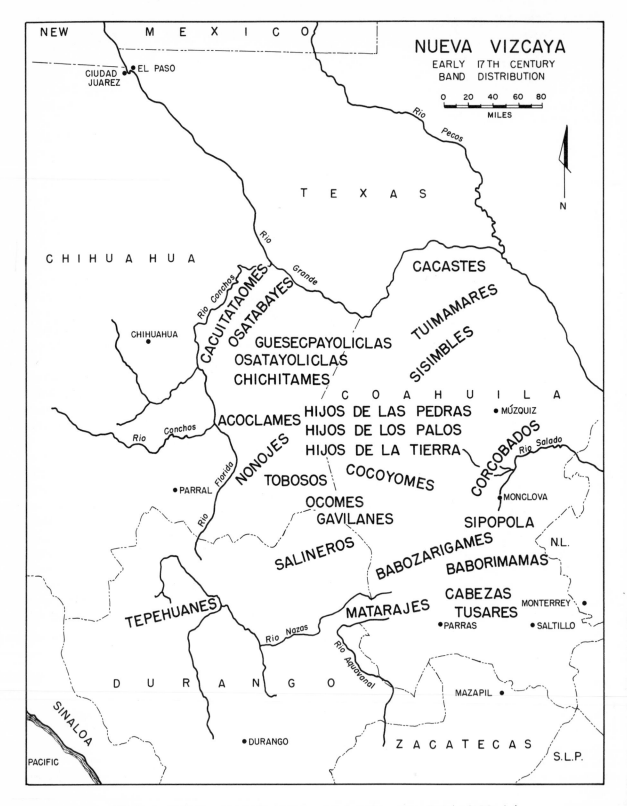

Figure 3.   Tentative distribution of some bands of the greater Bolsón de Mapiní.

1. INTRODUCTION

The portion of the central northern Mexican desert lying north of the Laguna district and extending eastward from the Florido River in Chihuahua into western Coahuila was one of the most inhospitable areas for settlement that the Spaniards encountered in North America. The aboriginal inhabitants eked out a living — most of the time in small, family bands — principally by gathering and hunting. As the Europeans pushed their frontier northward, their settlements eventually bordered the region on the west, south, and east, although they were unable to penetrate permanently into such harsh country.

In the march of Spanish civilization northward, various kinds of relationships were established between the Europeans and the native population. The over-all policy of the Spanish Crown was to Christianize and educate the Indians that they might eventually become participating citizens within Spanish society. The realization of the goals of this general policy was complicated by the differing aims and interests of the various segments of Spanish society, aims and interests that frequently conflicted with the wishes of the Crown. Peaceful relations between European and Indian often broke down for a variety of reasons, and the natives, particularly those whose way of life was essentially nomadic, would withdraw from or rebel against the Spaniards. Often outright hostile relations would be engendered either by slave raiding or by some form of mistreatment by the Spaniards themselves.

Furthermore, the native inhabitants of the backcountry sink of the Greater Bolsón soon learned, for whatever reasons, to exploit the Spanish holdings for their own economic and other benefits. Once hostility between the two groups became established, the Spaniards were forced to deal with the natives on a military basis. The Greater Bolsón de Mapimí country, for the most part free of Spanish settlements, served as a convenient refuge area for disaffected natives, and the nomadic characteristics of the aboriginal inhabitants added to the disaffection that developed among these peoples under the conditions of settlement set up by the members of Spanish society. In counter-reaction to the hostile responses of the natives to Spanish colonization, the Spaniards on more than one occasion were forced to modify their own policies toward the Indians. This Spanish reaction eventually included the establishment of a chain of presidios around the Greater Bolsón country.

The influence that the geography of the Bolsón exerted upon the people who met in it was one of the principal factors in the type of culture contact that occurred between the Spanish and the Indian ways of life. Because Spaniards could not maintain themselves permanently in this region, they had little direct control over the native population. The culture contact, then, was nondirected, since the Indians maintained "free choice" regarding the cultural elements they would incorporate into their own social systems — albeit while often coping with situations that the Spaniards, wittingly or not, had obliged them to meet. The program of "directed" culture change (where Spaniards were constantly directing the acceptance and rejection of cultural elements) — embodied principally in the mission system but also a part of other Spanish frontier institutions such as the *encomienda* — had for the most part minimal effect upon the majority of the native inhabitants who continued to live in the desert back country.

A number of individuals and groups from time to time did have more or less direct contact with Spanish civilization at both missions and haciendas, where they learned of new items and ideas that they later took back to their own territories. While missions for these Indians were founded in several places, it is unknown what percentage of the population over the total period were actually under mission control. Furthermore, in the majority of cases, except possibly in the Parras-Laguna district, such missionization was short-lived. The principal form of direct contact between natives and Spaniards was through warfare and peace negotiations. Geographical circumstances severely limited the use of Spanish resources, technological or otherwise. The culture change that did take place was an adaptation to Spanish society, involving an elaboration and intensification of the native way of life. It did not involve an adoption, wholesale or otherwise, of Spanish culture, although the Indians did accept a number of its elements.

The Greater Bolsón de Mapimí consists of a series of mountains and basins, the region as a whole tilting northward and eastward. The basin of Mayrán or

Laguna of San Pedro in the south is around 3,000 feet above sea level; one basin to the northeast in central Coahuila is only a little over 1,000 feet in altitude. Most of the area has interior drainage except for the western, northern, and eastern borders, which are drained by the Río Grande and its tributaries. In the south the Nazas and Aguanaval rivers flow into the San Pedro basin and keep it abundantly supplied with water. Elsewhere in the area, with the exception of several intermittent lakes and marshes in the interior, the water run-off from the desert ranges is quickly lost in the sandy alluvial fans. In some places non-saline ground water just below the surface can be tapped the year around. The Indians probably utilized this water source, although no direct evidence exists (James 1950: 572-573; Tamayo I 1949: 331, 414; and II 1949: 402).

Tamayo classifies most of the area climatologically in the Koeppen system as BWhw — that is, a hot, desert climate with mild winters, a regular summer rainy season, and sparse xerophytic vegetation. Average annual rainfall is low, from below 200 to somewhat over 400 millimeters in some of the peripheral areas, where steppe conditions sometimes occur. The Mayrán or Laguna district is the most favorable for human habitation and was the most densely populated in Spanish Colonial, as it has been in modern, times. Tamayo (II 1949: 123-124) also suggests the possibility that the climate of the general northern region was somewhat less dry during the Colonial period than it is at present (James 1950: 574-575; Tamayo II 1949: chaps. 17 and 18, and Atlas maps 7 and 8; Vivó 1949: 105, 290-291). Annual variation in precipitation fluctuates somewhat over thirty per cent in contrast to only twenty and ten per cent in areas to the west and south (Wallén 1956: 141ff). Such variability in water supply, aside from the general scantiness of moisture, would have repercussions upon the populations, human and otherwise, of the region. It would preclude the spread of much agriculture into the area because of the lack of firm expectation regarding annual rainfall; and a fluctuating food supply would probably affect, for example, the intensity of ceremonial behavior at certain times.

It is unknown when the peoples of this area began to feel the effects of Spanish conquests to the south of them, although it is quite possible that this was earlier than the historical documentation seems to indicate. New material items and new diseases may have spread fairly rapidly. Within five years after the fall of the Aztec capital of Tenochtitlán in 1521, fingers of Spanish penetration were extending into the Guadalajara area and northward beyond Jilotepec, and within thirty years Spanish adventurers and colonists were moving into the peripheral areas of the Greater Bolsón region.

Silver was discovered in Zacatecas in 1546, and this discovery was followed by a veritable rush of people northward from around the Valley of Mexico and the establishment of the city of Zacatecas two years later (Alessio Robles 1938: 60; Jiménez Moreno 1958: 99-100). While the principal task of the Spaniards for the next thirty or so years was the economic and political consolidation of the intervening region between Mexico City and Zacatecas — including the pacification of the native tribes who often reacted violently to the introduction of new people, wagon trains, ranches, mines, slave raiding, and enforced labor — the exploration and settlement of areas to the north, east, and west continued (Huerta 1963: 4-8; Powell 1952).

With each new mineral discovery of any importance, a repetition of the mining rush pattern followed, with a corresponding population movement and implantation of Spanish settlements and institutions. Likewise, native reaction to such alien incursions was repeated, followed by a Spanish counter-response to contain the Indians. This, as one of the basic frontier processes during the expansion of Spanish civilization northward, must be kept in mind when evaluating the early reports concerning local Indian populations. A great amount of activity had already taken place to the south of the Greater Bolsón de Mapimí during the seventy years between the conquest of México and the 1590's, when Jesuit missionaries who entered the Parras and Laguna district began to record demographic and ethnographic information about the peoples of the region. Some of the activity had occurred not too far distant from the newly opened mission field.

Following the founding of Zacatecas, a push outward from it was made in the 1550's and 1560's in a series of explorations by Francisco de Ibarra and other adventurers. Durango was founded in 1563 and soon became the capital of the province of Nueva Vizcaya by a commission granted to Ibarra, the first governor of the province. Santa Bárbara, in what later became the Parral district, was established in 1567, along with places of perhaps lesser importance, such as San Martín, Sombrerete, Avino, and Guanaceví in the 1550's and 1560's. The town of Valle de San Bartolomé, east of Santa Bárbara, was erected in 1570 and was one of the major agricultural settlements that served to support the mining towns of the region. More land continued to be opened up to agriculture and animal husbandry in the following decades — the Río Florido district in the 1570's, the San Gregorio valley north of San Bartolomé by 1581, the Todos Santos area after 1590, and the area around Atotonilco (Villa López, Chihuahua) before 1600. The mining *real* of Todos Santos (Cordero, Chihuahua) was founded in 1590, and it and Santa Bárbara were the principal mineral centers in the area until the establishment of Parral in 1631 (Dunne 1948: 10-11; Jiménez Moreno 1958: 99-101; Saravia I n.d.: 263; West 1949: 10-12; Bancroft 1884: 99-103; Mecham 1927: 101ff).

Franciscans were active on the northern mission frontier during the last half of the sixteenth century, and by the 1590's the Jesuits had also entered the field. In 1594 the Franciscans began the Cuencamé mission on the northern boundary of the Zacateco Indians. By 1598 the Jesuits had formally established their missions in Parras, at San Pedro de la Laguna, and on the Nazas River — missions which lasted until 1646, when this area was secularized. Franciscans had, however, founded a short-lived mission in Parras some twenty years prior to the Jesuit founding. Farther north and west, Franciscan missionaries established the mission of San Francisco de Conchos in 1604; they had one at Atotonilco by 1611, the year in which the Jesuits established the mission of San Pablo Belleza in Tepehuán country, west of Santa Bárbara (Alegre II 1956: 41-42; Dunne 1944: 20ff; 1948: 13ff; West 1949: 11-12; 184: 1641A).

On the eastern side of the area and slightly earlier, in 1555, the town of Nombre de Dios was begun as a Franciscan mission among the Zacatecos, and in 1567 Fray Pedro de Espinareda made the first exploration into Coahuila. A year later Francisco Cano discovered the Las Palmas River and a lagoon that he called La Laguna de Nuevo México, apparently the Laguna de Patos. Mazapil was founded in 1569, a year after the discovery of mineral wealth there (Alessio Robles 1938: 63-67, 140; Jiménez Moreno 1958: 99).

Northward from Mazapil, the Saltillo-Monterrey district was first settled in 1577 (Jiménez Moreno 1958: 101-105), and Monterrey was resettled around 1582-1583 as the Villa de San Luis. The next two or three years saw the founding of the Villa of Almadén (Monclova), although it was abandoned only five years later. Activity in this eastern area continued, and in 1590 an expedition was made northward into Texas by Castaño de Sosa. By 1582 there was also, apparently, a place called Cuatro Ciénegas located some seventy leagues east of the Santa Bárbara mines, and Alegre notes that a mission at Cuatro Ciénegas was in existence by 1602 (Alegre II 1956: 57; Alessio Robles 1938: 89-93, 102-108).

Between the western settlements of Santa Bárbara and San Bartolomé and the Saltillo area on the east was the place of Parras. A town was first founded here in 1577-1578 but was abandoned within a few years. However, the district apparently was never vacated entirely. In the spring of 1578 five Spaniards received a total of twelve *caballerías* of land running from the valley of Parras to the eastern side of the Guadalupe River. About two years later, the lands of the hacienda of San Francisco de los Patos west of Saltillo were awarded. More grants were made in 1586-1587 in the Sierra de Coapas and on the Muchachos River, at La Castañuela and at Parras in 1589, and again in the latter place in 1595. Previously, in 1583, Francisco de Urdiñola and two other Spaniards had also received lands between Saltillo and Parras (Alessio Robles 1938: 138, 140-142; Jiménez Moreno 1958: 99-100).

The Spanish drive northward in the sixteenth century, then, undoubtedly had some effect upon the native peoples of the Greater Bolsón de Mapimí. Certainly, when the first information on the Laguneros, Salineros, Tobosos, and other native peoples began to be recorded, enough time had passed for a number of modifications to have taken place — some degree of acceptance of cultural items such as the horse (Forbes 1959), population decline due to spread of disease, and population shifting. Although none of these changes can be documented for this earliest contact period, it should be kept in mind that in native life, some alterations, although of unknown magnitude, most probably had taken place. This is especially important with regard to such peoples as the Tobosos, because not until after the 1640's does any qualitative information about them occur in the documentary record.

Contributing to this early culture change would be new trade items obtained as booty in raids or possibly as handouts from the Spaniards and passed from one Indian group to another. Furthermore, many Indians at one time or another had fairly direct contact with Spanish society as laborers, whether forced or more-or-less free, in mines and on ranches. These economic units employed a great many workers, including local and imported Indians, and no doubt they exerted some influence on the natives in the spheres of work habits, new techniques, new material items, and the like. It was, of course, in these contexts that adverse reaction to Spanish civilization would occur. Missions also wielded much influence on the Indians. While the missionaries were more specifically concerned with effecting change in the native idea systems, they were also responsible for the introduction of many new material items and operational techniques.

These basic frontier social units — mines, ranches, and missions — did not affect all Indians either directly or equally, although they did serve as centers from which new cultural ideas and items — and diseases — spread as local Indians moved back and forth from these places to their own territories. There the Indians rejected or accepted or reworked the new elements into their own cultures in ways that seemed adequate or appropriate to them.

The contact process, of course, was not a one-way street. As previously noted, both natives and Spaniards reacted as they attempted to cope with the opposition. They were forced to deal with each other in some more or less effective way. Basically, the native and European societies were in a relationship of counter-reaction to each other, and over the years certain corresponding developments took place in their respective social organizations. As one example of this kind of frontier reaction, Colonial policy toward nomadic Indians made a couple of pendulum swings in the first two centuries of Spanish northward expansion.

From about the 1590's, it became the practice of the Colonial government to "buy" peace from the Indians with gifts and handouts, while using a minimum of military force for control. This policy was developed during the sixteenth-century expansion northward from Mexico City. Prior to this time it had been thought that rebellious aborigines could be reduced to peace and civilization only by the sword. But increased aggression by the Spaniards had led to greater hostility on the part of the Indians, in turn resulting in more violence by the Spaniards to quell the natives — a vicious spiral. When it was realized by Colonial officials that not only had this policy failed to bring about the results sought but

that it also had occasioned a continuous increase in war expenditures, a new practice of kind treatment and purchase was adopted. The military was never omitted entirely from the new program, and the threat of military punishment always lurked behind peace negotiations. However, the changes constituted a fundamental shift in Indian policy (Powell 1952: 189-203, 205).

The same policy was continued well into the seventeenth century. Since it included an actual reduction in the presidio system, it apparently explains in part the poor military defenses of Nueva Vizcaya throughout most of the 1600's. Powell has summarized this frontier Indian policy as it emerged during the last decade or so of the sixteenth century. Both military and religious personnel, with an increasing reliance on the latter, were employed as go-betweens in peace negotiations with the natives; the missions increased their direct efforts to reduce the natives to settlements; a program of transplanting sedentary Indians to frontier areas was adopted; and both the nomads and the sedentary colonizers were provisioned from royal funds (Powell 1952: 189-205, 222-223). Part of this policy was modified again at the beginning of the eighteenth century, when it was decided that the only effective way to handle the natives was by extermination — either biological or deportation from the province.

During most of the period encompassed by this paper, the region of the Greater Bolsón de Mapimí fell principally within the jurisdiction of the Province of Nueva Vizcaya, although the extreme northeast corner (very roughly, from Monclova northward) was considered part of Coahuila. Nueva Vizcaya, which included Parras and Saltillo, was formed in the early 1560's. Durango, established in 1563, was marked as the capital, but after the founding of Parral in 1631 the Spanish governors usually maintained their residence there (Alessio Robles 1938: 1ff; Bancroft 1884: 102-103; Hackett 1926: 3-5).

The rather weak military organization of the northern frontier during most of the seventeenth century eventually did grow in an effort to meet the increasing Indian menace. Presidios were practically nonexistent until the last decade of the seventeenth century, and the little recruitment of personnel that took place was carried out on a local basis and was sponsored by towns, merchants, and other organizations (Haring 1947: 124-125). Local citizenry, and many of the landowners and others who held military titles, were frequently pressed into duty; they were sometimes motivated by the price put on a rebel's head (Dunne 1948: 184). These men, plus many Indian auxiliaries from missions and native towns, formed the bulwark of Nueva Vizcayan defenses. In 1667 it was reported that there were approximately ninety-two soldiers in all of the province, and this included the installations on the west coast. Three years later there were three presidios with a total of seventy-five men, three captains, and one Indian spy. Most likely these men were distributed evenly among the three presidios of Cerro Gordo, San Sebastián, and Sinaloa (Hackett 1926: 21-25).

The presidio of Cerro Gordo on the southern border of the Greater Bolsón country was not founded until shortly after a major revolt in 1644. Until this time there had been no presidios in the immediate area of hostilities, except possibly at Guanaceví, where one is reported to have been founded in 1617. A recommendation for a presidio at Cerro Gordo was made in 1646, and the structure was apparently erected in 1648 (Hackett 1926: 17-18; Tamerón y Romeral 1937: 125 fn., where the figures in the date are reversed to read 1684, clearly an error since the governors mentioned are Luis de Valdés, 1642-1648, and Diego Guajardo Fajardo, 1648-1651 — see Bancroft 1884: 337).

The formal defenses of the province remained meager until the 1680's. Several presidios were erected in response to a general uprising in 1684, much like the founding of Cerro Gordo after the 1644 Revolt. Three — El Pasaje, El Gallo, and San Francisco de Conchos — were put up around the year 1686, following a Royal Order of September 22, 1685 (Hackett 1926: 24-25, 384, 296ff; DHM 1748).

By 1693, five major defensive points were set up against the desert raiders. Of major importance was El Pasaje, thirty leagues from the city of Durango, with a captain and fifty men, on the more eastern of the two roads between Durango and the city of Parral. Twenty-four leagues to the north of El Pasaje was El Gallo, also with fifty men and a captain. Cerro Gordo, twenty-two leagues from El Gallo and twenty-four from Parral, had only twenty-one men, including the commander. Parral, although it did not possess a presidio as such, was the base of a field company of fifty men plus their captain; usually around fifteen of these were stationed in Durango. Prior to this date the total number of men assigned to Parral had been only thirty. Twenty-two leagues north of Parral was the last presidio, that of San Francisco de Conchos, also with fifty soldiers and a captain. Sometime after 1693, another presidio was established at Mapimí.

Various other defensive measures included regular reconnaissance sallies from the several presidios. In the 1690's, three Spanish squads patrolled the areas of Parral and the Florido River, along the highway in the Nazas River district, and the area between Durango and Sombrerete (Hackett 1926: 25-26; DHM 1748; BL 1695a).

Farther east, and somewhat prior to the Nueva Vizcayan developments, a presidio was erected in 1674 at San Francisco de Coahuila, in the area of present-day (1967) Monclova. In 1703 the presidio of San Juan Bautista del Río Grande was built (Alessio Robles 1938: 237ff, 274, 376-377; BL 1676).

In summary, the implantation of Spanish civilization on the northern frontier of New Spain wrought deep changes in the aboriginal societies of the region. At the same time, Spanish society was also forced to adjust to conditions — geographical and social — that existed on this frontier.

NOTE

2. SPANISH-INDIAN CONTACT HISTORY: FROM THE FOUNDING OF PARRAS TO THE MID-EIGHTEENTH CENTURY

The native peoples of the Greater Bolsón de Mapimí country began to feel the effects of the Spanish conquest during the 1560's, 1570's, and 1580's, particularly with the establishment of various Spanish holdings in the regions of Santa Bárbara, Parras, and Saltillo. However, it is only with the founding of the Jesuit missions in the southern portion of the country in the last decade of the sixteenth century that information on the aborigines of this area becomes available. The men of this missionary order who worked in this field for many years remitted a number of excellent reports to their superiors regarding their missions and Indian neophytes. Elsewhere, data on the general Bolsón area are meager until the major revolt of 1644, and the pre-1644 contact history remains rather obscure.

Much more information is available on the history of Spanish-native relations after 1644. In a general overview, the pattern of relationship between the Europeans and the untamed Indians of the desert Bolsón country, which had been set up by 1644, endured in its basic outline until the native groups of the region disappeared about a century later. This pattern primarily involved native raids on Spanish settlements and other holdings, and Spanish retaliations. Frequently, peace negotiations would be entered into; less often the Indians would submit to a proposal to settle down at some location, sometimes at a mission, where they would remain for a short while before returning to their old territories and haunts to renew their raiding activities. In this process the aboriginal population was reduced in several ways — by death from warfare and disease, by permanent resettlement among the Spaniards, and in the latter part of the period by outright deportation from the province.

The Parras Missions and Early Bolsón History

The Jesuit founding of missions in the districts of Parras and San Pedro de la Laguna was one of the most important single events in the history of the relations between Europeans and the natives of the Greater Bolsón de Mapimí. This came during the period of Spanish expansion into the northern frontier. Jesuit missionaries had been working since the early 1590's in newly discovered mission fields along the west coast and in the mountainous Sierra Madre. At the same time, other Spaniards, after several northern expeditions, were making a long northward leap from southern Chihuahua in their first attempt to colonize New Mexico under Don Juan de Oñate. Although the first settlement was short-lived, lasting only from 1598 to 1601, Oñate was back again in 1608, this time to make the New Mexican endeavor permanent. In the year prior to this final and successful attempt to found an outpost in the north, the Jesuit Juan Fonte made his first contact with Tarahumara Indians, in the now flourishing Tepehuán mission district. The Lower Tarahumara Mission system would not be founded for another twenty years, following the discovery of silver at Parral in 1631. During this same period, men of the Jesuit order continued to penetrate northward in the west coast lowland country, opening up new missions among the Cahitan-speaking Mayos and Yaquis in 1614 and 1617 and among the Lower Pima in 1619 (Spicer 1962: 25-26, 28-29, 48, 87-88, 155-158).

As part of this general Spanish expansion, the Parras mission district was officially founded in 1598, although men of the Black Robe had been active in the area since the early years of the decade. In effect, this Jesuit mission establishment was a direct reflection of the new policy, forged during the previous decades, toward the natives on the northern Spanish frontier, and it constituted the first intensive European-native contact in the Greater Bolsón country. The Indians, of course, had already had some traffic with Spaniards before this event. The new missions, however, afforded a different kind of contact — one of greater intensity and regularity (Bancroft 1884: 112, 125-127; AGN 1619).

Outside this newly founded region which offered

intense daily relationships with members of Spanish society, the aborigines were in much less direct contact with Spaniards. Some natives probably worked occasionally for the Europeans, and in all likelihood some raiding was done by Spaniards for slave labor to be used at the mines and other holdings. At the same time, some of the Indian groups were likewise raiding Spanish settlements for livestock and other booty, although no actual revolt occurred until the year 1644.

The mission system at Parras and San Pedro de la Laguna, consisting of three principal districts, or *partidos*, was an important element in the organization of the Spanish power structure of the southern portion of Bolsón country for almost fifty years. The three main *misiones* were located at Parras, San Pedro de la Laguna or the Laguna de Mayrán, and on the Nazas River. In each of these locations *cabeceras*, or head churches, were erected. In addition, a number of towns and settlements were founded around satellite parishes and chapels. For approximately the first decade of the existence of the mission system, the population of the entire three mission districts was usually cited as 4,000 persons (BL 1602; BL 1604; BL 1606; BL 1610; BL 1614; BL 1616; AGN 1607c; AGN 1619; AGN 1622; DHM ca 1706).

Mota y Escobar, after his visit to the area about the year 1605, penned one of the most detailed descriptions now extant of the new mission system. Parras included two *visitas*, or satellite parishes, about eight leagues to the west of the *cabecera*, and the total population came to some 1,500 persons. A similar figure was given by Father Arista. The district of San Pedro on the lower Nazas and at the lagoon, west of Parras, had three *visitas*, two only one league away and one four leagues distant. The entire *partido* contained between 2,000 and 3,000 persons, approximately 1,000 of them in the town of San Pedro. Eight leagues up-river was the *partido* of San Ignacio, containing six towns (Mota y Escobar 1940: 167-170; AGN 1619).

Other sources add to the picture of these missions. The *Anua* of 1604 states that two of the three *visitas* of San Pedro were San Nicolás and Santiago and that the two of Parras were San Hieronimo and Santo Tomás (BL 1604), although elsewhere Santo Tomás is said to be a town of the *partido* of San Pedro (AGN 1622). Father Arnaya in 1601 described two pueblos of Zacatecos Indians on the Nazas — one containing over 400 persons, and the second, named Santa Ana,

around 300. On the river at the beginning of the lagoon, he wrote, a third town (apparently San Pedro) of over 2,000 persons was in the process of being formed, and many people from the hinterland were being brought into it. On an islet out in the lake or lagoon itself, some two or three leagues away, was another settlement of 200 to 300 persons. Parras, to the east, was the oldest town in the area (DHM 1601). By 1607, the Zacateco town of Santa Ana consisted of three pueblos (AGN 1607b; AGN 1607c). Later, the entire district was described as having six missions with an equal number of missionaries (DHM ca 1706).

Apparently it was not until sometime between 1601 and 1606 that the *visita* of Mapimí was founded (BL 1606; DHM 1601) and called San Miguel (BL 1616). This satellite establishment was very close to, or possibly in, Tepehuán country, judging from the number of references to the Tepehuanes in this region about this period (for example, AGN 1607a; AGN 1607b; AGN 1607c).

From the earliest years there is evidence of much population shuffling in the districts of this mission. According to Father Francisco de Arista, the original inhabitants of the Parras valley were the Yritilas and the Mayranos, although another group called the Maxiconeras had already been settled at the new town of Parras by 1595, three years before the actual founding of the mission. Arista, who arrived in Parras this same year, states that within a few months over 1,000 persons had taken up permanent residence at Parras. However, within a year or so these newly congregated groups had rebelled, encouraged to do so by some of their leaders during a plague. Afterward many of the natives returned to their old haunts in the back country (AGN 1619; DHM 1598; DHM 1601).

Aside from the populations adjacent to these missions, many persons were brought into the missions from a greater distance. The Pachos had come from the Patos and Saltillo region (see Chapter 5, Band History). More important for present purposes, however, were the groups brought down from the north, thirty to forty leagues away, from such places as Coahuila (the region of Monclova? — Jiménez Moreno 1958: 106), Cuatro Ciénegas, Nadadores, and possibly from as far north as the Río Grande, according to an anonymous Jesuit writing at a much later time (ca 1706) (DHM ca 1706; BL 1605; BL 1606).

These new Jesuit missions touched a number of

natives who had had little or no previous contact with Spaniards and their European civilization. However, some of the people "reduced" to the Parras-Laguna missions from the earliest years were reported to be quite acculturated (*ladinos*) with regard to the Mexican language and other cultural items accepted as proper by the Spaniards. Nicolás de Arnaya stated in 1601 that this was because of the many years of contact that a number of the Indians had had with Spaniards before the founding of the missions. The natives had been accustomed to traveling sixty to eighty leagues to work, and they would return to their own lands dressed in Spanish cloth (*paño*), which they preferred to the Mexican style of dress. Such contacts notwithstanding, only a few of the Indians had been baptized by the 1590's (DHM 1598; DHM 1601).

Some of this acquaintance with Spanish civilization probably had occurred during previous hostilities with Spaniards. Significantly, the Bishop of Guadalajara about the year 1584 had recommended, as an aid in the establishment of peace among the warlike Chichimeca tribes south of the Laguna district, the founding of six to seven settlements for these peoples. The places suggested were Las Charcas (between Mazapil and Saltillo), the valley of Parras, the region of La Laguna Grande (San Pedro), Indé, and the Tepeque district (Powell 1952: 181-182).

By 1598, most of the baptisms made by the Jesuits had been among the Zacateco Indians, apparently owing to the fact that the major portion of the other tribal groups had remained in the hinterland. The *Anua* of this year reports that fifteen caciques, plus other *principales*, had been settled at Parras with their people. These totaled around 1,000 people. For La Laguna eleven names are given, apparently also of chiefs, but the number of their followers is not recorded. Two years earlier, the *Anua* of 1596 noted the baptism of some seventy adults and a few children, seemingly in the Nazas River country. However, only a few people had been baptized at La Laguna because many had taken refuge on the islets in the lagoon to escape the plague that occurred in 1596. In 1601, the scattered Parras bands were still being brought back for resettlement (AGN 1619; DHM 1598; DHM 1601; DHM 1596).

This type of reshuffling of the local population was characteristic of the mission period in the general Laguna district. Plagues persistently caused the Indians to scatter, and the Jesuits afterward dutifully attempted to retrieve their flocks. Although figures

are not available, the population reduction at this time was probably fairly marked, and the missionaries constantly reported the bringing in of new rancherias of natives to settle at their missions. This movement of population is reflected by the continual appearance of new names of "nations" in the parish records of Parras for this period. Despite the initial heavy preponderance of Zacatecos and other tribes from the general region, as time wore on more and more names from peoples purported to be from "Cuaguila" occur in the records (Martínez del Río 1954: 41-43; BL 1606; BL 1615a; BL 1616) (see Appendix 1).

The same process of population shifting can also be noted during the 1620's. The annual reports for the years 1622, 1624, and 1626 cite a great number of deaths because of plagues. To escape these maladies many people at the missions fled to the hinterland where, however, many other persons were also perishing from pestilence. On the other hand, backcountry gentiles during these times would go to the missions to request baptism, also in an effort to stem the tide of sickness and death (AGN 1622; AGN 1624; AGN 1626).

The *Anua* of 1622 records somewhat more information on the gentiles who came from the hinterland to the Parras missions. Some had come in from Coahuila — two bands had done so this year — and others would arrive at the settlements at harvest time. Many persons were described as *ladinos* or "acculturated," and at least the chiefs spoke Mexican, although all understood it. The people were said to be docile and willing to learn. The report also states that these natives loved their own lands so much that even after six or seven months at Parras they would return to their territories, although they would come back to the mission punctually the following year. At the same time, many people dwelling in the mountains would admit no Spaniards, even missionaries, to their territories or camps. Spaniards and others who had inadvertently crossed into the areas possessed by these groups had been killed (AGN 1622).

Outside the Parras-Laguna district, nearby peoples also were in contact with Spanish civilization during this early period. Spanish contact with Salineros, Tobosos, and Chisos probably was not as sporadic as the lack of specific references in the sources might seem to indicate. Spaniards around Santa Bárbara and San Bartolomé no doubt employed nearby Indians as laborers on mines and ranches, as evidenced by the fact that a number of the back country Indians knew how to speak *mexicano* or Nahuatl – a language that served as a *lingua franca* in the north Mexican area at this time. Despite sparse documentation on the desert groups before the 1640's, the little that does exist affords a glimpse of the activities of these peoples up to the latter date.

It is likely that some Salineros were in contact with the nearby Laguna district missions, although this is not evident from the band or group names that appear in the records. However, there is evidence that some of the Laguna-Parras peoples in effect did become known in later years as "Salineros." It is also uncertain when Salineros were settled at the mission of Tizonazo, founded between 1630 and 1639 (Dunne 1948: 43-46). Around 1626, before the erection of Tizonazo, a town at Agua de Pelayo and another at La Mimbrera were established for the "Salineros" near Las Salinas, where it was expected that a great many people would come in to settle (AGN 1626).

Tobosos seemingly were first contacted by the Espejo expedition to New Mexico in 1582. At this time it was thought that they were a small nation – and they may have been – as only a few Indians were seen (Bolton 1916: 171-172). By 1593, Tobosos and Gavilanes had raided Spanish holdings, and an expedition was sent out after them under Captain Francisco de Leyva y Bonilla (Bancroft 1884: 128-129; Forbes 1959). A decade later, in 1603, according to Bancroft, Father Antonio Zalduendo went to Coahuila where he worked about three years as a missionary, but he had to give up his labors because of the raids of Tobosos and other Indians (Bancroft 1884: 336, 375). However, Alessio Robles, the historian of Coahuila, cites the lack of exactness of the dates of Zalduendo's activities in this area and does not mention the Tobosos (Alessio Robles 1938: 150-151, 180-181).

A mission was founded at Atotonilco by Franciscans in 1611, apparently for the Tobosos, who reportedly rebelled from the place in 1612. These Indians were finally pacified by Governor Francisco de Urdiñola, who managed to resettle them at Atotonilco and at San Bartolomé (Alegre II 1958: 41-42; West 1949: 11-12; AHP 1641A; UTD 1648).

Although the records of events of these early years are extremely sketchy, "Tobosos" and other Indian groups begin to emerge in the record as raiders in Nueva Vizcaya. About the year 1618, during the Tepehuan Revolt, Indians – probably Salineros and Tobosos of Las Salinas de Machete and Pozo Hediondo – rebelled together with Conchos from the Santa Bárbara mountains. Tepehuanes were probably also involved, and a group called Conejos were indicted at this same time. Captains Mozquera and Medrano led campaigns against these rebels (Hackett 1926: 98, 110; AGN 1617; AGN 1618).

Toboso groups showed up again in the 1620's. Five Tobosos appeared before the Spanish governor in Durango in May of 1621. One was Jacobo and another Cristóbal, a *principal*, the son of Don Jusephe, the governor and cacique of the Toboso nation. These envoys reported that the Nonoties (Nonojes), Achaclames (Acoclames), and Xipocales bands had gone to Atotonilco to make peace "in the name of all the rest," and that the Indians were now ready to go to the San Bartolomé Valley to work in the harvest (*siega*) (Hackett 1926: 124).

As previously noted, some of the desert bands were probably Tepehuanes. On January 16, 1622, Don Juan Negrito, cacique and governor of a group of Tepehuanes called Negritos, who were camped at the Mapimí mines, went to the Spaniards to make peace. This, it was reported, he did in the name of "the rest of his bands (*parcialidades*)" – indicating that more than one group of Tepehuanes were in this region at the time (Hackett 1926: 126).

On May 7, 1624, Fray Lázaro de Espinoza, Guardian of the convent at Atotonilco, appeared in Durango with Jusepe (Jusephe), the Indian governor of Atotonilco. Three other Indians were with them. One was Diego, son of Don Agustín, captain and governor of the Toboso nation; the second, Alonso, was captain of a Toboso rancheria or band; and the third was named Jacobo. These three men reported that they, their people, and the Nonojes, Ocochames (Acoclames), and Chisos nations, as well as some Tepehuanes and Salineros, had been at war against the Spaniards for over twenty years. They confessed to past deeds, including damage done to farms and ranches in the Santa Bárbara area and an instance of haughty refusal to surrender to the governor. When a contingent had then been sent out after them, a Spaniard was killed and some of the Indians wounded or imprisoned. Now, however, these Tobosos were willing to settle in peace. The Spanish governor ordered them to settle on the Florido River at a spot named San Felipe, six leagues from Atotonilco (Hackett 1926: 140-142). It is not known if this settlement was ever established.

A report of the following year — 1625 — describes Salineros, Tobosos, Acoclames, and Nonojes as allied bands comprising a great number of people. They lived in an area thirty leagues from the province of Santa Bárbara and had never accepted mission doctrine (Hackett 1926: 158). During the next decade these peoples are not heard of directly. However, many years later — in 1671 — a Spaniard named Valerio Cortés testified in Parral that the Masames ("Tobosos") had revolted in 1632, in one of the first "movements" (or so Cortés thought or remembered) of the desert Indians (CD[1671]).

Despite the lack of adequate historical documentation for this early period, Spanish-native contacts in the Greater Bolsón de Mapimí area obviously had been in progress for many years, probably close to eighty, by the time the revolt of 1644 broke out. Apparently the period of initial shock for the natives was followed by a period of adaptation to the new conditions introduced by the entrance of the Europeans. This adaptation had its high and low points, one of the peaks of intensity occurring in 1644 as the first major rebellion of the Indians of central northern Mexico.

The 1644 Revolt

The rebellion of 1644, four years before the first major Tarahumara uprising in the western Sierra Madre country, was the first general outbreak in which the northern desert tribes played any kind of prominent role. Some of these peoples had been involved in the Tepehuán Revolt of 1617, as previously noted, but the action on this later occasion centered on a number of the desert-dwelling nations. Several different bands of Tobosos and Salineros, as well as the more sedentary Concho Indians, took part. The revolt continued through the following year and was considered finally put down in the early months of 1646 when peace was established with various Toboso and Salinero bands. The Concho groups had been pacified for the most part by the middle of the previous year (Spicer 1962: 30; AHP 1646Ab; 1646a; 1650a).

Actually, for such peoples as the Tobosos, Salineros, some of the desert Tepehuanes, and probably the Chisos, 1644 seems to have been only a time of intensification of what by this time was a fairly well-established raiding pattern. However, it does not appear that the Conchos Indians, northwest of the territories of these desert peoples, had developed this kind of raiding complex, for the Jesuits, Alegre and Zepeda, referred to the perplexity of the Spaniards over the fact that the Conchos had taken to the warpath. According to these writers, the Conchos were a fairly settled people who had always been faithful to the Spaniards, and of whom many were employed in mines and ranches in the Parral and San Bartolomé Valley districts (Alegre III 1959: 37-39; DHM 1645; CD 1650a).

On the other hand, the desert bands apparently had never ceased to fight or raid Spaniards, despite their occasional short stays at settlements or missions. About 1640, Governor Bravo de la Serna wrote that the warring nations that had committed the most damage in the kingdom of Nueva Vizcaya were the Tepehuanes, Tobosos, and Salineros. The governor stated that he had been able to pacify some of these people in the vicinity of San Bartolomé (AGN ca 1640). Later, in 1643, Tobosos, Nonojes, and Acoclames, who had been settled at Atotonilco (unfortunately, it is not known for how long), rebelled. They joined a number of other bands and began attacking Spanish holdings in the Santa Bárbara Valley and elsewhere, stealing over 180 animals from the hacienda of Juana de Aldaz, located about three leagues from the Atotonilco mission. The reports at this time mention previous revolts of the Tobosos (AHP 1644A).

The writers of the period do not point to any specific cause for such a general conflagration in 1644, except possibly machinations of the devil. Father Zepeda, however, perhaps gives part of the answer. The region had suffered an extreme drought for five years (his writing this in 1645 would place the beginning of the drought at around 1640). This, combined with pestilence — Zepeda refers to a number of deaths among Salineros from plague in 1644, and no doubt other "nations" were not spared — may very well have been one of the factors that pushed tribes such as the Conchos over the threshold into active hostility (DHM 1645).

It is not entirely clear how this general rebellion began. According to Alegre, it started when the natives at the Franciscan mission of San Francisco del Mesquital left, an action that had repercussions on the mission of Tizonazo, where many Salineros were settled. According to Alegre, hostilities were then taken up by the Tobosos, who committed an inordinate number of depredations on Spanish wagon trains, mines, and other holdings (Alegre III 1959: 23-24). Zepeda somewhat more directly implies that the Tobosos were largely responsible for the rebellion. The Tobosos, the most cruel and warlike of all the tribes, had to be brought into peace almost annually and had caused trouble in the province for at least two years prior to 1644 (DHM 1645).

The motivations for revolt among some of the tribes were more than hunger resulting from prolonged drought. While nothing is known of the internal Toboso situation, reports on the Salineros indicate that some of these people had been feeling the effects of Spanish efforts at acculturation. Both Alegre and Zepeda (Alegre's information may have come largely from Zepeda) describe certain features that point to changes in the native social organization owing to Spanish pressure. During the revolt the Indians "elected" one Jerónimo de Moranta to lead the entire nation, and they designated him "the great one, or king." Another man, Nicolas Baturi (Baluzi, Baluri) (*Pies de Liebre*), was given the subordinate office of "captain" which, according to Father Zepeda, constituted a counterposition to that of the Spanish General, Juan de Barraza. A third Indian, named Hernandote, was chosen as "Bishop" and was placed in charge of religious matters — he said Mass, ridiculed the ceremony of the Holy Sacrifice through mimicry, and performed marriages and divorces for his flock at will (Alegre III 1959: 37,40; DHM 1645).

With the outbreak in 1644, the governor of Nueva Vizcaya sent the *Maestre de Campo* Francisco Montaño de la Cueva to the Río Grande against the Conchos, and General Juan de Barraza was sent, with three companies, against the Tobosos. Barraza penetrated to the last rancherias of the Tobosos, said to be near the Río Grande (according to a Spanish report — but there seems to be no supporting information that the northern boundary of the Tobosos was actually near this river).

At this time raids and encounters between Spaniards and Indians resulted in many of the latter being killed or imprisoned. One group of Indians, apparently mostly Conchos, attacked the Franciscan mission of San Francisco de Conchos, killing the two friars there and burning the church. They then moved northward to another Concho mission, San Pedro de Conchos, which they also ravaged, although the missionary there escaped. Other groups operated around Parral, San Bartolomé, and Mapimí.

One band attacked the mines at Indé, killed a number of Spaniards, and ran off most of the cattle. These Indians were well mounted on horses, and Alegre notes that following the raid they moved with

such "incredible speed that in two days they traveled seventy leagues." However, in this case the celerity of the rebels only worked against them; on their way back they encountered the Spanish troops returning from the northern campaign, who promptly took back the booty. A number of the raiders were then killed or taken prisoner and the remainder returned to their tribes in the back country. In retaliation, the Tobosos then went to the Cabezas at Tizonazo, where some 300 families were settled, and persuaded the Cabezas to join them on the warpath (Alegre III 1956: 25, 37-39; DHM 1645; CD 1644; CD 1650a).

According to Alegre, these Indians from Tizonazo were the last to enter the fracas. He states that they were of the Cabeza nation, although other material indicates that many Salineros were involved, and more than one band that had been at peace for over fifty years. Father Zepeda notes that it was after the attack on the two Concho towns of San Francisco and San Pedro that the Salineros proper joined the Cabezas, with whom they were related by blood, and the Tobosos (Alegre III 1956: 25-26; DHM 1645; AHP 1645 Aa; AHP 1646B; AHP 1652Dc).

Don Cebrián, the Indian governor of the "first" band (*parcialidad*) of Salineros at the mission at Tizonazo, retired to Indé with a few of his people and their missionary Father Diego Osorio when hostilities broke out. The remainder of Cebrián's band joined the rebels (AHP 1646B). Seemingly, Cebrián tried in vain to stop the rebels, who meanwhile stole his wife and took her to the back country. Another Indian governor at Tizonazo, Don Alvaro de Moranta, was sent with the Jesuit Nicolás de Zepeda, the former missionary at that place, to attempt to cement peace with the Cabezas. In reply to this overture more than 400 Cabezas and Salineros returned and promised to live quietly in their settlement. However, as soon as Zepeda left Tizonazo, the Cabezas fled to the hills. Don Alvaro was sent to them again, but they killed him on the road. During this time a continual round of attacks was being made on Spanish settlements and on wagon and mule trains, the assaults occurring frequently and over wide areas (Alegre III 1956: 25-26; DHM 1645).

The Salinero-Cabeza group divided into three squads for their raiding activities. One went to Ramos, another toward Cuencamé, and the third to the Parras-Laguna district. The third group attacked the town of San Pedro, burned the houses, and profaned the church, but they desisted from going on to Parras when they learned that the Spaniards were there in force awaiting them. On the way, however, the Indians captured a Spanish woman, Antonia Treviño (N. Tremeño by Zepeda), and her four children and took them to the head chief, Gerónimo de Moranta. Two of the boys were killed before their mother's eyes, and the third a few days later. The daughter was given to one of the other chiefs. According to an Indian, apparently a Salinero, who had been with Antonia part of the time, the children were not merely killed but were roasted (*en barbacoa*) and eaten. Antonia's Spanish clothing was taken from her, and she was given Indian dress. Her hair was cut, and she was assigned such woman's duties within the tribe as fetching water and firewood. The Indian who captured her had once been her servant (Alegre III 1956: 40-41; AHP 1652Dc; DHM 1645).

yuk!

After several months of servitude, during which time she was traded among several different masters, Antonia was given to the Tobosos as part of an alliance agreement. Some Indian declarants, under questioning later, stated that Antonia had been turned over to the Ocome band, although most disavowed knowing anything about what had become of her. One Salinero woman, however, stated that Antonia had been held by a Toboso band (unspecified) camped next to hers during the uprising and that later these Tobosos had killed Antonia when they decided to return to peace. Another Salinero woman declared that she had heard that Antonia had died of *cocolixtli* (an Aztec or Mexican term used during the Colonial period to refer to epidemic diseases, most usually smallpox). Both Alegre and Zepeda state that the Tobosos killed her so that there would be no witness to their own evil doings. The daughter, who had remained with the Salineros and Cabezas, was ultimately released, although pregnant, and went back to Spanish civilization (Alegre III 1956: 40-41; DHM 1645; AHP 1652Dc).

Spanish forces made a number of sallies in an attempt to reduce the rebels to peace. Maestre de Campo Montaño de la Cueva went to Atotonilco, and Cristóbal Nevares moved into the Conchos country. Juan de Barraza marched a few leagues from Cuencamé with the major portion of the Spanish troops, to go to Las Salinas at the end of August to cut off Indians reported to be on their way to Las Bocas. Governor Luis de Valdés himself took out a force that penetrated into the second salt flat (*salina*) two days' march from the Salinas de Machete. Here the enemy, now suffering because of the lack of food, was corraled on the top of a hill and forced to surrender (Alegre II 1956: 41-42; DHM 1645; CD 1650a).

At the salt flats, Moranta and his group, which may have included a few Tobosos, were pardoned for their activities and given a three-day truce. Some eighteen to twenty Indians were kept with the Spaniards as hostages while the others prepared for the coming peace. The Indians did not show up at the end of the truce period; they had made use of the time involved in the peace negotiations to make their escape, apparently breaking up into a number of small groups as they left. Lack of supplies then forced Valdés' Spanish camp to move to Cerro Gordo, a place commonly frequented by the rebels. Here some of the hostages were put to death. In the meantime, a band of some twenty-eight or thirty Indians, including six chiefs, was captured by a small Spanish force at Las Bocas (Alegre III 1956: 42; DHM 1645).

The governor began to prepare for another sally into Las Salinas. Moranta's group, aware of this, then sent Dominguillo to Atotonilco to request peace from Montaño, since they were afraid of punishment at the hands of the governor for their treachery during the previous truce. When Dominguillo arrived he requested that a certain Francisco Mama, who had remained with the Spaniards, be sent to the Salineros. According to Alegre, Mama was faithful to the Spaniards but also was much loved by the Indians, who were now sorry they had not followed his advice about refraining from going to war. A Salinero, testifying later, claimed that the Indians had received Mama and his message of peace because they were still fearful after the attack Governor Valdés had made on them at the salt flats. By this time the governor was again marching through these same flats, and the Indians traveled day and night to escape him and reach Atotonilco to make a truce with Montaño (Alegre III 1956: 42-43; DHM 1645; AHP 1646B).

Meanwhile the Spaniards had sent a number of envoys to the Tobosos with offers of peace, all of which were turned down. Finally, on May 8, 1645, a Toboso by the name of Juan Largo was sent to the rebels with a mule loaded with clothing and supplies as a possible inducement for surrender. On May 11, notice was received that Juan Largo had died en route to his people, apparently of old age (AHP 1645Aa).

Actually, Montaño had made an entry into Concho country, leaving Captain Luis de Escobar in command at Atotonilco, on the border of the territory of the Tobosos, Nonojes, Acoclames, and Ocomes. Barraza had already received instructions to go out against the Cabezas who, apparently, were not felt to be in direct alliance with the Toboso bands. Specifically, Escobar was to send an envoy, a Toboso named Cristóbal El Gangoso (The Snuffler), son of Juan Largo and a resident of Atotonilco, to the Tobosos and their allies. As these Indians were located nearest the Spanish holdings in the San Bartolomé Valley, their attack upon this area and the destruction of the ripening wheat would have been extremely detrimental to the mining centers of Parral and San Diego, which were supplied from the valley (AHP 1645Aa; CD 1650a).

El Gangoso arrived back in Atotonilco about June 24, having met with little success, and was sent out again. On his second return he brought two of the rebels — a Toboso captain named Zapata, and a Nonoje. These men had been empowered by their groups to make a peace offering. Montaño, returning from his campaign against the Concho, was met by El Gangoso at San Francisco de Conchos with word that the Tobosos would meet him at Atotonilco. At the same time El Gangoso met and talked with about one hundred Conchos who had just arrived in peace at San Francisco. The Spanish authorities hoped that when the Tobosos heard how leniently the once-rebel Conchos had been treated, this would be an added inducement for them to declare peace, although the Toboso, Nonoje, Ocome, and Acoclame chiefs had already promised peace to Escobar (AHP 1645Aa; CD 1650a).

Again, in the latter part of July, Indian envoys arrived in Atotonilco with the ambassador El Gangoso. These envoys included the Toboso cacique Cristóbal Zapata (the Don Cristóbal Doble cited by Zepeda?) and another captain, also named Cristóbal, who had come to offer peace in the name of all of the Tobosos. Ocome and Acoclame chiefs were with them to speak for their peoples, as was a Nonoje named Pedro, said to be a delegate from his chief, Juan Casa Zavala (occasionally Casabala). The allied "Toboso" groups were to come to Atotonilco as soon as they had consumed some squash they had planted and other food they had on hand. Two women and two children were left as hostages by the envoys when they departed for their home territories (AHP 1645Aa; DHM 1645; CD 1650a).

On August 25, Escobar received word that at least part of the Toboso groups were two days' journey from Atotonilco; Zapata, another man, and two women were only one day's travel away and would soon arrive at the pueblo. Pedro, the envoy, was sent out to bring in the others within a period of six days.

On September 3, Cristóbal El Gangoso came in with ten Tobosos, half of whom were women. The men were Chief Cristóbal Zapata, his son Antón, and Juan, Santiago, and El Peinado (two of whom were nephews of Cristóbal the Toboso), plus the Salinero Dominguillo. Montaño de la Cueva, who had now been in Atotonilco since August 30, received them. The Tobosos said they had come in the name of their governor, Don Cristóbal, to make peace, and that they were certain the Spaniards would keep their word because of what El Gangoso had reported to them concerning the treatment the Conchos had received. At this time Zapata's band was said to be called the Jaquue, and the Nonojes, Ococlames, and Ocomes were reported to be still at war (AHP 1645Aa; CD 1650a).

Dominguillo, the son of Chief Nicolás Baturi, reported that he had been sent by the Salineros to request peace. The Salineros were now camped close to the Tobosos, and the two groups were in constant contact with each other. The Salineros would come in immediately if their peace offer were accepted. The Tobosos and Dominguillo were then given meat and flour and told to go and rest before they returned to their peoples. Two days later they were given gifts, some of which were specifically to ransom the Spanish woman, wife of Antonio Fernández — apparently Antonia Treviño (the names given by Zepeda are Antonio Péres de Molina and N. Tremeño). According to the Tobosos, the Ocomes now had her, having purchased her from the Cabezas, who had captured her when they attacked a wagon train en route to the town of Mapimí. Moranta, they reported, had gone off with the Cabezas and Colorados, who were at this time camped a little to the west ("this side") of the Salinas de Machete. Another group of Cabezas and Colorados were in this same region. The Toboso envoys were soon dispatched to fetch their head chief, Cristóbal, and the remainder of their people (AHP 1645Aa; cd 1650a).

Chief Francisco Mama was sent with Dominguillo to the Salinero chief. Mama had just returned from Montaño's campaign against the Conchos, and the Spaniards felt that he would be able to relate to the rebel Salineros the results of the peace settlement with the Conchos. This plan apparently worked, and on September 19 Dominguillo and another Salinero showed up with the news that the rest of the band was on its way to Atotonilco. This was one day after the governor had left Cerro Gordo with five companies of military, including many Tepehuán and

Tarahumara auxiliaries, and marched his camp to Atotonilco. The Salineros arrived on September 30 with Captain Francisco Mama and the Salinero governor Don Pedro. These men reported that their principal chiefs, Don Gerónimo Moranta and Don Gáspar, were at that time out gathering up the remaining Salineros to take to Atotonilco. Early in October two Cabezas, who had come in with the Salineros, were sent out to seek a surrender from their band. These rebels, including some Salineros who were neighbors of the town of Mapimí and who had been terrorized by the arms of Barraza, surrendered within a short while. The governor issued orders for the arrangements regarding the peace settlement and for the punishment of the leaders. Some of the Indians were returned to their mission at Tizonazo and others were distributed to various Spanish settlements (Alegre III 1956: 43-45; CD 1650a; AHP 1645Aa; AHP 1646B).

In the early part of October, 1645, El Gangoso was back in Atotonilco with the Toboso governor Don Cristóbal and a few other persons. Cristóbal offered to cement peace with the Spaniards, as well as to bring in the Nonox (Nonojes) nation which lived in the same area as the Tobosos. Cristóbal was sent out again but was back before the end of the month. On October 31, the Tobosos were formally settled in peace at Atotonilco.

At this time it was reported that the Nonojes, Ocomes, Ococlames (Acoclames), and other nations still in rebellion had not yet come to the Spaniards because they had been cut off by a squad of soldiers from the troops marching with the Spanish governor Valdés, and in fright had returned to their own territories. Valdés, on the other hand, said that he had suspended military action against the Indians in order not to disrupt the efforts for peace being made from Atotonilco. On November 3, envoys were sent to the Nonojes and Cabezas. The Coyomes (Cocoyomes), the now settled Tobosos reported, lived farthest away and were now at peace with the Spaniards, but special envoys were sent to them also (CD 1650a).

Many of these bands remained at large for the next few months. Negritos were reported to be roaming about the area of Santo Domingo, La Cadena, and Mapimí. Ocomes, Nonojes, Cabezas, and another group of Salineros (possibly those referred to previously as being from Mapimí) continued in revolt, although by the end of November the Ocomes, Ococlames (Acoclames), and Nonojes had sent messengers to the Spaniards to affirm a peace; it was not consummated, however, until the middle of January

of the following year — 1646 (AHP 1652Dc; CD 1650a; CD [1671]).

The Salineros who had surrendered began to complain that they did not want to return to Tizonazo because of the lack of water and good lands. They also objected to being returned to their former missionary, Father Diego Osorio. Over these objections, the Spaniards, with some difficulty, eventually resettled over two hundred Salineros at the Tizonazo mission. Once there, many misbehaved, and small groups of Indians began to disappear. Part of this situation was due to the intervention of local Spaniards. The captains Montaño de la Cueva, Escobar, and Ontiveros — apparently for their own personal advantage — had surreptitiously told the Indians to ask the Spanish governor if they could settle at Cerro Gordo rather than return to Tizonazo, and they themselves had promised the Salineros that Cabezas Indians would also be settled with them at Cerro Gordo (Alegre III 1956: 44; AHP 1646B; AHP 1652Dc).

On December 13 three envoys from the still rebellious Salineros of Chief Francisco El Tuerto arrived at San Gregorio de Naysa. Peace was granted them, and El Tuerto brought in some thirty-three persons from Santo Domingo where they had been camped. Not long afterwards the Coyotes, who had formerly been settled at Mapimí and were now reported to be in the area of Santo Domingo and La Cadena, were ready to come to peace terms. Furthermore, other bands (apparently Salinero)—those of Chiefs Juan Bonifacio and Gabriel Pachon — were negotiating for peace at this time, but it is not entirely clear whether or not these constituted two different groups. Eventually they came in with El Tuerto, whom they requested to be their governor (AHP 1648B; AHP 1652Dc).

The Spaniards wanted these people to return to Mapimí, but the Indians objected and stated that they were afraid of retaliations by the local Spanish population. Not only this, but at Mapimí they would be able to enjoy only a partial peace, as they were enemies of the Alaguna nation (apparently Laguneros). For these reasons and because the land in the Mapimí region was rather infertile, the people under El Tuerto were eventually settled at an hacienda at Cerro Gordo (where seemingly they had been located at some time in the past) (AHP 1646B; AHP 1652Dc).

The month of January of the following year, 1646, saw a formal peace established with a number of the rebel bands. On January 12 peace was made with Chief Francisco Hauchuli (also Hauchile) and fifty-eight Nonojes at Atotonilco. The next day two Cabeza envoys who had been dispatched on October 7 of the previous year returned to Atotonilco. They brought with them nine Cabezas and two Matarajes. One of the messengers reported that the reason for their delay in coming back was that after conferring with the Cabezas they had decided to penetrate more deeply into the hinterland. Here they had visited nine other nations – Cabacuitac (or Cabacuitae), Totolcoyome, Gavilanes, Matarajes, Cocoyomes, Talcocoyomes, Tubaymamar, Macalypilguas, and Babosarigas – all of whom had acquiesced in going to the Spaniards to surrender. On January 16, forty-two Ocomes under Chief Miguel arrived in Atotonilco and made peace with the Spaniards. Two days later, 396 persons from ten "nations" led by the Cabezas – Cabezas, Gavilanes, Maçaltypilguas, Cocoyomes, Cabacbitac, Talcocoyomes, Salineros, Tubaymamar, Matarajes, and Babosarigas – also surrendered at Atotonilco (CD 1650a).

In November, after the first groups of Salineros and Tobosos had surrendered, Governor Luis de Valdés ordered an investigation of the motives behind the uprising. A number of Indians were questioned, and the results were those typically obtained by the Spanish procedure of interrogating witnesses and delinquents. Aside from variations in the stories, it seems clear that the Indians, particularly the Salineros, were aware that they should admit nothing that might implicate themselves. Responsibility for the rebellion, raiding, and other crimes was often placed on other persons or on other bands. Salineros blamed the Tobosos. The little information that came to light concerning the Spanish woman and her children in the main corroborates Alegre's story, as well as the apparent fact that it was indeed the Ocomes to whom the Cabezas had traded her. It was stated on several occasions that booty from raiding was shared with other groups. One Salinero declared that his band had divided its proceeds with a large tribe called the Come Cíbolas (AHP 1652Dc; CD 1650b).

Gerónimo Moranta, the Salinero governor from Tizonazo, claimed that an Indian unknown to him personally had advised his Salineros to leave the mission because the Spaniards were planning to hang them. Out of fear the Indians had left, and Moranta, under orders from the Spanish Alcalde Mayor, had gone out later to bring them back. It is not too clear what happened after this. The Spaniards in one of their campaigns at a place called El Peñol de la Porcíngula (probably at Las Salinas) corraled the Salineros who had promised peace. The people were in general agreement with this, according to Moranta, but one man, Francisco El Tuerto, had insisted that the peace offer was merely a ruse under which the Spaniards were planning to capture and execute them. Consequently, the Salineros had retired farther into the back country, and judging from other information it must have been soon after this that the band of Salineros under El Tuerto broke off from the main group. At the time of these testimonies the latter were now ready to settle down in peace. Moranta also claimed that the pillaging and murdering that had taken place during the uprising had been done by the Tobosos, Matarajes, and Negritos, and that only some six Salineros had been involved. He later admitted, however, that another group of Salineros, those governed by Don Cebrián, had committed some raiding but had kept all the booty for themselves. Despite this declaration, other information indicates that most if not all of Don Cebrián's band had been with the rest of the Salineros. Moranta did not know if the captives taken by the Indians during the revolt were dead or alive (AHP 1656B; AHP 1652Dc; CD 1650b).

Other Salinero witnesses filled out Moranta's story. Some stated that they had gone along with the uprising because the rest of their people had been in favor of it. Apparently not all of the Salineros had been at Tizonazo at the time of the rebellion. Some had been working at nearby haciendas, and as soon as they heard the news of the revolt they left to join their people. Others claimed that they had never learned exactly why the Salineros had left Tizonazo, although some cited trouble with certain Spaniards as the reason. The principal conflict they mentioned involved some Salinero cowboys who had been working at an hacienda at Ramos that belonged to a certain Doña María. She had implicated them in the theft of some animals in which it was thought that Tobosos and Cabezas had been involved. Some witnesses claimed that the Salineros had left the hacienda because of the fear of punishment, and others that Doña María had become angry and had sent them away (AHP 1652Dc).

The Toboso governor, Don Cristóbal, whose group had been living at Atotonilco, gave his Toboso version of the uprising. When he had heard that the Ocomes were planning to go on the warpath, he personally had gone to them in an attempt to get them to change their minds. Then, he discovered that his own braves had fled from Atotonilco during his absence.

While on his way to intercept them out in the back country he learned that the Spaniards were blaming his group as well as other "Tobosos" as the perpetrators of a number of robberies and murders. With this, he and his people, out of fear, retired farther into the desert. For a while they had been at El Peñol de la Porcíngula (which would seem to indicate that they had been together with the Salineros). Don Cristóbal, and later Zapata, admitted that the Tobosos had had a hand in some of the raids committed during the hostilities (CD 1650b; AHP 1652Dc).

After January of 1646, the province of Nueva Vizcaya enjoyed a short period of peace, although it is not certain whether all the nations who took part in the uprising surrendered. At the end of February, the Viceroy wrote that over 2,000 Indians of the province had been reduced to peace and that some 150 of the leaders had been executed for their deeds (Hackett 1926: 162). By the middle of the year several of the bands had gone back on the warpath. Tobosos, Nonojes, Ocomes, Acoclames, Otolcoclomes, and even Conchos are mentioned (CD 1646a; AHP 1646Ab). About this same time the inhabitants of Tizonazo rebelled, after suffering some five months of a plague of *cocolixtli*. The ethnic identity of the Indians is not mentioned, but certainly many were Salineros, and perhaps some were Tepehuanes. Some forty families remained faithful to the Spaniards and were taken to Indé by their missionary for protection. Many of the rebels were returned to the mission at the beginning of the following year (AGN 1645-1647a).

Information on the desert-dwelling Indians is practically nonexistent from this time until the early 1650's. However, one minor event in April of 1647 indicates that rebel groups were still in the hinterland. A group of Indians, of unstated ethnic affiliation, while on a pilgrimage were attacked by enemy Indians on the road to Parral. They were beaten, and their clothing and an image they were carrying were taken from them. Their assailants informed them that if they were caught again with such images they would be killed. It was not determined exactly who the attackers were, but it was thought that they were Salineros under the protection of Baltazar de Ontiveros, who a little over a year earlier had been named "protector" of the Cabeza Indians (the names Salinero and Cabeza were possibly used interchangeably here) (AHP 1647; AHP 1652Dc).

The 1650's

Not all of the desert bands surrendered in 1646, and the available documentation indicates that some raiding by these peoples continued during the next few years. Moreover, whatever peace the province of Nueva Vizcaya as a whole enjoyed was short-lived. In 1648 and again in 1650, the Tarahumara to the west of the Parral district revolted, the second time destroying the newly founded town of Villa de Aguilar near the Papigochic River. There is evidence that the raiding activities of the desert-dwelling Indians were becoming more intense in the 1650's. To make matters worse, while the tribes of the Greater Bolsón were stepping up their warfare, in 1652 the Tarahumara rebelled for a third time, although they were put down in the same year (Spicer 1962: 30,32).

In the midst of all of these enemy hostilities, Spaniards either made expeditions themselves against these rebels or instigated friendly Indians to do so. The frontier situation at times must have appeared desperate to the Europeans. As seen from the capital of Parral, the Indian wars, for a while at least, were being carried out on two fronts, to the west among the Tarahumara and to the east with the Tobosos and Salineros. Despite this, either by their own direct efforts or indirectly through those of their Indian allies, the Spaniards managed to soundly defeat the rebel Indians on several occasions. Battles occurred at such places as Acatita, Río Angosto, and Guapagua, but the most notable one was fought at the Peñol de San Miguel de Nonolat when several Toboso bands were virtually wiped out (BL 1649-1700; AHP 1652Ab; AHP 1653Ad).

A number of different Indian nations took to the battlefield in the decade of the 1650's, and the events of this period foreshadow in large degree much of the future history of Spanish-native relations in the area. The nomadic Indians were becoming increasingly efficient in raiding and warfare against the Europeans while at the same time expanding their geographical range of operations. Moreover, the reduction of the number of distinct Indian bands can also be noted. This trend took place for several reasons, one of the foremost being annihilation at the hands of the Spaniards and their allies. Another pattern that becomes increasingly clear at this time is the establishment of peace by Indians and resettlement among the Spaniards for short periods, followed by further rebellion and a return to the desert and to raiding activities. The Spanish practice of giving handouts during and after these negotiations was no doubt a factor in inducing Indians to consent to peace on many occasions. The total picture is one of a rather continual round of peacemaking and rebellion.

One Spaniard, Antonio de Medrano, described some of the desperation the Europeans felt under the onslaught of enemy Indian attacks. Writing from Durango in 1657, he cited the atrocities the Indians had committed in all parts of the Nueva Vizcayan province. These, he said, were executed with such cunning that their authors appeared to be phantoms; the only persons permitted to see the enemy were those unfortunate enough to fall into his hands. Medrano suggested that the most efficacious means of putting an end to these hostilities was to seek out the rebels in their own territories, as had already been done on several occasions by the Spanish governor. However, this tactic was becoming more difficult to carry out, because for some time the rebels had been operating outside their tribal territories, having been reported as far south as the areas of San Juan del Mesquital, Sombrerete, and Durango (AHP 1657Bb).

The situation of Spaniard pitted against marauding desert Indian is only part of the story; other Indians were sometimes involved. Medrano's letter may only hint at the complexities of the hostilities the Europeans were forced to face at this time, with the natives in effect ranging far from their own home territories. In January of the year of Medrano's writing, a large-scale assault involving about 100 enemy Indians had been made on Los Cerrillos, three or four leagues from the Nazas River. The assailants had spoken in the Mexican, Concho, and Salinero tongues, although one of the attackers was reported to have said in Mexican that the attacking force was made up entirely of Salineros and that no other group should be blamed. The reason the Concho language was employed by the attackers remains unexplained by this statement. On another occasion a Concho, imprisoned in Durango for murder and theft in the jurisdiction of Chalchihuites, declared that his accomplices had been five Salineros, including one woman, and four Cabezas. About this same time a band of Julimes and Chisos attacked a Spaniard and an Indian only six leagues from Durango. The fact that these Indians were operating this far south amazed the Spanish authorities (AHP 1657Bb).

Actually, this and other information indicates that some of the trouble was coming from Indian hacienda workers rather than from the permanently rebel groups living in the back country. These laborers would get together for specific assaults and disband afterward. The hacienda Indians were accustomed, particularly during the summer season, to retire from their places of work to look for food as well as for other (unspecified) reasons. The chance of their banding together on these occasions for raiding purposes was naturally increased. Furthermore, crimes committed by other persons were probably often blamed on the desert Indians, lending confusion to the reports about the activities of these nomads (AHP 1654Aa; AHP 1654Ac; AHP 1657Bb).

The situation of the "Salineros" and the "Cabezas" also appears to be somewhat complicated. During part of the 1650's, a number of these groups were allied on the Spanish side to the extent that they were employed as auxiliaries against the Toboso bands. Many of these people apparently worked for Spaniards on haciendas and other establishments. However, Spaniards felt that from these places, as well as from their mission of Tizonazo, Salineros and Cabezas would sneak off to raid Spanish holdings as they had done when they had been in full rebellion. Furthermore, at times these groups were considered "worse" than the "Tobosos." During the hostilities of the 1640's Governor Valdés had felt that the Salineros and Cabezas were more dangerous enemies than the Tobosos. In October of 1645 he had written that the excesses of the Tobosos, Nonojes, Ococlames (Acoclames), and Ocomes were minor (*por menores*), while those of the Salineros and Cabezas were extreme (*exsorvitantes*) (CD 1650a).

Conchos Indians, who as a group were fairly peaceful, were sometimes also cited as raiders, together with the Tobosos and Salineros, particularly in the region north of Parral. Despite the wide and intense raiding, the Spaniards at this time seem to have been quite well aware that they were not dealing with any general alliance of Indians but rather with a number of independent nations. Aside from the fact that raids were often widely separated from one another, the Spaniards knew that many of the Indian "nations" were traditional enemies of each other and would not dare trespass upon another's territory. It was also recognized that interband relations were not static, that temporary alliances were formed and dissolved, and that groups who would not join in a revolt often would be attacked by the rebels. The Tobosos, Acoclames, and Cabezas had attacked the Laguneros, forcing them to leave their lands and move under Spanish protection (AHP 1654Ad).

At various times the local citizenry petitioned the governor at Parral for an alleviation of the Indian menace. On such occasions the governor held conferences with various officials about the wild Indians. Opinions given by a number of persons in 1654 were typical of those held throughout much of the historical period. The desert Indians were described as people who did not wish to work or cultivate the land, but to live by what they could steal from the Spaniards. When they did surrender, which was frequently, they used the guise of peace to enjoy the protection afforded by the Spanish administration, until within a short while they would revolt and withdraw to their old haunts. The word of these Indians in peace treaties was worthless. In 1654, the priest at Parral testified that in his eighteen years of experience in the area, the Tobosos and their allies had made peace many times, but on not a single occasion had they kept it. An episode at Atotonilco was a good example. The Indians had been settled there with a missionary and had been furnished with everything they needed — food, clothing, and animals to plow their fields. Still, they remained only a short time before they revolted.

In the 1650's a large consensus apparently was developing to the effect that the only solution to the enemy hostilities was to make war on the Indians until they were annihilated. Although efforts were made in this direction, the actual extermination of the enemy Indians would not be realized for almost another hundred years (AHP 1653Ac; AHP 1654Ad; AHP 1718 Ab).

One event that occurred in the 1640's, the secularization of the Laguna district missions, probably contributed to the unsettled conditions in Nueva Vizcaya during the mid-seventeenth century and later. Although a detailed analysis of the factors involved is not possible at present, some of the writers of this period thought that this was the case. The missions at Parras and San Pedro de la Laguna were taken out of the Jesuits' hands in 1646, after some fifty years of missionary activity there. The Black Robes kept one small establishment at Parras, but the area was now controlled by the secular clergy. Jesuit writers somewhat exaggeratedly attributed the wars with the Neuva Vizcayan natives to this event, partly because of the dissensions that had been allowed to build up among the several nations after secularization. There is likely to have been some truth to this, for one would guess that Jesuit mediation

between Indians and Spanish citizens had been important (Dunne 1948: 86; DHM 1653; AGN nd; DHM ca 1706).

On May 1, 1653, the Jesuit Gáspar de Contreras, one of the two men who had remained on at Parras after the secularization, penned a description of the situation as he saw it. This, and another report rendered about fifty years later, seem in part to outline the context of some of the events of the following decades. Contreras blamed the secular priests for inefficiency and stated that after the Parras missions had been handed over to them, the "Laguneros" had returned to their old haunts in the interior, leaving the towns depopulated. The Jesuits who remained at the old mission town were still attempting to work with the Indians as much as possible; they had managed to get some to come in for Lent during this year, and a few had even confessed. Some of the Indians, however, had told the Jesuits that "the Faith" was now finished and they were no longer Christians. The people of San Lorenzo, one of the towns of La Laguna, had also revolted, Contreras said, and were ceaselessly executing robberies and thefts, including attacks on Parras. He stated that these rebels had sent a message to him to the effect that they would come in and surrender as soon as the Jesuits returned to take over the area (DHM 1653; AGN nd).

A later report, written by an anonymous Jesuit about the year 1706, notes that only two secular priests had been sent to take over the missions of six missionaries, three at Parras and three at San Pedro. By the time of the Jesuit's report, only a few persons from the nations that had settled at Parras remained. Of the nations at La Laguna — Salineros, Vaqueros, Molineros and Cabezas — the Salineros had departed and the Laguneros and Baganeros (Molineros and Vaqueros? — tribal identity here is not clear) had been forced to remove themselves to the town of Parras, owing to the hostilities of the Tobosos (DHM ca 1706).

Regardless of cause and effect, the secularization of the Jesuit missions in the Parras-Laguna district did occasion a change in the power structure and economy of the region. At a minimum there was a lessening of control over the Indians by virtue of the smaller number of clerics, and a reduction in face-to-face contact between native and secular priest (DHM 1653; DHM ca 1706). At the same time that the Jesuits relinquished their moral control in the area, their role as an economic force stopped too — a large ranch, for example, was abandoned. After the Jesuit evacuation, the Urdiñola hacienda nearby was forced to serve as the principal bulwark in the defense of Parras, and it prevented the abandonment of the town by its own military force (AGN nd).

Events are sketchy for the first two years of the 1650's. In the early part of 1650 a number of Toboso bands, some of which had been settled at the mission of Atotonilco, went on the warpath. These Tobosos and the Salineros and Cabezas were reported to be executing a constant round of hostilities, but practically no details are given for a year or so. Then the Spanish governor, Diego Guajardo Fajardo, reported that over 30,000 natives were in the kingdom of Nueva Vizcaya, and he underscored the fact that many Indian raids had taken place. Since the 1650 peace with the Tarahumaras, he noted, the Tobosos, Nonojes, Acoclames, Gavilanes, Salineros, and Cabezas had diminished their bellicose activities to some extent, although they had not ceased to commit robberies and atrocious crimes, a deeply ingrained custom with them. The Tobosos, Nonojes, and Ococlames (Acoclames) were at this time sending proposals of rebellion to the Tarahumaras and Conchos. The governor feared that all of the nations of the province would revolt, a fear not totally unfounded, as the Tarahumara did rebel again the following year, although it is not known that the Toboso proposal had any effect upon this Tarahumara decision. Guajardo Fajardo described the rebels as moving from town to town, raiding settlements as far south as Mapimí, some sixty leagues from Parral. About this same time, however, some Salineros and Cabezas had made peace with the Spaniards (BL 1649-1700).

In October of 1651 Captain Juan de Barraza summarized the declaration of an Indian woman. She told that the Indians from Tizonazo had congregated with a number of other bands for the purpose of avenging the deaths of two Indians who had been killed at the place of Palmitos. These groups were planning to join the Baburigames (Babozarigames), a large nation from the hinterland, to make war on the Spaniards, as they were now acquainted with Spanish territory and customs. This plan had had its origin at the Tizonazo mission. Barraza commented that he had no confidence in the Salineros, Cabezas (of which there were only a few at Tizonazo but many in the back country), or Babozarigames, who had some time previously offered to fight the Tobosos, because since

their offer they had not been heard of again (BL 1649-1700).

In 1652 many attacks, attributed to both "Salinero" and "Toboso" bands, were reported over a wide area, from Parral to San Miguel de las Bocas (AHP 1652Db; AHP 1652Bb; BL 1649-1700). In July, Felipa, an Indian woman fluent in the Mexican language, the daughter of Don Cristóbal the Toboso governor (appointed — again? — as such in Atotonilco in June of 1649), arrived in Parral to request peace. Her story was that her father, with another six or seven Indians, had separated from the Nonojes, Ocomes, and Acoclames with whom they had been associated — and presumably from the rest of the Tobosos — who had become angry with Don Cristóbal when he had reprimanded them for raiding the Spaniards. These rebels, consisting of some ten groups, including Cabezas and Salineros, were camped at a mountain called Tuacague, located somewhere to the west of the Sierra de Jaque (Jaco). Here they had their families and horses, abundant mesquite and water, as well as many items of Spanish military paraphernalia, including arquebuses taken from the people they had killed. They were led by three chiefs — two Nonojes, Cristóbal and Caza Zavala, and a Gavilán named Joxocomi — and planned to fight the Spaniards until they had annihilated them. Her father, Felipa claimed, would have come to the Spaniards, together with another Gavilán chief, and given himself up, except for his great fear of Juan de Barraza and the other Spaniards who, he felt, would hang him. Felipa was given several gifts and a document that formally assured her safe conduct (the usual Spanish procedure), and was sent back to fetch her father (AHP 1652Ac).

By August 12 Felipa was back with the Spaniards — without her father. She reported that just before she had arrived at her own camp she had been stopped by a group of Nonojes. These had treated her with a good deal of hostility, had taken the gifts from her, and had accused her of collaborating with the enemy. Then, after visiting her father, she had returned to Atotonilco. Actually it appears that the problem her father had with the other Toboso groups was that many of his own people had been killed by Barraza; those remaining, since her father was an old man (or at least was considered to be ineffective), had moved into closely related bands. This had left him without much of a following, as well as probably with a great deal of criticism. It was also learned at this time, partly from Felipa, that some hacienda laborers, seemingly mostly Conchos, had been in touch with the enemy and had sent them stolen cattle. Several of these men were questioned, and it was learned that the Tobosos and allied bands were camped at a place called Nagolcaguel, west of Jaque, from which they were planning to raid the Parral district (AHP 1652Ac).

Meanwhile, farther south the Salinero faction of Don Cebrián and the Cabezas had banded together for the warpath. In the early part of August of 1652 three members of this group arrived in Indé, stating that they wanted to join the Spaniards. They claimed they were Tepehuanes, although they had been raised at the mission of Tizonazo with Salineros; their governor, Don Cebrián, was now at El Canutillo. According to the three Tepehuanes, their group had left Tizonazo three weeks after Holy Week and had joined the Cabezas, led by Santiaguillo (AHP 1651A).

The two nations had gone to a spot called La Magdalena, from which Santiaguillo had sent his brother Diego back with a mixed squad of Salineros and Cabezas to raid in the area they had just come from. Santiaguillo had then taken the remainder, plus the women and children, to Santo Domingo. Here they waited for Diego, who showed up with his men five days later with a large herd of horses, a captive girl (apparently an Indian) of around seven years old, and the scalp of an Indian woman. This group had been raiding around the Nazas River as well as in the Indé region (AHP 1651A).

From here Santiaguillo and Diego took the group to a point about two leagues from El Gallo, where they had made mescal and eaten all of the horses. Afterward, Santiago sent his brother out again with the best braves of both the Salinero and Cabeza nations to attack Los Palmitos and the Ontivero's hacienda to obtain all the horses and clothing they could. This war party met Santiaguillo's group a week later at Las Salinas de Machete but was forced to report little success owing to the resistance put up by the Spaniards. They had brought with them only a few horses and mules, plus some saddles and a little clothing. Not a single scalp was taken (AHP 1651A).

About a day's journey from Las Salinas these Salineros and Cabezas had met another nation in revolt — the Baborimamas, led by Chief Baltazar. Santiaguillo regaled them with part of the booty of horses and clothing his people had collected. The combined group traveled the next two days in the direction of Toboso territory. Then the chiefs decided, since they had already made so many raids and could expect only punishment at the hands of the Spaniards, the only thing left to do was to continue the war until the Spaniards were exterminated. The chiefs sent two ambassadors to the Tobosos, Acoclames, Gavilanes, Nonojes, and other Toboso bands, located at that time a couple of day's travel from Atotonilco. The message they carried was that all the tribes should join and carefully distribute themselves along the borderland country facing Parral. From this series of positions, war parties could be sent out to wreak all possible damage on the Spanish enemy (AHP 1651A).

Santiago then decided to visit the Cíbolas of Coahuila to enlist their aid. However, the party had hardly begun its trek eastward when the three declarants began to feel that they themselves were in danger. They figured that they should get away from Santiago's people as soon as possible, particularly since the Cabeza-Salinero bands had killed an uncle and a brother of one of them for refusing to cooperate. The next morning the combined group broke into small parties in order to hunt more effectively along the way. The three Tepehuanes, plus two of their spouses and the wife of Don Cebrián, made good their escape. Don Cebrián had remained behind at Tizonazo during this uprising (AHP 1651A).

In mid-September of 1652 Governor Guajardo Fajardo, now engaged in a campaign against the Tarahumara, decided to take time out to move against the Tobosos. Toboso raiding had become so serious at this time that it was felt that pacification of the desert tribes was more urgent than putting down the current Tarahumara uprising. Spanish troops, led by Guajardo, left for Toboso country on September 13 and 15. After several encounters between the Spanish scouts and the enemy, the main body of soldiers corraled a great number of the Indians near a rocky crag (peñol) called San Miguel de Nonolat, a spot where Spaniards reportedly had never penetrated before. The enemy camp was surprised on September 26, and a number of persons were killed and their food and water supply destroyed. The remainder took refuge in nearby Nonolat where the Spaniards besieged them for three days, containing the Indians in such a way that they could not avail themselves of flight, their usual defensive procedure in tight situations. A pitched battle ensued, with a great many arrows and rocks. When the Spanish forces began to slow down, Barraza promised his men they could keep some of the captives (that is, to sell later as slaves). Finally, a truce was called on September 29. The Nonoje chief, Don Francisco de Casa Zavala, his son, and the chief of the Acoclames, came into the Spanish camp with a banner. The Indians agreed to bring all of their people down from the crag. The next day, however, the natives were still in hiding, and Guajardo broke the truce and attacked, causing a great many casualties (Alegre III 1956: 223; Saravia III 1954: 329-330; BL 1649-1700; AHP 1652Da; AHP 1652Ab).

A number of Toboso bands took part in this encounter, one of the most decisive in Toboso-Spanish military history. In one statement Guajardo Fajardo reported that there was a "great number of the enemy which comprised five nations: Nonojes, Acoclames, Gobossos [in another version this reads "Jogosos"], over half of the Tobosos, and Masames." Later reports estimated the number of enemy Indians killed as between 200 and 345, and from 100 to 270 prisoners taken (Alegre III 1956: 223; Saravia III 1954: 329-330, BL 1649-1700; AHP 1652Da). A field certification of October 4 claimed 300 warriors dead and 180 women and children taken prisoners (BL 1649-1700).

Governor Guajardo then returned to the Tarahumara country with the major portion of the Spanish troops. He left two subordinates, Captain Juan Gutiérrez Tamayo and Sergeant Major Cristóbal de Nevares, to reconnoiter the general Toboso and Salinero region, together with the men under General Barraza. Their orders were to punish the Salineros, Cabezas, and their allies, as well as all those Tobosos who had escaped from the Peñol de Nonolat affair (Saravia III 1954: 327, 329-330; AHP 1652Ab). For over a month these forces roamed a broad area which included the places of Río Angosto, San Pedro de la Laguna, Parras, Sierra de Acatita, Sierra de Sonteco, Sierra Colorada, Sierra de la Ventanilla, Sierra Prieta, and Aguachila. A few abandoned camps of varying sizes were located, including one large ranchería which was said to contain definite signs of mourning for those lost at a fracas at Acatita (AHP 1652Ab).

This battle of Acatita had taken place some time before the middle of November. Gutiérrez Tamayo reported that a minimum of 200 enemy warriors,

very well armed — including shields (*chimales*) — had participated (AHP 1653Aa). Judging from the size of the forces involved, this encounter was apparently more than a minor skirmish. Declarations taken later from "Coahuila" Indians shed some light on the event. An old man, testifying in the presence of Barraza in Parras, said he had gone to visit the Baborimamas and Babozarigames to retrieve his daughter whom they were holding. While there, he learned that a number of nations had held a large junta at a camp situated among the mountains of Acatita, Sonteco, and Colorada (AHP 1652Ab).

The Indians had been about to sally on Parras when they saw the dust of two or three persons moving in the direction of the water hole at Acatita. Half of the warriors went down to meet them, killing one Spaniard and an Indian. A second Spaniard escaped. At this moment a great many Spaniards and their Indian allies had emerged from Acatita, surprising the enemy, who was totally unaware that a Spanish force was in the vicinity. Heavy fighting ensued in which many of the rebels were killed, including the Talcoyote chief and his son, and the captain of the Baborimamas. The remaining warriors fled back to their camp, where the bands decided to split up and go their separate ways. The old man reported that he had also heard, before he left the enemy at Sierra Prieta, that the Baborimamas and Babozarigames had met some other tribes from the distant hinterland, the names of which he did not know. They had entered into a friendship agreement with these people, formalized with a peyote ceremony and the exchange and sacrifice of two boys (AHP 1652Ab).

Two days after this testimony, on December 14, two Indians from Coahuila arrived in Parras. They had been sent by Barraza over two weeks before to contact the "Coahuilas" (specific bands unstated) at Aguachila; three chiefs now returned with them. The rest of the "Coahuilas" were camped about four leagues from Parras. They had come to offer their services to Barraza as evidence that they were not part of the rebel groups. The captain, named Bega (Vega?), and the other "Coahuila" chiefs gave the Spaniards essentially the same story of the events at Acatita as had the old man before them. More than six nations had been involved — not only Babozarigames, Baborimamas, and Talcoyotes, but also Salineros, Tobosos, and Matarajes (AHP 1652Ab).

The "Coahuilas'" account varied concerning the

events following the skirmish. The several bands had held a meeting that same night and had decided to split up. The Salinero captain, Santiaguillo, was going to Indé to surrender to Captain Levarío. The bands had then sworn peace among themselves, performing the ceremony mentioned by the old man. Only, they said, it was the Salineros who had given one boy to the Babozarigames and Matarajes, and the latter had reciprocated by sending one of their own lads to the Salineros. After this, they had taken leave of one another (AHP 1652Ab).

The Babozarigames had then gone to camp at Sierra Prieta, which lay behind Sierra Colorada. Some twenty of them tried to cut off the "Coahuilas" when the latter were going down to see Barraza. Apparently a fight was in the air, although it did not take place immediately because the "Coahuilas" were greater in number and the Babozarigames simply went along beside them. This was in the morning. That evening, after traveling some four or five leagues, the Babozarigames on two or three occasions started to attack the "Coahuilas," but each time desisted. They decided to spend the night with the "Coahuilas" to determine whether the Spaniards were still in the general area. The next day the two bands parted company, and no hostilities materialized. It is uncertain what the "Coahuilas" did after their arrival in the Parras vicinity or, for that matter, where they were at the time of the Acatita affair (AHP 1652Ab).

A number of enemy bands were still at large. The Spanish forces left to campaign again, reconnoitering into the Mapimí region, Sierra de Pelayo and Pozo Hediondo, then to Pantita, and to Los Patos, three leagues from Cerro Gordo. At Los Patos, Barraza received orders to march to the Tarahumara in the early part of January. In a letter to the governor he summed up his feelings regarding the more than two months of reconnaissance since the Nonolat battle — considering the many leagues traveled, and over the worst country imaginable, the effort had been largely unsuccessful (AHP 1652Ab; AHP 1653Aa).

What had happened, apparently, was that for the most part the Indians had managed to outmaneuver and dodge the Spanish troops. The Spaniards opined at one point that the enemy could never be reduced by the force of arms. The Salinero governor, Don Francisco Mama, together with other Salineros who had remained faithful and were now marching with the Spaniards, concurred in this. They felt that a gen-

eral pardon issued by the governor of Nueva Vizcaya might more effectively bring the rebel Indians to surrender (AHP 1653Aa).

Reports from other areas of the Toboso country also indicate that the Indians were making themselves scarce at this time. While Barraza was in Parras questioning the "Coahuilas," four envoys from the Mamites and Julimes reported back to Governor Guajardo Fajardo in the Tarahumara. These messengers had been sent to the Chisos, the Tobosos' northern neighbors, but had failed to locate them. They had returned by way of Toboso territory and not only had not run into a single person but, they stated, had not even seen any tracks (AHP 1653Aa).

Despite the fact that Barraza and the Spanish forces remained in the area until January of 1653, the evidence indicates that raids upon Spanish settlements and other holdings had become more frequent as time progressed. From the reports it is often difficult to determine which Indian groups were involved in the individual attacks. Information from El Gallo stated that the Cabezas and Salineros were operating in this area. In the early days of December of 1652, a sally was made into Toboso country as far as the Sierra de las Cañas, in pursuit of the enemy, but nobody was found. The Spaniards felt that Salineros, Cabezas, Tobosos, Nonojes, Ocomes, Acoclames, Negritos, Gavilanes, Matarajes, Babozarigames, and Baborimamas were all taking part in the hostilities. Raids were committed in the areas of Santa Cruz, San José, San Juan del Río, and Los Palmitos, among other places, and Tobosos were blamed for some attacks in Tarahumara country. Cuencamé was practically depopulated. A number of raids in the Parras district were attributed to the Salineros and Cabezas (AHP 1653Aa; AHP 1653Ba).

In the latter part of October a report from Saltillo stated that a number of the Coahuila groups from around the town of Parras had left to join the rebel Salineros. These tribes were planning a large scale attack on Parras. An Orame Indian, testifying at the Hacienda de las Mesillas near Saltillo, stated that the peoples involved included Tusares, Tocas, Gueyapaes, Tetecos, and Sipopolas. Other wild nations were also being asked to join the Salineros, and clothing (*capisayos* and *fresadas*) had been sent to them by the Spaniards as inducement to refuse (AHP 1653Aa).

It is impossible to determine how many enemy Indians were actually operating. According to one rumor there were twenty rancherias consisting of some two thousand people at Sierra Colorada alone — but it may be that Spanish imagination under the duress of hostilities had run overboard. Another, perhaps more realistic, report referred to some six hundred of the enemy camped at Acatita. This, however, was after the attack and battle that Gutiérrez Tamayo had there. If the several bands at that place had in effect split up as reported and had remained separated, this rumor is open to some question (AHP 1653Aa).

The year 1653 saw no let-up in the hostilities of the desert peoples. In the spring, enemy attacks were reported in a number of different areas. The Tarahumara towns of San Felipe, San Ignacio, and Santa Cruz were raided, seemingly mainly by Conchos and Julimes, although it is likely that some Toboso raiding parties were also involved. Three soldiers were assaulted by a force of over one hundred and fifty enemy warriors, said to be Tobosos. Cabeza and Salinero bands were still active in the general Parras district, and two large groups of the rebels were reported at Sierra Colorada. It was felt that these people were in communication with the Cabezas and Salineros, said to be in "feigned" peace at Tizonazo and other places. Salineros and their close congeners, the Cabezas, Matarajes, Babosarigames, and Baborimamas, were blamed for activity in the general region of Indé, Cuencamé, the Tepehuán Atotonilco, Santa Catalina, and Papasquiaro (AHP 1652Ba; AHP 1653Ae).

The several Salinero chieftains, including Gerónimo Moranta and Francisco Mama, were asked by the Spaniards to send messengers to the Cabezas requesting the latter to go out and fight the Tobosos. Included in the message was the notice that the Spanish governor was coming with well over eight hundred troops from his punitive expedition against the Tarahumara, and that he would castigate the Cabezas in the same way he had the Tarahumara if they did not come over to the Spanish side. The chief of the Cíbolas was asked to help the Cabezas — his brother Agustinillo and an old man, who were at Indé at the time (April), were to carry the message to him. Meanwhile, Salinero and Toboso bands had killed five Indians from Tizonazo who had been out on patrol with Moranta, and had murdered another party searching for wild tobacco in the Los Patos area because they were friends of the Spaniards. One

Indian, Frasquillo, who had been with a group looking for palm branches for Palm Sunday, was captured and carried off alive (AHP 1653Ad).

The Cabezas and their allies accepted the proposition made to them by the Spanish governor. Santiaguillo sent word to Barraza that he and the rest of his people were furious with the Tobosos because his own brother had been one of the five from Tizonazo they had killed. He was leaving immediately to get the Cíbolas, Corcobados, and other nations (apparently including the Babozarigames) from the north of Parras to join them against the Tobosos. They were planning on attacking the latter from behind, from the Río Angosto region (AHP 1653Ad).

By July the Spaniards were of the opinion that it would not be long until the Tobosos were duly chastised for their wrong-doing. The force led by the friendly Salineros had grown, with the addition of some forty to fifty Pies de Venado and Tusares braves from Parras, and was now considered to be a good bit larger than that of the Tobosos and their associates. Furthermore, about forty Chisos, said to be known enemies of the Tobosos, arrived in Parral after having been called by their governor, a Concho named Hernando de Obregón. These Chisos wanted to go to war against the Tobosos, for the latter had recently killed some of their people. The Chisos claimed that before leaving their own country they had sent a message to the tribes on the Río Grande area to join them in the battle against the Tobosos (AHP 1653Ad; AHP 1653Bb).

The Chiso situation was somewhat more complicated than this, however. In early September, a little after the Chiso visit to Parral, the Franciscan, Fray Francisco de Cervantes, made a trip down the Conchos River to Julimes. From here he went to a Chiso camp led by Chief Alonzo, one of the captains who had gone to Parral in July. Alonzo warned Cervantes not to continue farther into Chiso country because all the other Chiso bands were friendly with the rebel Tobosos. These Chisos, he said, were resentful over the recent deaths of two of their chiefs at Los Peyotillos, as well as because, they claimed, when they had visited Parras they had not been paid. The Spaniards disclaimed this, stating that the usual gifts of clothing, flour, and meat had been distributed to the Chisos, and at another time Chief Alonzo did say that his group had received compensation. This seemingly was a Chiso excuse for not going to fight the

Tobosos. In the meantime, Cervantes did send a message to the hostile Chisos to see if they could be induced to join the Spanish side (AHP 1653Bb; AHP 1653Bd).

Obregón, the governor of the Conchería, then reported in Parral. He corroborated the story of the lack of payment of some of the Chisos as a reason they had not wanted to fight the Tobosos, but he added that the main reason was that the Chisos were related by marriage to some of the Tobosos. Furthermore, on their trip back from Parral, some of the Chisos had died, thus leading others to claim later that the flour given them by the Spaniards had been poisoned (AHP 1653Bd).

Before September 10, Gerónimo Moranta sent word that his combined force of well over 200 Indians had hit the Toboso bands in a surprise attack at Río Angosto. These Tobosos had been caught completely off guard at daybreak, after having held an all-night dance celebrating the success of a recently returned raiding squad. Moranta reported that 180 adult males, not counting the women, children, and aged, had been killed. A later report reduced the total to somewhat over 100, including only about thirty adult males. Many others had escaped with wounds, including one El Zurdo and Don Cristóbal El Toboso. The hand and scalp of one Gavilán chief had been sent along with the bearers of the news, who announced that Moranta's men were bringing in some fifty prisoners. Santiaguillo's and Cebrián's bands, together with the Babozarigames, were coming in with Moranta in order to ask for pardon for themselves and for their allies. The Cíbolas with the others were returning to their territories, although they informed the Spaniards that they were ready to help them in whatever they were asked, in the event of another campaign against the Tobosos (AHP 1653Ad).

The nations that had fought with Moranta and the Tizonazo Salineros had been the Cabezas of Santiaguillo, the Salineros of Don Cebrián, the Mayos, the Tusares, the Matarajes, the Babozarigames, the Cíbolas, and another band of "wild" Salineros. Considering the previous reports, it is quite possible that other bands were also involved. The combined Toboso forces were said to have included the Tobosos proper, Gavilanes, Nonojes, Acoclames, Ocomes, Coyotes (probably Cocoyomes), and Baborimamas. At the same time, six other "Toboso" chiefs with

their people were reported to have been in Ocotán, and one squad from the Río Angosto group had been out in the Parral district at the time of the attack (AHP 1653Ad).

After January 1653, Spanish troops apparently were not employed in the Toboso war. The entire action was carried out by Indians, led by the Salineros under Moranta. The Spaniards often furnished supplies, and, through the good offices of the Tizonazoans — and with the promise of a general pardon and of payment for all enemy scalps (*cabezas*) brought to them — the Spaniards had been able to induce a number of rebels to join their side to put down the more recalcitrant Toboso bands (AHP 1653Ad).

On August 4, the victorious Salineros and their allies marched into Parral "with much order," carrying a red (*colorada*) flag with a cross on it, and a pole from which hung Toboso scalps. With them marched the chiefs Gerónimo Moranta, Francisco Mama, Juan Concho, and Pedro Negrito, with thirty-eight warriors. Moranta and the others were thanked for their fine action and asked what they wished to do. They replied that they wanted to go back a second time to fight the Tobosos, for which they planned to join their allies, the Cabezas, Cíbolas, Mayos, Babozarigames, Tatalcoyomes, Tusares, Ygoquibas, Yguitoros, and others. Together they would track down the enemy. The Tusares, at any rate, and perhaps some of the others from the Parras district, were at this time in revolt and raiding around the Laguna country. The Spaniards wanted them either exterminated or reduced to peace. The Salineros were to try to get the Tusares to join them as allies by working through the Cíbolas, Mayos, and Babozarigames. The same was to be done with the Baborimamas, who were still holding a mestizo woman they had captured in Guatimapé (AHP 1653Ad).

The Spaniards at this time were making an all-out push to reduce in number or to eliminate from the desert the Indians who were such a menace. They were, and so they told the Salineros, attempting to bring Chisos, Julimes, and Mamites into the fracas to hit the enemy at Ocotán and Las Encinillas, as well as some Tarahumaras who were coming with a large quantity of poison (for arrows) for the enemy. All the Indian allies would later be adequately paid in cloth (*sayal*), blankets (*frasadas*), and knives (AHP 1653Ad). As an indication of the effort being made against the Tobosos at this time, the Spanish governor, in July, while conferring with Chiso chiefs in Parras concerning an *entrada* against the Tobosos, as an added inducement promised them that once the Tobosos were eliminated the Chisos could have their territory in recompense (AHP 1653Bb).

Three Toboso women, prisoners captured by the Salineros at Río Angosto, were interrogated. The women reported that the bands convoked at this place had been Tobosos, Nonojes, Ocomes, and Gavilanes. This battle, plus the previous attack at Nonolat, had seriously reduced some of the "Toboso" groups. The Toboso proper were now virtually extinct. The few Acoclames and Nonojes remaining had joined the Ocomes, although there is some confusion in the testimonies regarding this, since these groups seem to have gone back to their own territories after the encounter. There were also reportedly only a few surviving Govossos and Gavilanes. The Baborimamas had remained with the "Tobosos" for a while after the Nonolat battle, but had later separated, although the friendship between the two groups remained. From these testimonies, both the dwellers of Las Salinas and those of the Laguna district were long-standing enemies of the "Tobosos" (AHP 1653Ad).

The three Toboso women also gave their views of recent events and of the general intentions of the Tobosos. Before the Nonolat battle, Don Cristóbal had been at Bacata with his people. This was a place with poplar trees and water located west ("this side") of Río Angosto. Here the Tobosos had agreed among themselves that they wanted to submit to peace before war was made on them, but they had not known how to ask for it. After the several battles with the Spaniards and their allies, the various Tobosos bands had split up. When they had gotten back together again, some of the Ocomes had invited the others, including the Nonojes and Gavilanes, to a dance, and they all went to Río Angosto. Here three Salineros had visited the "Tobosos" with the message that their people wanted to be friends with them. The envoys departed that evening, but the next morning at dawn the entire group of Salineros came in force and attacked the "Tobosos" by surprise. Many were killed, and the three declarants were taken prisoners. These three women felt that Don Cristóbal at this time would probably be back at Conune, and the "Tobosos" would want peace since they now found themselves surrounded by so many enemies (AHP 1653Ad).

On August 23, Esteban de Levarío at Indé reported information he had received from the Cíbolas. The "Tobosos" who had escaped from the Río Angosto affair had fled to Ocotán and had joined four bands of their allies there. In vengeance, they had killed one of two Salineros who had been among them for many years. The second had escaped to the Colorados, and from there to the Cíbolas. Meanwhile, the Toboso forces had moved to a place west of Ocotán where they were making up a new supply of munitions for their last effort to avenge their losses in recent battles — they planned to fight the Cíbolas first, and then to go after the Salineros and Spaniards. When the Cíbolas learned of this, they called together all their neighbors and prepared to wait for the "Tobosos" (AHP 1653Ad).

With this news, Levarío decided to send out a contingent of Salineros from Indé under Moranta, which he expected to arrive at Cuatro Ciénegas by September 13. These Salineros would pick up the Tusares, Ygoquibas, and others of the Parras area on their way. If they had not yet encountered the enemy by the time they reached Cuatro Ciénegas, they were to send a message to the Chisos, who had promised to be in the Ocotán region. The two groups would then join forces against the "Tobosos" (AHP 1653Ad).

This plan was never carried out. On their way through the desert, the Salineros learned that the "Tobosos" were at Guapagua. Moving to this spot they ran into Don Cristóbal with ten warriors and their wives, but no children. The Salineros attacked and killed all but one man, Antón, and took the women captives. Here the Salineros learned that the Nonojes and Acoclames were at Las Encinillas and that the Ocomes, Gavilanes, and others had separated, but were in the Ocotán area (AHP 1653Ad).

Under questioning Antón revealed that since the Río Angosto battle, the Toboso groups had not dared to go out on more raids, partly because of their few numbers. However, a small sortie had been made into the Parral district by one Santiaguillo, who was later killed in the last attack on the Tobosos. This party had been met by those who had escaped at Río Angosto. Antón had also heard that the Ocomes, Baborimamas, and many wild Indians from the hinterland had been responsible for a raid on Atotonilco in the Papasquiaro area, in which a few Tepehuanes had been killed. The Ocomes had carried out another raid back in May. Antón later summed up Toboso raiding activities with the statement that these groups often sent out parties, although they were not always successful (AHP 1653Ad).

The Salinero Moranta opined at this time that most of the Tobosos bands had been pretty well wiped out, and that the only real threat left was from the Gavilanes of El Zurdo. Since these bands also had been rather thoroughly beaten, there probably was not much danger of more attacks by them. Consequently there was no need to carry out another campaign against the Gavilanes for the time being, especially with water so scarce in the hinterland at this time of the year (September). In any event, according to Moranta, once El Zurdo and his group were dead, there would be no more enemy to war upon the Spaniards and friendly Indians (AHP 1653Ad).

Other Indian allies rounded out the Spanish information of the desert and its enemy tribes. The two Salinero captains, Francisco Mama and Pedro Negrito, together with six Cíbolas from Cuatro Ciénegas, testified in Parral. The Tusares had been quiet and at peace since their raid on Parras in May, when they had stolen a herd of horses. The reason they had remained away from the Parras settlement, they said, was that they had not been paid for their work at the haciendas — actually only ten or twelve men had been working, out of a total of forty or fifty braves in the whole nation. The declarants had no news of the Baborimamas, as they had not ventured into the territory of the latter. They all felt that the wisest course of action with regard to the still hostile Toboso bands would be to send an envoy to call them in to peace (AHP 1653Ad).

The Spaniards decided to send an Ocome woman to tell the Nonojes, Ocomes, Acoclames, Cocoyomes, Hijos de las Piedras, and Hijos de los Palos to come in immediately and give themselves up — that otherwise Antón, the son of Zapata, would be hanged and soldiers would be sent out to exterminate the rest. This envoy was to leave from Atotonilco with another Indian, taking the usual flag and written and sealed documents giving her safe conduct (AHP 1653Ad).

On October 7, word was received in Parral that the Tobosos groups had for the most part separated from each other. Casa Zavala and Brazos Chiquitos were about a day's journey from Jaque, others had withdrawn to the Ocotán area, and Zapata was still elsewhere. Just prior to this, however, it had been learned through a Concho source from the Chisos that

Acoclames, Nonojes, Coyotes, and Hijos de las Piedras were convoked together (AHP 1653Ad).

On October 26, the Spanish captain Diego Galiano brought seven Indians into Parral — six Ocomes and one Toboso. One of the Ocomes was a woman; two were brothers of the Ocome chief, El Zurdo (apparently the same as El Mapochi — mentioned later); the Toboso was Cristóbal Zapata. They had come to request a pardon for their crimes, as the Spaniards put it. The governor received them, granted them the peace they sought, and told them that if they had surrendered sooner they would not have suffered such terrible devastation at the hands of the Salineros. Previous declarations had indicated that a few Tobosos had wanted peace for some time, and the reason Zapata had not been with the Tobosos during the last attack (when Don Cristóbal was killed) was because he had gone to the Ocomes to talk peace to them. However, the young Ocome braves had been the principal opponents to this suggestion (AHP 1653Ab; AHP 1653Ad).

This delegation stated that the other Tobosos had not come in because the several bands had split up and were now living apart from each other, corroborating the report received earlier in the month. However, it would not be long before they arrived to settle the peace. Casa Zavala, the Nonoje chief, had retired with some of his people, and the others had not been able to locate him. The declarants were not certain of the whereabouts of the Acococlames — this group had been so decimated at Nonolat that only twelve were left, and it was thought that they had gone to join Casa Zavala's band. Several envoys were selected to go out and contact these bands. The Spaniards tried to impress upon them a sense of urgency because Chisos and Salineros had already been sent to seek out and destroy the Tobosos (AHP 1653Ab).

In effect, this is precisely what happened to the Acoclames, or at least to one group of the Acoclames. Don Hernando de Obregón, the Indian governor of the Conchos, Julimes, Mamites, and Chisos, took a party of some eighty-five men (which may or may not have included Chisos) into Toboso country. Two days' travel from Las Encinillas (in the general area of Espíritu Santo) they encountered a small band of Acoclames. In the skirmish that followed, eight or ten men and a woman were killed, and one woman and three girls were taken prisoners. At least three escaped, but it was presumed that two would die of wounds because of the Conchos' poisoned arrows. Later testimony informed that there had been no more people at this rancheria because they had been killed in previous battles (AHP 1653Ab).

A captive woman reaffirmed that the Toboso bands were anxious for peace. The Nonoje chief, Cristóbal, the Acoclame chief, and chief Buelchomi (of unstated affiliation) had all agreed to submit to the Spaniards. Casa Zavala was reported to be at Jaque and was trying to convince his people to surrender, but he was running into a good deal of opposition. The band called Coyotes (or Cocoyomes) and one other group helped all of the rebels, but at this time they refused to leave their own territories to make peace (AHP 1653Ab).

The situation remained for the most part the same with the entrance of the year 1654. There was little or no let-up in the raiding of Spanish settlements. However, for a while it did seem that peace with the "Tobosos" finally was going to be consummated. On January 14, the Tobosos Zapata and Antonillo (Ocome?) returned to Parral, bringing with them the Ocome chief, Hernando de los Brazos Chicos, as well as a few children. Brazos Chicos requested lands at a spot two leagues from Atotonilco because his people did not want to live at the mission. He said the missionary would put the Indians to work and send them on errands to such an extent that they would not have time to work their own fields. In view of this, and for the interim until the Nonoje, Casa Zavala, and the remaining Indians came in to settle, the governor ordered that the natives now with the Spaniards remain with Captain Galiano near Atotonilco. It was finally decided, however, that these Tobosos should be settled at Atotonilco (AHP 1654Ac).

In February, Brazos Chicos returned from his trip to the back country in search of Casa Zavala, whom he had been told to convince to go to the Spaniards to surrender. He had located the Nonoje chief, together with El Zurdo or El Mapochi at Conuli. During their conferences to plan for peace, the Cocoyomes had arrived with the news that, while their own envoys had been in Parral making similar arrangements with the Spanish governor, the Chisos had attacked those who had stayed behind, killing seven persons. Now they had come to ask Casa Zavala and El Zurdo to join them against the Chisos to avenge these deaths. The two leaders agreed to the proposal and informed Brazos Chicos that they would surrender to the Spaniards as soon as they had finished their campaign with the Cocoyomes (AHP 1654Ac).

In the following month, peace negotiations were

totally frustrated — a pattern repeated many times in the history of Spanish-Indian relations. On March 16, the people already at Atotonilco left, taking a herd of horses and mules that belonged to their protector, Captain Diego Galiano. Only five persons stayed behind. By March 23, four of these also fled the mission, and the Spaniards felt that the one remaining — Diego Cestín — had been left as a spy. His story, however, was that he had been away in the town of Santa Ana and had not known of the planned withdrawal. He had wanted to follow the first group the next day, but his mother requested that he remain. When questioned at another time, however, he changed this story and said that two of the women had informed him of the projected escape. Galiano apparently had asked that some Indian women be sent out to make mescal, and Brazos Chicos and Zapata had feared that Galiano's motives were not wholly honorable, so they decided to flee. The Spaniards discarded this explanation, since there were other easier, less roundabout, ways to procure Indian women. This deponent stated on his second questioning that he had remained behind because he had been raised among Spaniards (AHP 1654Ac; AHP 1718Ab).

This same Diego Cestín was questioned again, this time under the threat of torture. He then declared that two "Tobosos," one the son of Zapata, had come to Atotonilco two days before the withdrawal, sent by the chiefs of the Ocomes and Gavilanes. Some Tobosos were still with the chiefs, who wanted the people at Atotonilco to join them to go to Guapagua, territory of the Tobosos and Salineros. With this news those at Atotonilco had departed, leaving Cestín behind to spy for them. An Ocome was going to act as courier between Cestín and the rest in the hinterland (AHP 1654Ac).

Their plan was to break up into a number of parties, each of which would operate in a different region — one group in Baus in the Roncesvalles mountain, another around Atocha, and the Tobosos in another (unstated) area. From these points they would then execute as many raids as possible, killing as many people as they could, and taking the cattle and horses they stole back to their own territories. Allied with them were the Cocoyomes (the small band called the Coyotes) and apparently the Hijos de las Piedras. Cestín also declared that the tale about the Ocomes and others going to fight the Chisos was not true. The Ocomes had not made the campaign, although it was possible that the Cocoyomes had been attacked by the Chisos. Cestín also related a number of assaults during the previous three years by Ocomes and Tobosos in the Parral district. The recent raiding, at any rate, had been carried out by the Acoclames, Nonojes, and the Hijos de las Piedras under Chief Casa Zavala (AHP 1654Ac).

In the early part of April, Spanish forces made an encounter with a small band of the enemy, considered to be Tobosos and Gavilanes. Five prisoners were taken alive and later hanged by General Barraza. During the interrogation proceedings before their execution, they gave a run-down on the current situation of the rebel bands. In essence, there were three principal groups. One was led by Casa Zavala and consisted mainly of Acoclames and Nonojes; the second was made up of several "nations," the chief of which was a Concho named Frasquillo; the third included the Ocomes and Gavilanes and their allies, led by El Mapochi. While these "clusters" were kept more or less separate in the minds of the declarants, a good bit of cooperation nevertheless took place among the groups. It was the first group that the "Tobosos" from Atotonilco had joined (AHP 1654Ac; AHP 1655Ab).

The existence of some Conchos operating out of Toboso territory helps clarify in some measure the conflicting and garbled reports of attacks in the general Parral region, along the eastern border of the Tarahumara, and in the Concho country itself. There was good evidence — based on language and types of arrows found — that both Tobosos and Conchos were the culprits. Sometimes the attackers appeared to be a mixed group; sometimes a raid would be attributed to one or the other group in different reports. At the same time, the Chisos were cited for hostilities in this region. The Concho governor, Obregón, testified that he had good evidence that the Chisos were not at peace, thus contradicting other reports concerning their activities. The Chisos had participated in at least some of the attacks, including the killing and capture of a number of Julimes (Conchos) Indians at the place of Ocotlán. Soon after this, the Chisos made a second visit to Ocotlán, where they announced to the Julimes that they were not at peace; then they apparently proceeded to kill two of the latter. Arrows discovered at Agua Escondida (near Babiscomalba?), where three Conchos had been murdered, indicated that Chisos as well as Acoclames and Nonojes had been the perpetrators (AHP 1654Aa; AHP 1718Ab).

The Indian declarants also filled in reports on some of the recent activities of the "Tobosos." After leaving Atotonilco, El Mapochi (or El Zurdo?) had returned to Gaqueque (Guapagua?) to call the others together. He was bent on avenging the deaths of his relatives, to die fighting if need be. From here he took thirty-seven braves from "all" the bands and was off to the area of Cerro Gordo. Another party of sixteen men was to go to Mapimí, under the chief of the Imudagas, after El Mapochi's group had departed (AHP 1654Ac).

El Mapochi first went to Santo Domingo, and then to El Charco. From the latter place his brother took a squad of eleven men to the Casanga River, Coneto, and the Pass of Balquitame, into the Sierra of Santiago Papasquiaro to Guatimapé, and then to San Juan del Río. All along the way there were too many people, and the cattle and horses were too well guarded for an attack. The party then decided to return to the river by Cuencamé, where they had previously agreed to meet El Mapochi's larger force. The latter reprimanded his brother for coming back empty-handed (AHP 1654Ac).

El Mapochi left immediately for home (apparently) because of some killings his group had made at San Lorenzo, where they had also stolen some clothing. He ordered a smaller squad under the command of the chief of the Gordo band to return to San Juan to look for horses, as the Indians were out of food. El Mapochi's brother was to go back with him, and the group departed for Pantita. The smaller squad stole two horse herds from near the town of San Juan del Río and began to drive them back to camp, traveling partly at night. At Pantita, recognizing that someone else had recently been there, they sent scouts to investigate. Shortly afterward the squad was attacked by Spanish troops, the chief of the Gordos was killed, and the others were captured (AHP 1654Ac).

Indian attacks continued on into May. Raids took place at San Miguel de las Bocas, attributed to the Cabezas; in the area of Babiscuamalba, upriver from San Francisco de Conchos, attributed to Tobosos who had had a large herd of horses and were dressed as Spaniards (!); at Xaguey, nine leagues from Parral on the Conchos (Florido?) River, and also attributed to Tobosos. But a Concho who testified later thought — on the basis of some of the arrows and the hair style of some of the warriors — that Chisos might have been involved (AHP 1655Bc; CD 1655-1663). In one assault in April the ten to twelve attackers remained unidentified, but their dress indicated that they might have been hacienda workers — they were unpainted, some wore pants (*calzones*), and most had blankets around their bodies and wore tonsure haircuts (AHP 1654Ab). Salineros and Cabezas were still being accused of raiding, although some of the tribesmen were fighting as auxiliaries for the Spaniards (AHP 1655Bc).

The heavy raiding kept up. In the latter part of 1654, in the month of October, attacks were reported at Los Charcos, near Las Bocas, and later in December around Indé and El Gallo (AHP 1654Aa; AHP 1654Ac). At the beginning of 1655, the raiders hit Los Palmitos in the jurisdiction of San Juan del Río, Las Cruces in the Nazas River region, and around the area of Cuencamé. The Tizonazo Salineros were called out again as auxiliaries. In the early part of January they met and battled the enemy, estimated to comprise about one hundred forty warriors, at Tonalquisa about three leagues from the town of Los Palmitos. Eight braves were killed and some thirty-five women and children were taken prisoners. The rest escaped (AHP 1655AB; CD 1655-1663). Later in November a raiding party was surprised in the region of the headwaters of the Florido River in the Sierra de Huejotitlán, where in its haste to get away it left a great quantity of stolen booty behind (AHP 1655Aa).

Chisos are mentioned increasingly in association with some of the more northern of the Toboso bands, but their exact involvement is uncertain. For at least two years the Spaniards had been attempting to enlist the Chisos to go out against the Tobosos, even sending them clothing and supplies, but with no success. Then, in September of 1655, eighty-six Chiso warriors appeared in Parral to see the governor. They were now ready, or so they claimed, to make war on the Tobosos; and they wanted supplies and payment from the Spaniards for the campaign (AHP 1655Ab; AHP 1718Ab).

These Chisos had an interesting tale to tell regarding the Tobosos, a story that affords some evidence that Indians could and did learn that they could exploit the Spaniards in ways other than by raiding. Before their arrival in Parral they had fought the Tobosos at Chicaumuca (Chocamueca) or Sierra Prieta, killing many (ninety-eight according to their own record on a notched bow) and taking many prisoners. The Tobosos had later retaliated and had retaken all the prisoners except three small boys,

whom the Chisos had brought with them as a gift for the Spanish governor. At this time the Chiso women and children had remained behind at a place called Bacabto, and the Tobosos were camped at Los Tlacotes. The Chisos were ready to go out after them in order to avenge the deaths the Tobosos had caused them (AHP 1655Ab).

The three boys, who were said to be a Nonoje, an Acoclame, and a Toboso, were eventually questioned by the Spaniards. It turned out that the entire story of the Chisos was a hoax, that no such battle with the Tobosos had taken place, and that the three boys were Chisos. Two of the boys were brothers, and their father's name was Casa Zavala (or was this the name they had been instructed to give?). The interpreters, when asked what language the testimony was being given in, replied that it was Chiso, as the boys did not understand Toboso. The boys went on, saying that this moment the Tobosos, Acoclames, Nonojes, and other bands were with the Chisos, dancing with the head and clothing of a Spaniard they had killed, and two Tobosos were with this group in Parral. The boys recounted that the Chisos had stolen much clothing from the Spaniards and had taken it back to their country. Their parents, before leaving on the present trip to Parral, had told them to go along with the first story and that eventually they would come and retrieve them from the Spaniards. Their mothers had said that they were going to a good land where there was much to eat. Despite this attempted deception, the Spaniards, in conformity with long-standing policy, regaled this Chiso party with gifts and ordered them to go back and remain in their own territory and fight against the Tobosos (AHP 1655Ab).

Reports on the activities of the desert-dwelling Indians drop off tremendously in the latter years of the decade of the 1650's, owing certainly in the main to the lack of extant documentation rather than to an actual decrease in their raiding. Many attacks continued to be reported in 1655. It was noted that the aggressors spoke in several languages: Concho, Salinero, "Toboso" (Gavilán and Acoclame), as well as Mexican. Specific persons among the enemy were sometimes recognized — a Concho from Los Corrales, and a left-handed leader, apparently the now famous El Zurdo or El Mapochi (the "left-handed one" in Spanish and Mexican respectively) (AHP 1655Ab).

Again Tarahumara and Concho villages, as well as Spanish settlements, were the targets of attacks, many of which probably were carried out by the

Nonoje-Acoclame-Concho combine with Casa Zavala. It is quite possible that other Concho groups were also involved. Certainly Casa Zavala's group can account for much of the raiding along the Concho-Tarahumara border area. Fray Hernando de Urbaneja, for example, reported that Tobosos and Nonojes had attacked his mission of Santiago Babonoyaba in June. The Jesuit, José Pascual, constantly maintained that the raids around his mission of San Felipe were executed by Conchos. The evidence from other sources, however, conflicted with Pascual's contention, and it seems probable that often it was the Casa Zavala group that was involved. In two testimonies it was declared that only a few Conchos were with Casa Zavala, namely Frasquillo and his son, but this information was given by two women in Parral. However, there may have been more than the previous information seemed to indicate, since Indians of other ethnic affiliation did often join the back-country raiding bands (AHP 1655A).

In 1656 raids were reported, among other places, at Los Palmitos, San Juan del Río, the Nazas River, Cuencamé, Ocotán, Canatlán, Mapimí, and San Juan de Casta — the raiding territory of El Mapochi's "Tobosos" and Salineros. The Cíbola Indians sent word that on one occasion they had seen a great party of the enemy traveling in the direction of Los Palmitos at El Cerro de las Minas. On another occasion the Cíbola, while fighting for the Spaniards in the area of El Peñol Blanco, encountered an enemy party estimated to be about forty persons. The Cíbola attacked, literally burned the enemy out of a grassy wooded area where they had taken refuge, and pursued those who escaped (AHP 1656Aa).

Spanish reports came in that the Salineros were partly responsible for the hostilities, although there were no testimonies from captured enemies that Salineros actually had been with their raiding parties. In February the missionary at San Pablo, Gerónimo de Figueroa, wrote that the Salinero auxiliaries in Spanish pay, while on a campaign led by Cristóbal Nevares from Cerro Gordo, had met with the enemy at a place called Las Animas. From here the two groups had gone together to Los Amoles where they feasted on a horse and a mule that the enemy had stolen. When they took leave of each other, the enemy moved toward San Pablo and the Salineros blotted out the enemy's tracks (AHP 1656Aa).

Chisos were sometimes with the Tobosos. In a battle at Sierra del Diablo between Spanish forces under Cristóbal Nevares and the Tobosos, the Chisos were reported to have sent help to their Toboso allies (the date of this battle is uncertain, although it took place sometime after September of 1655). In June of 1656, Conchos in Spanish employ went to Ocotlán, where on the far side they found an abandoned ranchería which they judged to have belonged to Chisos. They followed a trail from here to a dark mountain (Chocamueca?) where, they calculated, these Chisos had gone to join the Tobosos (AHP) 1656Aa).

In preparation for further hostilities, in September of 1656 a Spanish force with a number of Salinero auxiliaries under Captain Juan Gutiérrez Tamayo was sent to reconnoiter Toboso country for permanent waterholes in the event a campaign should become necessary during the dry season. One watering spot was located at Las Cañas, apparently considered to be about on the border of Toboso territory. No water was found in Toboso country except at a place seven leagues from Las Cañas. This was in the area of Sierra del Diablo, and apparently the springs here had their origin near this mountain range. The battleground at Sierra del Diablo where Nevares had met the Tobosos the previous year was also reconnoitered, but no tracks were discovered and no water source is mentioned for this place. Some thirteen leagues from the second water hole, a third was located with its source from the river that ran by the Cerro Gordo presidio (AHP 1656Aa).

The year 1657 apparently saw no let-up in Indian raids. In the north, the Tobosos were reported raiding in the general region of San Felipe, San Pedro, and San Francisco de Conchos. In July one Spanish squad went through the Sierra de Diego Pérez. Eight leagues on the Parral side of Los Peyotillos, the squad picked up enemy tracks that were interpreted as indicating movement of Indians on horseback at top speed without stopping to drink or to water their animals. Six leagues on the far side of Los Peyotillos the tracks split, about half going in the direction of Espíritu Santo and the rest to Los Tlacotes (Tobosos, plus Chisos?). In November, killings occurred between San Francisco de Conchos and Bamiscomalba and near the confluence of the Conchos and Florido rivers. The trail left at the latter place also went in the direction of Los Tlacotes (AHP 1657Bb).

In October of 1658, forty-seven Chisos showed up, with nine scalps and a hand, at the pueblo of San Antonio (Julimes?) near San Francisco de Conchos.

Their story was that they had followed the governor's orders and entered Toboso country. They had located only one small camp of Nonojes and Acoclames between the mountain ranges of Jaque and Conune. They wiped out the entire group — four men, five women, and a few children — and then continued on to Parral. The Spanish governor thanked them for their action and remunerated them with gifts. He also admonished them to return to their own territory, to stay there, to plant crops, and not to let any enemy nation pass through (AHP 1658Aa).

In March of 1658, Francisco de Méndez had written from Zape that there were a great many enemies who would surround the Spanish settlements from all sides, spy on them, and then enter them in the darkness of night. They often forced the Spaniards to keep off their own highways. One Spanish contingent had two encounters with hostile Indians near Canatlán. In the second, when the enemy left part of its gear behind, the Spaniards estimated, somewhat exaggeratedly, that the opposing force had consisted of some 1000 warriors. Several prisoners were taken, and evidence from the tracks after the battle indicated that many had been wounded (AHP 1658Aa).

From 1660 to 1690

Spanish-Indian contact history in Nueva Vizcaya for the thirty years between 1660 and 1690 was characterized by a continual round of raiding and peace-making activities. The period was marked by two major revolts and the demise of the Salineros and Cabezas as raiders in the province, although unfortunately not enough information is available on these events to place them adequately in an historical context. In both uprisings, one in 1666 and the second in 1684, only four years after the great revolt of the Pueblo Indians of New Mexico in 1680, Conchos and other neighboring Indians took part. Indeed, these rebellions can be considered as major precisely because the more peaceful people were actively involved in the hostilities. It is by no means clear how the desert-dwelling Toboso and Salinero groups fit into these outbreaks, although they were on the warpath on both occasions. Again, as in the 1644 episode, it appears that the 1666 and 1684 revolts for the desert nomads were more in the nature of an intensification of their regular raiding activities. This should not be too surprising as for some time raiding Spanish holdings had been a necessary and integral part of the native economic and ceremonial life.

In the revolts of 1666-1667, the Salineros, Cabezas, and associated nations allied themselves with the Tobosos, Acoclames, and other "Toboso" bands. Conchos Indians, including Julimes, were reported to have joined "Tobosos" and "Salineros," or at least to have tried to; but this is uncertain. The Concho portion of the rebellion was quickly put down in the Western Concheria; the day before Christmas of 1666 Governor Antonio de Oca Sarmiento reported that the members of this nation who lived along the Tarahumara border had now been pacified, although "the enemy Indians of the Tovosso Salinero nations and their allies" were still at war. Owing to the great numbers of the enemy and because of the deficiencies in Spanish defense organization, the governor wrote, the rebels encountered little opposition and the province was "infested" with wars. Although the causes of the 1666-1667 outbreaks are not known, there was about this time a drought, followed by a famine and a plague (Hackett 1926: 188-192; BL 1649-1700; DHM 1669; DHM 1667a; DHM 1667b; UTD 1671-1685).

The 1684 occasion was a general conflagration that covered the entire central northern Mexican area. It is uncertain what connection this outbreak had with the revolt four years before in New Mexico when the Spaniards were driven completely out of that province southward to El Paso. However, following upon the heels of the New Mexican hostilities as it did, the 1684 rebellion caused the Spaniards to feel that some communication existed between the New Mexican pueblos and the Nueva Vizcayan rebels. As in the 1666 affair, the Conchos and neighboring Jumanos were rather quickly quieted, although the desert raiders continued their activities much as they had done previously (Hackett 1926: 218-224; Spicer 1962: 152-163).

The Salineros and Cabezas were particularly prominent in the thirty years after 1660, and they held the leadership, such as it was at this time, among the desert tribes during much of this period. In this position they seem to have felt the effects of Spanish retaliation more than did the other nations, although much documentation is lacking on this point. The Salineros at Tizonazo totally abandoned their mission and were replaced there by Indians from the west coast. Some of the Salinero-Cabeza groups, such as the Matarajes, apparently disappeared at this time, while one of the most active bands, the Cabezas under Don Pedrote, about 1690 finally capitulated and settled at Parras, where it remained permanently peaceful.

During the latter half of the seventeenth century, the Salineros and Cabezas were considered by the Spaniards to be their greatest enemies and the principal culprits, motivators, and leaders of the enemy Indians, including Tobosos, Cíbolas, and various groups from the Coahuila area. According to Spaniards testifying before the governor in Parral at the time of the 1667 Revolt, these Indians during the term of office of governor Dávila y Pacheco (1654-1661) had revolted three times, and another three to six times when Francisco de Gorráez (1662-1665) was in office. The responsibility for the abandonment of many haciendas and mines in the province of Nueva Vizcaya was placed on these people (Bancroft 1884: 337; AHP 1667Aa).

The Tizonazo Salineros cooperated with the back-country rebels as spies, as supported by the fact that the Tizonazoans possessed an abundance of Spanish material goods given to them by the raiders. Desert-dwelling Salineros often went to Tizonazo, and many Salineros had been recognized in raids. Furthermore, Salineros had recently tried to kill their own governor (that is, the one appointed by the Spanish authorities) because he would not condone their activities. Then they elected another governor, forcing the former one to retire to the town of Indé. The provincial governors, from Diego Guajardo Fajardo on, had wanted to exterminate the Salineros by the sword, but the missionaries had constantly opposed this. Spaniards in 1667 felt that the Salineros should be done away with and the pueblo of Tizonazo razed. They wanted permission to kill members of this nation on sight (AHP 1667Aa).

Ten years later in 1677, similar opinions were put forth by a number of the citizens of Nueva Vizcaya, and Salineros and Tobosos again were indicted. It was felt by the persons testifying that the general policy that had been followed until this time had been largely ineffective. The rebels had surrendered a great number of times, always with the same result — after a short period the natives would break the peace, flee to the back country, and take up their raiding activities again. Even when they were at "peace" they would manage to steal a great many cattle and horses, and this notwithstanding the fact that they were always given an abundance of seeds and tools to farm with. Throughout this period opinions frequently were expressed that the policy of handouts to the Indians was ineffective, since the Indians — who occasionally admitted to this — would merely take what they could get before returning to their old haunts (AHP 1667Aa).

In the early 1660's several groups, including Salineros and Cíbolas, were operating in the general Laguna area, and apparently at this time some Cabezas were residing at Parras (AHP 1662C; AGN 1662). In the latter part of 1666 a Tepehuán from the town of El Peñol Blanco was released by one of the rebel desert bands with which he had spent a short sojourn. He claimed he could not identify his captors by nation, although all the raids he reported had been in the region of El Peñol Blanco and Cuencamé, which would make it likely that the captors had been "Salineros" or possibly El Mapochi's "Tobosos" (AHP 1669Ba).

In January of 1667, during the revolt of this year, a combined force of "Salinero" and "Toboso" bands attacked a wagon train near El Gallo (said to be the place from where the enemy would make its sallies into Spanish territory), killing the entire guard. A Spanish contingent went after the raiders, corralling and battling them at Acatita, although only three or four of the enemy were killed. After this skirmish at Acatita a number of attacks occurred in the Nazas River and Tepehuán country — at San Juan del Río, Covandonga, Palmitos, Guatimapé, and Texame, as well as on some of the Tarahumara missions. On one occasion three Franciscans were killed, and the Indians donned their clothing. In August a Spanish expedition was made to the Sierra del Diablo, called "the land of the Tobosos," and later another into the Las Cañas area where several waterholes, including that of Las Batuecas, and a campsite with many bones of cattle and horses, were discovered. In early November the Toboso governor, Don Francisco (El Tecolote?), went to the town of San Antonio (de Julimes) to request peace and a settlement at Bavisco-malba on the Conchos River. This was carried out, but the Indians withdrew immediately after the first of the year (Hackett 1926: 188-192; BL 1649-1700; DHM 1667a; DHM 1667b; DHM 1669; UTD 1671-1685).

On February 16, 1667, it was learned that Don Alonso Santiago, chief of the Cabezas, and several of the rebel nations had gone to the missionary at Tizonazo to request peace. They left two hostages, apparently to show good will. One of the hostages soon fled with three horses, after which attacks were made on a number of places in the area — including Palmitos, Huejotitlán, and Roncesvalles, and Santa Catalina de Tepehuanes. The latter place, according to a later certification, was hit by a group of 150 warriors (BL 1659-1700). By September, Governor Oca Sarmiento claimed that the Salineros, Cabezas, and other nations had been "punished" (UTD 1671-1685).

Although hostilities seem to have been rather heavy at this time, little specific information exists concerning the assaults and raids. One, in June of 1667, involved a band of Tobosos and Cabezas, many of the latter from the Tizonazo mission. These attacked a Spanish party of fifteen persons at La Encina de la Paz. The sole survivor was a priest, the Jesuit Father Rodrigo del Castillo. Castillo later opined that the Indians had spared him because they had been afraid of the "power" he possessed. They had told him a story of how on a prior occasion they had captured and then released some Franciscans who later in vengeance had caused many to die of the disease *cocolixtli*. The good Father was given his freedom at the Cerro Gordo presidio, where the Indians were planning an attack. Because of his prestige with the enemy he managed to stop the impending bloodshed, although the Indians stole all of the cattle belonging to the garrison (Alegre III 1956: 289-291; AGN 1667; DHM 1669).

Hostilities continued in the following year — 1668. Two wagon trains were attacked by over 300 Indians, according to one report (DHM 1669). By 1669, the Indian inhabitants of Tizonazo had again abandoned their mission (DHM 1668).

In August of 1670, the governor reported from Durango that the Conejos Indians at the hacienda of Antonio Medrano and the Negritos at the town of Cuencamé under chief Francisco Machado were responsible for the many murders and robberies in this area. Arrows discovered were the types used by Salineros, and Conchos Indians (the Conejos may actually have been Conchos) and Gavilanes living at the hacienda of Medrano were indicted, as well as Machado's people at Cuencamé, all said to be in contact with the rebels. Later several Indians from haciendas of the area confessed to having trafficked with the enemy and to having taken part themselves in some of the raids (AHP 167OB).

Attacks continued throughout the area, and the enemy was rumored as far south as Durango. The Salineros apparently were in the thick of raiding

activity. By 1671 they still had not returned to Tizonazo, and on March 10 the governor ordered that forty Tepehuán Indians with their families be sent to repopulate the mission. At the beginning of 1672, the rebel Salineros were at the Sierra de la Cadena and the Sierra de Ramos in the Mapimí area. At this same time some Salinero chiefs were being held prisoners by Spanish authorities, who were hoping to utilize them as a lever to obtain a surrender from the rest of the Salineros; however, little resulted from this endeavor. Around the middle of the year the Salineros, Cabezas, and their allies went to Las Bocas to make peace, but they did an about-face and withdrew soon afterwards. The governor attempted to induce them back to the Spanish fold with gifts, but to no avail (AHP 1673Aa; AHP 1674Ab; AGN 1672).

Although the year 1673 was again plagued with Indian raids, toward the end of the year various efforts for peace were made by the Indians. In October, a large number of Chisos arrived in San Francisco de Conchos stating they wanted to embrace the Catholic faith. The Spaniards accepted this request, but because of the difficulties involved in settling these Chisos all in one place, it was decided to distribute them among the several haciendas and other establishments in the Parral district (AHP 1673Ab; AHP 1673Ac).

In December, one chief Marcos and other captains of the Tetecores, Guisacales, Obayas, and Contotores from Coahuila went to Cuencamé and asked for a settlement under missionary Father Bernabé de Soto. They also offered to fight the Spaniards' enemies, the Salineros and Cabezas. About a month previous to this, it had been reported that some 150 Indians from several nations — Colorados, Negritos, Cabezas, Salineros, Bovoles, and Guisacales — had gone to Saltillo to make peace in order to settle in Coahuila. However, Don Marcos and his companions testified that the Cabezas and Salineros had not been in Saltillo, but that four to six persons from these bands had gone to see them in their home territories below the town of Coahuila. According to the present declarants, the Cabezas and Salineros claimed they had been avenging the deaths of the many people whom the former governor, Francisco Gorráez (1662-1665), had killed at the church cemetery in Tizonazo. However, now they were ready to make peace and live among the Coahuila groups — they had no more reason to fight because the present governor had never done them any harm (Bancroft 1884: 337; BL 1649-1700).

So much for these efforts toward peace on the part of both the Indians and the Spaniards, since nothing was accomplished until the following year. Salineros were operating heavily in the region of Indé. Back in the spring of 1673 Spanish troops had sallied and made an encounter, taking away the enemy's animals and clothing. During the skirmish a Salinero, Felipillo El Tartamudo (The Stutterer), was recognized. He had been accompanied by about twenty Indians, all of whom succeeded in escaping. In June, Juan de Nevares reported he had reconnoitered the Sierra de Ramos, Mojitome, and from Tizonazo to the Nazas River, but had not found a single trace of the enemy, who apparently had successfully eluded him (AHP 1673Aa). However, in December Governor García de Salcedo complained of the daily occurrences of Indian attacks. One report had come in that the enemy was running stolen horses by the town of El Peñol, seven leagues from Cuencamé. García personally took out a contingent and met the enemy at a place called La Junta de los Ríos, killing two and capturing an equal number (AHP 1673Ab).

The prisoners, a Cabeza and a Baborimama, testified that their squad had consisted of seven men, and that another five-man party was working the San Juan del Río area. The Mayos were allied with these groups, which had raided as far south as Guadiana or Durango. Santiago, brother of the now-acting Cabeza chief, had gone to see the Cíbolas to determine if it was true that the "Coahuileños" were planning on making peace and, apparently (this part is not too clear), if the Cíbolas also had any such intentions. Felipillo El Tartamudo, they said, had gone with three of his brothers to visit Don Juan Mapochi who, with Chief Galiano, was actively raiding in this area. This party spent a number of days with Mapochi. When they returned, Felipillo sent Mapochi three Indian women with gifts of stolen clothing to give to their host. El Mapochi had wanted El Tartamudo to join his band for a raid on a wagon train (AHP 1673Ab; AHP 1674Ab).

These declarants also told of an attempt on Governor Oca Sarmiento's (1665-1670) life when a combined force of Salineros and Tobosos (probably El Mapochi's group) had attacked the party he was traveling with at the Nazas River. Two Tobosos had been killed. Interestingly enough, during this period these two groups were in touch with the Spanish Sergeant Major, Valerío Cortés, because, they said, he would give them blankets, clothing, and food when they asked for them (possibly in the attempt to buy them off). However, on one occasion they had burned and destroyed Cortés' hacienda at Guajuquilla, although they still considered him their friend (AHP 1673Ab). Cortés may have been "too" involved with the Indians, judging from the case brought against him in which his many "disobediences" to Spanish authority were cited (Bancroft 1884: 337; Hackett 1926: 194-198).

The witnesses continued, ending up with a run-down on the recent raiding activities of the Cabezas and allied bands. From the time the Salineros had withdrawn from Tizonazo they had occupied the area between Las Cañas, Acatita, and the Laguna district. This year, 1673, they had gone to Mapimí because Chief Santiago had heard that a Franciscan had passed by there on his way to Parral with some "Coahuileños," Baboles, and Tetecores to request a peace treaty from the Spanish governor. Santiago had ordered El Tartamudo and the chiefs of the other allied bands to move to Mapimí while he went to confer with the tribes of Coahuila. During this interim these Salineros were to utilize Mapimí as a base from which to raid — but only for horses, according to one declarant, to be used as food; they were not to commit any killings. The Cabeza explained why his people had refused previous peace overtures from the Spanish authorities sent to them from Durango — the people had discussed the matter and decided it was a trick (AHP 1673Ab).

These same bands previously had attacked Avino twice — once killing ten or eleven persons and the second time making one kill and taking a captive. At Puana they killed some women and burned another in a hut at the spring of Sancho Jiménez. At La Laja they put to death some Indians and carried off their wives; then they attacked a mule train at La Silla, murdering twelve or fourteen persons. Between Saltillo and Mazapil they assaulted another mule train and killed ten or eleven persons; at Caopas they murdered two Lagunero Indians and a Spaniard; on the Aguanaval River they killed another Spaniard and two Indians and stole a large herd of horses (AHP 1673Ab). From another source the Spaniards learned that during the preceding month Salineros and Cabezas had hit a settlement at La Laguna, where they fought the Bahaneros and killed their captain (BL 1649-1700).

Then, another Spanish sally was made, and finally on December 29, 1673, Spanish troops attacked and soundly defeated the Salineros, Cabezas, Mayos, and others in the Sierra de Mapimí, killing about forty warriors (a later report said 100 persons) and capturing all the women and children. The rest escaped, but some surrendered later to settle in peace. Among those who gave themselves up were the chiefs Pedro, Bartolomé, and Fabián (AHP 1674Aa; BL 1649-1700).

In the early part of 1674 the chiefs of some five bands of "Tobosos," but also including the Guijacales (Guisacales from Coahuila?), arrived in Parral asking for peace. Four of these chiefs were Juan Mapochi, Juan Galán, Juan Campos, and Galeano. They wished to surrender at this time, they declared, because they did not want the same thing to happen to their people as had taken place with the Salinero bands. After listening to them and accepting their story, Governor García de Salcedo assigned them various places in the area in which to settle. Other Coahuila nations, including the Babozarigames, were in the process of settling in peace by July, although in March such groups as the Tetecores, Guicales (Guisacales?), Obayas, and Contotores were reported to still be in revolt (AHP 1674Aa; BL 1649-1700; BL 1709-1715).

About this same time the Franciscan Fray Juan de Larios made the long trek from Coahuila to Parral with a number of Salineros, Cabezas, and Mayos, to assist these men in requesting that their women and children captured in December of the previous year be restored to them. The trip was fruitless and the party returned home. However, when they arrived at Cuatro Ciénegas, and Father Larios tried to take leave of the Indians, they killed one of his mules (Portillo 1887: 80; BL 1674).

By the beginning of 1675 these groups were in rebellion again. In January a Contotore declared that a few Babozarigames had stolen some horses from Parras and that the Salineros, Cabezas, and Mayos had been raiding as far south as the towns of Nieves and Sombrerete. He felt that the Babozarigames could be settled in peace but that the Salineros, Cabezas, and Mayos would have to be exterminated since they did not trust the Spaniards and would never give up their war against them (Portillo 1887: 81-83; BL 1674).

During the spring of this year, 1675, a number of the more northern of the Coahuila peoples were making their peace with the Spaniards — but not the Salineros, Cabezas, and their close associates. In March Fray Larios told of information about some of the rebel groups that he had obtained from the Guiquesales and their "great chief" Esteban, at San Ildefonso some twelve leagues south of the Río Grande. The Cabezas, whom they had tried to call in to peace, were now at Mapimí, and the chief of the Contotores had gone to fetch the Babozarigames. The chief of the latter turned over to him a Spanish captive who had been held formerly by the Cíbolas. This Spaniard and his brother — now held by the Colorados as a "slave" — had been among the Indians many years; the brother was said to have lost the ability to speak Spanish (Portillo 1887: 77-78, 80-82, 85, 93; BL 1674).

The following month the chief, Salvador, of the Babozarigames testified in Ciudad de Guadalupe, Coahuila, when he arrived there to surrender. He had been baptized at Tizonazo, and the band called Pies de Venado was allied with his group. He reported that the Cabezas had no intention of giving up. The group at this time was very small — fifteen men and four old women, because the rest of the members were still being held in Parral — and they planned to continue fighting until they were exterminated. They were captained by Alonso Santiago. The Cabeza Don Fabián with three others had separated from this band and had gone to a place next to Los Charcos next to Mapimí and to Parral to live peacefully. From other sources it was reported about this time that the Cabezas were in touch with groups from the Río Grande area (Portillo 1887: 94-96; BL 1674).

In July, 1675, the Cabezas were still trying to get their families back. At this time they were at Cuatro Ciénegas attempting to get both Fray Larios and Don Esteban, the Gueiquesal, to go with them to Nueva Vizcaya. They were afraid to go alone since they felt that the Spaniards there were treacherous and would kill them under truce (Portillo 1887: 167-168). In the early part of 1676 the Salinero chief, Don Pedro (Pedrote?) escaped from prison, and in February the Tobosos again retired to the hinterland from the places (unnamed) where they had been settled. By mid-year they were raiding in full force and were said to have confederated with other nations "to commit all of the hostilities possible" (AHP 1676Aa; AHP 1676Ab).

In the spring of 1680 a band of "Tobosos" hit San Francisco de Conchos, killing twelve and wounding a like number of the faithful "Tobosos" (said to be of the same "nation" as the attackers) living there under their governor Don Francisco Gutiérrez (possibly the same Francisco who had settled there some six years earlier with Juan Campos and other "Tobosos"). The enemy had tried to burn Gutiérrez' house, and afterward only three of the latter's people were left at the town. The motive for this attack may very possibly have been revenge, although the events leading up to it are unknown (BL 1649-1700).

It also is not known how many Tobosos had been living at Conchos at this time, although previously forty-seven Toboso auxiliary troops had accompanied a Spanish contingent on a campaign. Where Francisco's people went at the time of the raid is unknown. However, many were back by June. On June 2 Governor Estrada reported another assault on Conchos. Spanish forces, including loyal "Tobosos," pursued the attackers to Agua del Venado where a fight ensued and the Spaniards lost six men (BL 1649-1700).

Some "Tobosos" were reduced to peace in 1683 and were settled at El Peñol Blanco, with a church and a missionary, prior to Governor Bartolomé de Estrada's writing in February of the same year. Estrada had personally accompanied these Tobosos from Parras to El Peñol when they made their journey to settle there (AGN 1683). (This may be, and probably is, the same event referred to in a much later source concerning a peace made in 1682 with the Acoclames and Cocoyomes.) Some Tarahumara were also settled there in order to teach the wild Indians how to farm. After some seven months, at harvest time, paying no attention to the crops, these Indians simply returned to their old haunts (AHP 1722Ba; BL 1722). The warpath apparently attracted them almost immediately. By the middle of August, Lagunero and Bahanero Indians at San Pedro de la Laguna had been forced to take refuge in the town of Parras because of "Toboso" activity in the region (PSA 1682; PSA 1683b).

Little is known of the exploits of the various groups of desert Indians during the Revolt of 1684. The "Tobosos" carried out several attacks — one between El Gallo and Santo Domingo and another two leagues from Parral. General Juan de Retana made a five-week expedition to Toboso country, but nothing of importance was accomplished. Several other sallies were made soon afterward, all with the same result (Hackett 1926: 218-224).

A number of Chiso groups were indicted about the time of this revolt. Evidence at this time and in a later investigation in July showed conclusively that before May, when the general uprising broke out, Chisos and

Tobosos had been responsible for many of the attacks and raids around the Parral district northward. Some of the Chisos confessed that they were acquainted with a number of the Toboso chiefs, including one El Mapochi who at this time was said to be in jail (AHP 1684Aa). (This may have been the same El Mapochi of earlier years, although another report stated that both Juan Mapochi and Galeano had been executed by governor Martín de Rebollar (1674-1676) — Bancroft 1884: 338; BL 1709-1715; in 1686 and in 1687 a Juan Mapochi showed up again as chief of the "Tobosos" — AHP 1686Bb; AHP 1687Ab). This and other information indicated close contact between the Chisos and the Tobosos at this time.

In the early part of 1686 a band of enemy Indians attacked a mule train at Los Sauces, near Santiago Papasquiaro, on its way to Durango. Aside from the killing of seven persons, some 350 mules were stolen. Under investigation it turned out that this attack, involving a large concerted effort, had been carried out with the help of a number of "hacienda" and other Indians. Tarahumares, Conchos, Julimes, Chisos, Tobosos, Cocoyomes, Cabezas, Salineros, Chichitames, and Oposmes (from the confluence of the Río Grande and Conchos rivers) were mentioned as having taken part. The total force came to some 200 men, led by two mulattos (AHP 1686Bb).

This case is too complicated for a detailed analysis here, but assuming that the basic outlines of the testimonies taken during the ensuing interrogations are essentially correct, it seems that the permanently rebel groups of Tobosos, Cocoyomes, Cabezas, and Salineros had managed to enlist the others from the haciendas to join them in this raid. It is not clear whether the Chisos and Chichitames (a Chiso band) were also from haciendas or had come down from the north and banded with the "Tobosos" and others, but the latter seems to have been the case. At any rate, the "Tobosos" and Chichitames are mentioned specifically as having taken the stolen mules. The Indians from the haciendas were reimbursed for their trouble with blankets and other booty acquired in the assault. The leadership also is not clear in some respects. The two mulattos, who led the party, did some of the recruiting of the hacienda Indians. Don Juan Mapochi was cited as the chief of the "Tobosos," but it is not certain that he actually took part in the raid (AHP 1686Bb).

When the group broke up after these activities, the hacienda and mission (Tarahumara) Indians went home, and according to one deponent, the remainder went to the area of Sierra del Diablo. After the raid, two Tobosos from the town of San Francisco de Conchos were reported to have stated that now everyone would rebel. There was some hint that the Tarahumaras from Las Bocas and San Felipe were on the verge of revolt at this time (AHP 1686Bb).

On May 1, in the vicinity of San Francisco de Conchos, an attack occurred on the hacienda of Santa Cruz, belonging to Captain Domingo de Apresa Falcón. While there was some possibility that Chisos were involved, many of the assailants were rebel Tobosos. One small Indian boy from Sonora was taken prisoner but later escaped. The raiders traveled six days to get back to their camp in a mountain that the boy had been told was called El Diablo. He stayed here seven days and then managed to escape when some Cocoyomes took him out to hunt deer (AHP 1686Bc).

Preparations were made for a campaign against the enemy in February of the following year – 1687. A mule train was attacked by a large force of Indians near El Gallo on May 4, 1687. One estimate placed the number of attackers at fifteen hundred. The expedition was to leave from the presidio of Cerro Gordo (AHP 1687Aa; AHP 1687Ab).

Around the end of the month soldiers captured an Indian four leagues from the presidio. His name was Marcos and he belonged to "one of the nations that fled from Tizonazo." According to Marcos, the chiefs of the Cabezas and Salineros, Don Fiscal, Don Pedro (Pedrote?), Don Francisco Sunuri (also Sunora), Don Bartolo Sinarvee, Don Martín, El Baquero, and another named Don Pablo (possibly these are nine rather than seven men) had moved their peoples into the vicinity of El Gallo. They and their warriors had been involved in the assault on the mule train – one-half of the men had been under the command of the "Toboso" El Mapochi. Following the fracas, they had gone all together to the Sierra de la Cadena, and then Don Fiscal, Juanillo (this is the first time this name occurs), and Sunora split off and went to the Sierra del Diablo. (In these declarations is mentioned another chief, named Contreras – Juanillo? or the Cocoyome leader of later years?) Eight nations had been camped in front of the Sierra de la Cadena. One-half of the men from this group had gone off to raid for horses. Those left behind, in the deponent's opinion, would still be in the general area (AHP 1687 Ab).

With this news the Spanish contingent left to seek out the enemy. On the road Marcos informed his captors that the Indians were well aware that the Spaniards had been planning on making war this year. He knew of one Indian from an hacienda at Parras who spied for the rebels. In the vicinity of the Ciénega de San José about five leagues from Mapimí, evidence was found where the enemy had held a great *junta* in the arroyo below La Cadena. Some of the tracks led to the Sierra del Diablo, the others went toward the east. Marcos claimed that the people who had gone to Sierra del Diablo would be Don Fiscal, also called Don Felipe, Sunuri, and Don Martín (AHP 1687Ab).

The tracks going eastward led to the Ciénega de San José (if this is interpreted correctly). Here, they divided and went in several different directions – some to Cuatro Ciénegas, some toward Mapimí, and some toward Acatita. Marcos stated that the people going to Cuatro Ciénegas would be the Cabezas under chiefs Sinarvee and Don Bartolo. He also declared that the people who lived at Mapimí and Acatita were the Cocoyomes and the bands of Don Pedro (Pedrote, the Cabeza?) and Don Francisco Tecolote (Cocoyome) (AHP 1687Ab).

At this same time the hostile Indian nations frequently "invaded" the area of Coahuila. These nations included the Colorados, Contotores, and Conianes, among others (these are clearly "Cabezas" or closely associated groups – see Appendix 3), who raided the roads from Nuevo León, Saltillo, and Mazapil to Zacatecas and Sombrerete, as well as the haciendas of Caopa and Patos, and the mission of Contotores. The Nadadores mission had been depopulated. Furthermore, these peoples had also joined the "Tobosos" for a raid on a mule train that was traveling on the road to Parral (near El Gallo?). Chiefs Pedrote, Bartolo, and Santiago were the captains leading the rebel bands, now camped at Baján (Portillo 1887: 187, 190-193).

One campaign was made in November by the governor of Coahuila, Alonso de León. At the end of October, a Barbozarigame captured at the Potrero de Patos was interrogated at the hacienda at Anaelo. He had been settled previously at Cuatro Ciénegas, where he had been baptized. He had left his homeland with the Colorado chief named Salvador, chief Marcos of the Odames, and some other men, following the Itocas and Idedepos bands that had sallied forth to rob and to kill Spaniards. Don Pedrote, he said, was the head chief and now had twelve nations under him (Portillo 1887: 192-195).

Furthermore, the captive said, the Indians of Nadadores and the Contortores were very friendly with Don Pedrote, which would make it impossible for the Spanish expedition to track him down, because he would be warned beforehand. The Quechal captain, Don Dieguillo, at Nadadores, kept in touch with Pedrote — booty was shared with him, and he and his people participated in victory dances with Pedrote's group — although he pretended peace and friendship with the Spaniards. Chief Dieguillo was trying to make an alliance between the Indians at La Caldera and the Contotores, and the people of Nadadores, for the warpath. However, after this information, this captive led De León and his men some forty-five leagues westward where they encountered Pedrote's allies, the Tobosos and Colorados. The Indians attacked while the Spaniards were watering their horses. The latter, however, killed five of the enemy while the rest escaped (Portillo 1887: 195-197).

In January of 1688, Alonso de León reported that he had gone to Parras to pick up the Contotores Indians to take them back to their own mission to resettle it. At Parras, an Indian man who had been raised with the Contotores recounted to De León that four Indian women had been sent to San Francisco de Coahuila by Don Pedrote and the Cabezas to request peace. However, Pedrote's people planned on staying in Coahuila only until the tuna were ripe, during which time they would attempt to gain the Caldera Indians as allies for an assault on the Spaniards (Portillo 1887: 198-199).

Later, two of these women testified that Don Pedrote (Cabeza), Don Alejo (Conián), and Don Santiago (Cabeza) had sent them to request peace. Messengers were sent out to the rebels, and by February 26 over fifty persons had come in to settle. However, De León told them that in order to consummate the peace it would be necessary for Don Pedrote (who had not yet shown up) and the rest of the Cabezas, plus the Tobosos and the Colorados, also to give themselves up. He would then have them settled at Nadadores (Portillo 1887: 199-201).

According to two Cabezas, Don Bartolo, the Tobosos, and some of the other nations with them planned on staying in the desert until the tuna ripened. During the tuna harvest ceremonies, they were going to try to gain the alliance of the Indians (Cacafes, one of two groups) at peace at the mission of La Caldera to make war on the Spaniards. Since Pedrote and his people had been in rebellion they had been in communication with Don Dieguillo at Nada-

dores and with the Pies de Venado at the Contotores mission. Don Pedrote always had distributed some booty to the Nadadores people; and two of Dieguillo's relatives, who lived with Pedrote's band, acted as go-betweens for the two groups. The Spaniards then sent messengers to the back-country nations on March 1 (Portillo 1887: 201-203, 205-206).

Don Bartolo arrived at Nadadores with fifteen of his people and some Colorados on March 26. Then, within a week, the Indians who had been settled at the new town of Santiago de Monclova, together with sixteen men sent by Don Dieguillo from Nadadores, assaulted the Spanish soldiers and settlers who were also in the process of moving to Monclova. Alonso de León later wrote that the very day that he had left the Indians, Don Santiago had requested permission to hold a dance with the people from Nadadores. He had conceded this because he felt it would be good policy and would gain the good will of these people whom he was endeavoring to settle in peace. It was later learned, however, that Don Dieguillo had then exhorted the Indians to rise up against the Spaniards. A few days later they moved out and attacked Monclova with about 100 warriors, killing two Spaniards; the following day they descended upon Nadadores. At this time Don Dieguillo had under his command the Colorados, Pies de Venados, Cabezas, Quechales, Conianes, and Manos Prietas (the latter at least were from the Nadadores mission). The Indians at the Contotores mission also revolted at this time, apparently with the others (Portillo 1887: 204-215).

Another Spanish contingent went out after the rebels in the latter part of April. Two of the enemy were killed, including the Terocodame chief Marcos, and a third was taken prisoner (called a Bobole by the Spaniards, but he declared himself to be a Conián). This prisoner corroborated the story that the Tobosos and Cabezas had "always" communicated with the Nadadores people, and that two relatives of Don Dieguillo with Pedrote's band served this purpose. Dieguillo and Marcos, the Terocodame chief, were the ones who had incited the Indians to this uprising, which included the Cabezas, Conianes, Colorados, Quechales, Manos Prietas, and Bocoras. This rebel group hoped to use stolen horses to attract other nations to their alliance (Portillo 1887: 201-220).

On April 28 Alonso de León ordered out still another campaign. The rebels were taking horses in the direction of the Río Grande. Spanish troops cut the Indians off, killed seven, and captured three. The latter confessed that Dieguillo had given them the stolen goods and animals they had been caught with and had told them to go and convoke the Teodocodamos (Terocodames), Jumanes, and other nations to assist against the Spaniards. Don Dieguillo and his followers were allied with the bands of Don Pedrote and Don Bartolo, and the Tobosos, although they all lived in different places; they comprised many people and had little food. The next day another squad of the enemy was encountered near Santa Rosa, on its way to join Don Dieguillo (Portillo 1887: 221-223).

On July 16, 1688, an Herbipiamo Indian envoy returned who had been sent to call in the Terodocodamos, Jumanes, and Manos Prietas to the mission of Nadadores. He reported that the first two and the Herbipiamos had refused to make peace with the Spaniards at this time because, they claimed, they had been forewarned that this was simply a trick of the Spaniards. The Herbipiamos had now gone off with the Tejas and would not be back until winter (Portillo 1887: 237-238).

Farther west in Nueva Vizcaya, back in the month of March, 1688, investigations had been made concerning the enemy situation. Raids and assaults were rampant in all parts of the province. In February the Spaniards had made a campaign into the interior. After fifty leagues from Parral a camp was discovered where the troops captured a boy in his early teens, three women, and two children. Here the Spaniards learned that an Indian who worked on an hacienda in the San Bartolomé Valley had warned the people of this rancheria of the approaching Spanish troops. This camp had consisted of Gavilanes and Tobosos (the latter probably used in its generic sense). Later it was discovered that the spy who had done the warning was a Suma or Cholome Indian from up north. No real motive was uncovered except that apparently he had visited this rancheria a number of times before the warning, although the culprit denied this (AHP 1688Cb).

In November Captain Juan de Retana was ordered north to the Río Grande to check on reports of a "foreign" nation in that area, apparently some Frenchmen. On the road he learned that a number of enemy Indians were camped at the Sierra de Guapagua. Although the camp was somewhat out of his way, Retana marched his troops to that spot, where he surprised three bands — Cocoyomes, Hijos de las Piedras, and Gavilanes. He broke them up and killed many of them (Hackett 1926: 250; 254-256; BL 1649-1700; BL 1693-1702; UTD 1683-1697).

Sometime around the year 1690 the Cabezas, or at least a band of them, and including Don Pedrote, finally surrendered to the Spaniards and settled permanently at Parras. Here they remained peaceful, although they were implicated in spy activity for the enemy some twenty years later (BL 1694-1698; Parras Parish Records). It was about this time, but principally during the previous decade, that the "Cabezas" and "Salineros" fell out of the picture of Nueva Vizcayan desert raiders for good. From this time on, the "Tobosos," and later the "Chisos," became the principal native actors in the contacts between Spaniard and desert Indian in central northern Mexico.

The 1690's

The last decades of the seventeenth century in many ways constituted a rather significant period in the history of northern Mexico. This was a time of a considerable amount of expansion of Spanish society on the northern frontier, despite various setbacks owing to native reaction and the fact that from the long picture the weakening of Spanish power that occurred during the next century was beginning to take place. Indian hostilities broke out in Nueva Vizcaya several times — among the Concho Indians of the central river valleys, and among the Tarahumara of the mountains in the west — and the people of the eastern desert intensified their activities on a number of occasions. Furthermore, nomadic Indians in the north — the Apaches, Janos, Jocomes, and others in northwest Chihuahua and northeast Sonora, and Apaches in New Mexico — were increasing their hostilities, a trend that was noted as early as the 1650's with regard to the Apaches in New Mexico (Spicer 1962: 161, 233-236).

In this general northern area, aside from two uprisings in the penultimate decade of the seventeenth century (the Great Pueblo Revolt in New Mexico in 1680 and the second rebellion four years later by the Conchos, Suma, Jumano, and neighboring tribes immediately to the south in Nueva Vizcaya), the Tarahumara Indians in the Sierra Madre country of the Nueva Vizcaya province took up arms twice before the end of the century. After a quickening of Spanish activity in their country, the Tarahumara first revolted in 1690. This took place a little over a decade after a new push of missionization and the formation of the Upper Tarahumara mission district, and five years following the discovery of silver and a corresponding mining rush at Cusihuiriachic in the eastern portion of Tarahumara territory. The Tarahumara went to war again in 1696 and were not effectively put down until 1698 (Spicer 1962: 33-35; 162).

In 1692 the Spaniards moved back into New Mexico and re-established their authority in that province. On the west coast, in these same final years of the seventeenth century, the Spanish mission system was expanding under the Jesuits. The first mission among the Seri was founded in 1679, followed by the establishment of the Upper Pima mission district eight years later by Father Eusebio Kino, and in 1697 by the conquest and Jesuit penetration of Lower California under Father Juan María Salvatierra. About this same time in Nueva Vizcaya, on the heels of the 1684 Revolt, the Spaniards re-organized the defenses of the province, which included the establishment of several new presidios. These were placed at various strategic locations with regard to the desert raiders — at El Pasaje, at El Gallo, and at the mission site of San Francisco de Conchos, as well as at Janos in northwest Chihuahua (the site of an older Franciscan *visita*) (Massey 1949; Spicer 1962: 105, 118-119; DHM 1748).

With the withdrawal of the Salineros and Cabezas from the scene about 1690, the Toboso bands became the undisputed leaders of the Nueva Vizcayan desert raiders. This constituted one of the major high-marks of the now well-established trends in the decrease in the number of native bands, with a concomitant diminishing of population and the amalgamation of remnants of bands and individual refugees with other groups, as well as a geographical extension in a southward movement of at least the zones of exploitation of the remaining bands. Some of these shifts in the Indian situation were noted by Spanish observers located on the northern frontier. One of the best resumés of population changes among the nomads was made by Captain José de Berroterán in the 1740's (see last section of this chapter). Other reports, such as that of Medrano in 1657, and that of Pardiñas and Escorza to be cited later, also

recorded rather effectively some of these modifications. Although better documentation is needed from the areas actually raided, general reports indicate that the Indians had in effect increased the geographical ranges of their activities — a process that Medrano had noted some thirty years earlier.

In July of 1691 Governor Pardiñas wrote to the Viceroy that new nations had joined the "Tobosos" and Cocoyomes; this coincided in time with the demise of the Cabeza band when it withdrew from the desert and settled down at the town of Parras. Other contemporary sources report that the "Tobosos" were now raiding as far south as Nueva Galicia, hitting both Spanish and Tepehuán communities. This extension of activities was purportedly because of the new military pressure being put on the rebels in Nueva Vizcaya, a change that reflects the increased defenses of the province. These reports of the southern extent of Indian raiding operations were confirmed during interrogations of captive rebels (BL 1693b).

The Sergeant Major Juan Bautista Escorza summed up much of this situation two years later. In 1693, while reporting on a campaign he had recently carried out against the enemy, he made evident his alarm concerning new peoples among the rebels. These were ten to twelve nations from the area extending from Coahuila and Santa Rosa de Nadadores to the Río Grande, a distance of some sixty leagues. Some of the newcomers had been recognized by the Spaniards' Indian auxiliaries; the "Toboso" bands had constituted only about one-fourth of the total enemy forces. One Luquillas, a man much worse than the famed Chief El Tecolote, Escorza claimed, had been responsible for bringing these Coahuileños into the Nueva Vizcayan picture (Hackett 1926: 318-324; BL 1695a).

Escorza ended his report with two points. The first was that raids were getting worse because the Indians had consumed the thousands of (wild) cattle and horses that had once been in the province and they were now forced to go after the animals raised by the Spaniards. The second was that in earlier times the Indians of the province had been many in number and had not had to rely upon alliances with other nations deep from the interior; actually the native groups closest to Spanish settlements had served as a buffer to the more distant nations. Now, however, they were so few in number owing to past hostilities and to "time" (plagues?) that they had been forced to invite these other tribes to join them (Hackett 1926: 318-324; BL 1695a).

Judging from other information Escorza's second point seems to be essentially correct — at least alliances at this time were including peoples more widely separated geographically. The first, however, is more difficult to appraise. There seems to be no real evidence that raids by the desert Indians had become worse since the 1650's. Unfortunately, there is no way that this can be determined precisely from the documentary sources and the general, somewhat impressionistic, statements of the writers of the period that have to be relied upon. Nevertheless, even if raiding activities had remained about the same from mid-century and the population of the back-country natives had in effect diminished, the implication remains that the desert nomadic people were now relying more upon raiding as a subsistence activity — that is, for the acquisition of food and other economic goods. Although the evidence for this specialization is not adequate, it was corroborated to some extent by the Indians themselves (see chapter III). Moreover, it is not certain that Escorza's statement concerning a decrease in the number of wild horses and cattle in the province is too accurate. These animals were reported to be abundant still in the second quarter of the eighteenth century (Arlegui 1851: 130, 134).

The appearance of new Indian nations from the north in the Greater Bolsón Spanish-native contact zone was perhaps one of the contributing factors in what apparently was a more concerted effort on the part of the Spaniards to quell the raiding Indians. The period between the two Tarahumara uprisings in the 1690's saw the extermination by the sword of two of the Toboso bands, the Jojocomes (Ocomes) and the Gavilanes. Concurrently, a number of requests and opinions aimed at or advocating the extermination of the "wild" Indian bands, were made on the local level. Although the history of Spanish policy toward these nomadic Indians is not clear, it seems that a growing consensus evinced that the only effective way to handle the nomads was to eliminate them, in some fashion, from the frontier scene. A recommendation to that effect was made to the Viceroy of New Spain by the *Maestre de Campo* Joseph Francisco Marín in 1693, and in essence the *fiscal* in Madrid made the same suggestion in 1698 after reviewing the reports of Marín and of others with similar opinions (Hackett 1926: 401, 419ff, esp. 429, 451-453).

Despite the accumulation of evidence of the desert Indian menace and the growing feeling that the elimination of the natives was the only possible solution, the Spanish government in Mexico City and in Spain maintained basically the same policy toward the rebel Indian that it had had for decades. Nevertheless, specifically with regard to the area of Nueva Vizcaya, this policy would be changed early in the following century. In the 1690's, however, while authorities in these higher levels of government recognized the fruitlessness of the handout system, they continued to issue orders to the provincial governors emphasizing that captured rebels should be given due process of law before punishment was meted out. In 1693 it was stated that the natives should not be deported outside the province because of the demoralization they would suffer in a new place with nothing to do, as well as because of the expense that deportation would entail for the Royal Treasury (Hackett 1926: 355-357, 359-361).

In the late spring of 1691, raids had been reported in the Tepehuán area near Santa Catalina and Papasquiaro, and in the vicinity of El Gallo. Soldiers from the presidios of El Pasaje, El Gallo, and Cerro Gordo were ordered out to reconnoiter, and the Cocoyome band of El Tecolote was discovered in the Sierra de Jicorica. The Indians escaped through the mountains, and no battle ensued, although the Spaniards managed to recover some thirty stolen animals and three captives — one a Spaniard from Saltillo (BL 1693b).

These ex-captives were later interrogated. The Spaniard, about eighteen years of age, had been taken prisoner by the Indians five years before at San Juan de los Ahorcados. He had spent a little over two years with a combined group of Cocoyomes and Cabezas, until the latter went to Parras to settle permanently there in peace. He recounted a battle at Pozo Hediondo around the beginning of 1689 between these Indians and Spanish troops, and another time, immediately following his capture, when his "group" had joined the "Tobosos" and had raided wagon trains from Mexico City around El Gallo (which, he said, had been before the presidio was founded there?). About 1690, a great meeting had been held by a number of enemy nations — including Cocoyomes, Hijos de las Piedras, Gavilanes, "and many others" with whom he was unacquainted — at the Nazas River at which time various future raids had been planned (BL 1693b).

Although the Cocoyomes eventually entered into peace negotiations with the Spaniards, this witness recounted that the Indians had been saying that they had no intention of surrendering but only "to die or to flee with everything." The witness had heard when he was at Jicorica that the Cocoyomes were going into the interior to obtain reinforcements of Chisos and Chuchitames (Chichitames) in order to attack and destroy the presidio at El Gallo, despite the fact that they were now very fearful of the Spaniards because so many of their people had been killed during the last two years. Once a certain Contreras had suggested to El Tecolote that it would be a good idea to make peace; the latter answered that he had no such intention but expected "to remain at war until death" (BL 1693b).

The Indians had raided as far south as the Nazas, Papasquiero, Zacatecas, Nieves, and Sombrerete. Later, from the Acatita located near Mapimí, a number of raiding parties had left to go outside the territory (*tierra afuera*), south to the region of Río Grande and Aguanueva near Mazapil. (Another ex-captive declared that the Cocoyomes once stated that the easiest region to raid was around Sombrerete and Zacatecas.) El Tecolote had gone to Jicorica, near Indé, from where squads left to raid in the Parral district. This band had remained in the Jicorica mountains because of the availability of cattle there, both wild and domestic, and because of fear of the Baján and Tagualilora (Tahualilo) area where they felt the Cabezas at Parras might lead the Spaniards out against them (BL 1693b).

In mid-year of 1691 the Suninuliglas (Chisos) made overtures of peace, and reportedly other Indians from the north around the Río Grande were ready to do the same. General Juan de Retana of the Conchos presidio sent a flag, hat, and other items to the head chief of the Sisimbles to induce a surrender; he requested that the Indian governor of Coahuila be ordered to send peace talks to his people who bordered the lower Río Grande, with the hope that this would encourage the Sisimbles to acquiesce (BL 1693b).

Somewhat later some Indians, thought to be Chisos, stole animals from Captain Sapién in the Conchos area, and a six-man squad was reported on its way to Santa Bárbara to strike there. It was later learned that a large group of "Chisos" and "Tobosos" had gotten together in Chiso country to form an alliance for the war against the Spaniards, although most of the Chisos, except the Chichitames, had been reluctant to go along with this. A number of "invasions" were also registered in the Parras area. People from Parras sallied forth with Don Pedrote and recovered some animals that the enemy was herding to Cuatro Ciénegas. It was thought that the culprits were Hijos de las Piedras and other groups from the "east" (BL 1693b).

Around mid-December the Spanish governor Pardiñas led a large force of some 300 men into the desert by way of Los Peyotillos to track down the rebels. On December 30, the Spanish troops met and defeated the Gavilanes of Don Felipe El Tuerto, taking a great many women and children prisoners. Some eight of the ranchería's fifteen warriors were killed; only El Tuerto and some ten others escaped, taking refuge with the Cocoyomes, and later the Jojocomes (BL 1693b).

On the basis of information received during this campaign, Pardiñas took out another expedition during the latter days of January of the next year — 1692. On this occasion the troops traveled by way of Agua de Terrazas and El Venado, roughly on the border area between "Chisos" and "Tobosos." From here they went to the Sierra del Diablo, where they moved in on the enemy, including the Hijos de las Piedras — although most escaped. Then, owing to lack of water, it was decided to suspend operations temporarily against the rebel Indians (BL 1693b).

In March of 1692, a number of envoys from the rebels appeared in Parral to see Governor Pardiñas. Among these were Lorenzo, "governor of the rebels of the Cocoyome nation; Antonio, brother of Don Francisco Tecolote, chief of the said nation, who said he has been sent by his brother; Juan Polanco Totoci, who is called Contreras, captain of the Acoclames and of the Hijos de las Piedras; Don Phelipe El Tuerto, who is called Don Fiscal, captain of the Gavilán nation; Alonso Querinbolo of the Nonoje nation; Nicolás of the Gavilán nation." These men had come to seek peace, according to Lorenzo, and El Tuerto underscored this, referring to the great losses his people had suffered, including the deaths of his own sons (BL 1693b).

For a while it appeared as though some actual progress toward peace was being made. Governor Pardiñas wrote on March 25 that the Indians still in rebellion were the Chisos, Batayolilas, and Cholomes.

However, by April 21, the "Tobosos" again had returned to the warpath. Pardiñas sent the Franciscan Fray Juan de Sumeta out to them. Sumeta was personally acquainted with many of the "Tobosos," and Pardiñas harbored the hope that through his good offices the Indians could be persuaded back to the Spaniards (BL 1693b).

Later El Tuerto confessed that most of the people of El Tecolote's and Lorenzo's bands did not want peace. The reason for the last withdrawal had been that a number of hacienda workers had gone after the Cocoyome envoys near Guajoquilla. With this the rebels had feared an ambush, losing faith in the Spaniards and in the establishment of any kind of peace. At the time of this questioning El Tuerto's few remaining people were camped at a location separated from the rest of the "Tobosos." When asked about recent raiding, El Tuerto stated that one foray on Santa Bárbara probably had been carried out by Chisos. He was uncertain about the perpetrators of an assault near Sombrerete, but he told of one chief, named Pescueso or Cuello de Venado, who lived with a small band (apparently "Toboso") separated from the rest of the rebels who might have executed it (BL 1693b).

One "Toboso" woman corroborated much of this testimony, stating that the Cocoyomes were not really seeking peace, because when she had been with them she had seen one of their raiding squads make a sally. She felt certain that it was this group that had made the raid near Sombrerete. However, she thought that Don Felipe El Tuerto, the Acoclames, Hijos de las Piedras, and Hijos de la Tierra actually did want peace. Most of the Cocoyomes were now at Poso Hediondo and El Picacho, two leagues from the former place, although El Tecolote was with a small band at Sierra del Diablo (BL 1693b).

With this it seemed clear that the real obstacle to peace was the Cocoyomes. War would have to be made on them, while at the same time El Tuerto's people and the Acoclames, Hijos de la Tierra, and Hijos de las Piedras would be brought in and settled in peace. Messengers were sent to these bands for this purpose. Retana wrote on July 15 that the Cocoyomes were only eight leagues from the Conchos presidio on the Río Florido, and that the other three bands were at El Venado on their way in. Two days later El Tecolote and his men arrived at Conchos. However, by August 9, the Acocolames and their associates had not yet shown up, and the Cocoyomes of El Tecolote had retired from Conchos. Only El Tuerto and his people remained at the presidio (BL 1693b).

In the latter part of August, it was thought, from tracks discovered and attributed to the Acoclames and the Hijos groups, that these had fled to join the Chisos at "La Sierra de los Chisos" and at Encinillas. Still, however, it was felt that there was a slight possibility that the Cocoyomes could be induced to peace through Gavilán envoys. Friars Juan de Sumeta and Gabriel Montés de Oca went out around the end of August and early in September to the area around the Ojo de Barraza, Las Batuecas, Las Cañas, and Los Remedios. They met the Cocoyomes and parlied with them concerning peace, but again the results were unsuccessful. Furthermore, the first part of September, even Don Felipe El Tuerto, the Gavilán chief, had fled with a few women and a Cocoyome man from Conchos. El Tuerto was later captured and brought back (BL 1693b).

General Retana then came to the conclusion that the entire peace offerings of the previous three months had merely served the Indians as a cover under which to carry on their thievery, since during this period several hundred head of animals had been stolen, quite obviously by the very same groups that had been negotiating for peace. The only solution was all-out war. The opinions of other military officers differed somewhat. Captain Juan de Salaices felt that the plundering could very well have been carried out by hacienda Indians. Often Indian laborers from the Río Grande del Norte area stole animals on their return trip home, or other rebel groups could have taken them. In accord with Salaices were others, particularly the Franciscans, who advocated that the Indians should be reduced to settlement by peaceful means rather than military action (BL 1693b).

Despite Retana's suggested strong measures, governor Pardiñas decided to attempt again to bring the Indians peaceably into settlement. Two loyal "Tobosos" from Conchos sent as ambassadors returned by September 24 to report they had located some of the Cocoyomes at the place of Tagualiloat (Tagualilo). The Indians claimed they had lost faith (confianza) during the last peace negotiations and were afraid to go to the Spaniards, although they had not committed any raids but had been living only off wild mustangs. On October 23, Pardiñas learned from the Toboso governor at Conchos and from several Cocoyomes that El Tecolote and four of his men, including his brother Antón and Juan Polanco Totoci (Contreras), had gone to Chiso country. However, the rest of the Cocoyomes were still at peace, and the recent raiding had been done either by Chisos or Cholomes (BL 1693b).

In November of 1692 a band of Jojocomes (Ocomes) under chief Lorenzo Delgado, said to be their *gobernador* and *caudillo*, went to the Spaniards to make peace despite the fact that rebel nations such as Chisos and Cholomes had tried to impede them from carrying this out. At this same time, the Jojocomes sent word to El Tecolote, the Acoclames, Hijos de la Tierra, and Hijos de las Piedras for them to come in also. A mestizo, captive of these Jojocomes for a number of years, claimed that both the Jojocomes and Cocoyomes (reported to be in the vicinity of Guajoquilla at this time) now would accept peace, as evidenced by the way they had respected and celebrated the envoys, and particularly because a flag, or banner, had been sent to them by the Spanish governor. However, the captive said, the Chisos had no intention of making peace (BL 1693b).

In December it was learned that El Tecolote had been at Jacue with the Hijos de las Piedras and Hijos del Lodo, at the same time the Chiso chief Santiago had visited them. These bands — with the possible exception of Santiago El Chiso — seemingly were still planning on making peace. However the Chichitames, Cíbolos (probably those from the far side of the Río Grande, since they are mentioned together with other northern groups), Cholomes, Batayolicuas, and Solinyolicuas had no intention of surrendering. Moreover, the Solinyolicua captain had gone to the confluence of the Río Grande and Conchos rivers during the wheat harvest where he was going to wait for his companions to go down later to the Tabalaopa area to raid (BL 1693b).

On December 6, Cocoyomes and a combined group of Jojocomes and Gavilanes made peace with Governor Pardiñas at Santa Cruz. Arrangements were made for settlement, and a set of Indian officials was appointed for each group. On the night of December 10, these recently-reduced-to-peace rebels revolted. Pardiñas personally led a contingent after the Indians. At Las Cañas it was learned that one band of Jojocomes and Gavilanes was camped about two leagues away. Don Lorenzo and the chief El Sombrero Prieto (also called El Tordillo) were here.

The group was manufacturing arrows and refused to return to the Spaniards. Another rancheria of the same Indians was discovered at the pass of Los Remedios. Both bands, when rounded up and asked why they had fled, claimed that the Cocoyomes, whom they had always followed and helped, had compelled them to flee. Apparently the Indians had been told that the Spaniards were intending to kill them. The Cocoyomes had now gone to Acatita (BL 1693b).

Pardiñas, after conferring with his aides, gave orders to execute both groups of Jojocomes-Gavilanes. Fray Juan de Sumeta, guardian of the Franciscan convent at San Bartolomé, confessed the condemned, and most were put to the sword, except a few of the women and children. Some of the heads of the chiefs were placed at Las Cañas and others at the spring (*ojo*) of Barraza, to stand as a reminder to the remaining rebel bands of their impending fate. In his report Pardiñas cited an example of the rebelliousness of these Indians. One man, prior to his execution, arose from confession and began to shout that he "was not afraid to die because he was a man of great bravery and as such he had always known how to kill Spaniards" (BL 1693b).

In January of 1693, Captain Juan de Salaices led out a campaign against the Cocoyomes, Hijos de las Piedras, and Hijos de la Tierra. Salaices reported from El Alamo on February 4 that he had attacked a band, but only their captain, Don Gregorio, was killed, and a few prisoners were taken. Before this, Salaices' troops had killed two Hijos de la Tierra and captured an Hijo de las Piedras, whose rancheria was at the Sierra of the Cuerno del Venado. This prisoner declared that there was a great *junta* of Cocoyomes, Hijos de las Piedras, Hijos de la Tierra, and Chisos at the Sierra de Jacue where Don Francisco Tecolote now was. Instead of moving to this place Salaices decided to attack a somewhat more distant Chiso camp, because he estimated that his own force was too small to go after the bands at Jacue. Two days later, Pardiñas decided to suspend military operations against the rebels because of a large epidemic at this time (BL 1693b).

On April 30, 1693, governor Gabriel del Castillo, reviewing the general Indian situation in the province of Nueva Vizcaya, ordered Captain Juan de Retana to go out on campaign from the "Sierra of Conula and Bapagua reconnoitering the trail to that of El Diablo," that is, Chiso and Toboso country. Retana left the Conchos presidio on July 3 with some twenty Toboso auxiliaries, plus Tacuitataomes and Indians from the mission of San Pedro, and later many from the La Junta Pueblos. The party went by way of Tabalaopa, Nombre de Dios, to near La Junta, partly to look for the Suninoligla band that had recently offered peace, said to be located a day's journey from the last town of the jurisdiction of Don Nicolás, governor of the La Junta nations. From here Retana began his campaign into enemy Chiso territory. Scouts reconnoitered the Sierra de Ocotán and eventually picked up an enemy camp at the Sierra de Chocamueca, containing a great number of people recently arrived from Jacue (BL 1695a).

Retana marched there at once. On July 29 the Spanish forces fell on the Chiso camp of Don Santiago at the Peñol de Santa Marta. The enemy, when corralled on top of the crag, requested a conference. Santiago came down with some of the Chisos, but many stayed up in the mountain contrary to Retana's conditions for the talks. During the meetings, some rebel Indian envoys arrived and went to the still hidden Chisos, and all together then made good their escape. Later inspection of the battle area revealed that some twenty-two men and eight women had been killed during the fighting. Also, a number of religious items stolen from a church were discovered. A retrieved captive testified that the Chisos, together with other nations, had made some recent raids in both Coahuila and Parras. He said that the group of Chisos he had been with were without horses because The Suninoligla had attacked them a few days previously, had taken all their animals, and had killed five men and a few women. He declared that the enemies at Santa Marta had been "los del dho Don Santiago Chichitames y Sisimbles" (BL 1695a).

Retana returned to La Junta to recontact the Suninoligla rancheria. Some eight days later three Suninoliglas leaders and a Batayoligla chief arrived to give obedience to Retana, now in the Posalme village. These envoys claimed that their peoples had not been with the enemy for more than two years. Actually they had fought the Chisos and Chichitames on several occasions. Retana granted peace to the Suninoliglas and Batayoliglas and designated the abandoned village of the Tapacolme Indians as their place of settlement (BL 1695a).

Later, a Chiso named Bartolome de Estrada, who had accompanied Retana on this last campaign and who had stayed in the back country to see if he could

track down the enemy, arrived at the presidio of San Francisco de Conchos in September. With him were 104 Indians of the Chichitame, Osatayoligla, Guasapayoligla, and Sisimble bands. Still more members of these nations were camped at the water hole of San Pedro, waiting to come in. These Chisos reported that the Acoclames, Hijos de las Piedras, and Hijos de la Tierra were camped out in the Jaque-Encinillas area. They had tried to impede the Chisos from coming in to surrender and had said they were going to send out raiding squads so the Spaniards would put the blame on the Chisos. Eventually, some 400 of these Chisos came in to San Francisco de Conchos (BL 1695a).

The "Tobosos" continued their raiding activities. On October 15, Captain Martín de Hualde made an encounter with the "Tobosos" at the Sierra de Baján — where only two warriors, one youth, and twenty women were killed, and some twelve children between the ages of three to five years were made captives. An Indian woman captive from Guadiana, when given her liberty at this time, declared that El Tecolote had died at Sierra del Diablo during a plague (BL 1693b; BL 1695a).

On November 10 Governor Castillo ordered three commanders — Retana, Escorza, and Hualde — each to take a contingent out to the back country to seek out the enemy Tobosos. Then it was learned that the newly reduced Chiso groups at San Francisco de Conchos had contrived with the Cocoyomes to uprise as soon as Retana left on campaign and to kill the soldiers and other people left at the presidio. Seventy of these Chisos who were assigned to accompany the expedition were to put Retana and his men to the sword once the contingent was out in the back country. Castillo, recounting this to the Viceroy, stated that it was against reason not to execute all of the Chisos since, aside from their being evil (*mala*) people, it was extremely difficult to determine their designs (BL 1695a).

The Spaniards switched their plans somewhat and Hualde marched to the Conchos presidio, arriving on November 25, two days after Retana had departed. Four days later, a group of the enemy hit a nearby hacienda, stealing 110 mares. Hualde went after them and managed to retrieve the animals. It was later discovered that the Hijos del Lodo had made the theft (BL 1695a).

On January 23, 1694, Escorza wrote from Los Patos that he had encountered a group of Acoclames and Cocoyomes in the mountains of Pelayo. From the one captive taken it was learned that chief Luquillas had been killed, together with eight others – the group had left to avenge Retana's attack at Guapagua earlier that month. The captive also told of a previous occasion when Retana attacked "these [people] of El Tecolote" (apparently this group was part of El Tecolote's) who were together with the Hijos de las Piedras, Hijos de la Tierra, and Hijos del Lodo. Three of the latter had gone to the Parral district to wreak vengeance for the deaths that Retana had brought about (BL 1695a).

Retana had made his campaign the previous December, going by way of Julimes, the arroyo of Santa Lucía, the water hole of San Pedro, Agua Redonda or Santo Tomás (this was apparently in Chiso country, as Agua Redonda was said to be the name the Chisos called it), to the vicinity of the Sierra de Chocamueca, to Jacue – trying to sneak up behind the Tobosos, as had been suggested by some of the friendly Indians. At Jacue, it was learned that tracks went to the Sierra de Conula, Acatita La Grande, and Guapagua. At Conula it was discovered that the enemy was in a *junta* at Guapagua, some nine leagues away, and that from a trail they had picked up a herd of horses brought in by the Indians from Parras or Coahuila. On January 8 the Spanish troops attacked the enemy, consisting of Cocoyomes, Acoclames, Hijos de la Tierra, and Hijos de las Piedras – the Chiso auxiliaries carrying the brunt of the fighting. Some forty persons, male and female, were killed, and around fifty were captured. The remainder escaped. Six captives were retrieved – said to be from the places of Guadiana, Santa Ana, and Mazapil – as well as five horses with brands from Nieves and Mazapil. The rest of the enemy's horses had been killed and eaten, according to the captive's report. The fifty prisoners were given to some of the soldiers, to the Chiso Indian auxiliaries (apparently because they were relatives), and to various Spanish establishments (expressly for their education) (BL 1695a).

In August of 1695, Governor Castillo wrote that a few Acoclames and others had come to San Francisco de Conchos to settle in peace. The Cocoyomes apparently were against this, and a short while later two other Indians arrived to take the first group back to the desert. When the Spaniards learned of this they executed the two messengers (BL 1695a).

Between 1698 and January of 1700, the Cocoyomes made peace twice with the Spaniards. Around the middle of 1698 they went to the area of

Cuencamé and the El Pasaje presidio to surrender. They were settled at Santa Cruz but within a short while rebelled again and withdrew to the back country. Later they returned and again asked for peace at El Pasaje. This was granted them, and they were taken to a place on the Nazas River to stay before settling at Covadonga. However, while at the Nazas River they fled back to the hinterland (AHP 1700a).

In April of 1699, the Spaniards interrogated a mulatto boy of about twenty years of age who had been turned over to them by the Cocoyomes when they had gone to Santa Cruz in peace. The boy had been a slave in the vicinity of Río Grande (to the south) and had been captured, according to his own estimate, about two years before at San Juan de los Ahorcados while in the service of his master. He said that he had never attempted to escape from the Cocoyomes, as other captive boys had, because he had found himself well off among them. He had participated in war parties on a number of occasions, and he recounted the activities to his interrogators. He had been with a group that had raided at Río de Medina and a place called Chapultepeque; each time they had killed two herders (*pastores*) and had stolen their clothing. Near the town of Canatlán, they had killed four men – two Spaniards, an Indian, and a Negro – who were traveling in a large party. On another occasion the raiders had stolen the horses that belonged to the presidio of El Gallo; the following day they fought with the soldiers who were pursuing them, killing two. Another time, they attacked a mule train near Papasquiaro. On still another, they fought with a squad of six soldiers from the presidio of El Pasaje, killing all, including the sergeant of the presidio; they took the latter's clothing and fifteen horses. After this, they went to Covadonga, where they stole a herd of horses (AHP 1699a).

About the same time the Cocoyomes made peace in 1698, "Toboso" envoys arrived in Parral. Some 130 were later settled at the abandoned mission of San Buenaventura de Atotonilco at the end of the year. (Governor Larrea wrote in May of 1700 that these "Tobosos" had been at Atotonilco for about a year and a half.) When the group was settled they reported that the rest of the nations were not coming in because they were so divided and distant from one another they had not been able to get together in one spot, apparently to agree together about peace. However, by the time of Larrea's writing in 1700, other "Tobosos" had been slowly arriving, and the total number of persons at Atotonilco was then 260. At this time 350 Chisos were settled at San Francisco de Conchos — they had arrived, or had begun to arrive, in May of the previous year. While these people were settled, the governor of Coahuila reported in mid-1699 that his jurisdiction was constantly hostilized from the west and north by rebel "Tobosos" (BL 1649-1700).

The Early Eighteenth Century

In the early years of the eighteenth century the situation of the Indian warfare in Nueva Vizcaya remained essentially the same as in the last years of the previous decade. The one major exception to this was that after the peace was established in 1698 the Tarahumara Indians remained relatively quiet. At the same time the previously cited trends of Spanish expansion and increased Indian hostilities in northeast Sonora and northwest Chihuahua continued.

At the beginning of the 1700's only two "Toboso" bands by name were in existence. These were the Cocoyomes, who had been able to maintain and add to their strength throughout the contact period, and the Acoclames. The latter had managed to increase in numbers since a near demise in the mid-seventeenth century. However, during the second decade of the eighteenth, the size of this band again was diminished radically, leaving the Cocoyomes for a time as the leaders of the Greater Bolsón desert nomads.

Knowledge of the situation is much less certain with regard to the Chiso groups. References to Chisos are most numerous from about 1684 into the first ten or twelve years of the eighteenth century. From the latter date, individual Chiso band names virtually cease to show up in the sources. Some Chisos were probably assimilated with their Concho brothers on haciendas and other Spanish establishments, although at least one group, the Sisimbles, persisted as desert raiders into the 1740's. Meanwhile, during the second decade of the eighteenth century, a number of Coahuileños from the Nadadores area joined the Cocoyomes and the few remaining Acoclames. With these "Tobosos" the Coahuileños became the principal native actors in the Greater Bolsón for several years.

Aside from the continuing trends of population reduction, band amalgamation, and the southward movement of peoples, one of the fundamental changes that occurred in the first decade of the eighteenth century was a modification in the feelings of the higher governmental authorities about the deportation of natives from the province. How this change in policy developed is somewhat obscure. However, on August 7, 1711, the Viceroy of New Spain, El Duque de Linares, ordered that the Cocoyomes, Acoclames, Chisos, and other nations who were at that time detained in the public jail in Parral, be sent to the viceregal court in Mexico City in order that they could be distributed to mills (ingenios y trapiches) and workshops (obrajes) to gain their own living and be instructed in the Holy Faith. There is little information on the details of this deportation. However, the following month the Spanish governor in Parral stated that he was sending the prisoners as ordered. These persons seemingly had been in Parral since at least January of 1710, and a legal case had been carried out against them during the course of that year. This is the first recorded deportation of Nueva Vizcayan Indians from the province, although the measure was repeated on at least two later occasions in the 1720's (AHP 1710a; AHP 1710b; AHP 1710c; AHP 1710d; AHP 1711a; BL 1709-1715).

Many of the details of this policy shift are unknown. It is not clear how much of the change stemmed from local pressure and how much may have been part of certain modifications in policy that occurred with the advent of the War of Spanish Succession and the Bourbon period in Spain — various measures, such as defensive rather than offensive war, designed to keep down military and other expenses in the Colonies in order that more monies could be allocated to the wars in Europe (Dunne 1948: 192; AHP 1708a; AHP 1708b). Deporting the rebels from the area would eliminate, once and for all, further military costs.

Opinions commensurate with this policy change had been expressed in Parral in 1704 at a time when the various desert "nations" had begun to make peace overtures. At that time a number of persons felt that the "Tobosos," and some included the "Chisos," should be sent out of the province as the only permanent solution to the rebel Indian problem, since these people were of evil inclination, hostile, lazy, and untrustworthy. Some individuals offered, if the Viceroy would not undergo the transportation costs, to contribute gladly their own funds for this purpose (AHP 1704Aa).

Following this first deportation, however, a number of efforts were made for the next decade to reduce the rebels to peace within the Nueva Vizcayan province. When these attempts failed, deportation was again resorted to, this time with more profound and lasting results on the desert-raiding Indian picture in Nueva Vizcaya.

The documentary sources are for the most part silent for the first few years of the eighteenth century. Then, as previously noted, the year 1704 began as one of peace offerings on the part of the untamed Indian tribes of the back country. Governor Juan Fernández de Córdova reported in January that peace negotiations with several nations had been opened. The Cocoyomes had sent messengers to Parras, while envoys of the Acoclames and Chisos had arrived in Parral and San Francisco de Conchos respectively. News had also been received that up north the Apaches of the Gila River had sent peace envoys to El Paso (AHP 1704Aa; AHP 1704Ab; AHP 1704Ac).

These overtures for peace came as a welcomed relief from the hostilities of the previous year during which the Spaniards had made several campaigns with rather large forces. The governor, leading a party from Durango, had encountered a band of the enemy that had just raided a mule train. The Spaniards managed to retrieve all the stolen goods. Another sally was made to the area of the Sierra de Jicorica. The enemy was not located on this occasion, but later reports indicated that the Indians had been hiding in some of the surrounding mountains (AHP 1704Aa).

Two Acoclames, Nicolás and El Curi, arrived in Parral on January 18. They had been sent by the people and chiefs of their nation to learn if a new governor (Córdova took office in July of 1703) had taken over and, if so, to request peace. All the Acoclames were now camped together next to the Sierra del Diablo. The two envoys, when questioned as to why the Acoclames who had been settled at Atotonilco in 1701 had revolted and abandoned the mission, replied that the missionary had had the people whipped a great deal while they had worked at the haciendas in the area. When asked why the people had not made a complaint to the governor instead of fleeing and turning to murder and to theft, the envoys answered that it was their custom not to make appeals to others but rather to simply get up and leave. However, this time, when they arrived back in their home territory they regretted that they had broken the peace (AHP 1704Ab).

Under the same questioning, the envoys gave a run-down on their raiding activities. Sometime during the previous year four Coyotes (Cocoyomes) and three Acoclames had attacked La Cuesta de Huejotitlán and captured two boys. The Acoclames had kept one and the Cocoyomes the other. Some fifteen to twenty days before this testimony, the Xexet Indians, a group associated with the Cocoyomes, had stolen a herd of horses from a Spaniard named Lope del Hierro. They had run the horses by the Acoclame camp on the way to their own territory, which apparently lay somewhere to the east. The Acoclames had thought to attack the Xexet and take the horses but, according to the declarants, decided to wait until they learned what the Spanish governor might want them to do. They were now ready to make an attack on the Xexet and capture the stolen horses, which were many. This Xexet band had been trying to persuade the Acoclames to join them on a raid against the Spaniards; in fact, one Acoclame had been with them when they raided Lope de Hierro's place. The reason the Acoclames had not surrendered before this was that one of the chiefs, named Taure, had opposed it; now he had agreed to it and these two ambassadors had been sent to Parral (AHP 1704Ab).

At the time of this interrogation, Captain Retana was out on campaign searching for the enemy. In the event that the two Acoclames should meet up with the Spanish forces, they were given a document to show that their group had been granted peace. However, apparently after the envoys had returned to their camp, Retana encountered this Acoclame group. They skirmished at the Sierra de las Cañas, and the Spaniards captured some seventy horses and a twelve-year-old captive mulatto boy from Guadiana. After the battle the enemy had split — most (apparently) went toward Atotonilco, but two or three went in the direction of Conchos (a more complete account of this event is given later). Of Retana's men, two Tarahumara from San Felipe and one Chiso were killed (AHP 1704Ab).

By February 13, some fifty-four Acoclames — men, women, and children — had arrived at the presidio of San Francisco de Conchos. They included the four chiefs, Don Nicolás, Rancón, El Ratón, and Panzacola, plus Dieguillo, the son of El Ratón. By February 20, these Acoclames had gone back to the hinterland, after two men from their nation had come for them. Before they departed, however, they killed some of the peaceful Acoclames living at Conchos. The Spaniards gave chase but encountered nothing (AHP 1704Ab).

One man, three women, and five children of the

rebel group stayed behind, supposedly because they had been at the home of another Indian and had not known of the withdrawal. The man claimed that the rest of the tribe was displeased with him because he advocated settling with the Christians — the reason they had left without him. Then he added a statement that summarizes much of the attitude of the rebel groups. He said, "every time the Acoclames and Cocoyomes requested peace they would say, 'lets go so that we will be given food and clothing and anything else we may want.'" Local Indians corroborated this (AHP 1704Ab).

Actually, Cocoyome peace overtures were begun at Parras in November of the previous year. On November 15, the Cocoyomes, who were then camped at the Sierra de Baján, sent a messenger to Parras to inquire about surrendering (AHP 1704Aa; AHP 1704Ad). Captain Martín de Alday from the presidio of El Pasaje was ordered on December 14 to go out to look for this Cocoyome band. On January 7, Alday reported from Parras that he had now given the necessary "talks" to two Cocoyomes who were there at this time. On January 16, nineteen Cocoyomes, nine men and ten women, including Chief Ignacio, arrived in Parras for further peace arrangements. One Acoclame had also come in for the same purpose. All were given a period of thirteen days in which to bring back to Parras the remaining members of their nations. By February 9, the Cocoyomes had not yet returned, and Cabeza scouts were sent to find out what had become of them. They discovered some horse tracks going in the direction of Cocoyome country. It was learned that on January 12 about thirty-three Cocoyomes were on their way to Parras, but chief Contreras and the rest of the band had refused to come in (AHP 1704Ac).

By March 2, this small group had gone back to the desert again. Two squads of Cabezas Indians were sent to locate them. One lone Cocoyome woman was brought in, captured at La Tinaja de San Sebastián, who declared that she had become separated from her companions. Her group had fled from Parras because they were afraid that the Spaniards there were going to kill them. She thought that this band had probably gone to San Juan de Casta to join the rest of the Cocoyomes (AHP 1704Ac).

The Cabeza scouts discovered tracks at the Sierra de Capuli (Conula, Conune?) which led toward Aguachila. A Spanish contingent made up of men from El Pasaje, El Gallo, and Cerro Gordo, plus a number of Indian auxiliaries, was then ordered out. Scouts re-

connoitered the places and water holes of Las Ventanillas, Baján, Sardina, Ayancas, Acatita, and Sozochata, and Santiaguillo, while the main body of troops went to El Pozo, the Laguna de Soconatocu, and San Pedro de la Laguna. An old camp site was discovered at Aguachila, the tracks leading from it going in the direction of San Lorenzo. Then it was learned that eleven of the enemy, including five warriors, were camped at the San Lorenzo River near the road from Parras to Parral. These people dispersed into the surrounding vegetation near the river at the first sight of the Spanish troops, and no encounter was made (AHP 1704Ac).

In the latter part of the month, Spanish forces attacked the Indians in the canyon of San Juan de Casta at the Nazas River, taking from them an Indian herder, whom they had been holding captive, and thirty-two animals. After about two hours of fighting, the enemy shouted for peace. The Spanish commander assented, partly because the place where the Indians had taken refuge was practically inaccessible and partly because he hoped in this way to have the opportunity to retrieve more of the enemy's captives. Later, chiefs Contreras and Lorenzo with some thirty-two braves went down to the Spanish camp at the edge of the river. The Cocoyomes claimed they were apprehensive about making peace, referring to some event regarding what Spanish soldiers at Parras had done to a certain Lomitas and his people. When the Indians took leave that day, the Spanish commander gave them gifts of flour and tobacco (AHP 1704Ac).

On the same afternoon, Contreras sent down one of the captives to the Spaniards, as well as an old Indian woman. The former, Francisco de Gaitán, an eighteen- or twenty-year-old Spaniard and native of Querétaro, had been with the Cocoyomes for two or three years. Commander Martín de Alday wanted Gaitán to stay with the Spanish camp. Gaitán refused, stating that if he stayed, the lives of four other captives held by the Indians would be in danger. However, he figured that they probably would be turned over the following day, since for a number of days now the Cocoyomes had been traveling upriver in order to surrender at the El Pasaje presidio (AHP 1704Ac).

On March 24, 1704, Contreras and Lorenzo sent Alday a message to the effect that a disagreement had arisen among some of their people. The "owners" (amos) of two captives whom they had agreed to turn over to the Spaniards did not want to give up their prizes. The situation had become so bad that they actually had taken up arms against each other. The two chiefs begged Alday to return to his presidio at El Pasaje, where they would notify him of the outcome of the conflict. According to the chiefs, many Cocoyomes did in effect want to surrender. Alday and his advisors acquiesced to the request, and the troops were sent back to their respective homes (AHP 1704Ac).

Little came of these negotiations, and enemy operations continued through the years 1704 and 1705. Around the first part of December of 1705, Ensign Antonio Rodela took out a platoon from Atotonilco, which included a number of Tarahumara auxiliaries. They followed tracks of the enemy, who had some cattle with them. Rodela's troops caught and battled the Indians some twenty-five leagues later. One Acoclame captive, Diego, and the heads of two others were brought back. During the same time that Rodela had been out on campaign, Spanish forces, under General Juan de Retana and Captain Juan Andrés de Aldás, fought the Acoclames, Cocoyomes, and others at Sierra Mojada. The Acoclames alone lost twenty-two warriors, plus several women and children. The Acoclame prisoner judged that probably many Cocoyomes had died from the poisoned arrows used by the Spaniards' Indian auxiliaries. One half of the latter's people had been at a water hole named Agua de la Lanza and the other half at the spring at Conula. The Cocoyomes had gone down to the Nazas River country. They had broken up as soon as the battle was over in order to rustle up some horses and cattle, because the soldiers had taken all of their animals. This witness had been with a group at Agua de la Lanza (AHP 1704Ab).

The testimony of this prisoner affords a rather detailed picture of the raiding activities of these desert bands at this time. Diego, between twenty-five and thirty years of age, was born at the Sierra de las Batuecas (a copious water hole discovered in 1666, five leagues from Las Cañas, was given the name "Las Batuecas" — BL 1649-1700) and was baptized at Conchos on one of the occasions his people had gone there to seek peace. He had spent his entire life in the desert with the Acoclames and neighboring nations — Cocoyomes, Xexet, Hijos de las Piedras, Hijos de la Tierra, and Gavilanes. Since he had been of age (probably soon after puberty) he had devoted his time to helping his relatives in these tribes in robbing and killing. Once he had been with a raiding party

that had stolen some animals from El Canutillo and had run them back to his country to a rancheria at Sierra Mojada. From here he had gone out again with Captain Zurrón de Venado and six other braves to El Torreón. Finding nothing there, they had gone to the Nazas River where they stole some animals, returning directly to Sierra Mojada (AHP 1704Ab).

Diego left from this camp with a large force under chiefs Panzacola and Mojocabara and all of the Acoclames, as well as most of the Cocoyomes under Chief Vas. At the Puesto de Barraza they fought a Spanish ensign with a platoon of soldiers, and the Indians suffered three casualties — one Cocoyome and two Acoclames. This skirmish had been recently preceded by another at Las Cañas, when the Acoclame chief El Ratón with twenty-eight men fought with Spanish soldiers, resulting in the loss of four Acoclames (AHP 1704Ab).

After the Puesto de Barraza affair, the Acoclames returned to Sierra Mojada — except Mojocabara, who had taken a raiding party off to La Concepción and the Florido River where they had stolen fifty animals, and Panzacola, who had gone with four braves to rustle some horses in the Parral area. The Cocoyomes also went to the Río Florido to look for horses. On another occasion, Diego went out with a squad of eight under Chief Bibiaca to Todos Santos to steal horses. After returning to the camp at Sierra Mojada, he sallied again with ten men led by Captain Sari to the Indé area. Between the latter place and the presidio of Cerro Gordo, they had fought three soldiers, one of whom was killed and the other two escaped; also one of the Indians was killed. On this trip, the raiding party picked up a great number of horses which they took back to their camp. Only a short while before this interrogation, Diego had gone out with nine braves to the area of Santa Cruz and the Parral River where they acquired a herd of mares and some mules. The last sally had been with eight men from El Agua de la Lanza to the Sierra del Diablo, after the Sierra Mojada battle (AHP 1704Ab).

Diego also recounted the exploits of other rebel warriors. On one occasion Lorenzo El Chapatón had gone with four men to the Parral district where they killed a Spaniard and ran off a large herd of horses. Another time, a Cocoyome with four other warriors went by way of Pozo Hediondo to the town of San Felipe, where they stole some horses from near Huejotitlán; soldiers later attacked and regained the horses, although the men returned safely to camp.

Once, an Acoclame with four braves went off toward Chancaplé, stole eight horses from the Conchos River area, and took them back to Sierra Mojada (AHP 1704Ab).

On another occasion, a party of twenty-two Acoclames and Cocoyomes, with three chiefs — Zurrón de Venado, José Moguillo, and Ceja Blanca as commander — went through the Sierra de Chancaplé to a point below the presidio of Conchos. They went in the direction of San Felipe and Santa Cruz, killing two Spaniards on the way and taking almost all of their clothing. On the far side of the Conchos River, they stole mules from a pack train, plus some horses in the same vicinity. Here they were pursued by a large contingent of Christian Indians, whom Diego thought were Tarahumaras. The latter eventually caught the raiders and a battle ensued. The Tobosos lost all they had stolen, and chief José Moguillo and three others were killed. Their take on this raid had been a total of fourteen horses (AHP 1704Ab).

A few months before this deposition, four Acoclames and Chief Bribo, whose wife and children were being held by the Spaniards, went to the Parral district where they captured a Spaniard, whom they took back to Sierra Mojada where they played *pelota* with him. Chief Bribo, the captive's master or "owner," later took his prize to a place below Parras with the Cocoyomes and a few days afterward came back with corn and squash, but minus his "slave." Bribo announced that he had given the captive to a Spaniard — to whom he had presented his "Spanish servant" (AHP 1704Ab).

Only a few "moons" before this declaration, Chief Rancón had left Sierra Mojada to raid and kill around the area of the confluence of the Conchos and Florido rivers. They had stolen horses and mules but were later overtaken on the other side of the river (Conchos?) toward the Tinajas de San Juan by some of the town-dwelling Indians, and Rancón and another Indian were killed.

In another raid, sixteen Cocoyomes and Acoclames had gone off in the direction of Atotonilco, where they split into two squads, stole some horses, and then were chased and caught near the Sierra del Baus by some Tarahumaras. The Tarahumaras fought with seven of the Cocoyomes, killing one, and retrieving the stolen animals. Two other men died of wounds on the way home. A few days afterward, Lorenzo (or Lorencillo), the Cocoyome chief, took his men by way of the Arroyo de las Cruces on the Camino Real, on which the presidios were located, to penetrate into Spanish territory. Here they captured a priest, whom Lorencillo wanted to take to their camp at Mobana, but because the wounded Father was unable to walk, Lorencillo killed him. At Sierra Mojada, Lorencillo gave the priest's habit to one Nicolás, who had been their governor when they had settled at Atotonilco, and lost the Father's hat to another Indian in a game of *patole* (AHP 1704Ab).

On still another occasion eight Cocoyomes left from Mobana to steal horses and to kill people. On their way back to camp after collecting a number of animals between Parral and Santa Bárbara, they were attacked by soldiers at a place called Nacababit, out toward San Blas, where their booty was taken from them. After this the Cocoyomes fled to Mobana, from where ten Cocoyomes went out and brought in a number of mules, but due to lack of water almost all the beasts ran away. On this same occasion Chief Lorenzo, with three other Cocoyomes, went to Sombreretillo near Parral, where they killed an old man, stole his clothes and two horses, and took them back to their rancheria (AHP 1704Ab).

The Cocoyomes had captured three Franciscans sometime during the previous "moon" — they ran one off and killed the other two. Actually, this was a somewhat complicated episode, judging from the several references to it in various testimonies. The Acoclames had some differences among themselves regarding what to do with the priests. One priest had a pistol and shot the son of Contreras. After this, the eldest Father complied with orders to leave, and the other two, whose clothes had been taken from them, followed behind the Acoclames and Cocoyomes, apparently not understanding the Indians' request that they go back also. Finally, Contreras ordered some of his men to kill the priests, exclaiming that it was not right that these two should live while his own son was dying. The order was executed immediately, and the habits and other clothing of the three Fathers were deposited in a cave at Sierra Azul, about six leagues from Coahuila. The Indians feared they might die if they wore these clothes, as they remembered another occasion on which those who had donned the clothing of a murdered priest had also perished — apparently in battle (AHP 1704Ab).

Diego explained why the several groups at the battle of Sierra Mojada — Acoclames, Cocoyomes, Xexet, Hijos de las Piedras, and Hijos de la Tierra — had parted company afterward. His own group had moved to a spot at Sierra del Diablo because the mescal at Sierra Mojada had run out, and also in order that they could rob, since they were hungry. The rest of the bands went by way of Mogona (Mobana?) to San Lorenzo to the Boca de San Gerónimo at the Nazas River where there was a small lagoon at which the women and children probably remained while the men raided Mapimí and adjacent places for clothing and horses, and to kill people. If the women and children were not actually left at this lagoon, they likely were taken to a nearby mountain, probably El Vizcaíno, on one side of the Sierra de Jicorica (AHP 1704Ab).

However, there was more to the story than this. At Sierra Mojada the Acoclames and Cocoyomes had fought separately. It is not wholly clear what happened, but the Acoclame chief, El Ratón, prior to this had had a violent argument with Lorenzo, the Cocoyome. The latter had shot an arrow into (or near) the face of El Ratón. Moreover, just before the fight, the Cocoyome group had been camped at the Sierra de Baján, and four of the Cocoyomes who were living with the Acoclames had "fled" to this camp. The rest soon followed – thus the Spaniards had found them all together. However, the two groups had fought independently of each other. Several chiefs, including the captain of the Avos nation, had been killed at this time, and Diego gave the total number of dead as seventeen. Furthermore, the soldiers took many of the horses that both bands had stolen from the area of Caguilayunas (Coahuila?), as well as those taken in the Parral district (AHP 1704Ab).

Diego filled in details of some other past events. The "Tobosos" groups had left Atotonilco because they had simply felt like going back to Sierra Mojada. Another time, when Nicolás El Chiso and El Curi (some two years before this present testimony) had gone to Parral to ask for peace in the name of the Acoclames and Cocoyomes, the Cocoyomes were at Sierra del Diablo. The governor had granted peace, but almost immediately after the envoys returned home their people battled Retana and his men who were on campaign in the area of Sierra de las Cañas. According to Diego, his own group had been at the pass of Los Remedios hunting wild mustangs when Nicolás and El Curi had met them. The message the latter carried was given to Chief Ratón. It is not clear exactly what happened except that the Acoclames had moved to the Sierra de las Cañas where they had

spent the night, and the following morning they were attacked by Retana's troops. The battle lasted until mid-day, the Acoclames losing twelve men in battle and another ten or more who later died of wounds. Nine women and children also were killed.

The Indians then asked for peace, which was vouchsafed them, and Retana supplied medical care for their wounded. The conditions for surrender were agreed upon, and Diego and another, named Felipe (the one who had remained at Conchos at the time of the last withdrawal), had gone to the presidio at Conchos. Then, with gifts and supplies loaded on mules, and accompanied by five Indians from the town of Conchos, they returned to the Acoclames and the others who were at the confluence of the Florido and Conchos Rivers. The next day they all moved to Conchos and met Retana (AHP 1704Ab).

At San Francisco de Conchos the Acoclames informed the Spaniards that they were completely through with living in their desert mountain ranges. Chiefs Ratón and Panzacola, with five Indians from the Conchos pueblo, plus mules and supplies, were sent out to the hinterland to bring in the remainder of the people. Despite the fact that they were treated well at Conchos and were given many gifts, after five days the group left for their old haunts. According to Diego, the people with the supplies had met the others at El Nido del Cuervo, between the Sierra de las Batuecas and the San Felipe pass. Two of the Acoclames had refused to go back to the Spaniards and declared that those who did were "the Devil," because the Spaniards were planning to kill them (AHP 1704Ab).

The next day the envoys, less El Ratón, who had stayed behind, began the trek back to Conchos, watching to see if the rest of the people would follow. After a short while El Ratón left the camp to cut them off, telling them that they were foolish because the Spaniards wanted to kill them. They all returned to camp, where El Ratón and another decided to kill the messengers. They started to fight and Panzacola went to the aid of Andrés Buey, one of the men from Conchos. Panzacola shouted for the others to leave Andrés alone because he was his brother (!?). El Ratón retorted to Panzacola to get out of the way or they would kill him too. Andrés and two others were put to the sword (AHP 1704Ab).

The Acoclames had then taken off for Sierra del Diablo on their way to Sierra Mojada. Panzacola left the remaining two from Conchos with his sister, and he himself went back to Conchos to tell those still there what had happened. Rancón and Nicolás answered that he could stay at Conchos if he so desired, but if he did they would kill him. The others were going back with their people. Panzacola left with them, and they returned by way of Sierra de los Peyotillos in small groups toward Sierra Mojada. Immediately a six-man party sallied to raid San Cristóbal, but soldiers pursued them and regained the take. The Indians then returned to their camp (AHP 1704Ab).

Occasionally some groups from Coahuila, or some Chisos or Sisimbles, would join the Acoclames and Cocoyomes on raiding expeditions. The "Chisos" were in an especially close relationship with the "Tobosos," and sometimes even lived with them. About five "moons" before this declaration, Chief Ventura, whose father also had been a chief, arrived at Sierra Mojada with five or six Chisos. El Chapatón and Juan and his people (?) received them, and they exchanged deer skins for the buffalo hides the Chisos had brought, while they discussed some marriage arrangements. Many others supposedly were coming from Chiso country by way of Acatita, and the six visitors returned by that route. Some Chisos, who lived with the Acoclames, also assisted them in raiding, although after the battle at Sierra Mojada they disappeared. No Chisos had been seen by the Acoclames since Ventura and his envoys had departed some five months previously — with the exception of some (apparently from Ventura's group) who had been with the Spanish forces at the Sierra (de Acatita). The Acoclames had asked why the Chisos were with the Spaniards, telling them either to return to their own country or to join the Acoclame side. Unfortunately, Diego did not report the Chisos' answer. This, he claimed, was the extent of his knowledge of the Chisos, except that the Cocoyomes were up around Chiso territory most of the time and possibly got together with the Chisos more frequently than did the Acoclames (AHP 1704Ab).

The Acoclames and Cocoyomes had no friends (at this time) among the Indian hacienda workers. However, the inhabitants of a pueblo of Tepehuanes, located about a day's travel on the far side of the Nazas River (which the Spaniards interpreted as being the pueblo of Atotonilco near Papasquiaro), had told the Cocoyomes to ask for anything they needed but not to commit any hostilities there. The Cocoyomes had gone there twice to dance and sing with the people at

night, but these Tepehuanes had never joined them in raiding (AHP 1704Ab).

By February 27, 1706, the Acoclames still had not surrendered and had continued to commit robberies and murders. The Spaniards had withheld execution of the Acoclame Diego in the hope that this would be an inducement for his people to come in and surrender — but to no avail (AHP 1704Ab).

During this same month, news of enemy Indian activities in the Coahuila area came in. Some priests had been killed and the culprits were reported to be four Chisos plus some others called Sisimbles, although known as Toidas in Coahuila. The culprits had taken off to the back country toward the area of the Río Grande, taking the habits and other items they had stolen at the time of the murders. It is uncertain if this is the same event previously referred to by Diego (AHP 1704Ab).

At the same time the Indians of the mission of Santa Rosa de Nadadores had requested the Spanish Sergeant Major at the town of Todos Santos to send a dozen soldiers to them to capture a Bacorame Indian, named Luis, accused of killing several Indians of the pueblo by witchcraft. Luis was taken back to Todos Santos for questioning. He blamed two Guechal (Hueyquetzal) Indians — Juanillo and Miguel Tartamudo — of the same mission. These two had acted as guides for the "Tobosos" when they had committed some murders on the road called the Camino de la Caldera. These "Tobosos" had killed the priests (this involves three Fathers, apparently the ones previously mentioned) and committed murders at a place named Zúñiga. The two Guechales accompanied the Tobosos to the Sierra de San José and were paid off with a bay horse and a handful of tobacco for their trouble (the horse eventually ended up in the hands of a Terocodame Indian). Luis also cited several raids in the general Saltillo region by the Gueripiamos (Hervipiamos) Indians. In the Parras valley one Jurive (married to a Conián woman), as well as the Cabezas settled there, acted as spies for the Tobosos. Furthermore, some of the scouts from there whom the Spaniards had employed had simply informed the enemy of Spanish movements, and the Indians had been able to keep out of the latter's way (AHP 1704Ab).

Later, on April 9, a final declaration was taken from Diego. He afforded some clarification of the circumstances of the deaths of the two Franciscans. These deaths had been carried out by the Cocoyomes, Acoclames, and a few Sisimbles, who — immediately prior to their trip to Coahuila — had been camped at the end of the Sierra de las Salinas, where they were visited by two Indians from the Coahuila mission of Santa Rosa. These visitors (probably the same two mentioned in the previous declaration) invited the others to go to Coahuila to raid and kill — it would be more lucrative there than in the Parral area. This they did, bringing back a large number of horses and a few mules to a small lagoon called La Lima about four leagues east of the Cerro de las Salinas on the far side of (*adelante de*) Sierra Mojada. Then most of them went northward (*arriba*), where they encountered the three Franciscans. The rest of the story is essentially that given before, except that the guides received four horses plus some deer skins in payment (AHP 1704Ab).

At another time the same two envoys from Santa Rosa took the Acoclames (and Cocoyomes, seemingly) to Coahuila to raid. They brought back a number of animals from the expedition. The deponent also remembered that when he was a child the Acoclames and the people from Santa Rosa would get together because of the blood relationship that existed (*tienen* — and still did) between them. The Coahuileños, he said, raided in the Coahuila, Saltillo, and Parras areas (AHP 1704Ab).

More interesting from the standpoint of interband relations is Diego's account of a visit of six Sisimbles to the Acoclames about a year before this declaration was made. The Acoclames were at Acatita La Grande at this time. These Sisimbles had told them that they should send some representatives to a *junta* of pagan nations at the juncture of the Salado and Río Grande rivers. Here they would be able to formalize peace with the chiefs of the tribes of this region and make alliances for raiding. No Acoclames went, and the six Sisimbles departed. A short while later two Hijos de las Piedras and one Cocoyome went off to look for the Sisimbles at the spot the six had said they were camped. They were unable to locate the Sisimbles (apparently — or the others) because the latter had entered Cíbola country. The "Tobosos" continued on until they came to the camps of some other nations. The latter recognized that the three were their enemies so they killed them. The identity of these nations was unknown to the witness, but the Sisimbles later had reported the affair to the Acoclames, swearing that they had had nothing to do with it (AHP 1704Ab).

In 1708 "Tobosos" were reported committing hostilities in the Coahuila area in the vicinity of the mission of Santo Nombre de Jesús at San Ildefonso. This mission had originally been in the Valle de la Circuncisión, sixteen leagues to the east, with the name of San Francisco Solano together with the missions of San Bernardo and San Juan. The original Indians at San Francisco had been the Xarames, Siabanes, and Payoguanes. When El Nombre de Jesús was founded in 1705 only a few of the original Xarames moved over to it. However, in this new location, Terocodames, Ticmamares or Tiquimamares, Tripas Blancas, Piedras Chicas, and a number of others, including Julimes de dipos (*tipos*?) Gavilanes were settled there. During 1708 all the nations except a few of the Xarames left because of the "Toboso" raids, in which in this same year eight persons were killed and two were carried off alive (UTD 1707).

Farther west, in December of this same year, five Acoclames — two men and three women — arrived at the hacienda of Santa Cruz in the Parral district (or San Bartolomé) to ask for peace. According to them, this time the peace of all of the Acoclames was certain. The last time they had surrendered (in 1704?), they stated, a Chiso had informed them that the Spaniards were planning to kill them so they had fled back to their own country. At the present time, five Cocoyomes who had been with the Acoclames had left the latter, because the five did not want to surrender. The Acoclame envoys stated that they would return within ten days with the remainder of their band — if by this time they had not done so it would mean that the Cocoyomes had prevented them from doing it by the force of arms, since the two groups were not in agreement about making peace at this time. On December 16, word was received by the Spaniards that the Acoclames would not be able to make it within the time they had previously agreed to because the animals they were traveling on had tired out (AHP 1708a).

It was learned that Lorenzo El Chapatón, El Ratón, and the latter's son Dieguillo, had arrived on December 26 at Santa Cruz with a captive whom they had left there. They declared that they were happy with the peace but that they had not been able to come in yet because their people had become separated. These were now being gathered up, although some people in the band did not want to surrender. The envoys, while certain of the peace, nevertheless refused to go to Parral to see the governor (AHP 1708a).

The Spanish governor was not convinced of the honorableness of the intentions behind the Acoclames' action. He feared that these Indians would use the cover of peace to continue their hostilities. He felt that possibly a "defensive" sally by the Spanish military might force the hand of the Acoclames, and, if they were not serious about consummating the peace, out of fear they would flee back to the hinterland. The governor was rather apprehensive over the situation, since the Acoclames were now in the Florido River area, roughly the borderland of Spanish settlement, and under the guise of hunting deer they could easily commit some depredations. The military officials at Parral concurred basically with this opinion (AHP 1708a; AHP 1708b).

By January 1, 1709, the Acoclames still had not shown up. Furthermore, some enemy Indians had made a small raid between the Santa Cruz hacienda and Pozo Hediondo. Spanish troops sallied to reconnoiter. Tracks were discovered at Pozo Hediondo, and considering the time of the attack, the Spaniards opined that it was the Acoclames who had been behind it. Quite a bit more evidence for this opinion was discovered farther out in the Sierra de San Felipe. At Los Chupaderos the Spaniards came upon an enemy camp that had been abandoned in such extreme haste that it appeared that almost everything possessed by its occupants, including the dogs, had been left behind. Later inspection of the surrounding tracks indicated that the enemy had dispersed in all directions. From smoke signals at Sierra del Diablo, it was presumed that the people were being called together to go to either Conula or Guapagua. Since water holes were dry, the Spaniards decided to desist and return home (AHP 1708a).

At the end of March, the Spanish governor, Antonio Deza y Uloa, reported that he had news from Guanaceví that some forty hostile Indians had invaded that place on March 28. They had sacked an hacienda, taken two children alive and killed one woman. Before they left they announced that they would be back in five days. A Spanish contingent sallied to make a reconnaissance of the general Nazas River region. While they were in the field, marching from San Nicolás to the hacienda of a Captain Flores, it was learned that the Indians the previous day had stolen over 150 animals from Flores and from another hacienda, as well as having killed over sixty animals. On the following day, April 9, while the Spanish troops were on their way back to Parral, news was received that the enemy Indians had raided a sheep ranch at La Mimbrera and had taken over 100 animals. The report continued that the enemy had broken up into a number of squads and that one had gone into the vicinity of La Sierra de Guajolotes, adjacent to the hacienda of El Canutillo. Investigation at Guajolotes, however, revealed nothing. The Spaniards opined that the La Mimbrera raid had been carried out merely to divert their attention in order that the enemy could move the animals it had stolen (AHP 1710a).

Some time before November a number of Acoclames and Chisos, and probably including some Cocoyomes, were apprehended and imprisoned. Later, the prisoners tried to escape from the Parral public jail; they also attempted to kill the governor, although the time and circumstances of the latter are unknown. Following this the governor began criminal proceedings against the rebels (BL 1709-1715).

A number of witnesses testified regarding the crimes and character of the desert Indians. One witness, Sergeant Diego de Estrada, had been a prisoner of the enemy for fourteen years — eight with the Cocoyomes and six with the Acoclames. Estrada gave a long account of the Indian hostilities as he remembered them, stating that most of the time the Cocoyomes and Acoclames would join forces in their sallies. Raids cited by all of the deponents covered a wide geographical area — from San Francisco de Conchos, the Florido River, Huejotitlán, Santa Bárbara, Minas Nuevas, Indé, San Felipe, Santa Cruz, the Nazas River, Parras, the Río Grande in the south, Fresnillo, Sombrerete, Anaelo, and the areas of Mazapil and Coahuila. A couple of the people cited the evil nature of these Indians because of their having descended from the now extinct Toboso nation, two of whose leaders had been Juan Mapochi and Galeano (BL 1709-1715)!

Unfortunately, further details on the results of this case are unknown. However, apparently it was these Indians who were deported to Mexico City in the latter part of 1711, although no figures exist regarding the numbers of persons of the several band or tribal groups that were involved (AHP 1710a; AHP 1710b; AHP 1710c; AHP 1710d; BL 1709-1715).

In October of 1713, two Chisos — a Batayoligla

and a Suniyoligla — were picked up near the Conchos presidio. The former was killed and the Suniyoligla was captured and questioned. He testified that his nation had always been allied with the Chisos (specific?). On this particular occasion a small squad had been operating in the vicinity of Conchos and Santa Cruz. He claimed it had been many years since the Chisos (his group only?) had banded with the Cocoyomes and Acoclames (!). However, about a month previous to this testimony, some Chisos had gone to Jaque and had fought the Cocoyomes, killing three and stealing their horses (BL 1709-1715).

Nevertheless, both the Sisimbles and the Suniyoliglas had received messages from the Cocoyomes to join them, the Suniyoligla group being so small that it was forced to accept the offer. It now consisted of only thirteen warriors, plus another three who lived with the Sisimbles. Prior to this declaration the Spaniards had made an attempt to get the Chisos in the hinterland to come into peace. The messenger they sent, one Don Baltazar, eventually visited the Sisimbles, who killed him. This witness told how Dieguillo, the son of El Ratón, had gone to his band's camp looking for the Sisimbles, saying that the message of peace of Baltazar was false and for the Suniyoliglas not to believe in it. Actually, it remains uncertain whether or not at this time the Suniyoliglas were allied with the Acoclames, Cocoyomes, and Sisimbles. In December, Antonio de Rodela wrote, however, that all four groups were allied together and that they had sent squads to various places, including Coahuila and Chihuahua (BL 1709-1715).

In 1714 the Indians at the Franciscan missions of Santa Rosa de los Nadadores and San Buena Ventura in Coahuila revolted. They began raiding in the areas of Coahuila, Saltillo and Parras. Peace settlements were made with a chief named Mateo, from the rancheria of Chief Don Pablo, who eventually was sent to visit the viceroy in Mexico City (AHP 1712; AHP 1716Ab).

Coahuileños, under chiefs Don Pablo and Diego, moved southward into the province of Nueva Vizcaya, where some of their kinsmen were already settled at the presidio of El Pasaje and others at Parras. Some of the Indians at El Pasaje were Babozarigames who in an undated petition (ca 1712) stated that they had been under Spanish authority for over twenty years (they were settled there as early as 1704 and were often mentioned as fighting with the Spaniards as auxiliary troops from El Pasaje) (AHP 1704Aa; AHP 1712).

Captain Martín de Alday and his men from El Pasaje went out to Cerro Colorado, next to Acatita La Grande, to meet the arrivals from Coahuila. Alday wrote from Aguachila at the end of October that he had some of these Coahuileños with him — twenty-six families comprising 120 persons, under chiefs Diego, Francisco, and Gáspar. According to Alday, this group did not even have horses, and he had put them on the backs of his own animals and brought them into Aguachila. The Indians refused to go back to Coahuila because of alleged mistreatment there. Alday took them with him and settled them at El Pasaje (AHP 1712; AHP 1722Da).

Some forty or so families, under the Indian governor Don Pablo (the father of the above Francisco), had remained behind at Cerro Colorado. Alday sent six of the Coahuileños with the governor to contact these stragglers, most of whom preferred to remain in the bush. However, by December it was reported that some nine families and five bachelors had decided to come in to settle with the others (it is uncertain if they did this or not) (AHP 1712; AHP 1722Da).

About this same time the Nueva Vizcayan governor, Manuel de San Juan y Santa Cruz, ordered that a settlement be established for the Coahuileños, including the Babozarigames, at El Pasaje. This was carried out in 1715, and a town was founded on the Nazas River between the presidios of El Pasaje and El Gallo with the name of El Pueblo Nuevo de los Santos Cinco Señores. The new pueblo was to serve as a buffer against enemy hostilities, and seemingly this was in part successful. San Juan y Santa Cruz wrote later that the area between the two presidios previously had been totally abandoned, but by the 1720's it enjoyed a number of settlements, and the highway was much safer for travel. Indians from Tizonazo and Tarahumaras also were settled there (AHP 1712; AHP 1722Aa; DHM ca 1720).

Most of the Coahuila Indians had settled down by April of 1716, although a few were still in the hinterland. These continued to raid in the region, as well as to enter into alliances with the Nueva Vizcayan rebels. By July, another 100 or so, consisting of Terocodames and Paboris, had been reestablished at Nadadores, and it was noticed that some of the goods and animals they possessed were clearly from Nueva Vizcaya. Eventually Don Pablo's group returned to

Nadadores, from where it revolted again in the year 1719 and joined forces with the Cocoyomes of Juan de Lomas (AHP 1716Aa; AHP 1722Aa; AHP 1722Da; BL 1722).

Enemy Indians in Nueva Vizcaya continued to commit depredations. Attacks and assaults were reported throughout the area, from Huejotitlán, the San Bartolomé valley, Santa Bárbara, Mapimí, El Gallo, Cerro Gordo, the Nazas River area, and many less well-known places. In June of 1715 testimony was taken from two youths from Guanacaví who had been captured but had later escaped from the enemy. The war party that had taken them prisoners had consisted of four Indians and a young mulatto boy. They were taken to the Sierra de San Pedro where that night their companion, a third lad, was killed by the Indians because he had complained of the cold and would not let the others sleep. The squad had continued to look for animals to rustle, and found some horses four days later at the Roncesvalles River. Then the enemy went off to Santa Bárbara, after first tying up the two boys. When they returned they took the two to a nearby cave where they tried to hang one of the witnesses, but the halter broke. They tied the two up again and went off on another sally. This time the boys managed to untie themselves and escape. The Indians had previously told them that they were taking them to their country where there were a lot of people and horses and it was not necessary to work. Both witnesses stated that the mulatto with the party, who spoke the native tongue, was the most bloodthirsty of all (AHP 1715Aa; AHP 1715Ab).

In July, another ex-captive, who had spent about a month with the Cocoyomes, testified. After he had been taken prisoner near Mapimí, the group had gone by way of Pozo Hediondo to Sierra Mojada where the women and children were camped and where there were another twelve captives from a number of different places, including a small Negro boy, two Borrado Indians from Parras, and a couple of women. Later they moved their camp from the waterhole at Sierra Mojada to Los Charcos of Sierra Mojada, and then to Mobana, where they were met by a large band of Chiso warriors and a small group of Acoclames. From this point scouts were sent out to reconnoiter Mapimí. The Indians refused to believe their captive's statement that thirty soldiers and twenty Tarahumara auxiliaries were at the Mapimí presidio. They could not comprehend that new recruits would immediately

be added when others were killed, and the Indians had killed eight men two months before. The chief of the Cocoyomes was named Alonso, and a man named Pujare was captain of the Chisos. The ex-captive did not know the name of the Acoclame chief (AHP 1715Aa).

On the basis of this information the Spaniards sent troops to the Mapimí area to seek out the rebels. An abandoned camp was located at Mobana. Three days later, following the trail of the enemy's horses, the Spaniards arrived at Las Salinas. Passing over to the other side where there were some pools of water (charcos), the troops came upon the enemy camp totally unexpectedly. Four warriors — including Chief Contreras — and fourteen women were killed. Twenty-three women and children were captured, and thirty-five of the enemy's horses were taken. The prisoners were returned to Parral for interrogation. It was now the middle of August, 1715. Five women — four Cocoyomes and one Acoclame — as well as one Coahuileño boy, testified. Although the women gave some new information, they claimed ignorance of why the peace was never kept with the Spaniards and stated that this was a question that had to be asked the chiefs and menfolk. One woman did mention that she had heard that on one occasion her people had withdrawn to the hinterland because they had begun to become ill with measles (sarampion) and smallpox (viruelas) (AHP 1715Aa).

Attacks by the rebels continued. In September the Spaniards sent a sally into enemy country under Captain Juan de Salaices, who left from San Bartolomé by way of Atotonilco. The mountain ranges of El Diablo and Conula were reconnoitered, but nothing was found. Tracks of Indians on horseback and on foot were discovered at Sierra Mojada, plus those of the animals they were driving. These tracks went in the direction of Acatita. Scouts sent to Acatita uncovered a fresh trail indicating that the enemy had been deer hunting (AHP 1715Aa).

It was surmised that the Indians had gone to Los Charcos instead of to Acatita. However, the troops moved to Acatita, where they found an abandoned camp with over sixty huts where some eighty animals had been slaughtered. Another abandoned rancheria was discovered at Los Charcos, and a day later scouts reported that the enemy was convened at Sierra Mojada. The Spanish soldiers marched that entire night, and the next morning (September 22) they met the enemy. After eight of their group were killed and twice this number wounded, the enemy called for peace. The Spanish commander told them to bring the women and children from the top of the mountain where they had taken refuge and from where some of the Indian women could be heard crying. The troops waited at the foot of the mountain, but no Indians appeared, instead making good their escape into the bush. Their abandoned camp was later inspected and a good bit of stolen booty recovered. The troops then returned home (AHP 1715Aa).

Raids continued at La Mimbrera, El Carrizo, El Puesto del Tecolote, near Las Bocas, and at Las Cuencas, the Valley of San Bartolomé, and in the area of Indé. At the end of October the Spaniards made another campaign with some 150 men. The contingent left from San Francisco de Conchos, cutting across the northern part of "Toboso" country – going by Aguachile, El Puesto de Mayo, Espíritu Santo, and Las Encinillas, to the sierras of Conula and Mojada. At Conula they met the enemy, but the latter moved into the roughest and most inaccessible part of the mountain, making it practically impossible for the Spanish troops to pursue them. As the soldiers withdrew, a herder who had been a captive of the enemy came out to meet them, afraid to do so before because of all the shooting. He reported that the enemy was the Acoclames, although he did not know how many there were, and that the Cocoyomes were at Sierra Mojada. The Spanish force then began the march back to Conchos with sixty-nine horses and mules they had retrieved from the enemy (AHP 1715Aa).

Around the first of December, a large party of sixty warriors hit El Matadero, four leagues from the presidio of Cerro Gordo. In January of 1716, Salaices made another sally, encountering the Acoclames camped at Conula. Twenty-two were captured and six killed, including chief Dieguillo El Ratón (who had once gone to Mexico City to see the Viceroy). Declarations taken later indicated that with this blow the Acoclames were now almost finished. Seemingly, only a few had been able to escape to join the Cocoyomes (AHP 1715Aa).

Starting on February 12, messengers were sent to the Cocoyomes in an attempt to persuade them to surrender and settle down. In April the governor interviewed eight of the enemy, all Cocoyomes except one, who had gone to Parral to discuss the terms of the peace. Their chief's name was Juan (Lomas?),

they reported, and their people were approximately four days' travel from Parral, on their way in to surrender. They were bringing two captives with them, a girl and a boy both about ten years of age. The governor gave these messengers, as well as other envoys sent in later, a good many gifts and supplies in the hope of achieving success this time. More ambassadors were sent to the Indians, and another captive was brought in to the Spaniards. In exchange, the latter released several prisoners whom the Cocoyomes and Acoclames had requested. Word was sent several times that it would not be long before the rebels arrived. Finally, on April 23, Diego El Ratón showed up in Parral. The next day he was taken to the San Bartolomé Valley together with other prisoners, to show them where they would settle. A missionary had already been assigned to them (AHP 1715Aa; AHP 1716Aa).

The Indians gave several reasons why the remainder had not yet shown up. One was a story concerning an incident when a Spaniard had attacked one of the messengers. Many of the natives were afraid to go to the Spaniards because the previous governor, Deza y Uloa, had not kept his word with them and had killed many and sent many others to Mexico City. Moreover, there had been a smallpox epidemic among them. One Indian was certain that all the rest would come in, including some persons of the Cuautomana nation from Coahuila who were with them. Despite these reassurances on the part of the Indians and the apparent general progress toward a peace settlement, all of these efforts failed. An envoy left to fetch his people on April 26, stating he would be back within eight days. On May 7, a ranch some three leagues from the San Bartolomé Valley was raided, an event that marked the termination of peace negotiations on this occasion (AHP 1715Aa; AHP 1716Aa).

A number of attacks then followed – on Atotonilco, San Bartolomé Valley, and El Canutillo. After a raid on San Francisco de Conchos, the settled Indians there followed the enemy's trail toward Chiso country. However, other evidence pointed to the Cocoyomes, and whatever Acoclames were left, as the culprits (AHP 1715Aa; AHP 1716Aa).

A communiqué was sent by the Spaniards in Parral to the Spanish governor of Coahuila to the effect that the Acoclames and Cocoyomes were allied with the Indians of that province. It was hoped that the governor could attempt to take some action from that end. He replied that these two Vizcayan nations, together with the "Coahuileños," would often meet with a number of other tribes. One Spanish commander while on campaign had encountered a large *junta* of these Indians at the headwaters (*cabezera*) of the Río Colorado in the north. Here were many animals with brands from Nueva Vizcaya. No battle ensued, apparently, but the soldiers bartered with these Indians for many of the fine things they possessed, all stolen Spanish goods. The governor also cited a large raid carried out by these peoples somewhere between Coahuila and Nuevo León (AHP 1716Aa).

More raids were reported — in the Nazas River area, at La Guitarrilla, Indé, El Carrizo, La Mimbrera, Cerro Colorado, and Ramos, among other places. Several hundred head of animals, mostly horses and mules, had been stolen. Spanish sallies were made, and on one occasion some abandoned rancherias were discovered at Pozo Hediondo containing many indications, including nine fresh graves, that the enemy had suffered an epidemic of some kind. From the evidence it was estimated that some two hundred warriors and seven hundred women and children camped here (AHP 1716Aa).

On October 9 testimony was taken from a twelve-year-old boy who had been among the Cocoyomes for about a year. He had been captured at La Mimbrera and taken to a camp of some twenty families near Sierra Mojada. Three days later, because another captive had escaped from them, the entire group moved to Sierra Mojada where there were more and larger rancherias of Indians, including Acoclames. The deponent stated he had seen the men of the group return many times with many different items they had stolen. At the same time, he had heard that the Chisos would come to join the others in raids, although he never saw them the entire year he had been held captive (AHP 1716Aa).

The boy stated that after an attack on the camp, the people were seriously considering surrender. However, a mulatto and a Negro with them were vociferously against this and terrified the Indians with stories of how the Spaniards would put them to work and mistreat them. By this time, they had moved to a place called La Tinaja, on their way in to the Spaniards. With the fear the mulatto and Negro had instilled in them, they returned to Sierra Mojada. Soon afterward, this boy escaped from the Cocoyomes. After about a week he ran into a Sisimble Indian who took him to his own camp near Acatita, which contained about fifty adult males and many women and

children. The boy spent about a month with these Sisimbles, and one day while out cutting *tunas* he managed to slip off. A week later he made his way into the town of San Antonio de Julimes (AHP 1716Aa).

Raids continued to be regular and frequent over a wide territory, and as far south as in the Sierra de Avino near the city of Durango. A number of small sallies were made from the several presidios. Then, in October of 1716, Martín de Alday, from El Pasaje, took out a large force of soldiers and Indian auxiliaries. A wide area was reconnoitered, including Mapimí, La Sierra de Tahualilo, Sierra de la Tinaja, La Sierra de Baján, Mobana, and the Nazas River. At the Cieneguilla de Baján an abandoned camp of some twenty old huts was found, as well as a large inventory of stolen Spanish goods from both this and other nearby sites. From here the troops moved to Cerro Colorado, then to La Sierra de las Cuatro Ciénegas, and to Acatita La Grande, where they arrived on October 31. From information garnered here, the enemy was moving in the direction of Los Charcos de las Salinas, Sierra Mojada, and Conula (AHP 1716Ab).

On November 3, Alday and his Spanish troops met and fought the enemy at Sierra Mojada. A truce was called and Alday held a conference with the Cocoyome chief Juan de Lomas and many of his warriors. The reason they had not come in to Parral to settle in peace, they claimed, was because a number of Spaniards there molested (*atarantaban*) them, but if Alday would personally sponsor them they would cease their raiding. However, Lomas explained that he had dispatched a party of ten men about a week and a half before to rustle horses, and these men would have to be excused if they raided in the near future, since there was no way to contact and stop them. During these talks, the Spanish troops bartered away a good amount of their equipment to the Indians. Alday stated he was in agreement with this as it would keep the enemy happy (AHP 1716Aa; AHP 1716Ab).

The following day it was decided that within two and a half months the Cocoyomes would go to settle at the El Pasaje presidio. After passing out supplies and gifts, the Spaniards moved to Mobana. Very soon afterward, some Terocodames who had been with the Cocoyomes all this time sent word they wanted to go with the latter but (apparently) they had to send for their families first. Alday was to meet them later at the Sierra de Baján. In his letter to the governor, Alday also requested that supplies and blankets be sent along at the time of the meeting at Baján because the Indians were practically destitute. Alday felt that the confidence of the Indians could be gained by giving out such items. On the other hand, the governor, while doubtful about this, granted permission to the Cocoyomes to hunt wild mustangs in order to support themselves until they arrived to be located in a settlement. In January it still looked as if peace would be effectuated, although some of the tribes of the Coahuila area — such as the Terocodames, Tripas Blancas, and Cíbolas — refused to surrender, according to word received through the Cocoyome Lomas. The latter offered Alday his services in tracking down the Coahuileños (AHP 1716Aa; AHP 1716Ab).

On February 1, 1717, Alday again left with his troops from El Pasaje for the specific purpose of bringing in the Cocoyomes. At the place named San Pedro he met three couriers sent by Lomas with the message that the Cocoyomes were all camped at Baján, but that the Terocodames with them had returned to Coahuila. He met Lomas at Baján on February 18 and visited the rancheria, which contained over 170 persons. Alday gave out many gifts including blankets, hats, tobacco, flour, and rosaries. The Spanish contingent left Baján on February 23, taking seven Cocoyomes with them. Lomas was to bring the remainder in May (AHP 1716Ab).

Around the first of May, Alday made still another sally following essentially the same route as on the previous campaign. A number of messengers shuttled back and forth between Lomas and the Spanish troops, and Alday sent the Cocoyomes supplies because Lomas had notified the Spaniards that his people were in great need. The two groups finally met at Los Morteros. They spent some three days together here in peace talks, while Alday's Babozarigame and Coahuileño auxiliaries competed against the Cocoyomes in horseracing and in games of *pelota*. A week later Alday began the march back to El Pasaje (AHP 1716Ab; AHP 1716Ac).

Little or nothing had been settled at this time. On June 12, Alday informed the governor that Lomas had promised that during the coming "moon" he and all his people would arrive at the "new pueblo" (apparently Los Santos Cinco Señores) on the Nazas River. On June 16 he received word, however, that the Cocoyomes, without the slightest provocation, had withdrawn, in order that they could begin their

raiding and killing again, probably to a camp at Sierra Mojada. Alday wrote on this occasion that the reason behind this rebellion was the Cocoyomes' "perverse dispositions and evil inclinations," and that they entered peace negotiations motivated only by what gifts and goods they thought they would receive. Alday was extremely saddened by the event, and as he put it, "in one instant so much effort had failed" — the enemy Indians were totally ungrateful for what had been done for them. They would always be this way and Alday was convinced that the only solution was to extinguish them by the force of arms (AHP 1716Ab).

The year 1718 saw no let-up of enemy hostilities. Raids were reported at Conchos, Papasquiaro, Guanaceví, Indé, San Juan del Río, Mapimí, and the Parras district. Tracks of the enemy were seen at the Aguanaval River. Governor San Juan y Santa Cruz wrote the Viceroy in the middle of the year that of the 50,000 Indians in the province of Nueva Vizcaya, the 150 to 200 Cocoyomes and Acoclames were the principal culprits in keeping the province in constant turmoil. These two groups, however, were at this time allied with the Chisos and Sisimbles (AHP 1718Aa; AHP 1718Ac; AHP 1718Ad).

One assault on Conchos was the most outstanding. It was a large-scale operation in early June directed at a squad of sixteen men who were guarding the horses belonging to the presidio. Most of the animals were either stolen or run off, leaving the soldiers without means to follow the enemy. The raid was later described by several of the soldiers who had taken part in it. The attacking force had consisted of between 100 and 200 men, presumably representing several different tribes, judging from the great variety of arrow types picked up after the battle. One Cocoyome, Diego El Ratón, was recognized and talked to. He had even protected one of the soldiers from being killed during battle, although the latter had been stripped and all his clothing taken from him (AHP 1718Aa; AHP 1718Ac).

The enemy had attacked on foot and on horseback, carrying three different banners, or flags, and sounding fifes and drums. This was an unprecedented manner for these tribes to go into battle (several soldiers stated that it had never been seen before) and was considered by the Spaniards as an excellent example of their haughtiness. The assault had been a total surprise, and with war whoops, very effective weapons, and the great amount of dust the enemy horses had raised, the Spanish troops had been so totally disconcerted and disorganized that after the first blow was struck they had had no opportunity to regroup themselves for a counterattack, or even to defend themselves adequately. It was thought that the enemy had probably returned to or at least gone by way of La Tasajera in the Sierra de Minas Nuevas. Jose de Beasoain, commander at Conchos, went out afterward to this area to track them down, but no enemy was located (AHP 1718Aa; AHP 1718Ac).

In August, Juan Gutiérrez Gandarilla, the commander of the Mapimí presidio, carried a campaign into the back country. His troops reconnoitered Tlahualilo and Acatita de Baján, and at Los Esteros found the trail of a large herd of horses coming from Parras, plus the tracks of three of the enemy going to Las Salinas del Machete. Word was received that a band of the rebels had left Las Salinas for Acatita La Grande. This was on August 24. The troops marched in hot pursuit, and on the 31st located a camp site at Los Charcos del País (a name given to this place by the Spaniards at this time). The enemy was moving eastward. The Spaniards trailed them for two more days. Some fifteen or twenty leagues from Las Vertientes of Coahuila, the enemy's trail turned toward the Sierra de Chocamueca. On September 2, the Spaniards were forced to turn back due to lack of water (AHP 1718Ac).

While this Spanish contingent was in the field, on August 29 a raiding party attacked the hacienda of Santa Ana y el Torreón, and on the following day hit the pueblo of Las Bocas. Another Spanish force sallied and encountered them in the Sierra de Muñoz. The enemy escaped, but the Spaniards retrieved some sixteen horses (apparently the total stolen) (AHP 1718Ac).

In the early part of November, Diego de Estrada, ensign at Cerro Gordo, led another large Spanish force into the back country. On November 11, they encountered a group of the enemy at Mobana. Three of the latter were killed and several captured, as well as forty-five of their horses taken. Three of the captives were Cocoyomes, including Diego El Ratón, and one Terocodame, who claimed he was from the mission of Santa Rosa de Nadadores. The Spaniards also retrieved three captives the Cocoyomes had been holding. One of these had been with the latter for six years, engaging in the same hostilities as his Cocoyome comrades; of the other two, one had been taken prisoner by the enemy at Santa Elena near

Mazapil. Some of the Cocoyomes were able to escape to warn their rancheria, which was located in the Sierra de Chocamueca (AHP 1718Ac).

Unfortunately, practically no information exists on the events of the following year, 1719. The Coahuileños of Chief Don Pablo at the mission of Nadadores revolted and returned to Nueva Vizcaya to ally themselves with the Cocoyomes (AHP 1722Aa; AHP 1722Da; BL 1723-1724). In 1720, however, a new governor, and one well known to the rebel Indians, took over the reins of government of Nueva Vizcaya. This was Don Martín de Alday, who had been captain of the presidio of El Pasaje. The Cocoyomes and Acoclames came in this year to surrender, and Berroterán in his later report on the Nueva Vizcayan presidios claimed that this was because of the Indians' great fear of Alday. As a matter of fact, while Alday was on his way to Parral, six leagues from the presidio at Cerro Gordo, the rebels stopped him and requested peace and a town to live in. They were given a place at the Cerro Gordo presidio where they remained about six months before they went back to their old territory in the desert (DHM 1748). (It is not quite clear how the more detailed events from other sources fit in with Berroterán's report.)

In February, and again in early March, two Indians came to the Spaniards from the hinterland to offer peace. The first was an Acoclame. Juan de Lomas, he reported, was the chief of the Acoclames and the Cocoyomes, and both groups were now camped at Sierra Mojada. The excuse he gave for his people not having seen the peace negotiations through to the end on the previous two occasions was because of the mulatto and Negro who lived with them. These two had warned the Indians very strongly against surrendering, telling them of the severe punishment that awaited them at the hands of the Spaniards. Now, because the soldiers of the presidios as well as because Indians from Coahuila had killed a good many of them in recent battles, they wanted to settle down and live in peace (AHP 1720Aa).

The second envoy, Gerónimo Jaques, requested to see Diego El Ratón and four others who were still being held prisoners. He visited and spent the night with them in the Parral jail. He was designated as both a Cocoyome and a Gavilán, and he himself stated he had been raised in Cuencamé, although he had been with the Acoclames for some time. His chiefs had given him a horse and sent him to Parral to see if a new governor had arrived yet. Meanwhile, his people had come from the other side of Sierra Mojada to the Tinaja del Sombreretillo, where they were waiting for him to return with an answer. A later report stated that still others were camped at Mobana at this time. Shortly after this Lomas was reported to be at Pozo Hediondo (AHP 1720Aa).

After Jaques, another envoy from Lomas arrived at Cerro Gordo. Diego de Estrada wrote from Cerro Gordo on March 20 that there was one Indian camp at San Bernardo and another in the direction of San Blas. Gerónimo Jaques had some twenty-five Indians with him at Las Batuecas, all supposed to be "relatives" of Diego El Ratón (AHP 1720Aa).

Toward the end of April, Juan de Lomas himself showed up in Parral. He was told to take his people to Cerro Gordo and from there they would be settled. On May 7, Lomas, back with his people, sent in five more ambassadors, led by his brother Antonio Lomas. With them also was one Ventura, possibly one of the chiefs, who was said to speak Spanish well and to be a mestizo raised in the vicinity of the pueblo of Conchos and captured by the rebels when he was fourteen years old. This group also brought with it seven young boy captives to be returned to the Spaniards, and announced that Lomas himself would bring in the remaining captives the Indians held. Some of the Cocoyome women and children whom the Spaniards had taken prisoners and who had been entrusted to various Spaniards to work for them were turned over to this group of ambassadors. However, it was made clear to the Cocoyomes that Diego El Ratón and the other four men would not be given back to them. These had been captured in open war (*guerra viva*), and only the Viceroy had the power to grant them their freedom (AHP 1720Aa).

On May 27, Lomas himself arrived again with six of his men and five captives, for whom he was remunerated. Lomas' brother was going to take a group to Mexico City to make arrangements concerning the *reducción* of their people to a town — and no doubt to see about getting Diego El Ratón and others released from prison. Lomas was not going to Mexico City himself because he thought he should stay behind to take care of his people who were going to the presidio of Cerro Gordo where they would be among the soldiers. Also, the now rather infamous pair, the mulatto and the Negro who belonged to their rancheria, were going to be turned over to the Spaniards. Four Cocoyomes in effect left to see the Viceroy (AHP 1720Aa).

Many supplies were sent out to the Cocoyome camp, and a group of the Spaniards visited it. Lomas went out to greet them. Father Juan de Ynsáurraga reported on the meeting. The Indians received them with great happiness and took them to a large and "fresh" (newly built) shelter that they had made ready for them. The Spaniards distributed some gifts and reassured Lomas that his men who were on their way to Mexico City would be safe from harm. At this same time, the mulatto returned to Spanish civilization with the Father (AHP 1720Aa). It seems to be unknown what became of the Negro.

Following this meeting, things apparently moved rather slowly. The governor in September ordered that another prisoner be turned over to Lomas to demonstrate the good will of the Spaniards. The envoys from Mexico City had now returned. The Cocoyomes offered to send some sixteen warriors along with the governor on his campaign to the Río Grande del Norte, but the latter declined the offer. At the same time, it was reported that there were over fifty Coahuileño Indians with the Cocoyomes, apparently all at Cerro Gordo (AHP 1720Aa; DHM 1748). Alday wrote later that the Cocoyomes remained at peace at Cerro Gordo for nine months (BL 1722), although actually it was much closer to five.

Then, on the night of October 16, the Cocoyomes stole all of the horses from the hacienda at Atotonilco. The trail of the Indians went eastward in the direction of the Puesto de Barraza. On October 27, Juan de Lomas showed up with six Indians. They recounted that all the Indians who had withdrawn to Sierra Mojada were now back near Cerro Gordo and only one Rivas with his children and his father-in-law were not with them. Lomas claimed that he still intended to keep his word concerning the peace. Rivas and the others were apparently the ones who had stolen the horses, and it was thought that they were probably at Chocamueca (the story here is not entirely consistent) (AHP 1720Aa).

On November 4, Lomas reported that some of the tribe members had pursued the culprits, but their supplies had given out at Acatita La Grande and they had been forced to return. Furthermore, another ten warriors and the wife of El Ratón, kinsmen of the people camped near Cerro Gordo, were still out in the hinterland. Lomas was going to see that these people surrendered but opined that nothing could be done about Rivas and his group. To get the others to come to the Spaniards would take some ten or twelve days. When Lomas returned from his mission he was to go to Parral to receive his title of governor and cane of office, and then the founding of the new settlement would be completed (AHP 1720 Aa).

On November 9, however, Lomas and his entire rancheria left, taking with them the horses of the Mapimí presidio. This, of course, only reinforced the opinion held by the Spaniards that the Acoclames and Cocoyomes were rebellious enemies of the Crown who would only take advantage of the kind treatment they received in the name of His Majesty. Lomas and the others, they felt, had been behind the robberies (AHP 1720Aa). Berroterán later wrote that when the Cocoyomes withdrew to the back country, they had stolen over 300 head of horses from the hacienda of Antonio Marín, in the jurisdiction of San Bartolomé. They went to join a group of Coahuileños (DHM 1748).

Berroterán recounted that the two bands of Cocoyomes and Coahuileños stayed together during the following year. On one occasion they left their families at the mountain of Chocamueca, or possibly Acatita La Grande, and went to attack the presidio of Coahuila at Monclova where they sacked a number of houses and buildings. Over thirty people were killed, and a large amount of supplies was stolen. Spanish estimates ran from 300 to 600 Indian attackers. A Parral document places this event in August, 1721 (AHP 1721Aa; AHP 1722Ab; AHP 1722Da; Bl 1722; DHM 1748).

The Major Deportations

By the 1720's the history of a century or so of Spanish-Indian contacts in the eastern portion of the province of Nueva Vizcaya could be summarized in a few words — a continuous round of raids and assaults by the Indians, and Spanish retaliations and attempts to settle the natives in peace. The Indians had become increasingly proficient and specialized in raiding and making war on the Europeans settled in the region. The latter continued to find themselves at a loss in coping effectively with the Indian menace, although the military defenses of the province had been improved during the previous thirty years. Moreover, from the available evidence there were now fewer natives in the immediate area. The southernmost group at this time, the "Tobosos," consisted in effect of one rather enlarged Cocoyome band. North and northeast of these "Tobosos" were still some Chisos and the Coahuileño peoples.

This reduced number of Indians, however, ranged wider than before, and more distant nations had taken up the battle. In June of 1717 Fray Antonio De San Buenaventura Olivares wrote from the mission of San Juan Bautista in the Río Grande area to the Spanish governor of Coahuila that the entire land was in rebellion from Coahuila to the country of the Texas Indians. There was not, he said, a single nation the Spaniards could trust. Among the Indians of the region of his mission were many stolen goods from Nadadores and Parral that had been received in trade from the groups of rebel natives allied at this time (UTD 1713-1721). The effects of Spanish colonization in Nueva Vizcaya and Coahuila (as well as, no doubt, in New Mexico) were penetrating farther and farther northward into the area of Texas.

From the standpoint of the Spaniards in Nueva Vizcaya the history of their relations with the nomads in the east and northeast had been one of an inordinate number of unsuccessful attempts to subdue these restless Indians and settle them in peace. The frustration resulting from these abortive efforts was finally relieved to some extent in the early 1720's when the Spanish Crown gave permission for what was, in effect, the extirpation of the natives and their way of life from the province. In response to a letter from Governor Martín de Alday dated the spring of 1721, His Majesty issued a Royal Cédula on May 3, 1722, authorizing deportation of incorrigible natives to places distant from Nueva Vizcaya (BL 1723-1724). Under this order a shipment of some 311 enemy Indians was made to central Mexico, eventually to Veracruz, about the beginning of March of the following year; another deportation was made in April of 1726. This procedure for handling the rebels may have become rather common, although the information here is weak (AHP 1722Ba; AHP 1723A; AHP 1727Aa; BL 1722; DHM 1748).

With these deportations the Nueva Vizcayans felt, or at least hoped, that the Indian menace by and large had been taken care of. What in effect happened, however, was that the refugee Cocoyomes and Coahuileños joined the Sisimble Indians who moved southward and took over the raiding territories of the former and then in turn became the leaders of the Nueva Vizcayan desert raiders. Although adequate specific documentation is lacking on this period after 1725 or so, and particularly regarding the eastern region of Coahuila, the existing evidence indicates that the Chisos were the principal actors in the Greater Bolsón warfare until about 1740 (DHM 1748).

In June of 1722, Governor Martín de Alday wrote

the Viceroy that some 500 Cocoyomes and Coahuileños were at this time settled and at peace. It was not long, however, before these peoples rebelled. Almost immediately they were reported in the areas of the Sierra de Acatita, the Sierra del Rosario, and the Sierra de San Lorenzo. A herd of horses from La Hagana in the Parras district had been stolen, and a Spanish sally was ordered forth (AHP 1722Aa; BL 1723-1724).

In this same month the Spaniards learned that the Coahuileños who lived at the pueblo of Los Cinco Señores were planning to withdraw to go and live with their rebel "relatives" now in revolt in the back country. The Coahuileños at Cinco Señores complained that they had gotten along very badly with the Babozarigames there because the latter did not help them with their farming, and the former now requested land on the far side of the river for their own fields and cattle! The Coahuileños also requested the release of one of their women whom the Spaniards had captured from the rebel Coahuileños in the desert (AHP 1722Aa; DHM 1748).

On July 3, 1722, word was received in Parras that the enemy had stolen a herd of horses from El Charco some five or six leagues away. The Alcalde Mayor, with twenty-five of the local citizens and seven Indians, went out after them. The following day at El Charco a combined force of "Tobosos" and "Coahuileños" attacked the Spanish party. The Alcalde and most of the others were killed, and four were taken prisoners. One of these, a Tlaxcalteco Indian, was sent back later by Lomas with messages to the Spaniards. He had been escorted to the outskirts of Atotonilco by four of Lomas' warriors (AHP 1722Aa; AHP 1722Ab; DHM 1748, in which Berroterán mistakenly places the event a year earlier).

The Tlaxcalteco had first been taken to a camp at Sierra de Mobana, and eventually Gerónimo Jaques and Diego El Ratón had taken him to Lomas. The latter gave him a message and two letters to take back to the Spaniards. These letters, written by one of the captives, were principally concerned with establishing the amount of ransom, which Lomas ordered set down in detailed form for each of the prisoners (AHP 1722Aa; AHP 1722Ab).

With this writing, Lomas excused himself and his people for the various times in the past in which they had not kept the peace, registering some rather vague complaints against the Spaniards regarding certain incidents during the terms of office of the three

governors preceding Martín de Alday. Furthermore, the Viceroy had given the Indians no satisfaction when the four Cocoyomes had gone to confer with him in Mexico City. In a verbal message that Lomas gave to the Tlaxcalteco for the Spanish governor, he stated that the recent attack at El Charco had been perpetrated by the Coahuileños. Also, he did not plan to surrender at this time because he considered that Alday had no one to assist him in effectuating the terms of a peace settlement, as well as because he feared misdeeds on the part of the Coahuileños (AHP 1722Aa; AHP 1722Ab).

One of the captives held by the Cocoyomes escaped (mentioned by Lomas in one of his letters) and was later questioned in Parras, into which place he had stumbled completely nude. He recounted that he had been held at Sierra del Diablo where four different nations were camped. On one occasion he had seen Juan de Lomas take a party of over 100 men toward Parras. Also, he had learned from Lomas that chief Don Pablo of the Coahuileños, as well as Pacheco, the Cabeza governor at Parras, had made visits to this ranchería, and that Don Pablo's intentions were to ravage the area between La Castañuela and Coahuila. Lomas and El Ratón did not plan to surrender until a new governor had taken office. Moreover, where they settled would have to be the place where they were located at that time — that is, apparently, at Sierra del Diablo (AHP 1722Aa).

In the meantime, Governor Alday ordered that the Coahuileños of Cinco Señores be apprehended. These people were implicated in the raid by a report that they were in communication with the enemy. Thirteen of the men were imprisoned at El Pasaje. These, with some of the Babozarigames from the same town, plus a few other persons, were called in to testify during the ensuing investigation (AHP 1722Aa).

The Babozarigames declared that they had heard the Coahuileño governor at Cinco Señores, Don Francisco, say many times that he and his people were going to withdraw to the hinterland to join their relatives and the Cocoyomes (AHP 1722Aa; DHM 1748). Some rebel Coahuileños had been visiting their kinsmen at Cinco Señores. Moreover, at the time of a campaign made in November of the previous year from the presidio of San Francisco de Conchos, these settled Coahuileños had forewarned the enemy of the Spaniards' whereabouts, and the latter had encountered only abandoned sites. Also, during other campaigns some Coahuileños had said that they had to go to Parras, at which place it was thought they had been informing the enemy. Witnesses stated that the Coahuileños had done no planting this year because, it was thought, they were planning to revolt. One witness mentioned that in all of the time they had been at Cinco Señores the Coahuileños had only built three or four small houses of *terradas,* and the rest were their own style grass huts (AHP 1722Aa).

The Coahuileños confessed to their projected flight, which was the reason they had sown no crops this year. Furthermore, there had been a great deal of communication between the settled and rebel Indians. Three of the Coahuileños, including one Terocodame, some four months prior to these hearings had gone to inform the hinterland dwellers of their plans; and Don Pablo, chief of the rebel Coahuileños, had visited the Cinco Señores pueblo. Some stolen clothing had shown up among the Coahuileños at Cinco Señores. Even the Cabeza Indians living at La Horca in Parras had been in touch with the Indians in the hinterland and had been paid in pesos and in gifts for their trouble (AHP 1722Aa; DHM 1748).

When first questioned, the Cabezas at Parras denied their contact with the enemy. Other sources, however, confirmed their complicity — the Cabezas had even boasted of it, saying that the Spaniards were "cows" (*vacas*) and simpletons and that the enemy Indians would soon finish them off. Upon a second questioning, the Cabezas admitted to their dealings with the rebels, and the Cabeza governor, Francisco Pacheco, confessed that he had entertained envoys of the latter in his home. Some of the booty stolen from the people of Parras had now found its way back to that place, but in the possession of the Cabezas. The rebels had also attempted to get the Indians at the Hacienda of San Miguel de Aguayo to revolt (AHP 1722Aa; BL 1722).

On July 23, a Spanish force of some 200 soldiers, including sixty Indian auxiliaries, left to take the ransom out to Lomas. They were to meet the latter at the Ojo de Barraza. When Lomas did not show up at this place, the Spaniards continued their march as far as the mountains of Los Remedios and Las Cañas, sending up smoke signals along the way. These signals were not answered, and Lomas was never located, so the Spaniards returned to the San Bartolomé Valley. It was well over two weeks later that the ransom was handed over at Atotonilco and the captives were

returned to the Spaniards. These captives reported that the Cocoyomes were planning to give themselves up, and one stated that the Coahuileños also were. Several sources, including the Tlaxcalteco, revealed that the Cocoyomes and Coahuileños were not getting along too well at this time (AHP 1722Ab; DHM 1748).

On August 24, Lomas arrived at Atotonilco. He wanted to surrender and at the same time to explain why the peace had not been kept in the past. He also was turning the Coahuileños over to the Spaniards since, he claimed, they were the ones responsible for much of the recent raiding and killing. He himself had protected the captives taken at El Charco from the Coahuileños who had wanted to kill them (which was supported somewhat in the Tlaxcalteco's testimony). On August 28, Lomas returned with a few Cocoyomes and Coahuileños, who were now camped at the Sierra de las Batuecas. Don Pablo and the rest had refused to accompany them — the former were apprehensive because they knew that the Spaniards were now holding captive some of their relatives from the pueblo of Cinco Señores (AHP 1722Ab; AHP 1722Ba; DHM 1748).

Don Pablo did come in, however, two days later with twelve men and three women. These were immediately imprisoned. The Cocoyomes then went out to capture the rest of the Coahuileños but managed to bring back only ten or eleven men, four or five women, and some children. Ultimately, however, Lomas delivered some twenty or twenty-two Coahuileño families to the Spaniards. Later, about twenty Cocoyome men with their families arrived in Parral for a handout. On September 20, Lomas brought in around twenty-five of his own warriors, plus their families, to bring in two captive boys they had been holding. He announced that he would bring in the rest of his band to Atotonilco where they would settle. On October 7 the entire group was said to be at the latter place (AHP 1722Ab; AHP 1722Ba; BL 1722; DHM 1748).

On November 9, it was reported that the "Tobosos" had stolen four horses. Lomas was informed of the event. He said he would look into it, although he supposed that they had been taken by the Cocoyome Rivas who had left the main body of Cocoyomes with some eight persons (men?). He had already sent out one of his chiefs to look for this group. At the same time, apparently, some Cocoyomes had killed three Coahuileño women, and it was rumored that they now wanted to return to their own country. The Spanish military were ordered out to the back country to look for the rebel group (AHP 1722Ab).

The following day several of the Cocoyomes in Parral were thrown into prison. One of these, who turned out to be a Coahuileño, was interrogated. Lomas, according to this deponent, was intending to escape back to the desert. His plans were to carry this out at the time of a coming celebration. The Indians were going first to the spring at Baus. At this moment, apparently, Lomas had some sixteen Cocoyomes with him at San Blas, seemingly where Rivas also was. Another thirty-one Indians were at Las Lagunas in front of the Sierra de Ontiveros. On November 12, the Spanish force attacked Lomas' camp. Sixteen of the rebel Indians were killed, including captain Antonio (Lomas' brother) and a "sergeant." Thirty-one warriors were captured, including Lomas and El Ratón, plus forty-four women and forty-six children. This attack apparently took place at Los Peñoles, in the Sierra de Baus near the Sierra de Ramos (AHP 1722Ab; BL 1722; DHM 1748).

Among the prisoners, as it turned out, were fifteen Coahuileño women, two men, and seventeen children. These had remained with the Cocoyomes when Lomas had turned the others in to the Spaniards (Lomas previously had denied that he had any Coahuileños in his company). One of the Coahuileños was questioned. He declared that Lomas and the Cocoyomes had no intention of settling down in a pueblo where the Spaniards would put them to work. Furthermore, the Cocoyomes had taken the Coahuileño women away from their husbands and later had put to death three of these women at Las Lagunas, because they had wanted to marry them (AHP 1722Ab).

Lomas and the others were ordered to confess. They gave a rundown on all of the raids and killings they had committed, including the recent attacks at Monclova and Parras. The Cocoyomes and Acoclames had had no other allies than the Coahuileños for some time. Lomas, judged to be about forty-five years old, had been governor ever since Alonso died "a long time ago." The time they had broken the truce at El Pasaje (when Alday was in command there), Alonso and Contreras were the chiefs. Lomas also blamed Rivas for violating the peace in the past. He claimed

that he had not told the Spaniards of the remaining Coahuileño women and children because they had been camped a long way away at the time; the other three women had not been killed but had simply run away. Some of the witnesses claimed they did not know why the peace had been broken in the past; others said it was because of rumor that the Spaniards were planning to kill them (AHP 1722Ab).

A Terocodame from Nadadores with this group offered a little more information. He, as had almost all of the "Coahuileños," had lived at the mission in Coahuila before they had revolted some three years earlier. Since leaving the mission he had been occupied solely in raiding the Spaniards. Antonio, the brother of Lomas, at a meeting held by the Indians, had been one of the first to decide to go back to the desert, just before the Spanish attacks on the camp. He had left first, with a few old women, for the mountains. The rest of the people, apparently, were to follow later. At the same time, scouts had been sent out to reconnoiter the livestock in the area, which they were planning to take when they withdrew. A number of others, including Rivas, then began to depart for the back country. The remainder of the rancheria was going to leave as soon as they consumed six cows the Spaniards had given them as part of their rations. The reason behind this withdrawal was their fear of punishment for having already stolen animals in the region. The motive for the peace offering was not the desire to settle down to town life but was a need for clothing for the coming winter (AHP 1722Ab).

At the beginning of 1723, a Covaya Indian, Juan Francisco de Contreras, who claimed he had been raised at the hacienda at Parras, was picked up at La Cieneguilla. He had been asking about the prisoners held by the Spaniards, because the rebel Coahuileños had sent him to tell the prisoners to escape to Sierra Colorada where they would be met. Most of the Indians at this time were at the river of Las Sabinas, but twelve families who had accompanied the deponent were at a spring in a mountain near Sierra Colorada. These people had as chiefs Joseph Baptista, alias El Ladrón, Antonio El Apachi, and Bartolo, all apparently under Don Pablo. From a different source, another Coahuila chief, Moyate, was also mentioned. This deponent had been with the Coahuileños about a year and had participated in the El Charco attack (AHP 1722Aa).

At this time Don Pablo and twenty of his men, turned over to the Spaniards by Lomas and the Cocoyomes, were being held prisoners in Parral. During this period there seems to have been a good bit of friction between the Cocoyomes and Coahuileños. According to the same Covaya prisoner, Lomas' band and the Coahuileños (at least part of them) had parted company at a place below La Laguna because Lomas had refused to divide up some of his booty of horses and clothing with them. Later, apparently, when the remaining Coahuileños had received word from two of their own who had escaped from the imprisonment resulting from Lomas' treachery, they had turned on the Cocoyomes with the intent to fight. These were so many in number, however, that the Coahuileños thought better of it and stole the Cocoyomes' horses instead (AHP 1722A; AHP 1722Da).

The declarations of Don Pablo and his men clarify the previous events to some extent. The circumstances under which they had revolted some two years earlier are somewhat obscure, but a possible factor may have been a raid in this area by the Cocoyomes. Don Pablo's story was that then he and his men had moved out to the area of Cuatro Ciénegas and later had sent in envoys to request peace, which was eventually granted them. They were on their way in to settle down when at the Sierra de Chocamueca they met the Cocoyomes who had been previously settled in peace at Cerro Gordo. Four of the latter, the Coahuileños had learned, had gone to see the Viceroy in Mexico City. The Viceroy, however, had not given them a cane of authority, a paper (or document), or even one *real* to purchase food or a bit of clothing. For this reason the Cocoyomes at Cerro Gordo had rebelled and fled to the back country. The Coahuileños had met them at Acatita La Grande, where Juan de Lomas – during a dance, or *mitote*, they held together – recounted to them the story concerning the visit to the Viceroy. At this same time, Lomas presumably had had a vision from God telling him that the Spaniards were planning to kill them. The Indians then decided not to surrender, so they moved to Sierra Mojada (AHP 1722Da).

These Coahuila admitted their part in the attack on the town of Monclova in Coahuila in August of 1721, as well as when they had joined the Cocoyomes for the previously mentioned raid on El Charco, this time leaving their families at Poso Hediondo. They also admitted the contact they had had with Indians at Parras and at Cinco Señores (AHP 1721Ab; AHP 1722Ab; AHP 1722Da; BL 1722).

On December 9, the governor ordered out a messenger to the remaining rebels in the back country to attempt to convince them to come in and make peace. This envoy eventually located Rivas with twenty men and ten women and twelve children at the Sierra de Baján. In the early part of January, the envoy reported that Rivas and his group were on their way to Cerro Gordo. The Governor at Parral released the Cocoyomes from prison, although the guard was doubled, to demonstrate the good faith of the Spaniards to Rivas (AHP 1722Ba).

More envoys were sent out. On January 18 word was received again from Rivas. He would surrender, but all prisoners must first be released and settled at Cinco Señores. He said they had not come in on receipt of the previous message, because they were angry over what had been done to their relatives. By January 28, 1723 – after a series of events involving talks, messengers, and an attack on the enemy ranchería – Joseph Romualdo de Alday reported from Cerro Gordo that with Captain Joseph de Berroterán and the Spanish troops they had acquired another fifty-seven prisoners, comprising men, women, and children, plus some forty-one horses at the water hole of El Carmen. By February 5, some sixteen to eighteen more had been brought into the Mapimí presidio by an Indian named Antonio Baldús or El Chiso and his comrades (who apparently were among the prisoners previously taken(?); Chisos are not listed in the actual counts of prisoners of this deportation, although later it was said that Antonio actually was a Chiso). Rivas was still out with eleven warriors and one old woman (AHP 1722Ba).

On February 11, under authorization of a Royal Cédula of May 3, of the previous year, which granted permission to deport rebel Indians to distant provinces (BL 1723-1724), Governor Alday ordered that all the prisoners held at the presidios of Cerro Gordo, El Gallo, El Pasaje, and Parral, be gathered together to be sent to Mexico. The count at this time was 122 warriors plus the women and children – a total of 286; the Viceroy later reported that the total number of prisoners had been 311 (BL 1722). Only Rivas' group still remained to be captured (at least of the Cocoyomes). On February 19, word was received that Captain Joseph de Berroterán of Mapimí had taken four or six of these and killed Rivas at Las Hornillas. The rest escaped. All the prisoners then in custody were deported to Mexico City about the beginning of March (AHP 1722Ba; AHP 1723; BL 1722; DHM 1748).

The fate of only some of these prisoners is known. Captain Joseph Romualdo de Alday, with an escort of some seventy-two soldiers and fifty-two Indian auxiliaries, took the Indians southward to Mexico City. On the road a plague broke out among the captives, and Alday reported to the Viceroy from Celaya that by April 10 only 227 prisoners were left – thirty men, twenty-seven women, and twenty-six children had perished (a total of eight-three persons, with a discrepancy of only one, making the original total 310, and bearing out the Viceroy's figure) (BL 1722).

The Viceroy then ordered the Indians not to be brought into Mexico City, because of this plague and because of their past crimes, but instead to be sent via Puebla to Veracruz. From here they would be taken to the Windward Islands of Santo Domingo, Puerto Rico, and Habana (Cuba). In effect, Alday took his captives, now consisting of 205 persons, to Puebla, where he turned them over to the Alcalde Mayor (BL 1722).

At Puebla a number of people – the sick, widows, and orphan children – were kept, some to be distributed to workshops and other Spanish holdings where they would receive a Christian education. The remaining 138 persons were placed in charge of a company of dragoons. On the march to Veracruz, sometime in the middle of May around midnight at Venta de Barrera, the greater part of the prisoners escaped. Some were recaptured, and a total of ninety-two were later handed over to the captain of the Windward Fleet to be taken to the Caribbean islands. The rest committed some robberies and murders before they were picked up or killed, and a few managed to escape back to the Nueva Vizcayan desert (BL 1722).

The deportation of 1723 was undoubtedly the largest single step in the extinction of the original Nueva Vizcayan tribes. However, it did not signify at a single blow their total disappearance from the eastern Chihuahua region – Indian raids and hostilities continued to harass Spanish settlements. While there is some difficulty in interpreting the importance of the 1723 event, owing to the lack of adequate documentation, succeeding happenings help clarify its place in the general picture.

In the early part of February of 1724, an enemy group, said to have consisted of about fourteen men, attacked El Corral de Rosas, near the hacienda of La Mimbrera, and another raid was made on the Santa Cruz ranch. Antonio de Molina led a force out from Conchos to the Puesto de Terrazas. Fresh tracks to El Venado or Agua de Mayo were searched for, but nothing was found. Molina later wrote that since he and his men had discovered no tracks in the Terrazas region, he guessed that the assailants had been Cocoyomes who had probably gone to Acatita by way of Los Chupaderos (AHP 1722Bb).

A fifteen-year-old boy was interrogated at Guanaceví on March 1. He had been captured some two weeks before while traveling with his father from Ramos to Parral and managed to escape his captors a couple of days before this questioning, when the Indians raided El Topetón. After being taken prisoner, the father was killed and the boy was informed that he would be taken back to camp to be married to one of the girls left there with two of the men. The rebel group, made up of some nine men, remained in the general Ramos area for several days. The boy learned the names of only five of his captors – Isidro, Cristóbal, Antonio, and two Mateos. The chief of the party was an old man whose name he did not find out (AHP 1724Ab; DHM 1748).

On March 11 governor Joseph Sebastián López de Carbajal reviewed the enemy's current situation. It appeared that eleven men, plus women and children, were camped at Acatita La Grande with a fairly good-sized herd of horses. Because he feared that these Indians might entice some of the peaceful pueblos into joining them "and again infest this kingdom" of Nueva Vizcaya, he ordered an expedition be made to Acatita (AHP 1724Ab).

Captain Joseph de Berroterán left Mapimí on March 24, reconnoitering Tahualilo, Acatita de Baján, Salinas de Machete, and Mobana. On April 4, Spanish troops discovered the enemy's camp – abandoned just before their arrival – at Pozo Hediondo, thirty leagues north of Mapimí. Although the Indians escaped, the soldiers captured forty-two of their horses before returning to Mapimí (AHP 1724Ab; DHM 1748).

Later, after three youths had been assaulted on the Parral-Santa Cruz-Las Bocas Viejas road at the beginning of August, two ex-captives were questioned. These had been taken sometime in July by ten Indians between El Zape and Las Bocas. After several attacks on Spanish holdings, including one near El Canutillo, the party had gone to the enemy's camp at Sierra del Diablo. Here were another seven or so Indians, plus three captives — two Spaniards and an Indian. These had refused to flee with the declarants, claiming that they were well off with the Indians because they did not have to work — they could see no reason to return to Spanish civilization (AHP 1724Aa).

Farther north, about this same time, the Sisimbles had been causing trouble along the lower Conchos River, including the theft of animals from some Apaches from the north who had gone to La Junta to a fair — a custom of theirs. They had chased the culprits down the Río Grande to the Sisimble camp in front of the mountain of Chocamueca. However, the Apaches decided not to attack, owing to the numbers of the Sisimbles and because they figured their enemies were probably allied with some other nations. These Sisimbles were said to have had many horses and mules with them (AHP 1724Aa).

In the first half of 1725 several raids were reported in the areas of San Juan del Río, Los Palmitos, El Llano de Florido, Puesto de Pánuco, and Tumba Carretas. In the late spring Spanish and Indian forces met and fought in the Sierra de Acatita. The natives suffered no casualties, although the Spaniards managed to retrieve some stolen horses and goods and one captive. The captive declared that the enemy band was composed of thirty-two Indians (it is not clear if these were "persons" or "warriors"). With this, the governor ordered that the Alcaldes Mayores of the various jurisdictions reconnoiter their respective areas for a period of eight days before and eight days after each full moon in an attempt to forestall further enemy sorties (AHP 1725Ca).

Around December 1 Antonio Molina led out another campaign from the presidio of San Francisco de Conchos via El Venado (on the Florido River) and then to Terrazas, Espíritu Santo, Jaque, Las Encinillas, La Candelaria, La Tinaja de San Blas, and Cocomora. The enemy was finally located at Chocamueca but managed to elude the Spanish troops. From the camp and various tracks it was estimated that some 250 Indians had been there (AHP 1725B), although this figure may have been somewhat excessive.

Scouts were dispatched, and the next day the Indians were encountered at another spot in the Sierra de Chocamueca. Four men, three women, and three boys were killed; eighteen were taken prisoners; and two captives and eighteen animals were retrieved. According to one of the captives, some fifteen men and over twenty women had escaped. However, two days before this battle a large group had gone to the Nueces River to get more people in order to attack San Francisco de Conchos; still others had left for Parral and Cerro Gordo to raid. Three tribes were reported to be together — Sisimbles, Coahuileños, and Cocoyomes (AHP 1725Aa; AHP 1725B).

On February 15, 1726, nine Indians from this group arrived in Parral to make peace. Two of these individuals, Esteban and Joseph Gavilán, had already made initial peace overtures a month earlier. The rest of their people, some seventy-five persons, had remained at this time at Guajuquilla, twelve leagues from Parral. The Spaniards sent a number of supplies to them. According to the ambassadors, the group had previously consisted of some 140 warriors, but they had suffered a great reduction in numbers in a recent battle with some Apaches — reportedly comprising more persons than did these Nueva Vizcayan people. It was because of this decimation, however, that the Indians now wanted to settle down at Guajuquilla (AHP 1727Aa).

The governor summoned a meeting of local officials to discuss the situation. The story of the battle with the Apache was given little credence; it was felt more likely that the Indians were actually after their women whom the Spaniards had captured in December and were now holding prisoners in Parral. Some of the envoys had already, within a day, requested permission to marry these women. In the *junta* it was decided finally that for the time being the Indians should be settled at Guajuquilla. Within a few days some horses were stolen from the Nazas River, and with this the Spanish authorities had even less confidence in the Indians' request for peace (AHP 1727Aa).

Actually, the rebels were at Las Batuecas and not at Guajuquilla. On February 22 it was reported that one Chepe had arrived at the San Bartolomé Valley from the Batuecas camp by way of Guajuquilla with four companions. He reported that his people would be delayed for another six days because the Chiso chief and some others had taken ill (AHP 1727Aa).

On February 23 word was received that the Indians were in the process of sending their women and children back to the hinterland. Two other Indians, one from Conchos, had informed them that the Spaniards were planning to kill them. With this they had become frightened, although they were also indignant because the governor had not sent them either the clothing or knives he usually did when they came in to make peace. According to the Spaniards, however, supplies had been sent to the Indians and those who had gone to Parral had received ample clothing. Actually, it was learned somewhat later that the Coahuileños and the Cocoyomes were willing to make peace, but it was the Sisimbles who were "afraid." The Indians had now returned to Sierra Mojada where they were awaiting messengers from the Spaniards. With the arrival of these ambassadors, according to this story, the Sisimbles would be convinced that the efforts for peace were serious. The Spaniards planned to go along with this, although they decided to keep as hostages the women they were holding in Parral in the hope that this would act as a deterrent to further raiding (AHP 1727Aa).

In early March the Spanish governor in Parral received a letter from Marcos, the "general" of the rebels, dated the 3rd of this month. Marcos claimed that one Juan Gavilán from Atotonilco had informed him that the Spaniards were only trying to trick them. The Indians really did want to settle in a pueblo, he wrote, but in order to satisfy his people it would be necessary to send them four of the women held prisoners, as well as supplies, which Marcos detailed quite thoroughly. The Spaniards, again in *junta*, decided to acquiesce to Marco's demands, except they would not send out the daughter of Chepe as requested in the letter, but would substitute another woman. This, they opined, would provide some measure of safeguard in the proceedings while demonstrating their own sincerity (AHP 1727Aa).

On April 1, six of the leaders of the rebels arrived in Parral. These were Captain Contreras, chief of the Cocoyomes and Coahuileños; Marcos, an old man and a great rebel leader who had never surrendered in his entire life; Chief Mateo, who had escaped from the last deportation (apparently a Coahuileño); Estebanillo, one of the envoys sent to the governor; and, two Sisimble warriors. They had come to take the Spanish captain, Joseph Sarmiento, and another three or four soldiers out to their ranchería to help persuade their people to surrender. At this point, the Spaniards smelled a trap, figuring that the Indians had planned this in order to gain hostages whom they could then exchange back for the Indian women. They decided instead to send two of these Indians,

Felipe and Joseph, who had been staying in Parral, out to the rebel camp, since they had more confidence in these two. In the meantime, the six recent arrivals should remain in Parral to rest — in the public jail. There were, apparently, two others of the group also in Parral at this time, as well as the families of Joseph and Felipe. These people were to be kept in ignorance of the Spanish plans, while all those who came in would be clapped in irons. Orders went out to the various presidios to have ready twenty men, plus supplies, for any contingency that might arise (AHP 1727Aa).

On April 7, Juaniquito, considered to be second in authority (*segunda persona*), arrived at the San Bartolomé Valley where he was immediately taken prisoner. He reported that Felipe and Chepe had arrived at the ranchería and that the Indians were now on their way to the Spaniards. The latter decided to wait for the two envoys to find out where the new camp was. Juaniquito was sent off to the Parral jail. On April 12, twelve Indians — ten men and two women — arrived at San Bartolomé. These also were immediately imprisoned but were kept where they were, as the Spaniards did not want to concentrate too many of these rebel Indians in one place (AHP 1727Aa).

On April 25 the governor ordered that the prisoners, now totaling thirty-nine persons, be readied for deportation to Mexico City to be placed in the custody of the Viceroy. They would be sent with a wagon train that was to depart in two days (AHP 1727Aa).

Extinction of the Aborigines and Arrival of the Apaches

With the two deportations of the 1720's, the original inhabitants of the Greater Bolsón region, that is, the peoples encountered by the Europeans in the sixteenth and seventeenth centuries, were well on their way to extinction. The southern Coahuileño groups — "Salineros" and "Cabezas" — and the "Tobosos" had just about vanished. This apparently was true also for the mission population of these tribes, although there is little information on this point. The principal groups that remained throughout the 1730's as still uncontrolled, wild back-country dwellers were Coahuileños and Chisos from the northern part of the area, fairly immediate to the Rio Grande.

By the 1740's new people, called "Apaches," from

the far side of the Río Grande were making their appearance in the Greater Bolsón country, although from around the beginning of this century Apaches had been penetrating into the northern portions of western Chihuahua and eastern Sonora (Spicer 1962: 234ff). Within relatively few years after the recorded entrance of Apaches into this area east of the La Junta missions at the mouth of the Conchos River to Coahuila, they had taken over the entire region to the south. During the latter half of the eighteenth century remnants of some of the original native peoples remained at the missions in Nueva Vizcaya and Coahuila, but by this time the Apaches had become virtually the sole possessors of the back country from which they, as their predecessors before them, had taken up the raiding of Spanish settlements in these provinces. In this process the Apaches apparently absorbed some of the survivors of the original population, and it would be interesting to know how much the Greater Bolsón Indians taught the newcomers about the land they were coming to inhabit. On the other hand, the Apaches probably were responsible for the extinction of many local Indians when they raided Spanish missions and other holdings. The story of this Apache intrusion, unfortunately, seems to exist only in the broadest outlines.

The tribal identities of the back-country peoples become more difficult to trace in the 1720's. In an uprising in March of the year 1726 by the Indians of the lower Conchos River and its confluence with the Río Grande, few or no Chisos seem to have been involved; the peoples mentioned were the Sumas and the Cholomes. Furthermore, in the expedition led by Joseph de Aguirre into this region at the time, no Chisos were listed as auxiliaries, although Tarahumaras, Chinarras, Julimes, Conchos (which may have included some Chisos?), and Tobosos were cited (UTD 1710-1738a).

Three years later, when Captain Joseph de Berroterán made a campaign from San Francisco de Conchos via Mapimí, San Pedro, Aguachila, and Cuatro Ciénegas, to the presidio of San Juan Bautista del Río Grande, Indians for the most part were scarce as far as the expedition was concerned. However, on April 1, at the Río de San Rodrigo (north of the Río Grande?), Berroterán received word that enemy Indians had stolen animals from Parras and Saltillo. The tenor of the report was that most of the enemy lived on or north of the Río Grande river. These included nations called Apaches, Jumanes, and Pelones

(groups still north of the Río Grande at the beginning of 1736 — UTD 1733-1738) that infested the areas around the presidios of San Antonio Balero and San Juan Bautista, plus Gavilanes (location not stated). Another group called the Pacuaches was said at this time to be hunting buffalo at the San Diego River (BL 1729).

Assaults by Indians were still carried out from the Bolsón de Mapimí area in the 1730's, although it is not entirely clear what tribal groups were participating in this. The Archbishop of Mexico, in a letter of February 13, 1737, told of the great damage committed by Indians in the Parras area during the previous year. Orders issued in July, 1737, from San Felipe el Real (Chihuahua City) revealed that the Indian situation of the Bolsón region (although possibly alleviated compared with earlier times) was still considered serious. These orders called for the extirpation of the barbarian enemy, and a Flying Company was to be formed for this purpose. The five presidios of El Pasaje, El Gallo, Cerro Gordo, the Flying Company de Campaña, and San Francisco de Conchos were each to send six men a month on reconnaissance tours. Of the presidios named, Cerro Gordo, the most centrally located, was said to suffer the most assaults. The installation at Mapimí was exempted from this special levee because it was situated more deeply within Indian territory than were the others and consequently was frequently involved in enemy hostilities (UTL 1706).

A year later, in August of 1738, Governor Manuel de Urango ordered a campaign into the Greater Bolsón area, again under Berroterán. The troops were to be drawn from the same six presidios, including Mapimí. This expedition was to go from San Francisco de Conchos through Espíritu Santo or Agua de Mayo, Jaque, to Acatita La Grande in the heart of enemy country. Unfortunately, the ethnic identity of this enemy is not mentioned (TWC 1738). Attacks continued into 1739, during which year seventeen Indians of all ages and both sexes assembled at Cuatro Ciénegas ready to make peace, and three other persons went to Coahuila. However, the outcome of this effort is not known. This band was reported to have raided around Cerro Gordo (UTD 1739-1767).

Unfortunately, there is no good, solid information concerning the tribal identity of the raiders of the 1730's. Apparently, the hard core was composed of Sisimbles, although probably other nations also were involved. Berroterán stated that "Sizimbres" were allied with Coahuileños and Cocoyomes during the term of office of governor Vertiz y Ontañon, seemingly in the mid-1730's (Bancroft gives ca 1737 – 1884: 581), although he may have been thinking of earlier years. In any event, more precise documentation is needed. Interestingly, however, farther to the east, Indians coming out of the Greater Bolsón area were designated at this time as "Tobosos," although the sources emanating from Nueva Vizcaya, as already noted, indicated quite clearly that actual "Tobosos" by this time were virtually nonexistent. The governor of Coahuila wrote in May of 1734 that the mission of El Nombre de Jesús was besieged by both Tobosos and Apaches (UTD 1733-1738). One would guess that these terms "Toboso" and "Apache" were most likely being used in a somewhat vague and geographical sense.

"Tobosos" turned up in 1735 as far east as the kingdom of Nuevo León. In January of this year, Joseph Antonio Fernández de Jáuregui Urrutia wrote that there were Tobosos together with Pamoranos and Cotoayaguas in the Valley of La Pesquería Grande some eight leagues from Monterrey. Six leagues from La Pesquería Grande was the Valley of Las Salinas, which contained Tobosos, Pamoranos, and Borrados. He stated that "the enemy Indians are many who attack this frontier as happened last year in which the Toboso Indians who inhabit the jurisdiction of Coahuila . . . ." He also mentioned Tobosos at the town of San Nicolás de Gualeguas, at the Valley and Real of Santiago de las Sabinas. At the Real de Boca de Leones and the town of San Miguel de Aguayo, he wrote, there were "Tobosos and some Apaches," plus Tlaxcaltecos and Alazapas at the latter, and both places suffered hostilities at the hands of the Tobosos. The mission of La Punta contained "Tobosos with Apaches" (UTD 1730-1736). Writing somewhat previous to 1736, Arlegui stated that at missions there were still Tobozos, Chizos, Cocoyames (Cocoyomes), Acoclames, Cizimbres, among others (1851: 100-101).

The term "Toboso" also turns up in the northern periphery of the Greater Bolsón. Despite the fact that according to some sources the "Tobosos" were now extinct, Captain Joseph Ydoyaga learned in November of 1747 at La Junta at the time of his campaign there that the Apache Pasqual – the same who in previous years had been visiting the Conchos presidio – was now "somewhat angry and disturbed because, having gone to Acatita La Grande he met up with the few Tobosos . . . left who killed four of his

bowmen warriors and he could not discover any way to avenge the insult (*agravio*)" (BL 1746b). It seems probable that these "Tobosos" were for the most part "Chisos" or Sisimbles.

This scanty evidence still leaves much to be desired regarding the extinction of the last of the original peoples of the region and the arrival of the Apaches. The latter apparently did not operate in the area to any extent before the 1740's, and the "Apache" attacks reported farther east were probably carried out by groups moving across the Río Grande for their sorties. A summary of the history of this period – written much later than that cited in the following paragraphs – states that the Apaches did not penetrate into this part of Nueva Vizcaya until the year 1740 ([Riezgo] 1822); from other evidence this appears to be a fairly accurate date.

Captain Joseph de Berroterán wrote in April of 1746 from the Conchos presidio describing Apaches in the province of Nueva Vizcaya. Aside from their penetration as far south as the Tarahumara into what today is the southwestern part of the state of Chihuahua, they had also moved into Bolsón country. Some Apaches had been maintained in peace for a while at the Conchos presidio by gifts and handouts. However, by this writing they had withdrawn and had turned to raiding, taking over the region enclosed by the presidios of Coahuila, Saltillo, Parras, El Pasaje, El Gallo, Cerro Gordo, the San Bartolomé Valley, and Conchos. This was the area "that the extinct enemy used to occupy," a frontier that had become infested again. Westward, the Suma and Gila Apaches had done the same in the area that extended over to the province of Sonora (BL 1746a; UTD 1701-1730).

This contradicts to some degree the report Berroterán wrote in Mexico City two years later. The previously empty Bolsón had now been reinfested by more than 400 Apaches under Chief Pascual, who at the time of this writing were living on the peripheries of the Spanish settlements. It "appeared," Berroterán said, that these Apaches had not yet begun to commit thefts and murders because of the personal peace, friendship, and spiritual tie of *compadre* that Chief Pascual had with him (DHM 1748). Despite this contradiction, it seems that whatever hostilities the Apaches had committed up to this time were minor, especially compared with the situation that reigned in later years.

However, more important for present purposes than the specific date(s) of the arrival of the Apaches was the process of population replacement mentioned by some of the local Spanish observers during this period. In October of 1746 four Nueva Vizcayan military officers — Joseph de Berroterán, Joseph de Ydoyaga, Juan Antonio de Unanue, and Francisco Joseph de Leizáola, captains of the presidios of Conchos, San Bartolomé Valley, Cerro Gordo, and El Gallo, respectively — made a lengthy report to the Viceroy summarizing the history of Spanish-Indian contact in the province. While this is a somewhat simplified and occasionally erroneous version of the historical facts as indicated by more direct evidence, it nicely takes into account the problem of peoples migrating southward during the Colonial period (BL 1746a).

The report begins with the general revolt of 1684 and the establishment in the following year of the presidios of Conchos, El Pasaje, and El Gallo. The one group that had remained hostile after the rebellion was the Acoclames. These people lived closest to the chain of presidios that ultimately caused their demise. However, the Cocoyomes who dwelled farther in the hinterland to the north replaced the Acoclames, absorbing the few who were left, while taking over their territory. The Cocoyomes were also finally extinguished by force of arms, although just prior to their disappearance they were joined by the Coahuileños, Indians who had been under mission control. The writers claimed that both nations had been extirpated with the deportation in 1723, and that following this there had been no hostilities until 1725 (sic). Between these dates eight Indians from these two nations had remained hidden in the Sierra of Aguachila, adjacent to Parras, their existence unknown (apparently until they were picked up at the Mapimí presidio). Afterward, the land had been free of enemies — the only nation that was known in the area was that of the Sisimbles who inhabited the southern bank of the Río Grande. These, pursued by Apaches and Cíbolos from the far side of the river, moved down into the Bolsón country in 1725. Some of them were immediately rounded up and deported (the 1726 deportation?) (BL 1746a).

The remaining Sisimbles then joined the few Coahuileños and Cocoyomes who had escaped during the 1723 round-up and began a new series of raids. These were pursued by Spanish arms until it was learned from the confessions of prisoners in 1743 that only eight Indians (indios) of the Sisimble nation still remained. All prisoners held at this time, with the exception of these eight, were shipped to the Viceregal Court in Mexico City — the last deportation up

to the date of this writing. Since this time the province had enjoyed complete peace, which Berroterán noted again in his 1748 report (BL 1746a; DHM 1748).

Nevertheless, despite this riddance of the ancient enemy, a new danger had appeared with the arrival of the Apaches who, as they had done previously to the Sisimbles, had in turn been "pushed" southward by the Comanches. At the time of this writing some 400 Apaches were camped at the place of La Cruz some thirty leagues from the Conchos presidio. Some of these Indians with their chief had visited the presidio where Berroterán had given them clothing and supplies in an attempt to keep them at peace. However, due to past experience of the successive movement of nations from the north into the Bolsón region, little hope of a permanent peace was held for the kingdom. This was, these officers opined, because the former Toboso country was so dry and sterile that it could be occupied only by Indians; Spanish settlements could not be placed at the passes (entradas) utilized by the Indians, because there was nothing in these areas to support such a settlement (BL 1746a).

Berroterán, a year and one-half later, quite succinctly summed up the history of the Greater Bolson de Mapimí. Referring to certain measures in the reorganization of the military in Nueva Vizcaya, he stated that it was necessary, among other things, "to make war on the enemies in the frontier area who were located in the depression or pocket of land that lies between the two kingdoms of Cuaguila and Vizcaya and the Río Grande, from where it is populated by barbarous, gentile, and apostate enemies from the towns from which they leave, the pattern (causa) of which will remain always as [that of] the waves of the sea — after one passes another follows" (DHM 1748). Later, in this same report, Berroterán warned again of the growing Apache menace in the desert area of Coahuila and Vizcaya. Actually nothing could be done about the entrance into this region by northern Indians from the far side of the Río Grande del Norte, even though a chain of presidios were put up at the river (DHM 1748).

By 1748, practically all of the Sisimbles were extinct. The last sixteen persons were attacked at the Sierra of Acatita (near the Mapimí presidio) by the captain of Mapimí with eight soldiers and eight vecinos on May 21. At this time three men, three youths, and two old men were captured, and another was killed. It was thought that still another died of wounds. The eight prisoners taken were sent to

Durango to prison and tried in a criminal case there. This band had originally contained eighteen persons who had fled the Conchos presidio and had raided the province for about eight years, committing some twenty-five or thirty killings and many thefts (BL 1748; BL 1751a). This may have been the same group reported by Ydoyaga in a letter to Leizáola on April 9, 1741, telling of some "Tobosos" who had abandoned the presidio at Conchos for the hinterland (UTL 1706).

If any period can be said to be one of transition it seems to have been that of the decade of the 1740's. Hostilities, in effect, apparently had diminished considerably in the southern portion of the Bolsón country. However, there were assaults farther north: the La Junta pueblos were attacked in 1746 and various *entradas* (e.g., Ydoyaga's) were made in the next couple of years to control the rebels and to investigate the possibilities of establishing a presidio in the La Junta area. Raiding was reported around the lower Conchos River and to the west, roughly from Chihuahua to El Paso. The principal groups around 1750, more or less concentrated along the Conchos and Río Grande rivers, were the Sumas, Cholomes, and Apaches, although other groups such as Pescados, Venados, and even Chinarras from farther south were also mentioned. In 1754, the Corregidor, Antonio Gutiérrez de Noriega, stated that the Indian nations carrying out hostilities in the vicinity of San Felipe El Real (Chihuahua City) were the Sumas, Cholomes, Venados, Natagees, Apachis, and Gileños, all apparently coming down from the Río Grande area. Pascual's group of 400 Apaches who had been operating farther south in Nueva Vizcaya in previous years were said to inhabit the region from the Río Grande northward (BL 1746a; BL 1746b; BL 1749-1750; BL 1751a; UTD 1749b; UTD 1755-1760).

Within a few years, all of the hostilities around the Parral area and the greater Bolsón de Mapimí were considered to be carried out by Apaches. In a chronological report on Indian hostilities in the Parral district covering the years of 1778 through 1787, the majority of the attacks were said to have been perpetrated by Apaches, although some raiding was attributed to Tarahumaras (AHP 1787A).

Prior to this the Military Engineer, Nicolás Lafora, traveling throughout the area in 1766, stated that the Apaches, Lipanes, and Natages occupied the entire region of the Greater Bolsón, as well as many other places in Coahuila and northern Nueva Vizcaya, and along the Río Grande (Lafora 1958: 276, 304). Eleven years later Father Morfi cited the great many depredations by hostile Indians from the Nazas River area northward and noted the Apaches specifically at El Gallo, the Sierra de Acatita in the Mapimí district, San Juan de Casta, and the region around Parras. The Bolsón de Mapimí, he stated, was the "residence of the Apaches" (Morfi 1958: 361, 364-368, 374-379, 383).

Morfi also noted, in an interesting fashion, the extinction of the "Tobosos." He reported that his party went through an area near the Aguanaval River where, "on the right hand we saw many caves, which we were assured had been the dwellings of the Tobosos Indians, a barbarous nation that no longer exists." Shortly afterward he gave a run-down on the hacienda of Los Hornos. "This hacienda was, in its beginning, like the one of San Juan de Casta, a pueblo of Indians and a *visita* of the Parras parish; it was destroyed by the Tobosos, a barbarous and cruel nation, which the famous captain Berroterán finished off, and which was succeeded by the one which we generally call Apaches" (Morfi 1958: 376). Later, again referring to the ancient pueblo of Los Hornos, Morfi stated that it was a large town "but the Toboso and Cocoyome Indians, who infested these territories with such cruelty, and more ardor (*espíritu)* than the Apaches today, obliged the colonists to give up the new settlement and to withdraw to the capital" — that is, to Parras (Morfi 1958: 578). After some forty years the fame of the Tobosos and Cocoyomes was still alive in the memory of the Nueva Vizcayans.

Finally, Z. M. Pike gave a succinct description of the Apaches in the Bolsón a number of years later. He skirted the region during his expedition of 1805-1807, making the loop through Chihuahua, to Parras, and back through Coahuila to San Antonio (Texas). He said of the mountain region of the Bolsón area: "but it is very scarce of water, and your guards must either be so strong as to defy the Apaches, or calculate to escape them by swiftness, for they fill those mountains, whence they continually carry on a predatory war against the Spanish settlements and caravans" (Pike 1807: 253). In general terms, it seems that little had changed, except the names and ethnic affiliations of the actors, since at least the 1640's.

3. TRIBAL AND BAND HISTORY AND GENERAL DISTRIBUTION

This chapter is an account of the history of the tribes and bands of the Greater Bolsón de Mapimí country. It is focused upon the native groups rather than upon their contact relations with Spanish society – that is, upon their territories or the places occupied, their population and their interrelations. The major groups or tribes covered are, running roughly from south to north, the peoples of the Parras-San Pedro de la Laguna district, the Cabezas-Salineros, the Tobosos, and the Chisos. A few references to neighboring peoples – Zacatecos, Cuachichiles, Tepehuanes, and Conchos – have been included in order to place these principal groupings in a broader distributional context.

Several problems are involved in the analysis of the native peoples of central northern Mexico. One is that the region was characterized by a great number of "group" names, the use of which ran from the naming of small bands to the designation of large tribal groupings (see Appendix 1 for band and tribal names), and these names often overlapped or were used inconsistently. Another is that much of the information that exists in the published sources (e.g., Orozco y Berra) has been presented simply as lists with little or no time depth. Because the interrelationships and the distributions of these peoples were constantly changing under contact pressure, and because the present concern is one of historical and cultural change, the information here is presented as a detailed chronology of the various groups in order to give as clear a picture as possible of tribal and band distribution, population, and territory. Unfortunately, even with this chronology, little definite can be said about the several aspects owing to the complexities of intergroup relationships and to the lack of data. The principal outlines of this chapter are summarized in Chapter V.

The Zacatecos bordered on the south of the Greater Bolsón region. They inhabited the Nazas River and made up the population of the Jesuit *partido* of the Nazas district (DHM 1596; AGN 1607b; AGN 1607c). Pérez de Ribas noted that the southern border of the Laguneros was "at the place and mountain ranges of the Zacateco Indians who border those of La Laguna and Parras" (Pérez de Ribas III 1944: 253).

The Tepehuanes were to the west "in the area in which they border with the pueblos of the Mission of Parras and the Nazas River and Mapimí" (Pérez de Ribas III 1944: 290). Father Ahumada in 1607 referred to the Tepehuanes who were near Mapimí and the Nazas River pueblos, and added (interestingly enough) that they were like gypsies and the most ungovernable (the Zacatecos being the most governable) of the whole land. This contradicts the 1596 *Anua*, however, in which the Tepehuanes were considered to be the most civilized in the area (DHM 1596; AGN 1607c). Ahumada went on to the effect that some Tepehuanes had been settled at one of the pueblos on the Nazas River but within days had warred against the other Indians there and had retired to their own country. They were later settled at Mapimí from where they also fled (AGN 1607c). Many of those settled at Mapimí at this time were Tepehuanes, however (AGN 1607a); and about the same time Mota y Escobar wrote that a Tepehuán town had been founded at or near the now-abandoned mines of Mapimí (1940: 196). In 1618, Father Arista noted that Tepehuanes lived at Las Salinas that faced the mission of Parras (AGN 1618).

The *Anua* of 1606 states that Mapimí was the old pueblo of the Teguanes (Tepehuanes?) and mentions three rancherias – those of Tibulena (also Tobulina), of Serofaunu, and of El Negrito (apparently all are chiefs' names). Two other groups, mentioned later in the same *Anua*, the Haicos and the Gabilachos at Mapimí, were possibly also Tepehuanes. It seems somewhat probable that only one or two of these groups were from Mapimí originally and that the remainder had been settled there from nearby areas by the Spaniards (BL 1606).

One place five leagues from Mapimí and named La Cadama (La Cadena?) was apparently a camp site of the "Teguanes." In the same general region and somewhat over a day's journey from a place called Pelayo was another camp of some sixty persons and two chiefs, one named Naytra Iclotre Quimarato. Another sixty to eighty persons were camped at Pelayo but said to be of different nations because of the different hair styles (some of the different "styles" because of the practice of hair-cutting in mourning?). A group of rebels comprising persons from the "Misión de Tepehuanes" and several rancherias from Mapimí some years before was said to have made its headquarters (?) at Pelayo (BL 1606).

Information from 1607 noted that the language of a great many of the Indians of Mapimí was Tepehuán (AGN 1607c), which seems to indicate that the border of Tepehuán country was at or quite near to Mapimí. The *Anua* of 1616 stated that the Negritos were Tepehuanes, and that they had raided the pueblo of Mapimí (BL 1616). Another source also cited the Negritos as Tepehuanes (Hackett 1926: 126) (apparently named after their governor Juan Negrito of the early 1600's). Judging from the location, it is possible that some of the Tepehuanes, especially in the early years, were designated as "Salineros." (In 1654, it was reported that a certain Indian was a "Salinero Indian from the Negrito rancheria") (AHP 1654Aa).

Alegre leads one to believe that the Conchos bordered the Laguneros on the north, which may actually have meant west around the river valleys, unless he was referring to another group of "Laguneros." He says "The Conchos... is a quite numerous nation which extends up to the banks of the Río Grande del Norte. On the north side it borders the Laguneros [Sumas?] and on the south with some Tepehuán pueblos and the Santa Bárbara Valley" (Alegre II 1956: 236).

The Tobosos are mentioned only once by Alegre — the last rancherias of their territory were near the Río Grande del Norte (Alegre III 1956: 25). However, the Chiso-Toboso boundary was a good bit south of the Río del Norte, since Chiso territory was said to begin at the Sierra de Jaque (Jaco) and extended northward to the far side of the Río Grande (Río Turbio) (AHP 1653Aa). A Parral document of 1644 stated that the Florido River was in the area of the (western) border of the Tobosos (AHP 1644A).

A much greater problem is the identification of the tribal area in the eastern portion of the Greater Bolsón region. This is intimately tied up with the questions of the ethnic identity and territories of the peoples to the north of the Parras-Laguna district, and with the identification with later groups of the tribes or bands reported from around Parras and La

Laguna at the turn of the seventeenth century. Another side of the same problem is the documentation of the disappearance of the Parras-Laguna groups as separate ethnic identities. The names of these groups were many, and most of them do not appear in later documents (see Appendix 1). As already noted, a number of these people were Zacatecos, and (as will be discussed later) others were no doubt Cuachichiles. However, there were still a number of other bands or groups such as the Irritilas, as they have been called by Orozco y Berra and others (Orozco y Berra 1864).

Father Arista gave the names of three groups located around Parras in 1595 — Yritilas (Irritilas), Mayranos, and Maxiconeras, the first two said to be the original inhabitants of this place (AGN 1619). The 1598 *Anua* recited the names of a number of men, apparently caciques, who had settled at Parras and La Laguna. Many of these, especially when given as surnames, may have been group names; certainly some were. Those cited for Parras were Juan Mayconera, Francisco Cui, Colazaque Zacateco, Martín Pacho, Mainara or Macarue, and Antonio Martín Irritila; at La Laguna were Pedro Meriano, Oymana, Aomania, Gaspar Cavisera, Juan Inabopo, Daparabopo, Bartolomé (no other name given), Guamira, Mateo (with no other name), Bacacuyo, and Porras. Later, the same source stated that the Pacho were from this general area but does not say whether from Parras or La Laguna. The Irritilas, Miopacoas, Meviras, Hoeras, and Maiconeras were said explicitly to be from Parras, while the Paogas and Caviseras, Vasapalles and Ahomamas, Yanabopos, and Daparabopos were from La Laguna and were said to consist of four nations (DHM 1598).

The *Anua* of 1604 referred to two groups apparently some distance from or at least in the environs of the Parras-Laguna district. One was the Ohoes, said to mean "enemies," the other the Alamamas (Ahomamas?) which consisted of seven bands (*parcialidades*) (BL 1604; see also Alegre). The 1605 *Anua* reported the arrival of a group called the Mamaceras to Parras, where they were settled. These people for many years had been under religious instruction by other missionaries (Franciscans?, where?) some thirty leagues from Parras (BL 1605). The Dapavarapos were mentioned in the *Anua* of 1606 together with a group called the Managues. They were said to be mountain people who had come to Parras to settle after a fight with another band in which many of the former groups had been killed (BL 1606). The first group is almost certainly the same as the Daparabopos, in which case it would appear that these people had moved from La Laguna to Parras. This same *Anua* mentioned another group called "de la Peña" (BL 1606). Mota y Escobar stated the Zacatecos, Pachos, Irritilas, and Guasahuayos were from Parras. Two other groups, Mexues and Ocolas, he reported were at both Parras and La Laguna (1940: 164, 167).

This lack of congruence in the sources with regard to which "nations" dwelt in the Parras-Laguna district probably is due to at least two factors. First, duplicate names sometimes were likely used for the same nations. Secondly, in effect, a fairly great movement of peoples in the general area resulted from plagues and other reasons, and new groups were brought in from time to time (AGN 1619; DHM 1596; DHM 1598; DHM 1601).

Later sources do not clarify this confusion. Actually they should be held suspect because they are so late and because the bases for the statements contained in them are not certain. Father Morfi, in the mid-eighteenth century, stated that the principal tribes of the Parras area had been the Airitilas (Irritilas), Mazamorras, Neguales (Yeguales), Salineros, and Cabezas (Morfi 1958: 380-381). An anonymous Jesuit, writing around the year 1706, cited the Arritilas (Irritilas), the Mazorros, and the Yeguales as the original inhabitants of Parras (DHM ca 1706). Pérez de Ribas confirmed that the Irritilas (Iritiles) lived at La Laguna and its environs (1944 III: 265). Zepeda in 1645 designated the inhabitants of San Pedro de la Laguna simply as "Laguneros" (DHM 1645).

Probably some of the groups named for the general Laguna district were Cuachichiles from farther south or east, and the names Guachichila and Cuachichil occur in 1617 and 1618 respectively in the Parras Parish Records. In fact one group, the Pachos, recorded in the Parras area (Mota y Escobar 1940: 164; DHM 1598; Parras Parish Records) are very likely to have been Cuachichiles. They were stated to be from the Saltillo and Patos areas, together with Cuachichiles at Saltillo (quite definitely used as a generic term here) around 1588. Saltillo was on the border of the Cuachichiles and the Rayados Indians (Alessio Robles 1938: 109, 112-113, 127, 130, 139). Possibly such groups as the Mamaceras (Mamacorras) and Managues, previously cited, were also Cuachichiles. Cuachichil personal names recorded in Mazapil

in 1587 were Machitel (from the Valle del Pedregoso), Machichini, Maquamara, Mayaguas, Maquemachichipa, Majacopa, Maquamimisa, and Maquicaco (UTD 1592-1643), which are quite similar to some of the names listed in the Parras mission records — Mamaya, Mamaura, Hapiquamara, etc. (Appendix 1).*

To the north and northeast of the Parras-Laguna district were the "Coahuileño" groups. Their relationship to the peoples of the former region is not entirely clear, although some Coahuileños were found at the missions of Parras from the earliest years (DHM ca 1706). However, it seems best to postpone a discussion of this problem until more data on the region are presented.

Likewise, it is uncertain how the Tobosos (and Chisos, for that matter) fit into the early distributional picture. None of the Toboso groups, at least by the names that occur in the latter years, show up in the Parras Mission records, with one possible exception in 1617 with the occurrence of the term Toboco, which possibly should read Toboço, since in the manuscripts the cedilla is often omitted. Tobosos as such, however, were known since the Espejo expedition of 1582 (Bolton 1916: 171-172). Apparently the Atotonilco mission had been established for them in 1611 (West 1949: 10-11) and after a withdrawal the following year, some, at least, were settled at this mission and at San Bartolomé (UTD 1648).

Later, around 1618 during the Tepehuán revolt, rebellious Tobosos and Nonojes were reported with Conchos in the vicinity of Santa Bárbara. The peoples of Las Salinas de Machete and Pozo Hediondo who were in rebellion at this same time probably included "Salineros" and possibly Tobosos and Tepehuanes (Hackett 1926: 98, 110; AGN 1617; 1618).

Three years later, in 1621, the Tobosos, Acoclames (Achaclames), Nonojes (Nonoties), and Xipocales bands visited Atotonilco, and the Tepehuán Negritos were living in the area of Mapimí (Hackett 1926: 124, 126). In 1624, Tobosos declared that they, as well as Nonojes, Acoclames, Chisos (this printed source

---

* Alessio Robles gives a somewhat similar list of Indian chiefs who surrendered to Urdiñola about this same time (apparently from a 1592 testimony). These were "don Martín, Francisco el Tuerto, Machoquía, Yalacitamo, Viejo del Pedregoso, Ramírez, Melchor, Francisco Rayado, Cilavan, Zapalinamé, Minamea, Chiriniquinata, Quinaco, Maquicoca, Mocoanicaco, Gerónimo, Machichini, Mayagua, Maquemachichigua, Majacopa, Maquamimira, y Maquisaco" (Alessio Robles 1938: 120 fn.).

reads: "*nonojes o cochames chicos*"), and some Tepehuanes and Salineros, had been fighting the Spaniards for over twenty years (Hackett 1926: 140-142). In a report on the Indians of Nueva Vizcaya in 1625, it was stated that the Tobosos, (A)Coclames, Nonojes, and Salineros were allies and that they were usually together. These included a great number of people who inhabited an area thirty leagues from the Santa Bárbara "province" who had never been under mission doctrine (Hackett 1926: 158). A Spaniard, Valerío Cortez, testified in Parral in 1671 that some of the earliest trouble with the desert Indians occurred in 1632, when *he* first arrived in the province, and he cited specifically the Masames (CD [1671]). However, it appears that Tobosos had been raiding Spanish holdings for a good many years before this. Also in 1626, two towns were founded for the "Salineros" near Las Salinas, at Agua de Pelayo, and at La Mimbrera (AGN 1626).

The scant data for these early years do not afford much indication of the changes that may have been occurring in the hinterland during this period. Disease probably took its toll in some parts of the area — judging from reports from Parras — and plagues were reported at Parras in 1622, 1624, and 1626. The native population had diminished there, although some groups from the surrounding vicinity, including people from Coahuila, had come in or would do so periodically. Others, however, were recalcitrant and wanted no contact with Spaniards — missionaries or otherwise. Some were reported to have fled their territories to the missions during the plagues (AGN 1622, AGN 1624, AGN 1626). No doubt the peoples living farther in the back-country were affected by these happenings on their southern periphery.

It is not until the 1640's, during the Revolt of 1644, that more abundant information appears. Around the year 1640, however, Tobosos, Salineros, and Tepehuanes were committing depradations; in 1643 Tobosos, Nonojes, and "other nations" were reported again to be raiding in the province. During the 1644 Revolt, as noted elsewhere, it has been common in some of the published literature to cite seven tribes as the participants — Tobosos, Cabezas, Salineros, Colorados, Conchos, Julimes, and Mamites (Alegre III 1956: 37; Decorme 1941: 264-265). This list was apparently taken from Father Zepeda's 1645 letter where he stated that captured rebels had given these names (DHM 1645).

However, other documentary sources indicate that a good many more groups were involved. The last three names of the above "seven nations" were probably all Concho or closely related people, or possibly Jumanos. To this group should be added another series of names, the total list of names from other sources being Ayozomes, Bacabaplames, Bachichilmes, Chisos, Conchos, Hovomes, Julimes, Mamites, Mosnales, Nabobayoguames, Olazasmes, Oposmes, Tapacolmes, Tatamastes, Tocones, Zabasopalmes, Zolomes (Cholomes), and Xiximbles (Sisimbles). At least two of these, Chisos and Sisimbles, were closely associated off and on with the "Toboso" bands, and possibly others under different names were also. Of the desert peoples farther south, the Tobosos, Nonojes, Acoclames (or Ococlames), Ocomes, Otolcoclames, Masames, Pimotologas (or Pimotocologas), Gavilanes, Coyomes, Coyotes, Cocoyotes (these last three are possibly the same group), Salineros, Cabezas, the Salineros of Don Cebrián, Matarajes, Colorados, and Negritos are mentioned (Sauer 1934; AHP 1644A; AHP 1645Aa; AHP 1646Ab; AHP 1652Dc; CD 1646a; CD 1647-1648; CD 1650a).

To this list of desert bands, which at one time or another during this revolt were said to be in rebellion, should be added the names of a few bands not cited until a group of people, led by the Cabezas, arrived in Atotonilco in January of 1646 to surrender. Some of these names are likely to be alternates for some of those already cited, although a few possibilities can be eliminated — such as the Tobosos, Nonojes, and Ocomes, since these bands made a separate peace with the Spaniards. The Gavilanes, Cocoyomes, Salineros, and Matarajes can also be eliminated from the possible duplications because they formed part of the group led by the Cabezas, or at least for whom the Cabeza chief acted as spokesman. The other bands were the Cabacbitac (or Cabacbitae) under Chief Nicolás, the Talcoyomes under Chief Pedro, the Tubaymamar with Chief Hicabiaca, the Maçaltipilguas (or Maçalypilguas) with Chief Martín, and the Babosarigas (Babosarigames) under Chief Baibiadaga. The chiefs of the other bands were Don Baltazar of the Cabezas, Juan of the Gavilanes, Simón of the Cocoyomes, Baltazar of the Salineros, and Cahico of the Matarajes (CD 1650a).

Just prior to this surrender, in the latter part of 1645, these groups, less the Salineros, had been visited by envoys in the back country. The latter included still another group, the Totolcoyome, which name seems to be mentioned in no other place. All the bands cited in Atotonilco, with the exception of the Toboso but including the Nonojes and Ocomes, in January of 1646 totaled 498 persons (CD 1650a).

Reports during the revolt sometimes refer to groups "associated" with one another. In a very general way, apart from the above cited "Concho" peoples, there seem to have been two clusters, at least in the western part of the area. One was the "Salineros" associated with the Cabezas, Matarajes, and the Salineros of "Don Cebrián," among a few others; the other was the "Tobosos," including Nonojes, Acoclames, and others. The Tepehuán Negritos were with the first group (AHP 1645Aa; AHP 1646B; AHP 1652Dc).

Tobosos, Acoclames, and Nonojes were often said to be together, and in May, 1644, a group of persons from these three nations went to Atotonilco. They had previously been settled at this place with some Conchos. In November several nations — "Tobosos, Nonoxes, Ococlames [Acoclames], and Cabessas Salineros" — were at the place of Las Cruces, thirty-five leagues from Parral (CD 1644). In the following month Las Cruces, apparently the same place but now said to be twenty-four leagues from Parral and seven from Cuencamé, was said to be the site of Cabezas, Tepehuanes, and "other nations" (CD 1647-1648). Also in 1644, Cabezas and Saguales were reported to be raiding around Castaño, east of Parras (Portillo 1887: 31-40).

During 1645, "Salineros" and "Tobosos" were reported to be living next to each other and in constant communication (AHP 1645Aa) and Guapagua was one of their sites (AHP 1654Ac). Tobosos, Acoclames, Nonojes, and Ocomes were reported together this year, or at least until seventy-six Tobosos, together with eighty-four Salineros, surrendered and settled at Atotonilco in the latter part of the same year. At this time, the Tobosos declared that the Coyomes (Cocoyomes) lived the farthest away from the Spaniards and had had the least contact with them. Also, two combined groups of Cabezas and Colorados were out near the Salinas del Machete at this time. Governor Valdez, while on campaign, reported that the territory of the Colorados was at the *cordillera* of Coahuila (AHP 1645Aa; CD 1650a; DHM 1645).

Negritos and Coyotes were operating in the area of Mapimí, La Cadena, and Santo Domingo. Salineros were said to be neighbors of Mapimí, although the Coyote band had previously been settled at Mapimí. These Coyotes apparently were Salineros and quite clearly distinct from the Coyomes mentioned above, although linguistically a case could be made for their mutual identification. Actually, although this is not entirely certain, there seem to have been several groups of "Salineros" in the general Mapimí area, aside from the Negritos. These were under chiefs Francisco El Tuerto, Juan Bonifacio, Gabriel Pacho, Gerónimo Moranta, and Don Cebrián. Matarajes and Negritos were fairly closely connected, and in fact may have been under one of these chiefs (AHP 1646B; AHP 1652Dc; CD 1650B).

The complexities of band "association" at this time is further revealed when Toboso envoys from Governor Don Cristóbal arrived in Atotonilco in September of 1645. One of the ambassadors was Cristóbal Zapata, cited only as a Toboso in every other source. On this occasion, however, during the declarations it was stated that the Toboso governor had a band of people with him called the Tobosos and that Zapata had another band (*parcialidad*) of Indians named the Jaquue (or Jaqueie) (CD 1650a). This may be an indication that names that seem to have been used rather specifically at this time were in fact somewhat generic.

After the several aforementioned groups were settled in peace at the beginning of 1646, by the middle of the year the Tobosos, Nonojes, Ocomes, Acoclames, and Otolcoclomes had gone back to the warpath (AHP 1646Ab). There may also have been others. Unfortunately, there is practically no further information on these "Tobosos" until the following decade.

In this same year Indians at Tizonazo, apparently Salineros, uprose after five months of a plague of *cocolixtli.* They surrendered at the beginning of 1647, and seventy Christian families returned to the mission, plus the families counted at Cerro Gordo this same year. Another forty families who had remained with the Spaniards during the uprising were taken to Indé by their missionary for protection (AGN 1645-1647a).

The *Anua* of Tizonazo for the years 1645, 1646, and 1647, gives the population of the mission. During this period the mission consisted of the *cabecera* of Tizonazo, and the towns of Santa Cruz on the Nazas River and of Espíritu Santo del Cerro Gordo. In 1645, there were 130 Christian families and over seventy gentile families. In 1646, Tizonazo and Santa

Cruz del Río contained 115 Christian families, plus twenty more who had fled to the Sierra de las Salinas, plus another sixty-six families of gentiles. In 1647, the two above towns consisted of eighty families, plus another fifty at Espíritu Santo which was settled this year. There were also 110 gentile families with no location cited. At an *estancia* near Cerro Gordo there were forty Christian families (AGN 1645-1647a).

Two years later, in March of 1649, Baltazar de Ontiveros, *encomendero* of the Cabeza Indians, wrote that these people had no pueblo for settlement nor fields for corn, and the like. His brother, Cristóbal de Ontiveros, now deceased, formerly had held the town of Tizonazo, apparently also as an *encomienda* (BL 1649-1700).

While information concerning many of the tribal groups of the Greater Bolsón is comparatively ample for the first half of the 1650's, it is not sufficiently so to solve such problems as the relationship of the Salineros and Cabezas with the groups at Parras. Jesuit reports following the secularization of the Laguna district state that many of the people in this area went back to their old haunts, some at least taking up raiding (DHM 1653; AGN n.d.). One would guess that many of these people or bands had joined other rebel groups, such as the Salineros and Cabezas — and this they probably did. However, from the terms recorded in the various documentary sources, including the Parras Parish records, there is little overlap of names (see Appendix 1).

At the same time, many of the earlier named groups in the Laguna district had pretty well disappeared by the 1650's, being replaced in part by people from Coahuila. Even in the 1640's more and more "Coahuilas" show up in the Parras records. In 1653, a Jesuit report noted the arrival in Parras of a number of recently converted "Coahuilas" (DHM 1653). During the 1650's, some names do occur in the local Parras records as well as in the administrative and other reports from elsewhere. A few Cabezas and Salineros are mentioned in the Parras records, as are also a good many Tusares, who in one place were identified as Mayos. Similarly, the Cíbolas might possibly be identified with the Sibopora (Siboporame, etc.) of the Parras and other records (see Appendix 1).

In 1652, Tobosos, Acoclames, Nonojes, and Ocomes were closely allied and were inhabiting a mountain called Tuacague (Guapagua?), which from the context was west of the Jaque range. The Gavilanes

were also associated with these people in some way because the declarant who gave this information went on to state that there were three chiefs: Cristóbal, a Nonoje; Joxocomi, a Gavilán; and, the third named Casa Zavala (Nonoje). There was also apparently another Gavilán chief, but the information here is very confused. Later, ten nations — Tobosos, Acoclames, Nonojes, Brieiatiolyaguas, Chachatiolyaguas, Coyotes, Cocotiolyaguas, Salineros, Cabezas, and Yguocomes — were reported camped at two *peñoles*, Quunanli and Chubahoctpan, located close to each other and not far from Atotonilco. Nagolcaguel, somewhere west of Jaque, was also a campsite of the allied rebels (AHP 1651A; AHP 1652Ac).

"Tobosos" were involved principally or exclusively in the battle of Nonolat. Governor Guajardo Fajardo reported that five nations, "Nonojes, Acoclames, Gobossos [in another version this reads as "Jogosos"], and over half of the Tobosos, and Masames" were there in great numbers. However, at the battle of Acatita of this same year, Babozarigames, Baborimamas, Talcoyotes, Salineros, Tobosos, and Matarajes had all been involved (AHP 1652Ab; BL 1649-1700).

Cabezas under Santiaguillo and Don Cebrián's Salineros (containing a few Tepehuanes) were together raiding and at Salinas del Machete, where the Cabezas were afterward. There they had contacted Chief Baltazar and the Baborimamas, and then planned to visit the Cíbolas of western Coahuila (a different group of Cíbolas from that which was located in Texas in the area of the confluence of the Conchos and Río Grande rivers) (AHP 1651A; AHP 1652Da). The Babozarigames had some contact, reportedly somewhat hostile, with a group called "Coahuilas," but there is no further information concerning who these people might have been. The Salineros at the Acatita battle had been led by Chief Santiaguillo, possibly the same Santiaguillo of the Cabezas (AHP 1652Ab). Coahuila bands, including Tusares, Tocas, Gueyapaes (Quaaguapaias), Tetecos, and Sipopolas, from the vicinity of Parras left the latter and joined rebel Salineros (AHP 1653Aa).

In 1653, from Atotonilco southward to Papasquiaro and Cuencamé, Salineros, Cabezas, Matarajes, Babozarigames, and Baborimamas were reported to be operating (AHP 1652Ba; AHP 1653Ae). Cabezas, Don Cebrián's group of Salineros, and the Mayos were together on one occasion at the Sierra de Zotole, and the Babozarigames had been with these some time previously. Later, the Cabezas attempted an alliance with the Cíbolas and Corcobados from out in the direction of Cuatro Ciénegas to join the Salineros to fight the Tobosos for the Spaniards. These Cabezas consisted of some 100 warriors, plus families, but it is unknown how many bands this term actually covered. Pies de Venado and Tusares had also joined this group, although not long afterward the Tusares were reported to be raiding the Spaniards at Parras again. A band of wild Salineros (*Salineros Bozales* — apparently unreduced) was also reported — and other groups occur with the Cabezas and their allies: Tatalcoyomes (pl. of Talcoyote), Ygoquibas, and Yguitoros (AHP 1653Ad).

In this same year Tobosos as well as Conchos were raiding in the Tarahumara country. Tobosos with Ocomes, Nonojes, "Salineros who are called Mamorimas" (Baborimamas), plus others, were in the Guapagua and Río Angosto region. The Baborimamas later broke off and were said to have gone to Cíbola territory, but they ended up with the Cabezas and others who were at Zotole; the Cabezas by this time were allies of the Spaniards. However, either this group or another called Baborimamas was not long afterward said to be with the Tobosos, Gavilanes, Nonojes, Acoclames, Ocomes, and Coyotes. The general region for all the latter groups was Río Angosto, Guapagua, Ocotán, and Las Encinillas (AHP 1652Ba; AHP 1653Ad; AHP 1653Ae).

Three "Toboso" women captured in this year at Río Angosto testified that the combined group at that place had contained Tobosos, Nonojes, Ocomites (Ocomes), and Gavilanes. Other bands may also have been included, of course; one of the deponents was a Masame, although she claimed she had always been with the Ocomes. Seemingly only six Tobosos (probably meaning adult males) were now left alive — ten had survived the battle of Nonolat, but four of these had later been killed at Río Angosto by the Salineros. There were only a few surviving Acoclames, Nonojes, Govosos, and Gavilanes, and no more information is given on the last two bands. Tobosos and Nonojes, however, had now joined the Ocomes. The Acoclames were stated specifically to be at Ocotán and apparently had not joined any of the other groups, according to one of the women (AHP 1653Ad).

The regular camp sites of the Ocomes were said to be at Conune, at Naciolcaguit — one and half days' travel from Jaque (and the same distance from Atotonilco) — and at Guapagua. Naciolcaguit had no

water, and moisture was obtained from the *lechuguilla* growing in the area. The Nonoje territory was in the area of Nonolat. The Cocoyomes, under Chief Mutat, lived farther to the east on the far side of Las Encinillas at Chosiguat, a place that lacked water in the dry season. The Baborimamas, who had joined the "Toboso" bands after the Nonolat battle, dwelt to the east on the far side of Río Angosto and were still in touch with the "Tobosos." The Tusares of the Parras area, a nation consisting of forty to fifty braves under five chiefs, and several rancherías called by different names, were friends of the Baborimamas. They were not, however, friends of the "Tobosos," who used to war with them in ancient times. The Chisos formerly carried on regular wars with the "Tobosos" at Jaque, and they and the nations living between Las Salinas Grandes and the Parral district had always been enemies of the "Tobosos" (AHP 1653Ad). The latter statement may refer to Salinero bands.

Other information rounds out some of this testimony. The Tusares were said to border the Cíbolas on the south, and on one occasion six Cíbolas from Cuatro Ciénegas went to Parral — which information to some extent helps place these groups geographically. Also, Chisos visiting Parral concurred with this testimony, stating that they were enemies of the Tobosos. However, more direct information obtained in Chiso country held that the majority of Chiso bands were friendly with the Tobosos. Chisos and Coyomes (Cocoyomes) were said to be intermarried (AHP 1652Aa; AHP 1653Ad; AHP 1653Bb; AHP 1653Bd).

The declarations of these three women for the most part are not too clear, but a little new information came forth when they were questioned about the alliances in past raids. They told of one attack when a certain Francisco del Castillo had been killed, and said the assailants had been Nonojes, Acoclames, and Coyotes or Cocoyomes — one woman said "Coyotes," another "Cocoyomes," and the third simply "others," which would seem to indicate that this was the same group. Recounting an attack on Atotonilco, one woman offered three new band names that do not occur elsewhere: Babosaricas (Babosarigames), Mamisas (Mamorimamas or Baborimamas?), and Onat; another gave the term Tatamulis. The last two are possibly Toboso variants of "Salinero" or "Coahuileño" — names already encountered — but from the context it is impossible to determine to what groups they might refer. The declarant who gave the term "Tatamulis" also mentioned the Ocomes, apparently excluding these two groups from mutual identification. A later witness (Antón) mentioned the Baborimamas on this same raid, which lends support to the interpretation that the Mamisas were Baborimamas. The latter had been allied with Ocomes and Gavilanes in a raid on Los Charcos some three years earlier (AHP 1653Ad).

These same women gave a rundown on the "Toboso" chiefs. Two mentioned the Toboso captain, Cristóbal, as a man of great reputation. The third woman, the only one who referred to a Nonoje chief, called the latter Cristóbal, but did not mention the Tobosos. (From Antón's declaration — see following paragraph — there was another Chief Cristóbal besides Zapata, who apparently was killed at the time Antón was captured.) This seems to corroborate a very close association between the Tobosos and Nonojes. Only one of the women gave the name of the current Acoclame chief, Jaunaljipil (or Jaunalpipil) (Brazos Chicos?); she also mentioned another chief, Ymutacari, but did not know to what nation he belonged. The Gavilán captain, Chapsani, who died at Río Angosto (this may have been "El Gavilán,"), had the greatest fame among them, and he had now been replaced by his brother. Bartolo (also called Taribiquic), the Coyote chief, had died in the same battle. Two of the declarants did not know if the famed chief Casa Zavala "the elder" (Nonoje) had been killed at Río Angosto or not; the other stated that he was still alive. All three declared that "his son" had been killed at Nonolat (AHP 1653Ad).

Shortly after these interrogations, Antón, the son of Zapata captured by the Salineros at Guapagua, was questioned. His father, Cristóbal Zapata, was the only Toboso left alive, having missed death because he had been with the Nonojes at Las Encinillas at the time the Tobosos had been attacked. All the rest of the Tobosos had been killed either at Nonolat or at Río Angosto. There were, however, four persons — half Toboso, and half Nonoje — whom Antón considered to be Nonojes. The Nonoje band itself consisted of only some twelve or fourteen warriors. Francisco Casa Zavala and his "three sons" — at another time he said "one son" — had been captains of this band, but they had died at Nonolat (contradicting the statements of the three women). The Nonojes were now led by Pupuye, grandson of Casa Zavala, and were still located at Las Encinillas (AHP 1653Ad).

The Acoclames consisted of twenty warriors and were situated on the far side (*más adelante de*) of Jaque. Their last chief had died of an illness, and they were now led by a youth named Espinazo de Culebra. The Ocomes and Gavilanes, Antón estimated, totaled some thirty-four braves, although in another place he said he did not know how many there were. In effect this was a single nation but was called the Gavilanes because the chief had been named El Gavilán. Since the latter's death at Río Angosto, this group had been captained by El Zurdo, who on one occasion was said — by Antón — to be El Gavilán's "son" and on another "his nephew." El Zurdo was now considered the head chief of all the "rebels who are still in revolt." These Ocomes and Gavilanes were located at a water hole between Jaque and Río Angosto (AHP 1653Ad).

Other nations seemed to be less well known to the declarant. The Cocoyomes (Coyomes) and others called — in his tongue — Hijos de las Piedras and Hijos de la Pared (Hijos de los Palos? — this is the only occurrence of *Pared*, "wall") were partly at Ocotán and partly north of Río Angosto. In another place Antón stated that all three bands were together deep in the hinterland. In still another section he said that the Cocoyomes had held a convocation with the Chisos, although he did not know the outcome. He was also ignorant of how many people these bands contained, as they had not been with the Tobosos all of the time, but had participated in some raids with them. He estimated, however, that more members were in these groups than in the ones he had already cited, because they had not taken part in the battles that had decimated the others. At any rate, these bands were the only allies of the Tobosos. Other nations farther out in the back country were their enemies and had caused them a good bit of damage. Antón denied that his group had any contact with the Baborimamas, except that one of the latter was living with them at this time. The Baborimamas had joined the Ocomes for raids, however (AHP 1653Ad).

Apparently most of these bands were fairly small, and if the Salinero Moranta's opinion reflects at all the general situation, then the Gavilanes under El Zurdo posed the biggest threat at this time. The Cocoyomes, Hijos de las Piedras, and Hijos de los Palos seem to have been located farther away from Spanish settlements than the Nonojes and Acoclames, although, of course, these groups had been involved in some action against the Spaniards previous to this. One of the three Toboso women who testified stated that the Cocoyomes often went around with the Aco-clames and Nonojes (AHP 1653Ad). In another de-claration a short while later, it was said that the Tobosos, Acoclames, and Nonojes had always been together (AHP 1654Ac). Now, Nonojes, Ocomes, Acoclames, Cocoyomes, and apparently the Hijos de las Piedras and Hijos de los Palos were fairly closely allied (AHP 1653Ad).

If the Ocomes and Gavilanes were not the same band, as previously testified, they certainly were closely associated at this time. El Zurdo was referred to as the chief of one or the other (AHP 1653Ab; AHP 1653Ad). Six Ocomes and Zapata, the sole or one of the few surviving Tobosos, testified in Parral at the end of October, 1653. They claimed at this time that the several bands had split up, which likely was necessary because of the time of year and the dimin-ishing food resources. Casa Zavala and his Nonojes were by themselves, except for the twelve Acoclames left alive (probably plus some women and children) who, it was thought, had probably joined them. Shortly afterward, a small band of Acoclames was devastated at Las Encinillas — eight or ten men and a woman were killed, four females were taken prisoner, and three persons escaped. If the previous informa-tion is correct, the Acoclames should have been just about wiped out with this last blow. Casa Zavala and the Nonojes were at Jaque at this time, which was apparently not far from Las Encinillas. The Coco-yomes and another unnamed band, both said to have many children, were reported to "assist" all the rebel groups (AHP 1653Ab). Not long after, three Coco-yomes testified in Atotonilco that their people had had nothing to do with any of the hostilities; their territory was one hundred fifty leagues from the Parral district (AHP 1654Ac).

The foregoing statements are conflicting with re-gard to the number of Tobosos alive at this time, although later evidence suggests that the larger figures are the more nearly correct. Unfortunately, there is no way of determining whether or not the name was being used in a generic sense. In the incident at Ato-tonilco in 1654 when the "Tobosos," apparently with a good number of Ocomes and/or Gavilanes had fled to their own country, it was stated — or at least indi-cated — by the Indian Diego Cestín who had been left behind, that there were still some actual Tobosos with the Ocomes and Gavilanes. A Toboso woman questioned at this same time claimed there were nine-teen surviving Tobosos. All of these people, Tobosos,

Gavilanes, and Ocomes, including those at Atoton-ilco, were on their way to Guapagua, said to be the territory of the Tobosos and Salineros (AHP 1654Ac). Later, the Spanish governor wrote that the Tobosos had withdrawn from Atotonilco to join their allies the Ocomes, Ajocames (Acoclames), Hijos de las Piedras, Coyotes, and Gavilanes (AHP 1718Ab).

At this same time the Cocoyomes as well as a small band of Coyotes were said to be with the Ocomes and Gavilanes. According to the declarant who gave this information, the Ocomes were such a large nation that they had two chiefs — Andrés and Juan Mapochi (also Mapoch or Mapuz — apparently Nahuatl for El Zurdo, "the left handed one": *maitl*, "hand," and *opoch* or *opochtli*, "left": Molina 1944; Barra y Valenzuela 1944). All these groups had plans for raid-ing the Spaniards; one band was to operate out of Baus in the Roncesvalles Mountains, another around Atocha, and the Tobosos in still a third but unstated area. The Hijos de las Piedras, who inhabited the area of the Ocotlan (Ocotan) Sierra, were also somehow involved in this. At any rate, they were said to have joined the Acoclames and Nonojes under Chief Casa Zavala in some of the recent raids in the Parral dis-trict (AHP 1654Ac).

Five more prisoners testified this same year. They had been captured during a skirmish with the enemy, considered to be Tobosos and Gavilanes, although this identification might have been in error. Each pris-oner gave a different band affiliation from the afore-mentioned, as well as different from each other — Ocome, Coyote, Sombrerete, Baborimama, and Tucu-muraga. The Baborimama had been raised partly at Tizonazo, but while he was still quite young his father had taken him back to Baborimama country. The Tucumuraga claimed he was actually a Salinero and had been baptized in the pueblo of Santa Ana, but since a small boy he had been out in the back country (*en estas partes*). Both the Baborimama and the Tucumuraga said they had relatives living at Ti-zonazo whom they had never seen. This information seems to point to ethnic connections with the "Sali-neros" (AHP 1654Ac).

Although these declarations are somewhat obscure at times, in essence it seems that there were two — possibly three — main groups of raiders. Each of these groups included several of the named bands, and the raiding territory of each seems to have been some-what distinct. One group, led by Casa Zavala, con-sisted of seven Nonojes and eight Acoclames, totaling sixteen braves with the chief included. Later a Mamite (Concho) woman, captured in September by a squad of Nonojes — apparently this group of Casa Zavala's — testified that for the greater part of the three months she had been held captive, these Nonojes had been dwelling near Jaque. Toward the end of her captivity, she had been forced to go with a small group to raid in the San Bartolomé Valley, and the camp at this time was maintained at the Sierra de San Felipe. Supposedly, it was with this group that the "Tobosos" who recently had fled from Atotonilco were going to join, according to the five prisoners mentioned above (AHP 1654Ac; AHP 1655Ab).

Closely associated with this Nonoje-Acoclame combine was a band of twenty men led by a Concho named Frasquillo. This band was composed of people from several nations, but unfortunately actual ethnic identity is not cited. On several occasions three individual Conchos are mentioned, the above Chief Frasquillo, plus a Juanillo and a Nicolasillo. These Conchos were said to be from El Valle (de San Bartolomé), either from Sunes' place (*lo de Sunes*) or from Los Corrales, and kept in constant touch with their relatives in these places. When raiding they traveled either by way of San Francisco or Los Peyotillos, always going in the direction of Las Minas de San Diego. Nicolasillo had his wife from the San Bartolomé Valley with him, but Frasquillo was married to a Nonoje woman. The group was allied with Casa Zavala's band, and it was added that they were all such good friends that they danced together. The total fighting force of these two groups was forty warriors, not counting the Tobosos from Atotonilco (AHP 1654Ac).

Another major alliance (the third, if the "Concho" are included as one) was under Chief Mapochi. This was made up for the most part of Ocomes, Gavilanes, and Baborimamas (the latter with under twenty warriors). Recently three other small groups — the Gordos, the Tucumuragas, and Imudagas (the latter with less than thirty braves) — had been raiding with the rebel "Tobosos," apparently principally associated with El Mapochi's people (AHP 1654Ac).

Other bands were also mentioned, but it is not clear from the testimonies how they were associated. The declarants seemed to hint at another major grouping, but this was very vague and no name of either band or chief was cited. In any event, there was apparently a certain amount of fluidity to these arrangements as the declarants described them. One

group of attackers in February, 1655, was known to have contained both Conchos and Gavilanes. One Indian was recognized, called El Zurdo, as well as a Concho from Los Corrales named Martín. These identifications were made by friendly Salineros (AHP 1654Ac; AHP 1655Ab).

Continuing with the same testimonies, the Coyotes and/or Cocoyomes, totaling somewhat over thirty warriors, seem to have been with both El Mapochi and Casa Zavala. The Coyote witness once stated that his chief was also a Coyote, and another time that he was under El Mapochi (Gavilán); he was probably thinking of different contexts when he made these two statements. The Hijos de los Palos and Hijos de las Piedras, numbering somewhat under thirty warriors together, are impossible to place here in their association with any of these alliances (AHP 1654Ac).

These groupings, the prisoners stated, had no alliance with the Chisos to the north, as the latter people did not leave their own territory — implying that they were at peace. The Salineros, Cabezas, and Conchos were their mortal enemies because of the deaths these nations had inflicted upon the "Tobosos" and their allies. At the same time, and interestingly enough, they mentioned the Tepehuanes, whom they described as a large nation two days' travel from Toboso country. These Tepehuanes had constantly refused to join them because they were "afraid," although El Mapochi and the Conchos allied with Casa Zavala had been able to induce a few to help in raids, by paying them (AHP 1654Ac).

Contrary to some of this testimony, however, was a report of an assault on Agua Escondida. Arrows discovered afterward indicated that Chisos, Acoclames, and Nonojes had been the culprits. Also, Chisos twice had attacked some Julimes at Ocotlán (AHP 1654Aa; AHP 1718Ab).

In 1655 a number of captive women reported that El Mapochi's group that had fought the Salineros at Tonalquisa had been made up of Ocomes, Nonojes, Hijos de las Piedras, Coyotes, Cocoyomes, Acoclames, Gavilanes, Colorados, and Gordos, plus some Conchos, all "mixed up." Apparently, almost half of the warriors of the above groups had been at Tonalquisa at this time. A day or so before the skirmish the rest of the men had left to raid in one or perhaps two squads, breaking off from the main party led by El Mapochi, which was estimated in one place to be made up of around one hundred fifty men. One of the squads was captained by Casa Zavala, who had many of the Nonojes with him, as well as men from the other nations. The second group mentioned as having left the main force seemingly was captained by Antonillo, the son of Zapata the Toboso. These declarations were not entirely clear, however, and one declarant indicated that only one party had separated from the rest, led by El Mapochi's nephew. Unfortunately, the latter's name and other details are not given (AHP 1655Ab). What does seem to be apparent, however, is that the back-country Indians had been operating on a fairly large scale.

Interestingly, the Acoclame chief, Brazos Chiquitos, was not mentioned as having been with this large group, which, according to the witnesses, had had the women and children along because they had planned on staying in the general area for an extended period of time. Although superficially it seems that almost all of the "western" desert Indians were now together, one prisoner declared that some persons had stayed behind at El Cerro del Diablo. And, the region where El Mapochi and these people were located had already been indicated in previous testimonies as being part of his particular alliance's territory. One female deponent claimed that the Indians — actually she named only the Gavilanes, Cocoyomes, and Hijos de las Piedras — had fought the Cíbolas and then in fear had fled their own territories, which may have been a factor in so many bands being together at this time. It is impossible to determine what truth there might have been to this, although the Cíbolas did complain about this time that an enemy, almost certainly "Tobosos," had been attacking them (AHP 1655Ab).

These same witnesses stated, however, that raiding in the Parral district was carried out by Casa Zavala's Nonojes and Brazos Chicos' Acoclames, now said to consist of "many people." Other bands or people often joined them, including Conchos, Julimes, and Chisos. Again, the Hijos de las Piedras were said to spend most of their time at Ocotán where there was permanent water, and at Sierra del Diablo, which was dry much of the year. One Gavilán said that they (his people?) dwelt usually at Sierra de Guapagua and Río Angosto. The Coyote (Cocoyome?) territory was reported to be the farthest away (AHP 1655Ab).

While the Chisos do not appear to have been involved to any great degree in raiding during these years, this is likely to be a bias of the documentary material, most of which originated in Parral, as well as the fact that these people inhabited a region rather distant from Spanish settlements. There were, however, general claims about the Chisos committing hostilities, and there is one direct testimony regarding a "Toboso"- Chiso alliance in the latter part of 1655. Chisos who testified in Parral at this time mentioned as many as seven bands of "Tobosos," although none of those who testified were certain of the names. Tobosos, Acoclames, and Nonojes were mentioned several times, and one Chiso gave three names that appear nowhere else in the documentary record. These were allies of the Tobosos and were called the Zamoi, the Chiles, and the Perros. Jaque was said to be the place where all these nations camped (AHP 1655Ab).

By this time the "Salineros" seem to have dropped pretty much out of the picture as raiders, for a while at least, judging from the affiliations of captured rebel Indians. Despite this, Spaniards felt that "Salineros" were actually engaged in hostilities and, as noted elsewhere, there were reports of collusion between "Salineros" and "Tobosos." From the larger picture over the last half of the seventeenth century, the latter seems to have been the case. Unfortunately, there is often not much specific information on the "Salineros." Certainly, many individuals belonging to the more southern groups were serving at this time as scouts and auxiliaries for the Spaniards — in one list of payment to Indians for military services the band names of Salineros, including those of Don Cebrián, and of Cabezas, Babozarigames, and Pies de Venado are recorded (AHP 1655Ab; AHP 1655Bb). However, at least individuals from the "Salinero" groups, as well as from other "tribes," such as Conchos and Julimes, did join the permanently rebel groups (AHP 1656 Aa).

In one incident when a small building on the hacienda of one Juan Leal was burned, a number of Salineros who worked on neighboring haciendas were implicated, but apparently nothing was actually proved (AHP 1656Ab). Nevertheless, the testimony of one Salinero woman is significant here. A certain Salinero "captain" had been trying for some time to get her to go off with him to his homeland. She claimed that she constantly refused because she knew that he and other Salineros were some of those who robbed and killed Spaniards. She added that she had witnessed that Salineros, Cabezas, Mayos, Cíbolas, and "Tobosos" would meet together at Tizonazo and afterward go out to raid. This woman also cited trade in stolen booty among these groups, particularly with the Cíbolas who would bring buffalo hides to exchange at Tizonazo. Some five years before this interrogation, she had seen El Mapochi, Casa Zavala, and Brazos Chicos together at Tizonazo (AHP 1655Ba; AHP 1656Ab).

In the last half of the 1650's, the general situation regarding what are called here the "Salinero" bands is rather obscure. Possibly these Indians had begun to adapt to some degree, as hacienda workers who often served as auxiliary troops, to life with the Spaniards. The Spanish practice was to settle a group or band under a chief at or near a hacienda or other installation where the Indians could work as laborers. Under these conditions such Indian groups would be in a situation of directed culture change, and it is unfortunate that the material consulted contains practically no information concerning the process of acculturation. It is uncertain how much contact these people had with the Spanish religious hierarchy, for example. Apparently, such groups maintained tribal identity for some time, judging from occasional references to them. Occasionally they made minor withdrawals, which the Spaniards often termed "revolts," although they did not go *en masse* to the back country to join the groups that dwelt there permanently.

One such case occurred with the Negrito (a Tepehuán rancheria) people located at the Núñez de Huidobro hacienda in the Indé area. In September of 1658, this group retired into the back country carrying out an almost complete evacuation, including the dogs and chickens. Only three Indians remained at the hacienda. Following the withdrawal the people broke up into three groups, going to Naisa, Mapimí, and El Gallo, although not long afterward they were all rounded up and brought back to their settlement. Some fled again. From the ensuing investigation, the whole affair did not appear to be very serious, although it caused a good deal of consternation to the Spaniards. The case is somewhat more complicated than that presented here. According to the Indians, on the first occasion, they had left merely to look for *tunas* (and other food). Then, because the Spaniards had become so concerned and because of their own fear of punishment, some had left the pueblo a second time. There was some communication at this time between these Negritos, who were under Chief Francisco Machado, and the Cabezas of Chief

Santiago who lived at El Canutillo. In any event, nothing came of the entire affair, and the Negritos eventually returned to their settlement (AHP 1658Ab).

Some eight years later, in 1666, a band of Negritos was reported living at Cuencamé. This was apparently the same band, as its governor's name was also Francisco Machado. A Tepehuán captive testified that at least some of the members of this group were in communication with and had assisted a band of the back-country raiders. Unfortunately, there is no further information regarding these Negritos, or why they changed their residence from Indé to Cuencamé (AHP 1658Ab; AHP 1669Ba). As noted in another section, these Cuencamé Negritos were also implicated in raids in 1670, but again the details are missing. At the latter date this group was simply indicted along with other hacienda and settled Indians — particularly Conchos and a group of Gavilanes from the Medrano hacienda (AHP 1670B).

Moving back to the "Tobosos," in the latter part of the 1650's a number of these rebel groups were still operating in the desert. One "Toboso" prisoner captured during a battle near Canatlán in 1658 revealed something of the nature of the situation at this time. He belonged to the "Acoclame and Nonoje nation" and had served on the hacienda of Juana de Aldaz, located near Atotonilco. Shortly before his capture he had been with the Ocomes, and three of his companions in this fracas had been Tobosos (AHP 1658Aa).

According to the prisoner's testimony, Zapata was still the chief of the Tobosos. The group was still small — it had only six warriors and was now incorporated with the Nonojes, who consisted of twenty-five warriors. From this witness's figures the Acoclames had shown an amazing increase in numbers, as they now had forty braves. The Cocoyomes and Gavilanes had so many people that he refused to attempt to make a count. He stated that for these two groups there were three captains, but it was El Mapochi whom they (all) obeyed. The places where these bands maintained their camps were Jaque, Sierra del Diablo, Sierra de Conune, and Las Encinillas; there was no water in the area between these places and the Florido River, except one small water hole on the far side of the Sierra de San Felipe en route to Conune. Unfortunately the Ocomes are not mentioned again in this testimony, but it is possible they were included with the Gavilanes. Also, in this same year of 1658, some Chisos reported they had killed all the inhabitants (five women, four men, and a few children) of a small rancheria of Nonojes and Acoclames located between the Sierras of Jaque and Conune (AHP 1658Aa).

From the evidence of the last years of this decade, some of the Salineros apparently were now fairly well settled. However, in the 1660's, there were rebel Salineros, often allied with "Tobosos," living in the back country regularly, and this was seemingly the case all through the previous years, which for the most part are a documentary blank. In 1661, Cíbolas and Salineros were raiding in the Parras area, as were several other Coahuileño bands such as Contotores, Tetecoras, Obaides, and Omoomas, said to live fifty leagues from Saltillo. Some of the "Salineros" were probably from Tizonazo, and Matarajes may have been included with them, since the inhabitants of this mission were at war at this time. Apparently some Cabezas were settled and living at Parras at this same time (AGN 1662; AHP 1662c; AHP 1667Aa).

In the latter part of 1666 a large, unidentified group of enemy Indians was operating in the region of El Peñol Blanco, nine leagues from Cuencamé (AHP 1669Ba). The next year, Salineros, Cabezas, Tobosos, Acoclames, Gavilanes, Nonojes, Ocomes, Cíbolos, and other nations were allied and working together. One combined group was reported around El Gallo and Acatita (Hackett 1926: 188-192; BL 1649-1700; DHM 1667a; DHM 1667b). Father Rodrigo del Castillo was captured this year by a combined force of 150 Cabezas and Tobosos. In his report of the episode he mentioned several subchiefs and a respectable old man, of unstated tribal identity, who was the head chief (Alegre III 1956: 89-91; AGN 1667).

A similar situation prevailed during the 1670's. Salineros and Cabezas were in revolt in 1671 and 1672. According to declarations by a Cabeza and a Baborimama in 1673, the rebel Cabezas were led by Bartolomé, the brother of Santiago (the same Santiago who was one of the Cabeza chiefs some twenty years earlier?), who was absent at this time visiting the Cíbolas. This group was allied with two other bands, the Baborimamas under Chief Don Pedro (Don Pedrote?), and the Mayos of Don Fabián. These three rancherias consisted of a total of thirty "Indians" (*indios*) — that is, adult males or warriors. They were said to be in contact and sometimes allied with El Mapochi and his "Tobosos," and also with

(other) Coahuileños. The Salineros, at least those from Tizonazo now in revolt, were also involved, although the picture is not very clear. The territory occupied included Las Ventanillas, Las Cañas, southward to include Acatita and Mapimí, and eastward to the Laguna district. To here they would repair when the (desert) fruits were ripe. This was the area they seemingly considered as "their territory." On some occasions Mapimí was employed as a base from which to raid, and the Spaniards held this as one of the major locations of the enemy. El Mapochi's people also occupied or raided out of part of this region. Salineros had gone as far north as Guajuquilla, and Cabezas and their associates had raided down to Guadiana (Durango) and to the east between Mazapil and Saltillo (AHP 1667B; AHP 1673Aa; AHP 1673Ab; AHP 1674Aa; AHP 1674Ab; AGN 1672).

A large portion of the Salineros, Cabezas, and Mayos were either captured, killed, or surrendered in the Mapimí mountains at the end of 1673 (AHP 1674Aa; BL 1649-1700). This may have been the "punishment" referred to in 1678 by the Jesuit Visitador, Ortiz Zapata, when he noted the repopulation of the Tizonazo mission with families from Sonora and Sinaloa by the Spanish governor after the latter had chastized the Salinero nation (AGN 1678). However, a number of the men were left, without families, and these were the ones who trekked from Cuatro Ciénegas the following year with Father Larios to attempt to get back their women and children (Portillo 1887: 80; BL 1674).

It was this devastation of the Salineros and their allies that caused the "Tobosos" to enter into peace negotiations at this time. The groups represented by the envoys afford some notion of the associates of the "Tobosos." Aside from the Tobosos proper, Ococlames (Acoclames), Guijacales (Guisacales, Quequesales from Coahuila, apparently), Cocoyos (Cocoyomes), and Hijos de las Piedras were mentioned. The Toboso bands of chiefs Juan Campos and Don Francisco (the son of Juan Mapochi? — BL 1693b) were to settle at San Francisco de Conchos, those of Juan Mapochi and Juan Galán at the site called Bernardo Gómez' place, and the people of Galeano at Baus. Unfortunately, the specific band affiliations of these chiefs were not made clear. Somewhat later, Babozarigames were also said to be submitting to peace. To the east in Coahuila about this same time, the Tetecoras, Guicales (Guisacales), Obayas, and Contotores who bordered the Cíbola nation were in rebellion. The chiefs of these nations testified in Cuencamé in December of the previous year (1673) that their peoples totaled 1000 persons (AHP 1674Aa; BL 1649-1700; BL 1709-1715).

Any peace obtained at this time was rather short-lived. In 1675, Salineros, Cabezas, and Mayos were again or still committing hostilities (Portillo 1887: 81-83; BL 1674). One thing that appears to stand out is that the Salineros and Cabezas were covering a wide range of territory and involved in alliances with a number of nations. Aside from their southern and western extension along the Nazas River to Tizonazo, and their raids as far south as Durango, they were also operating as far east as Mazapil and Cuatro Ciénegas — as already mentioned.

In 1675, more information becomes available on the eastern extension of these nations and their connections with other Coahuilan peoples. The Cabezas, now at Mapimí, had been in contact with the Guiquesales, a large and powerful nation in the east, as well as with other bands around the Río Grande. According to the Babozarigame chief (who said he had the Pies de Venado with him) testifying at Guadalupe, Coahuila, in April of this year, there were only nineteen Cabezas left — fifteen men and four old women (Portillo 1887: 94-96; BL 1674).

Although there is no attempt here to unravel the complexities of the tribal situation farther east, some information is given that seems to contribute to the interpretation of later data, including the make-up of the "Cabezas" at Parras in the 1690's. As previously mentioned, Cíbolas, Colorados, Babozarigames, Contotores, and others were operating in this area in 1675. However, a much more complete survey of these eastern groups comes from a letter written by Father Larios in Patos in January of this same year. This is a *memoria* of the nations that had rendered obedience to the Crown as of December 30, 1674, and who lived in the "Province of Coahuila de la Zibola and Cuatro Cienegas, the Rio del Norte and La Caldera." While many of these bands do not enter the picture directly here, they are cited to demonstrate the possible ramifications of tribal connections on the eastern border (Alessio Robles 1938: 232, 242).

Father Larios cites four major groups of bands and the chief that was over each group. The first was the Bobole chief, Juan de la Cruz, over the Boboles, Xicocosses, Jumanes, Bauanes, Yoricas, Xupulames, Xiancocadam, Yerguibas, and Bacaranan nations. The second was Don Esteban, a Hueyquetzal, over the

Hueyquetzales, Manos Prietas, Bacoram, Pinanacam, Cacaxtes, Coniares, Ovayas, Tetecoras, Contotores, Tocaymamares, Saesse, Teneymama, Codam, Guiguigoa, Eguapit, Tocamomom, Huhuygam, Doaquioydacam, Cocuytzam, Aquitadotdacam, Babury, Dedepo, Seromet, and Teymamares. The third was Don Fabián, apparently a Mayo, and the same Don Fabián cited in other contexts. The nations that followed him but who also recognized Don Esteban as *Capitan General* were the Mayoes, Babusarigames, Bamarimamares, Cabezas, Bauiamamares, Colorados, Pies de Venado, Igoquib, and Toques (Toocas). The last group was under Chief Don Miguel and was composed of Catujanes (Catujanos), Bahaneros, Chacahuales, Toarmas, Masiabes, Madmedas, Mabibit, Milihaes, Apes, Pachaques, Tilihay, Garafes, and Mexcales (Allesio Robles 1938: 232, 242).

From other sources, these were nations that had just surrendered to the Spaniards at the city of Nuestra Señora de Guadalupe, Nueva Estramadura. These included Chief Esteban of the Gueicosales (Hueyquetzales) who spoke for his people and their allies — Manos Prietas, Bocoras, Siaexer, Pinanacas, Escabaca, Cacaxtes, Cocobiptas, Cocomaques, Oodames, Contotores, Colorados, Babiamares, and Taimamares. These people, they reported, were or had been enemies of the Yrbipias and said they had never trusted the Cabesas and Babosarigames. The Catujanos and their friends — Tilijaes, Apes, Jumees, Pachaques, and Toamares — also requested peace at this time (Portillo 1887: 77-78, 80-82).

Some two weeks after the arrival of Esteban and the other envoys, another group arrived of Queiquesales, Bapacorapinanacas, Espopolames, and Manos Prietas, led by Chief Pablo of the latter nation. They told of a skirmish their peoples had had with the Yrbipias, in which they had taken three women of the Yoricas and Bapocares nation from them. These nations also requested to settle with Don Esteban (Portillo 1887: 85).

In March, more envoys from the Catujanos, Apes, and Tilijaes were back at Guadalupe. In the latter part of April the Catujano chief Miguel brought in some 395 persons, including some from the Bajanes, Pachaques, and Jumees bands, while Chief Pablo of the Manos Prietas brought in 232 persons. These Indians were to be settled at the town of San Miguel de Luna, at the city of Guadalupe. With regard to location of the Manos Prietas and associates, a statement here reads ". . . de la nasion manos prietas y las mas de la asistencia del rio del norte . . . " (Portillo 1887: 91, 96-106).

In May of the same year, a group of Jeapes and Yoricas were said to be found some four leagues north of the Río Grande, while in December of 1674 the Yoricas, Gicocoges, and Boboles were reported at the Río de las Sabinas. Also, north of the Río Grande, some three leagues, Fernando del Bosque's expedition discovered the chief of the Bibit and of the Jumee, at the place of San Vicente Ferrer, plus six Indians from the Pinanacas, Xaeser, Teneimamar, and Gueiquesale nations. Four leagues farther north they met the Xoman, Tereodan, Teaname, and Tumamar; Chief Salvador and some of his Babosarigames were encountered near the Ciudad de Guadalupe (Portillo 1887: 70-72, 113, 116-120, 127-128).

Salineros, Ocomes, Cocoyomes, Acoclames, Gavilanes, Hijos de la Tierra, Hijos de las Piedras, and Hijos de los Palos were all raiding during 1677. According to Sergeant Major Valerío Cortés, a man of some thirty years experience in Nueva Vizcaya and with many intimate contacts with the local natives, there were three or four major alliances. The Salineros had banded with the Ocomes, Cocoyomes, and Coyotes to form one group. The Gavilanes made up a second, independent group. Tobosos, Nonojes, and Acoclames constituted a third, although they were much fewer in number than the other two, owing to past hostilities (apparently still feeling the blows they had received in the 1650's?). Cortés also mentioned the Hijos de la Tierra, Hijos de los Palos, and Hijos de las Piedras bands, which comprised a good many people among them. Apparently, he thought of these as a fourth group, although this is not entirely clear and he may have considered them as associated with the Toboso alliance. From his first hand experience with these bands he estimated that all together they would have about three hundred warriors. If Cortés' information was reasonably accurate, and not merely perpetuated myth from the 1650's, this indicates a good bit of continuity for the previous twenty years. Another witness at this time told of an encounter in which Salineros, Cabezas, Ocomes, and Cíbolas had been allied. The now famous leader, El Mapochi, was reported operating in the general area (AHP 1677A).

In 1678, Sierra Osorio stated that eleven Toboso nations dwelled east of the Parral-Guadiana highway. They were all designated "Tobosos," since this nation was the bravest of them all. In his post-1683 writing, Osorio stated that the "Tobosos" comprised twelve

nations (Hackett 1926: 210-224). In 1682, Acoclames and Cocoyomes participated in a relatively short settlement at Covadonga (AHP 1722Ba; BL 1723-1724; AGN 1683). Prior to this a group of "Tobosos," possibly involving the Toboso proper, had been settled at San Francisco de Conchos, some time before 1678 (Hackett 1926: 210-224).

Chisos were cited little in the records until the 1684 Revolt, except for a number in 1673 who went to live at San Francisco de Conchos (AHP 1673Ac). At the time of the Revolt and for many years before, they had joined the Tobosos on occasion for raiding. With the 1684 uprising there occur a number of specific Chiso band names — Batayolicla, Cacuitataome (who lived on the Río Grande), Chacuiyacua, Chichitames or Chichitamen, Chisos (apparently also a specific band), Cototoholome (or Totoholome), Guesecpayolicla (with several variants) or the people from the land of Las Auras, Osataba (or Osatabay, Osatapa, or Osatames), Osatayoliclas, Seuliyoliclas, and Tonmamal (or Tunmamal). Particularly the Chisos, Chichitames, and Osatayoliclas are cited together (see Appendix 1) (AHP 1684Aa).

One statement seems to refer to a general distribution of the Chisos, although there is a specific prior reference to the Chichitames and Osatayoliclas (who were often mentioned together) —"the Indians who are called Chichitames and Osatayolic who are all designated as Chisos . . . and that these said Indians live on the San Pedro River and in their own country on the other side of the Río del Norte [Río Grande]." Occasionally Osatames and Osatayoliclas appear to be the same group, but more often they are mentioned by witnesses as two separate bands. Chisos, Chichitames, Osatayoliclas, Osatames, Guesecpayoliclas, Cototoholomes, and Tonmamal were reported to have joined the "Tobosos" for raids (AHP 1684Aa).

Two years later, in 1686, the permanently rebel groups of Tobosos, Cocoyomes, Cabezas, and Salineros are mentioned together with other Indians such as Julimes, Oposmes, and Tarahumaras (hacienda workers), as joining forces for a raid at Papasquiaro. Juan Mapochi was cited on this occasion as one of the chiefs, and again the following year in conjunction with some six other chiefs, apparently of rebels from Tizonazo, with a large combined force that made an attack near El Gallo. At the latter time El Mapochi was reported to have commanded about one-half of the men involved. At least some of the people from

Tizonazo were Cabezas. The Cocoyomes, Cabezas, and others were reported at locations of Sierra del Diablo, Sierra de la Cadena, Acatita, and Mapimí; and one rancheria of Tobosos and Gavilanes was encountered some fifty leagues from Parral in the hinterland. "Tobosos" may have been communicating with both the "Salineros" and the "Chisos" in 1688. Cocoyomes, Gavilanes, and Hijos de las Piedras were camped together at Guapagua, where they were attacked by Retana. Tobosos, Salineros, Cabezas, Chisos, Chichitames, and Cholomes were reported fighting or raiding Spaniards during this year (Hackett 1926: 250, 254-256; AHP 1686Bb; AHP 1686Bc; AHP 1687AB; AHP 1688Cb; BL 1649-1700; BL 1693-1702; UTD 1683-1697).

Farther east, in the previous year of 1687, a number of nations were reported raiding in the general Coahuila area — from Nadadores and Cuatro Ciénegas southward to around Mazapil, at least. In one place three chiefs — Don Pedrote, Don Bartolo, and Don Santiago — were reported to be the leaders of rebels camped at Baján. Don Pedrote was later said to be the head chief with twelve nations under him: Colorados, Tocas (Itocas), Odames, Dedepos (Idedepos), Cabezas, Pies de Venados, Iboquiba, Conianes, Bajamares, Sodomamares, Bidamamaras, Quechales, Manos Prietas, Bocoras, and Maqualistacas. These people on at least one occasion had been allied with the "Tobosos." Contotores were also on the warpath at this time (Portillo 1887: 187, 190-195).

The Quechales, or at least some of them, were at peace at the Nadadores mission but were secretly friendly with Don Pedrote's group. The "Tobosos" and Colorados lived in the "western" part of the area. These rebels were trying to get the Indians at the Calderas mission, made up of two bands, one the Cacafes and the other unspecified, to join them. Pedrote's group also kept in touch with the Pies de Venado at the Contotores mission (Portillo 1887: 195-196, 201-203, 205-206).

Don Bartolo's people (who?) and some Colorados showed up together at the Nadadores mission in March of 1688. With the uprising soon after this, the Quechal chief, Don Dieguillo, was reported to have under his command the Colorados, Pies de Venados, Cabezas, Conianes, and Manos Prietas (the latter at least were from the Nadadores mission) as well as the Quechales. Terocodames (said to be "relatives" of the

Cabezas — AGN n.d.) and Bocoras were also involved, and possibly the Boboles, as were the Herbipiamos and Jumanes (Portillo 1887: 201-223, 237-238).

It is quite evident that the entire area from Coahuila to Parral was the region over which the desert Indians roamed. The previous year an Indian belonging to "one of the nations that fled from Tizonazo" was interrogated. He gave a run-down on the rebels, apparently "Salineros" and/or "Cabezas." He named several of the chiefs, apparently seven. These were Don Fiscal (also called Don Felipe), Don Pedro, Don Francisco Sunuri (also Sunora), Don Bartolo Sinarvee, Don Martín, El Baquero, and another called Don Pablo. These people had been in the vicinity of El Gallo and had carried out a raid with the people of El Mapochi, after which they had gone all together to the Sierra de la Cadena (apparently near Mapimí). Then Don Fiscal, Juanillo (the first time this name appears), and Sunora had split off and had gone to the Sierra del Diablo. Eight nations had been camped in front of the Sierra de la Cadena. While all of these chiefs cannot be identified with regard to nation, Don Pedro was apparently Don Pedrote of the Cabezas and Don Fiscal was Don Felipe El Tuerto, chief of the Gavilanes and known from other sources to be called Don Fiscal (AHP 1687Ab; BL 1693b).

Later, during the Spanish campaign in pursuit of these rebels, upon inspecting tracks leading toward Mapimí, Acatita, and Cuatro Ciénegas, the same informant opined that the Cabezas under chiefs Sinarvee and Don Bartolo had probably gone to Cuatro Ciénegas. The Cocoyomes of Francisco El Tecolote and the people of Don Pedro, apparently Cabezas, lived around Mapimí and Acatita (BL 1693B).

By 1691 the Cabezas under Don Pedrote had gone to Parras to settle. According to the testimony of a Spanish captive of the Cocoyomes, this was sometime in 1689, although it may have been a little later (BL 1694-1698). The baptismal and other records at Parras for this Cabeza band do not begin until 1693 (Parras Parish Archives).

The year 1691 also marked the end of the Gavilán band. In a skirmish in December, most of the Gaviláns were killed or taken prisoners, the prisoners being mainly women and children. Four or five men escaped, including Chief Felipe El Tuerto, and joined the Cocoyomes, Jojocomes (Ocomes), Acoclames, and "Hijos" bands (the Piedras being closely associated with the Acoclames), seemingly the only

"Tobosos" now left. However, in 1693 Governor Pardiñas referred to the Tobosos as though they were still a separate band, but in the supporting testimony to his letter no specific Toboso group is mentioned (BL 1693b).

It is in this decade that the Cocoyomes begin to predominate as leaders among the western desert nations, although for a short while the Ocomes also remained important. In the middle of 1691, Don Francisco El Tecolote was considered the most powerful of the rebel chiefs, together with Contreras and another man named El Julime. One captive in this year stated that the Cocoyomes had considered getting the Hijos de las Piedras, Chichitames, and Chisos as allies to attack the El Gallo presidio. El Tecolote's Cocoyomes were using the mountains of Jicorica and El Diablo, and Moba (Mobana?) as camping grounds, although for most of the time that one ex-captive had been with them, about six months, they had been in the Nazas River area. The Gavilanes were said to use the Sierra del Diablo also as a base (BL 1693b).

A Satayolila (Satayolicla) Indian gave a run-down this year (1691) on the desert nations. He belonged to the rancheria of Don Santiago that ordinarily camped at the Ciénega de Santiago and often joined Chichitames and Chisos for raiding. Now seven nations were banded together — the Satayolilas, Chisos, some Chichitames, Guasipayoles (Guesecpayoliclas), Hijos de la Tierra, Hijos de las Piedras, and the Cocoyomes of El Tecolote. Later he added that the Acoclames were also involved. A Tepehuán woman captive told that the group included Gavilanes under El Tuerto. The Spanish governor claimed that the Gavilanes were the principal allies of the Cocoyomes (BL 1693b).

This seven-nation alliance had been convoked apparently by the Cocoyomes of El Tecolote, as a great dance had been held when they had arrived. The Cocoyomes were interested in such an alliance because, as they had stated, their "backs were not secure" owing to the Cabezas at Parras, now settled in peace and consequently enemies of the Cocoyomes. They feared that the Cabezas would lead the Spaniards to them so they did not now dare to go into the Baján area. At the "friendship" ceremony, it had been sworn that the seven groups would be "like brothers" in their mutual defense against the Spaniards. They planned to have the bands split up but to keep within a short distance of each other for mutual

assistance in the event of battle. El Tecolote had also advocated taking possession of the Camino Real to assault wagon and pack trains, promising much booty to the other bands. The Satayolilas, Chisos, and Guisipayoles refused, although the two Hijos groups and the Chichitames agreed (BL 1693b).

The Satayolila continued. El Tecolote had many men with him, plus a number of arquebuses and two cueras. One of his men had a white left eyebrow (ceja), apparently the chief later known as Ceja Blanca. The other nations were afraid of the Cocoyomes because of all of the men in the band, although later it was indicated that it was the "Tobosos" in general whom the Chiso groups "feared." The Cocoyomes could and did call the bands (gentes) together in convocation when they desired because they were always laden with booty. On the occasion of the alliance meeting the Cocoyomes had had a great quantity of cattle (vacas) and some horses with them. The witness opined that they had come this time from an area where there were palm trees (palmas) because they had a great many with them with which they used to make petates (BL 1693b).

He also reported that the Acoclames were the happiest with this new alliance because there were now only fifty or sixty of them left — the band having been decimated in the many years of warfare. These Acoclames were particularly angry with the Indians (including Tobosos) at San Francisco de Conchos because of all the damage the latter — as Spanish auxiliaries — had done to them (BL 1693b).

Cocoyomes, Gavilanes, Acoclames, Hijos de las Piedras, and Nonojes were represented in the group of envoys who went to Parral in March of 1692. Possibly the Acoclames and Hijos de las Piedras were now rather closely associated; at least on this occasion they were represented by the same envoy. More interesting, however, is the fact that one of these persons was said to be a Nonoje, a group that had not been mentioned for a number of years (BL 1693b).

From subsequent information, the Acoclames in effect were closely associated with the Hijos de las Piedras and Hijos de la Tierra, and eventually all three were thought to have gone to Chiso country, "to the ancient union that they have with the Chisos and their allies." By August of 1692, after the peace negotiations, the Cocoyomes had returned to the desert. Some twenty-eight "Tobosos," largely Gavilanes, although possibly including a few others, were at

Conchos. A few Gavilanes were out with the Coco-yomes (BL 1693b).

Around November a band of fifty-seven Jojocomes (Ocomes) under Lorencillo Sau Muyaget, also called Lorenzo Delgado, with his chiefs Alarconsillo and Juan Sombrero Prieto, were met by Spanish author-ities in the Sierra de Almoloya for purposes of peace making. In a *diligencia* of November 23, Pardiñas stated that these Jojocomes were one of the principal nations, the most respected of them all for their brav-ery. Owing to this, the Cocoyomes, who about this time were at Guajoquilla, would probably follow their example in surrendering. Furthermore, the Jojo-comes had stated they would request the nations of the north (apparently Chisos and Cholomes) to make peace, or else they would assist the Spaniards in mak-ing war against them. Lorenzo then went to get El Tecolote, and another man was sent to the Aco-clames, Hijos de la Tierra, and Hijos de las Piedras (BL 1693b).

In a passage that is not altogether clear, Lorenzo declared that the reason the band of Don Juan (Sombrero Prieto?) had not (yet?) come in "was and is because of the said Don Juan having fallen ill with smallpox because he was in danger of dying but that in any event his people will come in." It was said (seemingly by Lorenzo) that many of the Jojocomes had never been among Spaniards before. At the same time, the ancient town of the Cocoyomes and of the people of Don Lorenzo (Jojocomes) was reported to be Atotonilco (BL 1693b).

A seventeen-year-old captive also gave his story. He had been taken prisoner when very young by the Cabezas, who at that time were allied with the Coco-yomes and other rebel nations. When the Cabezas had made peace with the Spaniards they had given the captive to a Jojocome named Pedro. Since that time, he had always remained with the Jojocomes, who at certain periods would go to the Nazas River, Acatita de Baján, and Las Ventanillas, but beyond these points they never passed. From them they would come to the Parral area. When they went out to raid they were accompanied by the Cocoyomes, the worst of all the nations, who were acquainted with the whole land and southward to Nieves and Sombrerete, from where they would bring horses and other items. Such raiding was easier to carry out in this latter region "because the Cocoyomes would say that from *tierra afuera* they could obtain them [horses] with-out risk" (BL 1693b).

El Tecolote was reported to have been with the Hijos de las Piedras and the Hijos del Lodo at Jaque. At this time these bands had been visited by Don Santiago El Chiso, also called Conulayaca. Actually, Jaque, Agua de Terrazas, and El Venado, lay roughly on the "Chiso"-"Toboso" border. To the north, and probably with some contact with the Tobosos, were Chichitames, Cíbolos (north of the Río Grande), Cholomes, Batayolicuas, and Solinyolicuas, who according to reports did not plan on making peace during this year, 1692. According to Lorenzo the Jojocome, the Cocoyome Lorenzo had declared that the Chichitames, Batayolicuas, and Cholomes were holding a get-together on the far side of the Sierra de Ocotán at a place called Cuerno de Venado. Lorenzo himself was bringing in some twenty-seven men and women, but few children (BL 1693b).

In December of 1692 Governor Pardiñas, on reviewing a number of the "invasions" by enemy Indians in the previous seven months, ordered that declarations be taken from some of the Cocoyomes who had met the Spaniards at the place of Santa Cruz (where?). At this time Pardiñas stated that the Coco-yomes "have the most influence among the nations in the area (*parte*) to the north in order to multiply their number when they are at war . . . ." The first to testify was Chief Lorenzo, now called the "gover-nor." He recounted his visit to Jaque where he had found Don Francisco Tecolote with the Hijos de las Piedras, Hijos de la Tierra, and some Chisos. El Tecolote had had these people convinced, he said, to go to the Spaniards to make peace. The governor of the Jojocomes was also coming in to surrender. According to Lorenzo, Chief Don Juan (Sombrero Prieto) had died of smallpox (this is possibly the same reference as previously given, where El Tecolote was supposed to have died from the same cause). Lorenzo admitted that a few of his people had done some raiding but that most assaults had been carried out by Chisos. The Hijos de las Piedras, Chichitamés, and Sonololilas had declared in the meeting of nations at Jaque that they were awaiting people from the north in order to send some large squads into the Parral district by way of Tabalaopa (BL 1693b).

Lorenzo testified that he understood from the elders of his band the reason peace had been broken so many times in the past was the mistreatment and oppression they had undergone at the hands of the Spaniards, including those whom they had worked for. However, he remembered during his own time in "his pueblo" of Atotonilco that the Julime governor, Don Hernando de Obregón, had once told them that the Spaniards had hanged their chief who had gone to Parral. The people uprose but later learned that the news had been false. They were on their way back to Atotonilco but first had gone to Parral to give obedience to the Spanish governor. The latter had made prisoners of Juan Mapochi, his son Don Francisco, Galeano, Alarcón, "and many others of the said nation" and had executed them (1674?). With this the remainder had withdrawn to the Sierra del Diablo and had maintained themselves in open war ever since. Later, when El Tecolote was governor, having taken over at the deaths of the aforementioned chiefs, he went with his people to Parras when Indians from this town had come to see them about making peace. They stayed at Parras for over a year, after which time the Spanish governor, Bartolomé de Estrada (1682), had settled them at Covadonga del Peñol Blanco. However, the Spanish captain Antonio Rodríguez de Cangas, their "protector," had treated them badly, so they had withdrawn to the back country again (BL 1693b).

Lorenzo stated also that the Chichitames and Sonololilas were allied with the "Tobosos" who were in the process of surrendering at this time but that the Chichitames were angry with these "Tobosos." The Chisos and Sunilolilas communicated with and visited the camps of the "Tobosos" in the hinterland, but Lorenzo thought the Chisos and Satayolilas were about to make peace, as El Tecolote had conferred with them about it. When Santiago, the head chief of the Chisos, had agreed to this, the Chichitames had gotten up and left. Chiefs Juan de Ibarra and Juan de Contreras also spoke, supporting much of Lorenzo's testimony. They stated that the Gavilanes, who had been so sorely defeated the previous year, had been the most warlike (*mas militar*) of them all (BL 1693b).

Following this, Pardiñas appointed officials for the two groups. The Cocoyomes were placed under Don Lorenzo; the Jojocomes, whom the few remaining Gavilanes had joined, were put under the old Gavilán chief Don Felipe El Tuerto. The latter arrangement reflects the strong continuity in the old Gavilan-Ocome closeness. A possible further tie of the Ocomes (Jojocomes) with the Gavilanes is that in the 1650's reference was once made to a Gavilán chief named "Joxocomi" (AHP 1652Ac; BL 1693b).

During Retana's campaign to the confluence of the Conchos and Río Grande rivers in the middle of 1693, the Chisos were reported to have been raiding the La Junta pueblos. The Chichitames, Guasapagoliglas, and Sisimbles were in alliance together, but the Suninoliglas had separated and were now making peace. These bands had been raiding in various areas, including Coahuila. Representatives of the Suninoliglas and Batayoliglas appeared together before Retana at La Junta, and the two groups were given the old Tapacolme site on the river for settlement. The two nations were said to consist of 300 warriors, plus their women and children. This possibly indicates a rather close geographical relationship between the Suninoliglas and Batayoliglas (BL 1695a).

According to the report made to Retana at this time by these Indians, there were many "enemy" nations who were allies of the more southerly desert Indians. Their camp sites ran along both sides of the Río Grande down to the confluence of the Río Grande and Salado rivers (i.e., apparently, the Pecos). This was the territory of the Chisos which extended very close to Jaque. It was said to be an easy area to penetrate because there was no lack of water holes. During the cold season these peoples would move to the Río Grande-Salado confluence, living in a nearby mountain, where they would provision themselves with meat and hides from the buffalo they hunted there. The declarants judged this place to be about thirty leagues from both Coahuila and the confluence of the Conchos and Río Grande. The bands were most vulnerable to attack during the cold season, although Spaniards from Coahuila had battled them in this area on several occasions with little success, owing to the roughness of the terrain (BL 1695a).

At this time General Retana received a list of these nations. The order of occurrence of the names seems in part to reflect geographical distribution in a general sense, as some of the better-known Chisos groups near La Junta are cited first. However, it is doubtful that much can be inferred from this. The groups named were, in the following order, the "Chichitames, Sisimbles, Guasapayoliglas, Osatayoliglas, Hijos de la Tierra, Hijos de las Piedras, Acoclames, Tuimamar, Cholomes, Cococomesno, El Tecolote's people [who?], Cabezas Blancas, the people of El Pellejo Blanco, Guacales, Cabezas de Guacal, Colorados, the Enemigos del Serro, Bapacolani, Cucubipi, Curuipicas, Martaja Mesquite, Malas Flechas, the nation of El Pescado, Babimamar, Cotomamar, Los

Cocoyomes of El Tecolote, Gavilanes, and Toto-holomes . . . ." The report continued: ". . . all of the above nations they said were enemies, and allies of each other, who invade this kingdom [of Nueva Vizcaya] and the outland [*tierra afuera*] around the area of Parras and Coahuila, the majority being those that withdraw to the said *junta* of the [Salado and Río Grande] rivers in the cold season for the killing of buffalo cattle . . . ." Two other bands – the Vívoras and the Bamichicoame (possibly "Sibolas"?) are cited about this same time in the Río Grande area (BL 1695a) (see Appendix 4 for a comparison of this list with that given by Marín in the same year).

Later in this year the Chiso, Bartolomé de Estrada (listed among Retana's auxiliary troops as being from San Lucas and consequently probably a Cacuita-taome), brought into the Conchos presidio 104 Chisos belonging to the Chichitame, Osatayoligla, Guasapayoligla, and Sisimble bands. From them Retana learned that the Acoclames, Hijos de las Piedras, and Hijos de la Tierra, with chiefs Don Juan Cola de Coyote and Alarcón, were camped three days' journey from the Peñol of Santa Marta. The usual territory of these groups lay between this camp site and the "Sierra of Xacue and Las Encinillas . . . ." The Indians also stated that El Tecolote and a few of his Cocoyomes were located at the Jaque mountain, and that Lorencillo and Contreras were with the rest between Acatita La Grande and Guapagua (Hackett 1926: 342-348; BL 1695a).

The Chisos apparently had moved down from the Río Grande, as in a statement of September 25 it was noted that all the rest were on their way to San Francisco de Conchos, except a few sick and wounded who had stayed near the river. By October 7, 101 warriors and 184 women and children were at Conchos (a total of 285 persons); another forty-three warriors and their families were still at Ocotán – some who were said to be sick. On October 28, another twenty-eight warriors and seventy-four *chusmas* were on the road to Conchos. This left, according to the Spaniards, some fifteen warriors still in the desert. The Indian envoy at Conchos at the time explained this delay by the fact that just before he had gotten to Ocotán, messengers from another group of Sisimbles had also arrived. These had told the Sisimbles at Ocotán to join them in order to take vengeance on the Cotomamar nation who had deceived their group and had handed over to the Spanish military in Coahuila eleven warriors plus many women and children. The Spaniards had executed eight of the men. The missing fifteen warriors had departed from Ocotán before the envoy's arrival, although they had left word that they would go to San Francisco de Conchos as soon as they had returned from the Cotomamar affair (BL 1695a).

Retana commanded that more information on these Coahuila Sisimbles be secured, stating in his order that these peoples " . . . were living immediate to Coahuila at the spring of water where a river is formed in the company of the Cotohomamar nation . . . ." At this same time a Sisimble chief named Bartolomé testified that " . . . he had never seen the *capitán* of Coahuila nor the some fifty of his people who have lived with him in the environs of the Río del Norte about four days' journey from Coahuila [that is, the town] . . . [but] . . . he knows . . . that some Indians (*yndios*) of his Sisimble nation were related (*emparentados*) and mixed up (*rebueltos*) with the Cotomamar nation and that these live one day's journey from Coahuila on a river that is formed by a spring of water and that they are at peace although they do not have a minister, and that a short while after I [Retana] attacked them at the Peñol de Santa Marta this declarant learned from a messenger who arrived to them from one of those who had escaped [from Coahuila], how the Captain of Coahuila in the company of Don Diego Valdez, governor of Nadadores, had gone with soldiers to the place where the Cotomamar nation was, and they battled (*entresacaron*) the Sisimbles and killed (*apelotearon*) some eight of them, taking away the women, children, and three young bucks as prisoners, and that for a long time his [the declarant's] relatives [the Sisimbles] had lived with the Cotomamar nation under the protection of the Spaniards . . . ." (BL 1695a).

Of the four Chiso nations at San Francisco de Conchos – Chichitames, Osatayoliglas, Guasapayo-liglas, and Sisimbles – the Franciscan Gabriel Montés de Oca sometime later certified that these consisted of over 400 persons and that he had baptized more than 244 of them, including 89 children. A subsequent report gave 401 "Chisos" at this mission, comprising 148 families. These figures are apparently in agreement with the number of persons in the four bands as given by the Chisos taken into Conchos by Estrada. At this time it was said that there were (seemingly referring to total numbers) thirty Chichi-tames, forty-two Osatayoliclas, thirty-eight Guasapayoliglas, and fifty Sisimbles. These were the numbers of warriors immediately following the count, it was stated, "... and all of the *Chusmas* [women and children] of the above-cited nations less those that are at this presidio today ..." — that is, 104 persons. Taking the warrior figures as totals, including those at the Conchos presidio at this time, plus a possible 250 women and children, would make a total in the neighborhood of 400 persons (BL 1695a).

Also in 1693, the principal "Toboso" leaders were reported to be El Tecolote, Contrerillas, Lorencillo, Luquillas[,] Cola de Coyote, and Maimara (a gentile); Lorencillo and Contrerillas were operating in El Tecolote's group. Marín gave the same list, minus Luquillas and Maimara, but adding Ceja Blanca (who may have been one of the latter). The total fighting force was not over 100 men (Hackett 1926: 296-298, 401, 342-348; BL 1695a).

In 1694, a captive testified that the Acoclames were with the Hijos de las Piedras "... and another nation called Tobosos ...." In the middle of the following year, some Acoclames and one Indian of the "Hijos de la Tierra and Piedras nation" arrived in San Francisco de Conchos. Later, a Cocoyome and a Colorado came to convince them to return. The presence of a "Colorado" apparently is evidence of Coahuila Indians with the Cocoyomes. During this same period Terocodames and some ten to twelve nations from north of Coahuila between Santa Rosa and the Río Grande were said to be joining the "Tobosos" in hostilities (Hackett 1926: 318-324; BL 1695a).

In 1698, both Cocoyomes and Acoclames were settled in peace, the latter at the Atotonilco mission and the former at Santa Cruz near Cuencamé. Many of those at Atotonilco apparently stayed until 1701, although not all of the desert people were settled at this time. Governor Larrea in Parral wrote in May of 1700 that persons from the back country had continued to settle at Atotonilco; the total population of the mission was 260 souls at this time. The Coahuila governor in 1699 reported hostilities from "Tobosos" coming from the north and west into the Coahuila region (AHP 1699a; AHP 1700a; AHP 1704Ab; BL 1649-1700).

In 1704, Acoclames and Coyotes and/or Cocoyomes often were allied for raiding. A small group called the Xexet were mentioned for the first time by Acoclame declarants. It comprised about eight "adult males" and was said to remain always under the protection of the Cocoyomes. The Indian governor of the mission of San Francisco de Coahuila about two years later mentioned a group called the Jajames with the Acoclames and Cocoyomes. There is some possibility that the Xexet (Jejet) and Jajames were the same people (AHP 1704Ab).

Some hints regarding relative territories occur during these early years of the 18th century. Acoclames made peace offerings in Parral, and later fifty-four persons with four chiefs went to San Francisco de Conchos to make peace. In general, Acoclames were reported in the western part of the territory, such as at the Sierra de las Cañas (east of Atotonilco), and several references cited the Acoclames at Sierra Mojada. The Cocoyomes were mostly to the south and east at places like the Sierra de Baján and San Juan de Casta. They made peace overtures at Parras, another indication of their territorial location relative to that of the Acoclames. At this same time Chisos went to San Francisco de Conchos to carry out peace negotiations (AHP 1704Aa; AHP 1704Ab; AHP 1704Ac).

In December of 1705 the Spaniards fought the Acoclames and Cocoyomes, as well as the Xexet, Hijos de las Piedras, and Hijos de la Tierra at Sierra Mojada. The Acoclames alone lost twenty-two warriors, but it is uncertain how many of the Cocoyomes and others were killed. The Gavilanes were mentioned as associated with these groups around this period, but they were not cited as having been in the Sierra Mojada fracas; another "nation," the Avos, is referred to, but with no further information. After this battle, the Acoclames went to Conula and Agua de la Lanza, while the Cocoyomes moved to the Nazas River area (AHP 1704Ab).

The Acoclame captive, Diego, gave the number of Acoclame warriors as thirty-three. He also reported eleven Cocoyomes (males) as living with the Acoclames, but it is unknown if they were included in the number of Acoclame warriors. In a passage that is not wholly clear, the total number of men, women, and children in this group is given as 250. This figure seems high and may well be in error. However, from this testimony some forty warriors had been killed in recent battles. The latter number added to the first would make a total of around seventy braves — guessing that these would be adult males roughly over fifteen years of age. There were probably at least this many adult women in this age bracket, and adding another seventy or so children of all ages would place the figure somewhere over 200 persons. Although this is conjecture, it seems worthwhile to make some reasonable estimate of population where possible. The same witness declared there were some sixty men among the Cocoyomes, but fewer children than among the Acoclames because of a recent epidemic. This may mean that these two groups totaled around 400 persons at this time (AHP 1704Ab). In 1704 several Nueva Vizcayan citizens stated there were only eighty-five Cocoyomes and Acoclames; this, if accurate, and taken with the preceding information, certainly referred to "warriors" (DHM 1704). Unfortunately, there is no way of checking such figures or of knowing how many bands were actually included.

Several chiefs were mentioned for the two groups. The Acoclames had three — Nicolás, El Ratón, and Panzacola — under a head chief named El Chapatón (Cola de Coyote and two other chiefs were now dead). The Cocoyomes had Contreras, Ceja Blanca, and Lorenzo. According to the declarant, when the two groups would get together El Chapatón and Contreras "commanded all," leaving Contreras, then, as the principal chief of the Cocoyomes. During the course of the testimony, the names of several other men, also called "chiefs," occurred as leaders in various raids — some seven or so for the Acoclames and two for the Cocoyomes (this difference is not surprising, as an Acoclame was testifying; also, it is quite possible that some of the names were duplicates or nicknames for the same individual) (AHP 1704Ab).

In the discussion of both population and leaders, the other "Toboso" groups (Hijos de las Piedras, etc.) were not mentioned, and it is uncertain whether they were included or not. Other tribes were cited as sometime allies of the Cocoyomes and Acoclames — the Sisimbles (known in Coahuila as the Toidas, according to the Indian governor of the Coahuila mission) and Chisos to the north and the "Coahuileños" to the east (the "Tobosos" had joined the latter for a raid on the mission of Nadadores). The Cocoyomes were around Chiso country the most, although the Acoclames were also in contact with them. The witness also mentioned that the Chisos were relatives of the Acoclames. These Chisos, he said, joined the latter for raids at Sierra Mojada and other places, but they were not the Chisos at peace at the presidio of San Francisco de Conchos but were those named Sisimbles. These were called Chisos because they lived to the north of the Acoclames. Also, around 1704 and

1705, twelve Chisos and their families lived with the Acoclames for more than a year. This apparently included four girls who were to marry Acoclames. At the same time, six Chisos who had been with the Acoclames later fought against them on the side of Spanish troops (AHP 1704Ab).

In the latter part of 1708 the Acoclames and Cocoyomes were mentioned as being together, although the Acoclames made peace overtures the last month of this year. Information for the next few years is extremely scanty, unfortunately, but near the end of 1711 an unknown number of Acoclames and Chisos were deported from Nueva Vizcaya (AHP 1710a; AHP 1710b; AHP 1710c; AHP 1710d; AHP 1711A).

Some information came out concerning these people during the court process brought against them the previous year. Several witnesses testified, including the Sergeant Major Diego de Estrada who had been a captive of the enemy for fourteen years. Unfortunately, the time levels of much of the information are not kept too distinct, but the general picture is essentially that from other sources. Cocoyomes and Acoclames spent a good bit of time together. One witness referred to three bands: Acoclames, Cocoyomes, "and the rancheria of Ceja Blanca who are also Cocoyomes . . . ." Another witness, who had escaped the Indians about two years previously (ca 1708) after having been held captive a little over a year, noted the last band as well as a group called Gavilanes. These declarants seldom cited specific alliances between the "Toboso" groups and Chisos; one stated that the Chisos only joined the others for large "functions." Mention was also made of the Cocoyomes going up to the Río Grande to cement an alliance with people from there (Chisos?) to raid in Nueva Vizcaya. Two witnesses stated that they knew that the Acoclames and Cocoyomes were related to the now extinct Tobosos. Various places — Pozo Hediondo, Mobana, Sierra de Baján, Las Ventanillas (next to Baján), Conula, Los Remedios, Sierra de Conejitos, Acatita, Acatita El Grande, and particularly Sierra del Diablo and Sierra Mojada (in the sierra de Tagualiloncate) — were cited as camping sites of the rebel Indians (BL 1709-1715).

Batayoliglas and Suniyoliglas were carrying out raiding operations in the year 1713. In the confession of one Suniyoligla, it was stated that his group was always allied with the Chisos but that it had been many years since the Chisos (including his group?) had banded with the Cocoyomes and Acoclames. In fact, about a month previous to this testimony, Chisos had gone to Jaque and fought the Cocoyomes, killing three. However, both the Sisimbles and Suniyoliglas had received messages from the Cocoyomes to join them. The Suniyoliglas comprised only thirteen warriors, plus another three who lived with the Sisimbles; thus the group was so small that it had been forced to accept the offer. It is uncertain how much getting together Sisimbles, Acoclames, Cocoyomes, and Suniyoliglas did, although the Spaniard, Antonio de Rodela, wrote at this time that all four bands were allied and sending out raiding squads (BL 1709-1715).

Prisoners — "Toboso" as well as others interrogated in 1715 — gave the names only of Acoclames and Cocoyomes as rebel Indians. These groups lived at Sierra Mojada and Conula and apparently were together much of the time, although this is implied more than explicitly stated. Five women were questioned, four Cocoyomes and one Acoclame. One of the Cocoyomes declared, however, that up until a short time previously (possibly as recently as three months?) she had lived "with her father" in another territory (en otras sierras), perhaps indicating that she was in effect not a Cocoyome. All five women claimed that the Acoclames and Cocoyomes lived solely by what they stole from the Spaniards. One Cocoyome said that ever since she could remember her people and the others as well had always held killing and theft as an inviolable custom because they had no other occupation or way to support themselves in their own land. A couple of women also noted that the Chisos and Sisimbles, their partners, still hunted deer and other animals when they were not raiding, either on their own or with the Acoclames and Cocoyomes (AHP 1715Aa).

The fact that Chisos and Sisimbles were the only allies of the "Tobosos" was corroborated by a Coahuileño boy questioned at this time. These two groups, he said, had been with the latter only some three years, having "first" gotten together at Sierra Mojada, and that these were the Chisos and Sisimbles who lived at Las Encinillas and Agua de Mayo. He added that the total number of warriors of these groups was 350 (? unclear). There was no communication between the rebel and peaceful Indians (AHP 1715Aa).

Also, Indians at the Conchos and Río Grande confluence stated that they knew that the Chisos, Sisimbles, Acoclames, and Cocoyomes were the ones who raided in Nueva Vizcaya and that the "first" (most northern) water holes where these groups usually camped were at the Peñol de Santa Marta, Sierra de Jaque, and Las Encinillas (AHP 1715Ac). Possibly these informants were thinking primarily of Chisos or of the places where "Chisos" and "Tobosos" would get together.

Although it is not mentioned in the testimonies, it seems unlikely that Coahuileños were not involved in some way with the "Toboso" groups. In 1714, the "Tobosos" in the hinterland were joined by some forty families, later said to be ninety-six families, from Coahuila. These included apparently Terocodames, Paboris, and Cuautomanas, under Chief Don Pablo; they were from the Nadadores mission and remained out in the back country until 1716 (AHP 1712; AHP 1715Aa; AHP 1722Aa; AHP 1722Da).

Unfortunately, none of the women declarants referred to previously could give an estimate of Cocoyome and Acoclame population. Both bands contained a number of baptized persons, however — the result of the many times they had "surrendered" and settled for short periods with Spaniards. Only one chief was referred to — an unnamed Cocoyome and a gentile — who led both the Cocoyomes and Acoclames. No Chiso leaders were mentioned. All declarants told that once a year Chisos, Sisimbles, Cocoyomes, and Acoclames would hold a large meeting during the dry season, at which time they traded goods and discussed plans for the coming year for raiding and other matters. Afterward they would break up and go their separate ways. However, for specific raids they would contact each other and usually meet near the place they were going to attack (AHP 1715Aa).

A released captive of the enemy, testifying in July of 1715, claimed he had counted the Cocoyomes several times. At Sierra Mojada there had been seventy-three warriors, eighty women and children, plus three very old Indians, and twelve captives. Later, they all moved to Mobana where they had been joined by seventy-eight Chiso warriors, without women and children, and by ten Acoclame braves with eighteen women, but no children (AHP 1715Aa). Although Chisos and Sisimbles often are not mentioned in the testimonies of the "Tobosos" as being their allies, apparently there was in effect fairly regular contact. A couple of years later, Antonio Arias, writing from the town of Santa Ana y San Francisco Javier in November of 1718, stated that the Chiso groups were then allied with the Cocoyomes and Acoclames and that they constituted about one-half of the fighting force (AHP 1718Ad), which is consistent with the 1715 testimony.

More prisoners were interrogated in February, 1716, after the battle at Conula — most were Aco-clames, one a Cocoyome woman, and another a Tepe-huán who had been captured by the Acoclames a number of years before. The Acoclames and Coco-yomes, they stated in their view of themselves, were the two nations that from "very ancient times" had been fighting in Nueva Vizcaya. The Acoclames were now finished, in their opinion: twenty-two had been captured, some six killed, and only five (one prisoner stated six) had escaped — two men, two boys, and a woman. Only the Cocoyomes, consisting of ninety to one-hundred warriors and led by one Dieguillo (almost certainly an Acoclame), the brother of one killed (one what?), were left to carry on the "war." (A few days later the Cocoyome chief was said to be named Juan; apparently, Juan de Lomas.) The prisoners stated it had been about a year since the Chisos and Sisimbles, who numbered about 100 warriors, had been with them. They carried out their continual raiding and robberies to obtain clothing and other needed items. Between 130 and 150 "Coa-huilas" warriors, plus women and children, under Chief Don Pablo, were with the Cocoyomes at this time. According to the declarants these had been with the latter about a year. The principal camping spots of the Cocoyomes were Sierra Mojada and Conula (AHP 1715Aa).

In October of 1716 a twelve-year-old boy, captive of the Cocoyomes for approximately a year, was questioned. He reported about sixty adult Coco-yomes, plus women and children, as well as some Acoclames (apparently refugees from the above battle of Conula?). These had all been camped together in the Sierra Mojada area. He had also heard that Chisos would join the Cocoyomes, but he never saw this during his period of captivity. While this declarant did not mention Indians from Coahuila, a month later, after the Sierra Mojada battle, it was learned that Terocodames were also with the Cocoyomes (AHP 1716Aa).

It is not at all clear exactly what Coahuila bands were actually participating with the Cocoyomes at

this time, aside from the Terocodames who were mentioned in several succeeding documents. At the beginning of 1717, the Cocoyome chief, Juan de Lomas, indicated that he had been in communication with the Tripas Blancas and Cíbolas, as well as the Terocodames. Sometime before this the governor of Coahuila had written that the Acoclames and Coco-yomes were allied for raiding with a number of other nations such as the Julimes, Chisos, Guejolotes, Cíbolas, Escomiagamos, Yerbiapames, Tripas Blancas, and Gavilanes (the latter a non-"Toboso" group?) (AHP 1716Aa).

Information concerning the next two years is scanty. In February of 1717, Alday reported that Chief Lomas' ranchería had 174 persons in it — sev-enty warriors, thirty-one boys, fifty women over fifteen years of age, sixteen over seven years old, and seven nursing infants. These possibly were almost all of the Cocoyomes at this time (AHP 1716Ab). In July of 1718, the Nueva Vizcayan governor wrote that the total number of "Tobosos" at this time was between 150 and 200. These were allied with the Chisos and Sisimbles (AHP 1718Aa).

In 1720 the Cocoyomes and Acoclames seemingly formed a single group. The term Gavilán occurs again — an individual (Gerónimo de Jaque), raised in Cuen-camé, was stated to be both a Cocoyome and a Gavi-lán (a Gavilán ranchería had been settled at the Medrano hacienda near Cuencamé a number of years previously). This Gavilán had, however, been with the hinterland people (Acoclames) for some time. Juan de Lomas was said to be the head chief (cabo y caudillo) of these "Tobosos," although three others (Ventura, Pedro Joseph, and El Gallo) were also mentioned as chiefs, apparently subchiefs. Over fifty Coahuileños were with the Cocoyomes at this time (AHP 1720Aa), the same people who were still with them in 1722. Later, an ex-captive of the Indians reported over 120 warriors with these groups. Another captive declared there were about 300 "Indians" (indios) belonging to four different nations. However, he later said that on one occasion a group of 114 men had been taken off by Lomas, and the men remaining in camp were fewer than this number (AHP 1722Aa; AHP 1722Ab).

Prisoners rounded up for the 1723 deportation gave the last glimpse of the "Toboso" picture in this final stage of their history. Lomas was the "head" chief. The only enduring allies the "Tobosos" had had for some time were the Coahuileños, of whom

[margin note, rotated:] 14 census?

many were shipped off at this time. The Chisos and Sisimbles do not come up in the testimonies. Lomas and others confessed why they committed so many raids and killings — this activity was the one they had been taught and the only one they knew, and their parents and grandparents had charged them to carry on with it (AHP 1722Ab).

The numbers of prisoners deported to Mexico City reveal in good measure the nature of the population at this time. From the lists from the several presidios some 297 persons were shipped off, although the Viceroy wrote that there had been 311, and Alday's figures from Celaya of the still living and dead on the road to Mexico City indicate 310. Regardless of the exact total, apparently not over 139 were Cocoyomes. The remaining 158 were Coahuileños, both the people under Chief Don Pablo who had been permanently with the Cocoyomes and those — ninety-nine — from the town of Cinco Señores who had been collaborating in one way or another with the desert groups. Those Coahuileños under Don Pablo, and several lesser chiefs, no doubt contained at least individuals from several different named groups (AHP 1722Aa; AHP 1722Ba; BL 1722).

The Parral list unfortunately is the only one that cites the number of prisoners who died between the time they were captured and the day of deportation. These were twenty-four, and should be added to the above 297, making a total of 321. This is also the only list in which the Acoclames are mentioned, although this is only in the title and there is no internal breakdown. Apparently the Acoclames were now considered insignificant as a separate group, and the term "Cocoyome" had come to have generic usage. According to the Spanish reports, then, this would place the total of those of the desert, excluding the Cinco Señores people, at around 250 persons. This figure probably should be considered a minimum, however, as a number of persons had been killed in hostilities just prior to the deportation. Also, it is very possible that some prisoners had died at the presidios (Cerro Gordo and El Gallo) other than Parral, but, as already noted, this is not recorded (AHP 1722Ba).

There is at present no way of determining what percentage of the desert-dwelling Cocoyomes and "Coahuileños" had been captured. The Spaniards seemingly felt that they had gotten almost all, at least of the Cocoyomes, and so states Berroterán. Governor Alday wrote on February 9, 1723, that the num-

ber of prisoners was at that time 286 "...leaving, according to the calculation of the number which these rebels comprised, eleven whom it has not been possible to apprehend because of their having used their deceit and retired to unknown places...." Berroterán noted in his 1747 report that later in the year 1723 a group of Indians under one Bautista who had escaped from the first deportation were captured at Acatita, and again this same year another twenty-eight were rounded up at Aguachila and sent to Mexico City (AHP 1722Ba; DHM 1748).

It is difficult to make very much out of the preceding information with regard to population during this period. However, it would seem that immediately prior to the deportation there may have been from 300 to 500 persons living in the desert back-country, not counting "Chisos." The figure 500 was given by Governor Martín de Alday in a consulta to the Viceroy in June of 1722. This number, he said, were Cocoyomes and Coahuileños now at peace, implying thereby that all had previously been "rebels." While subsequent information seems to indicate that the Cocoyome picture was fairly accurately portrayed at this time by these figures, the actual Coahuileño situation remains obscure. It will be impossible to put more light on the population problem until more detailed historical research is carried out on these eastern bands (BL 1723-1724).

In effect, in 1723 the Spaniards had gotten a large portion of the hinterland people. In August of 1724 a rebel camp at Sierra del Diablo and later at Sierra Mojada was reported to contain some seventeen to nineteen people, plus three captives (two Spaniards and an Indian). It is not known how long the latter had been with this Indian group, but according to two other captives who had escaped from the band, the three had refused to accompany them, stating that they now knew the Indians' language, implying that they had been with the Indians for some time (AHP 1724Aa).

One declarant gave the names of his captors: Esteban, Francisco, Marcos Viejo (master of one witness), Mateo, Isidro (chief of the others) — all Coahuileños who had escaped from the previous shipment (la collera); three Acoclames: Juanito, Don Pablo, and Mateo; another Diego Vaquero (master of the second witness) with no nation mentioned; Marcos El Manco (declared to be an Acoclame by the second witness only); two old men and two youths of unnamed affiliation; plus a boy, Joseph, from Coahuila. Of the five women, two — Micaela and María — were Coa-huileñas, and the other three (two young and one old) were (*son*) *Ynglecles* of the Chiso nation (AHP 1724Aa). This seems to have been clearly a refugee group.

At the end of 1725, a Spanish military force picked up eighteen prisoners at the Sierra de Choca-mueca. Judging from their testimony, plus the number killed during the battle, this camp had consisted of about sixty persons, representing three tribes — Sisimbles, Coahuileños, and Cocoyomes (AHP 1725Aa; AHP 1725B).

In February, 1726, the Cocoyomes were said to be attached (*agregados*) to a band of Chisos and Coa-huileños. This group apparently comprised some seventy-five persons of both sexes, although a previous report stated 140 warriors. Part of this "band" was eventually rounded up and deported, and the breakdown of the tribal identities of these persons reflects rather significantly what was occurring in the greater Bolsón de Mapimí during this period (AHP 1727Aa).

These captives numbered thirty-nine. Of these, only two were listed as Cocoyomes, and no Aco-clames were cited. The two Cocoyomes were Juan de Contreras and Marcos, both of whom had escaped during the deportation to Veracruz three years earlier. Marcos was once said to be the chief, the "general" of these "nations," and it was his name that appeared as a signature on a letter requesting supplies and the release of some women being held prisoners. Later, however, Contreras was called the chief (AHP 1727Aa).

The internal breakdown of the ethnic composition of this group is not too clear, and only some of the people on the list of captives are assigned band affiliation. However, a rough estimate may be made of this band's makeup. Aside from the two aforementioned Cocoyomes, eight persons were cited as "Coahui-leños" — including Mateo, Esteban, and Juaniquito, who also had escaped during the previous deportation. Because most of the Coahuileños were considered by the Spaniards to be Christians, owing to the fact that these Indians had once been under mission control in Coahuila, it seems probable that most of another eight persons stated in this list to be Christians, but without tribal affiliation noted, were also Coahuileños. Two more people were specifically cited as Chisos, one a Christian and one a gentile. Of the remaining nineteen persons on the list, sixteen were

said to be gentile Sisimbles, the other three were gentiles but with unstated affiliation. However, as the total of twenty-one gentiles included only one Chiso and one Coahuileño, it is probable that these remaining three gentiles were also Sisimbles (AHP 1727Aa).

The identity of raiding Indians in the western portion of the Greater Bolsón region remains rather obscure for the following decade or so. Some, along the lower Conchos River to its confluence with the Río Grande, were Sumas and Cholomes (UTD 1710-1738a). The Sisimbles apparently were one of the principal bands involved; possibly other "Chisos" also were, as well as various Coahuila bands.

While most sources indicate that the "Tobosos" were pretty well extinct at this time, people called "Tobosos," as well as "Apaches" were said to be raiding in Coahuila in 1734 (UTD 1733-1738). The following year "Tobosos" were reported even farther east in the Kingdom of Nuevo León (UTD 1730-1736). Later, seemingly during the 1740's, the Apache Pasqual was said to have encountered a few "Tobosos" at Acatita La Grande (BL 1746b).

It would seem that the term "Toboso" was being used rather loosely in these cases, and in effect to designate in a vague way any raiding Indians living in a somewhat distant geographical area. Most reasonably, these "Tobosos" were in part Sisimbles and some "Coahuila" groups, plus possibly remnants of actual "Tobosos" who had managed to survive. The last of the desert-dwelling Sisimbles, a small band of sixteen persons, disappeared in 1748 (BL 1748; BL 1751a).

The decade of the 1740's, from the available information, then, marked the end of the original inhabitants in the western part of the area considered here, except along the Conchos River and Río Grande area. In the eastern region, as previously noted, the picture is much less clear, and specific documentation of the disappearance of these groups cannot be offered at this time. However, in both the eastern and western areas, some of the original inhabitants no doubt were still in existence around 1750. These had been settled at missions and elsewhere — a process that had been going on for many years.

Within a few years, most, if not all, of the Greater Bolsón de Mapimí area was taken over by people called "Apaches." Apparently, these were in the main the Athabaskan-speaking people whose descendants are today known as Apaches. This, however, is a conclusion based on historical association, as it is known that such Athabaskans did occupy the region in later times. The statement is *not* founded on solid linguistic or ethnographic evidence, and it seems unwarranted to assume that all occurrences of the term "Apache" refer to Athabaskan-speaking Indians.

It is quite possible, although it cannot be demonstrated by documentary evidence, that non-Athabaskan groups from Texas who crossed the Río Grande were also called "Apaches" at this time. In Nueva Vizcaya the term "Apache" seems on occasion to refer to any northern Indian.* However, regardless of the use of "Apache" for non-Athabaskans, most of the Apaches who did enter the Bolsón region from the north during the eighteenth century were probably Athabaskans. In 1766, Lafora stated that the whole area was inhabited by Apaches (1939: 81, 197-200); this was repeated by Morfi in 1777 (1958: 361, 364-368, 374-379). Raids reported in the Parral district for the succeeding nine years (1778-1787) were attributed to Apaches and a few marauding Tarahumaras (AHP 1787A).

Not all of the desert-dwelling Indians were exterminated or deported. While this point is poorly documented in this study, certainly a number of the "original" inhabitants were assimilated into Spanish society at missions, haciendas, and mines. Chisos were reduced to settlement at such places as the missions of San Pedro and San Francisco de Conchos and were often cited as employed as auxiliary troops (AHP 1684Aa; AHP 1687Ab; AHP 1723A). From the latter half of the seventeenth century, apparently some "Tobosos" were living at San Francisco de Conchos and were also used as auxiliary troops against the desert dwellers (AHP 1686Bb; AHP 1687Aa; AHP 1697Aa; AHP 1697Ab; AHP 1715Aa; AHP 1723A; DHM 1704). Sierra Osorio's report of the Tobosos settled at San Francisco de Conchos sometime before 1678 indicates that this venture had been successful (Hackett 1926: 210-214).

Father Guendulaín, in 1725, reported Tobosos on the list of persons at the Jesuit mission of Santa Ana de Chinarras (near Aldama, Chihuahua), together with Conchos, Sumas, and Chinarras. Of thirty-eight families listed, the total for all of these groups, only seven were actually at the mission at that time — the rest were away looking for food. He does not state whether any Tobosos were there at the time of his visit or not (AGN 1725). No ethnic identity of the Indians is mentioned in a later report of this mission in 1758 (AGN 1751-1757). In the church records of Parral and the Valle de San Bartolomé, a few "Tobosos," "Chisos," and "Salineros" are listed during the latter part of the seventeenth and early eighteenth centuries. Elsewhere in this study various places of settlement for these three "tribal" groups have been cited, such as the Cabezas at Parras in the 1690's. Although specific information on these settlements is not available, certainly some assimilation into Spanish society took place.

Indians, both peripheral and central to this study, continued to inhabit north central Mexico during the eighteenth century, although the details are sadly lacking. In an anonymous description of the province of Nueva Vizcaya after July 2, 1766, among other nations listed are those of the Conchos, Chisos Otaquitatomes, and Sisimbres (Sisimbles) (DHM 18th.a; this is almost identical to Lafora's report, 1939: 79-84). Lafora noted that in Coahuila nine missions were administering to 382 families of Indians, including the nations of Terocodames, Pacpoles, Tacquites, Ocanes, Payaguanes, Cíbolos, Canos, Ostujanes, Pachoches, Apes, Colorados, Obayas, Tobosos,

---

*This seems to have been especially true in Nueva Vizcaya in earlier years of the Colonial period, and particularly the case with Indians from the province of New Mexico. Later, as Athabaskan speakers did in effect move in and take over much of the area, the term Apache crystallized to refer specifically to this linguistic group.

This is a point, however, that needs much further investigation. For example, a perusal of the baptismal records from the cathedral in the city of Parral for the seventeenth and first half of the eighteenth centuries leaves the impression that "Apache" referred to a geographical location, that is, principally New Mexico, and not to any specific linguistic or ethnic group.

This material is listed roughly by five-year periods, as the data were incomplete in a number of instances. However, the conclusion from the over-all picture seems to be that when the number of "Apaches" is high, that for the "Indians from New Mexico" is relatively lower, which indicates that "Apache" apparently was applied to any Indians, regardless of linguistic group, from the general New Mexican area. It might have been used more for nomadic peoples than for settled groups, but certainly it was not exclusively employed for nomads.

This conclusion is further substantiated in a court case brought against a Tigua (pueblo) Indian from New Mexico in Parral in 1686. The defendant identified himself as a Tigua, while the Spaniards referred to him as Apache as many times as they used the term Tigua (AHP 1686Ba).

"Apache" also seems to have a vague meaning as used in the Franciscan records of baptisms of Indians at the mission in Valle de San Bartolomé. Of thirty-four occurrences of baptisms of Apaches, eleven are of children of unknown parents, and presumably the "nation" identity would also be unknown. Furthermore, this was in the latter part of the seventeenth century (1662-1686) when administrative and other reports give no indication of "Apaches" being in the Nueva Vizcayan area. Thirteen entries list one or both parents as Apaches.

Indians from "New Mexico" Listed in the Baptismal Records in the City of Parral, 1634 – 1745

Time Period*	Apaches	Apaches from New Mexico	Indians from New Mexico	Quiviras	Total
1634 – 1639	0	0	11	0	11
1640 – 1644	0	0	0	0	0
1645 – 1648	2	0	5	0	7
1649 – 1655	9	4	8	0	21
1656 – 1660	14	1	34	0	49
1661 – 1665	20	0	8	1	29
1665 – 1670	4	2	95	1	102
1671 – 1675	45	0	22	2	69
1676 – 1680	100	1	15	5	121
1681 – 1685	54	0	10	2	66
1686 – 1691	18	0	2	0	20
1695 – 1700	21	0	1	0	22
1701 – 1705	30	0	4	0	34
1706 – 1710	24	0	0	0	24
1711 – 1716	18	0	1	0	19
1717 – 1720	2	0	0	0	2
1721 – 1725	4	0	1	0	5
1726 – 1730	13	0	0	0	13
1731 – 1735	7	0	0	0	7
1736 – 1740	2	0	0	0	2
1741 – 1745	1	0	0	0	1

* No data available after July 10, 1691, through 1694.

624

Xixames, Silangayas, Sadujanes, Siguares, Pitas, Pacuafin, Pajalatames, Carrizos, Cohumeros, Timamares, Pampopas, Tilixais, Mescales, Borrados, Pausanes, Manos de Perro, Piguiques, and Julimeños. The Cohumeros and Timamares were located at the mission of San Miguel de Aguayo, next to Monclova. The Julimeños were immigrants from the town of Julimes in Nueva Vizcaya (Lafora 1939: 179, 196-197, 239). In 1786, two Colorado Indians still remained at the mission of San Miguel de Aguayo. The remaining some 500 persons living there were either Tlaxcaltecan Indians, or Negroes, mulattos, Coyotes, and other castes. The Nadadores mission, seven leagues west of Monclova, apparently had no Indians at this time. The report of this year states that there had originally been Gavilanes, Terocodames, and Colorados here, but these had revolted and few or none had ever returned (BL 1786). A report in the 1790's covering this area cited a number of groups — Guey-quisales, Contores (Contotores), Ysipopolames, Pies de Venado, Colorados, Babozarigames, Tedocodamos (Terocodames), and Gavilanes (AGN 1793).

Not all the Indians at these mission establishments disappeared by assimilation into Spanish society. The 1790's report states that most of those mentioned had now disappeared by being absorbed by the Apaches or the Borrados from the coast of Nuevo Santander, or they had died or were dying off in epidemics. Many of the Indians joined the Apaches or at least served as spies for them (AGN 1793).

Throughout the period considered here, one of the acculturation-assimilation patterns was the absorption of Indians and others into the permanently rebel groups. This process continued with the advent of the Apaches. As early as 1746 the Viceroy of Mexico, the Marqués de Altamira, wrote that almost all of the former nations of the central north Mexican area —

Acoclames, Tripas Blancas, Tobosos, Tosimoras, Gabilanes, and Cíbolos — were now extinct. There were in the area, however, a few apostates — fugitives from the missions — who were raiding the bordering settlements. The Apaches were also in the region and had invaded the five missions of La Junta, at the confluence of the Río Grande and Conchos rivers, forcing the missionaries there to retire to Chihuahua City (BL 1746a).

Lafora also noted in 1766 that the few Indians left in the area at the missions were still active in hostilities. He stated that "not only the enemies [Lipans and Natages] but the apostates and thieves (*rateros*) from the many neighboring missions, from where they sally forth to rob and to kill . . ." were committing hostilities in Nueva Vizcaya and Coahuila (Lafora 1939: 197-200). Although he does not state it, no doubt these apostates sometimes joined the Apaches.

4. GENERAL ETHNOGRAPHY

The ethnography of the Greater Bolsón de Mapimí area has been only partially illuminated in the present study. Many aspects of the ways of life of the region — such as social organization — remain virtually unknown, and for any single group only a very small amount of information exists. However, the information encountered in the documentary sources is presented herein. By piecing together the few data that do exist, the broad outlines of the ethnographic picture for the general region can be reconstructed, aided by some general supporting information from surrounding areas. This ethnographic account, with a judicious amount of inference, will be used to establish a rough cultural base line in order to evaluate later some of the general processes of cultural change that occurred during a portion of the Colonial period.

Material Culture

Very little has come to light as to the nature of "uncontaminated" material culture — dress, hair style, and the like. Of the few references that have been found, a number evince synthesis with introduced Spanish items or models. Owing to the conglomeration that often occurs, it is virtually impossible to keep Spanish and Indian, as well as individual Indian, material separate. Such a mixture, of course, does represent the cultural situation of the Colonial Indians in this area at this period. Inventories of native camps usually list many Spanish goods and are also interesting from the standpoint of seeing just what items did get into the back country. Unfortunately, the significance of these goods and the part they actually played in native life can only be inferred.

Dress and Decoration

Dress exhibited a great deal of variation. Apparently from the time of first contact with Spanish culture, directly or indirectly, and particularly when the Indians took up raiding on a rather regular basis, they began to acquire some items of Spanish dress. In fact, the acquisition of clothing was often stated by the Indians as one of their prime motives for raiding. However, the native dress style was never given up

entirely — in 1726 Spanish captives reported that their captors (a mixed group of Cocoyomes, Coahuileños, and Chisos) made them put on breech clouts of cloth (*paño* and *bayeta*), stating that trousers (*calzones*) were no good. The women here had worn deer skins secured around the waist (AHP 1724Aa). Another reference to the use of deer skin pertained to an occasion when a Suniyoligla man gave a Batayoligla one such skin (*gamuza*) to wear (BL 1709-1715). Coahuileño groups — Boboles, Gicocoges, and Yoricas — around the Sabinas river utilized both deer skins and buffalo hides for dress (Portillo 1887: 71-72).

Pérez de Ribas gave a description of female dress for the Laguna area. The women wore animal skins adorned with other small pieces of the same skin, the hair was braided, and around the neck were strings of snail and other shells. The feathers of parrots (*guacamayos*) and other birds were worn during dances (1944 III: 254, 265). Mota y Escobar stated that the people at La Laguna used rabbit-skin blankets for dress (1940: 169). On the other hand, the *Anua* of 1600-1602 reported that the people of Parras went nude (BL 1600-1602). Farther to the west, strings of beads and bones (*sartas de cuentas y huesos*), probably to be worn as adornments, were cited for Mapimí (Pérez de Ribas III 1944: 275).

Attackers were reported at different times to have different dress. Some, judged on one occasion to be Cocoyomes, were wearing short jackets (*cotones*) of baize (*bayeta*), new hats, and blankets tied around the waist (AHP 1715Aa). In an assault upon two Conchos by Tobosos, the latter were dressed like Spaniards (AHP 1654Ac). Sometimes the enemy was in the nude (i.e., wearing a loin covering only) (AHP 1654Ca), other times mostly dressed (AHP 1656Aa), and still others in various combinations (AHP 1657Bb; AHP 1669Ba). For the most part, it seems, Spaniards associated "nudity" with the Tobosos, clothing somewhat more with the Salineros and Cabezas, but particularly with Indian hacienda laborers (AHP 1654Ac).

The Tobosos were reported to possess sandals (*cacles*) of *palmilla* and to have made others from the deerskin (*gamuza*) trousers of another Indian they had killed (AHP 1686Bc). Batayoliglas, or at least "Chisos," also wore sandals (*cacles*) (BL 1709-1715). A Spanish woman held captive by the Cabezas — from one report — was given a small doublet or jacket (*juboncillo*), a skin (*cuero*), and sandals to wear (AHP 1652Dc), and, according to another writing, "some deer skins which the Indian women use and *un saquillo de sayal*," plus sandals (*cacles*) (DHM 1645). Feather headdresses (*plumero, plumajes*) were worn by Tobosos and Cabezas (Alegre III 1956: 290; AGN 1669), and the feathers of parrots (*guacamayos*) and other birds were worn during dances in the Parras district, as were the tails of various animals (Pérez de Ribas III 1944: 265; DHM 1598).

Face painting was referred to a number of times, but the descriptions unfortunately are very poor. In one unnamed group, but apparently Salineros from the circumstances, two men each had two lines drawn from their lower lips to their chins, and two more lines near their eyes (AHP 1669Ba). A thirteen-year-old girl who escaped from the enemy gave a description of the face decorations of her captors, although she could not identify them as to tribe. They may have been Cíbolos, or nearby peoples, as they had told her there were buffalo in their land. The girl apparently communicated with them in Mexican. There had been thirteen men in this group. One had a line (*raya*) from his forehead to the end of his nose. Two others each had a line drawn along the left side of the face, from the nose to the ear, like a moustache cover (? *bigotera*). The rest were not painted (AHP 1654Ac). One Spaniard, held as a slave by the Colorados, and formerly among the Cíbolos, was described as painted (*rraiado*) with a black line from his forehead to his nose and another in the manner of the sign of a slave (? *Clabo*; nail?; or from the lip — *labio* — see Portillo 1887: 93) above the chin on the cheek (BL 1674).

In general, assailants were often said to be painted (e.g., AHP 1652Bb; AHP 1652Da; AHP 1653Ae; AHP 1654Aa; AHP 1654Ca; AHP 1686Bb), although frequently they were not positively identified. Not all attackers were painted however (AHP 1654Ac; AHP 1654Ad; AHP 1656Aa) — specifically the Cocoyomes and Acoclames in 1710 (BL 1709-1715). The Alamamas from around Parras painted their faces with lines (*rayados*) (BL 1604).

Arlegui describes war paint as he knew of it. The pigment consisted of different colored clays with which serpents, snakes, toads, and other low animals were represented on the body. Bright colored feathers were also placed on the heads of those going to war. All of this, Arlegui states, was done in order to cause terror in those who saw them (even mules trembled at the sight of them!) as well as because the Indians felt that the special qualities of the animals painted on them would be transferred to themselves (Arlegui 1851: 150). Alonzo de León reported that each Nuevo León nation had a different style of decoration (García 1909: 36).

No clear identification of peoples by hair style is possible at this time. The previously mentioned thirteen-year-old girl described the hair of the people she had been with. Three of the men had their hair cut in the form of a tonsure (*cerquillo*), and the rest had their hair cut very short, except for the part in front and heavy sideburns (*balcarrotas*) (AHP 1654Ac). On another occasion, of some fifty assailants said to be of "several" nations, most had long hair and bound foreheads; only some eight or ten wore the tonsure (AHP 1656Aa). These people were not identified, although the description might fit the Concho-"Toboso" group known to be operating at this time.

Another group of attackers was reported to have their hair cut in the manner of friars (tonsure?), and one witness stated that they might be Concho because of this style (AHP 1654Ca). However, of another group of Indians wearing the tonsure style, one was reported to have spoken the Salinero tongue, and no other language was mentioned (AHP 1655Ab). Much later one Cocoyome chief was said to be distinguished by his long hair (AHP 1704Ab). A woman captured by the Salineros in the 1644 Revolt had her hair cut back to her ears (DHM 1645). The *Anua* of 1606 referred to the great diversity in hair styles at a camp of fugitives at Pelayo. Some wore their hair in the Christian fashion without long locks (*cabelleras*); others had long locks partly braided and partly loose; some had only two large locks of hair (*mechones*) on either side of the head; and others parted their hair down the middle in the style of young Indian girls from Mexico (City). Some, with rather long hair, wore snake's rattles in it (BL 1606). The Alamamas wore their hair held by a comb and twisted once on top of the head (BL 1604). While the foregoing may be of some help in the future when more information is uncovered pertaining to this general area, it is offered here in part to show the general mixing of peoples and of cultural elements during the Colonial period.

Miscellaneous Material Items

Gourds (*calabazas*) were used by the Acoclames to obtain water at a water hole (AHP 1658Aa). Many were found at a camp near Nonolat, belonging to the several "Toboso" bands there at the time of Barraza's siege; they had been used for storage of water supply (BL 1649-1700). Pérez de Ribas mentions gourds used as water containers in the Parras area (1944 III: 277). Gourd cups (*tecomates*) were also cited as used by the Ocomes and the people of Mapimí (Pérez de Ribas III 1944: 275; AHP 1652Dc), and *tecomates* for carrying water were employed by the desert-dwelling Tepehuanes at Pelayo in 1606 (BL 1649-1700).

At one place seven Indians were discovered making small bags of hide (*botanas*) from some mules they had killed in order to transport water (AHP 1653Ae). Chisos in 1748 stated that the Indians carried water in cured (*curadas*) horse intestines and stomachs when they moved to camps without water supply (BL 1748).

Leather straps or thongs (*correas*) of mule hide were also reported (AHP 1654Aa), as were deer skins — although the specific use of these is often not stated (AHP 1704Ab). The Salineros and the people of the Laguna district made blankets from the skins of rabbits (Mota y Escobar 1940: 169; DHM 1645).

Mortars (of unspecified type) for mesquite were discovered at an enemy camp at Baján, apparently belonging to the Cocoyomes (AHP 1716Ab), and Mota y Escobar cited mortars for mesquite for the people of the Laguna (Mota y Escobar 1940: 168). *Palmilla* was employed to tie up a piece of jerky (AHP 1657Bb), and the Cocoyomes made *petates* from *palmas* (BL 1693b). One Spanish woman captive with the Cabezas was made to carry a wooden carrying crate (*cacastle*) (AHP 1652Dc), and *guacales* were reported for the Cocoyomes (BL 1693b). Baskets, combs (*peines*), jugs (*jícaras*), platters (*platos, escudillas*), and obsidian knives (*navajas de pedernales*) without description were cited for the Laguna district (Alegre II 1956: 151-152; Pérez de Ribas III 1944: 273-275; AGN 1607c). A type of eye shade was also cited, a frame work of grass (?) "which they [the Indians] tie to their heads when they want to see a long distance" (*un enarme* (?) *de silla de sacate que se atan a la cavessa quando quieren divisar*) (AHP

1654Aa). Flutes (*flautas*) are mentioned for the composite group at Pelayo in 1606 (BL 1606).

Pérez de Ribas and Mota y Escobar noted balsas or rafts made from cattails (*espadañas*) at La Laguna (Mota y Escobar 1940: 169; Pérez de Ribas 1944 III: 288). The *Anua* of 1605 stated that these Laguna craft were made of three bundles (*manojos*) of *juncia* (cyprus, sedge) tied in the manner of a raft (*balso*) and were called *naboyas* (BL 1605). Both fish and ducks were taken in the Parras-Laguna district with nets and bow and arrow, and ducks were knocked down in flight with *sondas* (*bolas*) (Alegre 1956 II: 107; BL 1604). Mota y Escobar described large baskets (*nasas*) made of willow branches (*mimbres*), in the form of a large jug (*tinaja*), with which fish were caught in the San Pedro Lagoon (Mota y Escobar 1940: 167).

Dwellings

No information is available on house types, except for the Cocoyomes who lived in huts (*jacales*) over which skins were used as coverings (*los cueros que tapaban sus jacales*) (AHP 1715Aa). The Sisimbles were also stated to have *jacales* (BL 1709-1715), as were the Salineros with little huts (*jacalillos*) (DHM 1645). The Coahuileños at the town of Cinco Señores possessed grass huts (*jacales de sacate*) (AHP 1722Aa), and two grass huts were found at San Ildefonso, twelve leagues north of the Sabinas River, apparently belonging to Coahuileños (Portillo 1887: 109-110).

One "shelter" (*enramada*) was reported built by the Cocoyomes in 1720 (AHP 1720Aa), and a shelter (*ramada*) and *jacalo* (*sic*) were both mentioned for the Tepehuanes of the Pelayo area in 1606 — used as churches, according to the missionary (BL 1606). The *Anua* of 1600-1602 mentioned a place near Parras where the houses were small huts in the form of caves (*chosuelas a manera de cuebas*), a site used by hostile Indians, judging from the great quantity of horse and mule bones nearby. Elsewhere, however, the same source stated of the Indians that their beds were the ground and their shelter the trunks and branches of some mesquites that had not yet sprouted and which afforded no shade (BL 1600-1602).

The utilization of caves was mentioned on four occasions, none of which referred to actual habitation. The Tobosos buried their dead in a cave after a battle (AHP 1653Ad), the Cabezas and Tobosos used one (how?) while out scouting (AGN 1667), the Acoclames and Cocoyomes deposited some stolen priests' garments in one (AHP 1704Ab), and a Cocoyome raiding party kept two captives tied up in a cave while they went out to continue their marauding (AHP 1715Aa). However, fifty years after the Toboso demise, Morfi reported "many caves" which, according to what he had been told, had been Toboso dwellings (Morfi 1958: 376). Alonso de León described the Nuevo León house as bell-shaped, made of grass (*sacate*) or cane (*carrizo*), with low entrances (García 1909: 35).

Weapons

Bows and arrows were used by all of the Indians of Nueva Vizcaya (Alegre II 1956: 107; Arlegui 1851: 137; Mota y Escobar 1940: 169; Pérez de Ribas III 1944: 254; AHP 1653Ae; AHP 1676Aa; DHM 1669; UTD 1710-1738b). Pérez de Ribas came closest to a description of a bow, in reference to the people around the Laguna district — "they make them longer than do other nations, and they use them with great power and skill" (III 1944: 354). Males began to practice with the bow and arrow from a very early age (Alegre II 1956: 107; Arlegui 1851: 137; UTD 1710-1738a), and Mota y Escobar noted their great dexterity (1940: 169). Obsidian points also were employed in this area (Alegre II 1956: 151; Pérez de Ribas III 1944: 273; DHM 1607c). No information is available on Toboso bows, although the Chisos to the north were reported to have used bows of brazil wood and arrows of cane (*carrizo*) (AHP 1704Ab); in another place Chiso arrows were said to be of *lechuguilla* with turkey feathers (AHP 1644Aa). Both the Salineros and Tobosos used arrows of *lechuguilla* (BL 1693-1702; AHP 1652Db; AHP 1655Ab; AHP 1670B; AHP 1716Aa). Acoclame and Cocoyome arrows (at least) had an identifying mark, a twisted or zigzagged line (*culebrilla*; *aculebreada*) on the shaft (AHP 1715Aa). Conchos were also said to use arrows of *lechuguilla* (AHP 1654Ac). Arrows were carried in quivers, on which adornments (of unstated description) were sometimes placed (AHP 1652Bb). Chisos, together with nations from the north, once used poison on their arrows while fighting in the employ of the Spaniards (BL 1693-1702).

Lances (*lanzas*) were mentioned, but much more deadly in battle were the pikes (*chuzos*), which were made by hafting whole Spanish swords (*espadas*) on long poles (*palos*, *astas*) (AHP 1704Ab; AHP 1718Ac; AHP 1724Aa). While the bow and arrow was the common shooting weapon in warfare, occasionally hostile Indians would be found using Spanish arquebuses (there is no mention that these were employed on horseback). However, the use of arquebuses by Indians was no doubt severely restricted, since the guns and the necessary powder and balls could be obtained only by theft (see Secoy 1953).

Tobosos who attacked two Concho Indians had two arquebuses with them (AHP 1654Ac). In 1653 it was reported that Nonojes, Acoclames, and Cocoyomes or Coyotes had had an arquebus among them (AHP 1653Ad). Two gentiles with the Cocoyomes in the 1690's were reported to have each an arquebus — one gun may have been a carbine (*carabina*). One of these men, a chief, seemingly was not a Cocoyome; he was said to be called El Julime, and to have been either a Chiso or Julime. He also had powder and balls for the gun. A Satayoligla later testified that the Cocoyomes had met with other bands, at which time they had with them "many" arquebuses plus two *cueras* (BL 1693b).

About a decade later it was reported that two Cocoyomes and two Acoclames each possessed arquebuses that they used in fighting the Spaniards, including in the battle at Sierra Mojada. Another man, apparently a Cocoyome, had had one also, but he had broken it up and made knives from it (AHP 1704Ab). It was reported that on another occasion the Ocomes, Acoclames, and Nonojes were together with many arquebuses, Spanish leather military jackets (*cueras*), swords, saddles, and *medias lunas* (AHP 1652Ac). Acoclames and Cocoyomes also possessed *cueras* (AHP 1704Ab). Shields (*chimales*) were utilized (AHP 1653Aa; AHP 1686Bb). Saddles, *cueras*, arquebuses, carbines, swords, and spurs were reported to have been seen in Cocoyome-Acoclame camps by captives, and Sisimbres, Suniyoliglas, Cocoyomes, and Acoclames had both *cueras* and *adargas* (BL 1709-1715). The use of rocks and stones in battle has not been documented here, but it was mentioned a number of times (e.g., AHP 1718Ac; BL 1649-1700; CD 1647-1648); in at least one instance the Indian women also threw stones during the fighting (AHP 1653Ad).

Stolen and Traded Goods

Aside from the items already mentioned, many other Spanish goods, some of much less practical value, were discovered at abandoned enemy camps. The inventories of some of these camps are instructive as to the infusion of Spanish material culture into the native setting. Many of these things, and probably most, were stolen from Spanish settlements, wagon trains, and the like, but the Spaniards themselves were directly responsible for the introduction of some items. Apart from the source of goods from natives who returned to their people with "goodies" after having worked for Spaniards in mines or on ranches, when the wild bands came in to make peace, the Spaniards usually gave them gifts. Also, groups on their way to Spanish localities to settle would often be sent supplies — material items as well as foodstuffs — including blankets (*frasadas*), knives (*cuchillos* and *navajas*), cloth of various kinds (*paño, sayal, bayeta*), hats (*sombreros*), ribbons (*listones*), cloaks (*capotes*), beads (*abalorios*), saints (*santos*), rosaries, tobacco, paper, meat, flour (*harina*), corn (*mais*), salt, chile, chololate, and raw sugar (*chancacas*) (e.g., AHP 1652Ba; AHP 1653Ad; AHP 1655Ab; AHP 1658Aa; AHP 1704Ac; AHP 1716Aa; AHP 1716Ab; BL 1694-1698). Once a Toboso woman was given, for example, a green skirt, a *huipil*, red ribbons, belts of *chochomite*, and glass earrings (*zarcillos de vidrio*) (AHP 1652Ac).

Items actually found by Spaniards out in the bush, for example, included steel (*yslabon*) and flint (*yesca*), which a group of the enemy, caught by surprise, had left after having begun a fire (AHP 1653Ae). A raiding party camp, near Canatlán, apparently belonging to Tobosos produced nine quivers, seven bows, three swords, three *armadores* (? jackets), and some blankets (AHP 1658Aa). Another camp contained an arquebus, a broken sword, a doublet (*jubon*), and a torn-up cloak (*capote*) (AHP 1654Aa). Indians would steal practically anything that was small and movable — all kinds of clothing, medallions, weapons, knives, halters, and the like (AHP 1655Aa; BL 1693b). Probably the fifes (*pifanos*), and perhaps the drums (*tambores*), and even the banners used by the natives in some attacks — as reported by the Spaniards — should be mentioned here (AHP 1715Aa; AHP 1718Ac).

Some of the less practical items were reported in later documents. At a site in Sierra Mojada the Spaniards found — after a battle — part of an ornament, one large bell and one medium-sized bell, a painting on linen of the King (*un lienzo de Su Magestad*), pictures (*quadritos*) from Michoacán, a small copper box (*un cassito pequeño de cobre*), two saddles, "and many other things of little value," plus over seventy horses and mules. Following another skirmish at Sierra de Conula (near Sierra Mojada), a cup (*taza*), a silver spoon, some well-cared-for clothing of men and women, and twenty-two horses and mules were discovered (AHP 1715Aa). A camp at the Peñol de Santa Marta produced "some church valuables (*alajas*) which are a missal, a stole and maniple, a little bell and a wafer-box (*hostiario*), and other letters and papers" (BL 1695a).

Three rancherias at Bajan were found to contain a knife (*cuchillo cavizero*), a large knife (*balduque*), a linen stocking (or shoe ? *escarpin de Bretana*), a sword guard from Puerta Cerrada de Madrid (*una guarnicion de espada*), and "a rosary with a medallion (*medalla*) of silver with the Holy Sacrament on one side and on the other the image of Our Lady with her Holy Son in her arms when He was taken down from the Holy Tree of the Cross" (AHP 1716Ab). Again, religious items show up at a camp at Chocamueca — a Christ child, a new ornament, an old chausable (*casulla*), and a small bell (*campanilla*) (AHP 1725Aa; AHP 1725B). Other items reported stolen by Indians were wax candles, books, a bag of [holy] oils (*oleos*), silver tips for canes or staffs (*casquillos de plata de baston*), and escopettes (*escopetas*) (AHP 1710a; AHP 1716Aa; AHP 1722Aa).

A captive of the last Sisimble band told of the goods she had seen at the Indians' camps. These were "a new cape (*capa*) of Castillian cloth (*paño de Castilla*) of a dark cinnamon color;" "some used red sleeves (*mangas coloradas*), a black *cotrencilla*, two small escopettes (*trabuquillos*), and a kettle (*caldereta*);" "a vest (? *solapa*) of deep-red scarlet ... a girdle-belt (*ceñidor*) of red Chinese silk (*saya saya colorada*), and a black hat *de concha*," a white hat, "some sheets (altar cloths) of linen (*sabanas de Ruan*), and a blue *chaqualito* also of linen (*deste mismo*) ... a blue *coton* (cotton print ?), and a deep-red sash ... a black wool girdle;" and "two pairs of small cushions, a white coverlet (*colcha*), two pieces of blue cloth, and many new huaraches (*Guarachas*)." The Sisimbles stated they had stolen *cotones, capotes, frezadas, mantas,* and *camisas* (BL 1748).

These pieces of material culture have been listed here to show the extent of their penetration into native culture and the possibility of rising expectations in this sphere of the natives themselves. That the latter did in fact occur to some extent is lent support by the two letters requesting ransom for prisoners that the Cocoyome chief, Juan de Lomas, sent the Spaniards in 1722. For the ransom itself, cloth such as *paño* and *bayeta*, blankets, knives (*belduques*), *suacales*, and hats were asked for. Apart from this ransom, as gifts to the Cocoyomes, Lomas requested silk ribbon interwoven with gold and/or silver (*liston labrado de tisu*), blue *suacales*, *cardonillo* (cochineal ?), loaves of bread (*panecillo*), cakes (of some type—*pastilla*), brown sugar (*piloncillo*), saffron (*azafran*), and bells (*casacabeles*) and beads for the children. One of the captives, the one who wrote the letter, mentioned other items for the Cocoyomes such as a shawl (*reboso*), beads, and a little *pita* (thread?) for Lomas' wife, as well as some small white skirts (? *faldillas*), a number of pairs of *xeras*, needles and thread, and playing cards (*barajas*) (AHP 1722Aa; AHP 1722Ab).

Lomas ended one of his letters with the request that good clothing be brought out to them as his men had much money to buy with and valuable things (*alajas*) to trade with. Trading in some form with neighbors no doubt had gone on before Spanish contact times. The general increase in material goods, and the greater mobility with the horse, would seem to indicate that trade possibly became more important, either among the several Indian groups since booty was distributed among them (AHP 1652Dc), or between them and the Spaniards, during the Colonial period. Some of the trading at this time can be glimpsed from several sources, as well as gift-giving and the distribution of goods at ceremonies.

On one occasion the Gavilanes of El Mapochi, after a raid in the San Juan del Río area, invited the Cocoyomes and Hijos de las Piedras to visit them. They regaled their guests with some of their recent take — apparently mostly clothing — and invited the other two groups to join them in a future expedition (AHP 1655Ab). The Spanish woman captured during the 1644 Revolt was traded among the Indians several times for various material items (DHM 1645). In 1684, it was reported that the Tobosos had been negotiating with several Chiso bands to establish an alliance, for which purpose the Tobosos had been sending them arrows while the Chisos had been giving the Tobosos buffalo hides in return (AHP 1684Aa). Individual Tepehuanes were said sometimes to join the "Tobosos" (specifically El Mapochi's and Casa Zavala's groups) if they were "paid" (AHP 1654Ac), probably in booty. The Cabezas of Don Pedrote were

said to divide up their booty constantly with Don Dieguillo of the Nadadores mission as part of their friendship, and the latter used booty in an attempt to induce the Teodocodamos, Jumanes, and others into alliance (Portillo 1887: 201-202, 222).

Salineros, Cabezas, Mayos, Cíbolos, and Tobosos were reported to have taken stolen goods such as arquebuses, swords, saddles, trousers, hats, stockings, footwear (*zapatos*), military jackets (*cueras*), doublets (*coletos*), coins (*dineros*), figurines of saints (*hechuras de santos*), silver boxes (*cassos*), crocks or plates (*escudillas*), jugs (*jarros*) in which to make chocolate, as well as horses, mules and cows, to Tizonazo to trade there. Some of the "merchandise" was kept here where the Cíbolo Indians would come to exchange it for buffalo hides. Four captives were also turned over to the Cíbolos at this place (AHP 1655Ba; AHP 1667Aa).

The Acoclames took a Spanish captive to the Parras area and traded him for some ears of corn (*elotes*) and squash, and they and the Cocoyomes exchanged deer skins for buffalo hides with the Chisos (AHP 1704Ab). Soldiers and Indian auxiliaries traded with both of these groups during peace negotiations while out on campaign (AHP 1716Aa). The Cocoyomes and Coahuileños were reported to have traded with the settled Cabezas Indians at Parras, and in part to have reimbursed the latter for spying for them, with such items as deer skins, quivers of arrows, and coins. The Cabezas would supply them with *cotones* (cloth?), blankets, figs (*higos*), raw sugar (*chancacos*), and bread (*pan*), some of which they would purchase locally (AHP 1722Aa).

Subsistence

The early Jesuits reported that the general Bolsón area was exceedingly impoverished and so dry that it would support only wild and spiny brambles. This was not the case around the district of La Laguna and Parras, however, as the latter eventually became the center or *cabecera* of the missions of this region. The San Pedro lagoon, fed by the Nazas River, was some forty leagues in circumference at high water. The surrounding land was fertile and would produce nearly any kind of plant in abundance. The Indians would farm here during the periods of low water, although moisture was available and used for farming some distance from the lagoon itself (Alegre II 1956: 107; Pérez de Ribas III 1944: 245-246; BL 1600-1602; BL 1604).

Some of the reports for the San Pedro lagoon may also have applied in part to the much smaller lagoons and marshy areas to the north — those which today are called La Estacada, Las Palomas, Los Frailes, El Rey, La Leche, La Mula, Jaco, Los Gigantes, Los Patos, Clavos, Pastores, Chicuas, and Colorada, for example. Documentary evidence indicates that in the vicinity of these spots a small amount of agriculture may have been practiced. The Laguna area was said to be especially abundant in fruits, seeds, roots, and various kinds of fish and ducks — all of which were used by the local population. Fish became especially important, partly because they were easy to secure at times of low water, as were fruits and roots (Alegre II 1956: 107; Mota y Escobar 1940: 168; Pérez de Ribas III 1944: 246-247, 289; BL 1600-1602; BL 1604; BL 1615a).

Mota y Escobar specified some of the fish — *bagre*, *matalote*, a kind of sardine or trout (*trucha*), and a great number of very tiny fish (Mota y Escobar 1940: 167-168). Indians of other areas probably made use of all of these items whenever they could, although few specific references exist for the Chiso, Toboso, and Salinero groups. Fishing is specifically mentioned for Coahuileños, however, after they settled along the Nazas River (AHP 1722Aa), a practice they may have brought with them if there was any truth to statements concerning the abundance of different kinds of fish in places such as the Nadadores River (BL 1674).

Gathering

The subsistence pattern of the general area was basically one of gathering and hunting, plus fishing in some places. Probably most of the edible items in the environment were utilized. Mezcal, tunas, and mesquite were important for all groups — Laguneros, Salineros, Tobosos, and Chisos (Portillo 1887: 199, 202; AGN ca 1640; AHP 1651A; AHP 1652Ac; AHP 1652Dc; AHP 1653Ad; AHP 1655Ab; AHP 1658Aa; AHP 1658Ab; AHP 1684Aa; AHP 1704Ab; AHP 1716Ab; AHP 1722Aa; AHP 1724Ab; BL 1600-1602; BL 1606; BL 1676; BL 1693-1702; BL 1694-1698; BL 1748; CD 1650a; DHM 1645). Mota y Escobar reported the use of mesquite, maguey, and *agua miel*, as well as fish, by the people of the San Ignacio *partido*, up the Nazas River from San Pedro (1940:170).

Maguey was mentioned specifically for the Cabezas (BL 1693b), and *nopales* for the Ocomes (AHP 1652Dc) and Chisos (AHP 1684Aa). Dates (*dátiles*) were found at a Cocoyome camp (BL 1693b). One Sisimble woman told of eating roots (*raizes de las yerbas*) (BL 1748), and the same item was attributed to the Tobosos by Governor Larrea (BL 1649-1700). The Coahuileños were reported to use *agua miel* from the maguey plant (AHP 1652Ab), and *lechuguilla* and maguey were cited for the Parras area (BL 1600-1602). Mota y Escobar noted the great quantity of mescal (cooked maguey leaves) at Parras, and that these Indians possessed another kind of mescal called *noas*, much softer than that from the maguey plant (Mota y Escobar 1940: 170). Pinole was mentioned as used by the Gavilanes (AHP 1688Cb) and Chisos (AHP 1723A). Wild tobacco was sought, although its use was unspecified, by Salineros (AHP 1653Ad) and Coahuileños (AHP 1653Aa). The Salineros were also said to eat their own excrement (DHM 1645), that is, a "second harvest" in order to utilize the undigested seeds of the first eating.

Roots, fruits, and seeds, as previously noted, were especially abundant in the Parras-Laguna district. A type of cat-tail or reed-mace (*espadaña*) was cited as important. Flour from the roots was utilized in drink (gruel?) or as solid food in the form of loaves or cakes. These foods could be kept for many days without becoming too hard to eat. Mesquite, mescal, and tunas were also used as "bread" (*panes*) or "wine" (Alegre II 1956: 57, 107; Mota y Escobar 1940: 168; Pérez de Ribas III 1944: 247, 258; BL 1600-1602; BL 1604; BL 1605; BL 1606).

Specifically, for bread, mesquite was ground in mortars. For wine, the fruit was first cooked and then left to ferment. Bread was also made from the roots of a reed (*tule*), like a cat-tail (*espadaña*), and from other seeds native to the land. One of these was *alpiste* (*Phalaris canariensis*?), which without sowing grew in such quantity that it gave the impression of a wheat field. The Parras Indians also utilized pinyon nuts (Mota y Escobar 1940: 166-169).

The use of tuna cakes (*pan de tuna*) was cited for the Chisos (BL 1695a), and Balcárcel once wrote that the Coahuileños ate only roots that were available in different places at different times (Portillo 1887: 89-90). Arlegui mentioned the great number of herbs in the general area of the central Mexican plateau (1851: 139) and the use of alcoholic beverages made from almost any available plant (1851: 146). Peyote was cited a number of times (e.g., Arlegui 1851: 154; Pérez de Ribas III 1944: 248; AHP 1652Ab; AHP 1653Aa; BL 1600-1602).

Lack of water in much of the desert area, especially at certain times of the year, would restrict or be a fairly decisive factor in the organization or execution of many activities. The Spaniards constantly had difficulty in finding water for themselves and their animals when traveling or campaigning in the area (e.g., Arlegui 1851: 134; Pérez de Ribas III 1944: 277; AHP 1656Aa; AHP 1708b; BL 1694-1698). Even for the Laguna region, Father Arnaya reported in 1601 that it was so dry that only four spots (Nazas-Laguna area) adequate for large settlements had been found (DHM 1601). The Indians north of the Laguna district were characterized as living from "pools of rain water" (AHP 1708b). Sierra Osorio stated that they utilized "the filthy and impure water from some few lagoons, and that which was conserved for a short while after rains in the hollows or rocks, and failing this, the moisture from wild plants, roots, and the bark of plants and trees" (Hackett 1926: 220). In most of the area the Spaniards considered the major portion of the water holes as exhausted the greater part of the year.

Despite this, the Indians apparently could get along in the area considerably better than could the Spaniards. In some places when and where there was no water, the natives simply relied on plants such as *lechuguilla* (AHP 1653Ad) or wild maguey (Pérez de Ribas III 1944: 254, 277). The same practice was noted for some of the Tepehuanes by Arnaya in 1601 (DHM 1601) and also in the *Anua* of 1600-1602 (BL 1600-1602). In the 1690's the Cocoyomes were reported to have opened up a great quantity of magueys because the water hole where they were camped was very short (BL 1693b).

Agriculture

The peoples of the general region in the main have been considered to have had no, or only a slight amount of, agriculture. The *Anua* of 1596 states that the people of La Laguna "neither sow nor harvest other than that which the land voluntarily offers them in roots and game," although their neighbors, the Tepehuanes, grew corn. The Laguna people wandered the entire year over the places where food was most available (DHM 1596). In the 1615 *Anua* the same people were said to neither plant nor harvest but only to hunt what they could obtain with their

arrows (BL 1615b). The 1622 *Anua* stated that these were "untamed people, enemy of settlement, hunters in the mountains and fishers in the lagoons" (AGN 1622). Other references also claimed no agriculture for this area (BL 1605).

On the other hand, however, some references did note agriculture for the Laguna district, maize in particular (Alegre II 1956: 107). The 1606 *Anua* told of a gentile near whose house and field (*milpa*) the Christian doctrine was taught (BL 1606), which may be an indication of pre-mission agriculture. The Zacatecos to the southwest and south were considered nonagricultural for the most part (as noted by Beals 1932: 156-158 who cites *Documentos para la Historia de México*, cuarta serie, 3:47; Arlegui 26-27, 137; and Icasbalceta 2: 543; for no agriculture but Tello, 108, for corn grown by some Zacatecos; see Tello 1891: 108). The 1598 *Anua* said that the Zacatecos were like "beasts, seeking their life's sustenance where they found it, which is maguey, *lechuguilla*, mesquite, tunas, etc." (DHM 1598). The Salineros, Cabezas, Mayos, and Babozarigames of Coahuila were also cited as having had no agriculture (BL 1676), as were the "Tobosos," in a report by Sierra Osorio in 1683 (Hackett 1926: 212).

It is possible, however, that a number of the groups of the general area did practice some crop cultivation. Furthermore, some of the statements made by Spaniards about the Indians in general are either contradictory or rather obviously extreme. The *Anua* of 1604 stated that the Laguna area was so fertile that ears of corn up to one half a *vara* (yard) were grown there (BL 1604), while another reference declared that La Laguna was not appropriate for cultivated crops, although it abounded with birds, fish, and other game (AGN n.d.). Mota y Escobar agreed with the first statement, however. He noted that, "those who live next to the river sow corn on its sandy banks, with no more work than making a hole where they bury the grains." The ears were exceptionally big, and the land so fertile there was no need to work it. Melons, squash, and other fruits were also of very large size (Mota y Escobar 1940: 168-169).

Sierra Osorio wrote that the "Tobosos" were totally without agriculture, that they had no year-around water source, and — from what he had seen — that their land was without birds or animals (Hackett 1926: 212). At the same time, although huts were noted for specific groups, the existence of "houses" (*casas*) was denied for Indians in general reports. The *fiscal* in Mexico City, after reviewing a report that said that the Boveles (Coahuileños) dwelt in huts, once stated that the Coahuileños "lived without planted fields (*sementeras*), without houses, and nude" (BL 1676; BL 1693b).

A statement by Pérez de Ribas may have been descriptively the most accurate for agriculture in the general region, including precontact times, since it is difficult to see by what process agriculture as cited here for the Tobosos could have been introduced to them during the contact period. De Ribas noted for the people around the San Pedro lagoon that "although they also plant a few seeds, they do not care for them as much as do the other nations"; this attitude he attributed to the abundance of (wild) roots and other items (III 1944: 247).

Several documents mentioned Toboso agricultural activity, always (with one possible exception) with reference to squash. In a series of declarations in 1646, two Tobosos cited squash planting. In the testimony of Cristóbal, the Toboso governor, it was stated, "and this declarant having some *milpas* of squash (*calabazas*) planted and his people waiting to eat them, they did not go to look for the *señor* governor to grant him peace." The other Toboso testified "that the reason for not having come previously to seek the *señor* governor has been because they wanted to finish a *milpa* of squash that they had" (AHP 1652Dc). These testimonies were made in November. Back in July envoys from the Tobosos, Nonojes, Ocomes, and Acoclames had stated that "they are all together ready to come in upon finishing eating the squash (*calabazas*) that they have planted and the corn and mesquite, tunas, dates (*datiles*) and pitayas" (AHP 1645Aa). The mention of corn together with the uncultivated food is somewhat puzzling and may mean that the Toboso sowed maize to some extent. However, this is the only such reference.

Again, with regard to squash, in 1653 a group of enemy "Tobosos" were reported to be planting *calabazas* at the Sierra de Guapagua. In this same year several Toboso women, while assessing their local food resources, testified that the Tobosos had not planted any squash this year (no other cultivated crops were mentioned); one declared, however, that the Nonojes had sown squash at the Peñol de Nonolat. Nevertheless, Esteban de Levarío reported from Indé in June of this year that a *junta* of Tobosos was at this time planting squash behind the Sierra of

Guapagua (this information came via the Salineros) (AHP 1653Ad).

In 1666, a campaign into the Las Cañas region revealed an enemy camping ground at a water hole with a squash field (*calavazal*), apparently planted by the Indians. This site was some six leagues from Las Batuecas (BL 1649-1700). Chisos, testifying in September of 1693 at San Francisco de Conchos concerning the whereabouts of the enemy "Toboso," stated that the Acoclames, Hijos de las Piedras, and Hijos de la Tierra were camped at a water hole in the Jaque-Encinillas area where they had planted their crops (Hackett 1926: 342; BL 1693-1702; BL 1695a). Another reference in December of the same year noted that the Acoclame had planted (*sembrado*) at the Sierra de los Picachos, apparently in the Jaque-Encinillas region, and four leagues from Chocamueca (BL 1695a).

There are no further references to "Toboso" agriculture, and the Spaniards usually considered them as nonagricultural (e.g., AHP 1654Ad; AHP 1676Aa; BL 1649-1700). Chisos, questioned in 1684 about their livelihood, cited mainly wild plants and animals. However one Batayolicla included corn, and another stated that he "lived on the maize he planted in his own territory" (AHP 1684Aa). The *Anua* of 1606 mentioned that the Indians around Mapimí (Tepehuanes?) gave a missionary some ears of corn. Later, reference was made to the "fields and squash" (*milpas y calabasas*) of an enemy group at Pelayo, consisting of people from the "Mission of Tepehuanes" and several rancherias from Mapimí (BL 1606).

Hunting

Hunting, no doubt, was important for all groups, although there are only a few references to it (e.g., for the Cabezas and Salineros — AHP 1651A; AHP 1653Ad; BL 1676). Rabbits were taken by the Salineros, who were said to prepare them by removing only the skins; everything else was eaten, including the intestines (DHM 1645). Mota y Escobar noted rabbit hunting as especially important in the Laguna district (Mota y Escobar 1940: 169). Deer, in particular, were cited for the Cocoyomes and Acoclames (AHP 1686Bc; AHP 1704Ab; AHP 1708a; AHP 1715Aa; BL 1649-1700). One group, apparently Cabezas or their "allies," had eaten a deer at Las Cañas (AHP 1652Da). Chisos hunted and ate rabbits (*conejos*), jackrabbits (*liebres*), deer, mice, and snakes (AHP 1684Aa; BL 1748). Rats, *tuzas*, and snakes were also noted as eaten in the general area, and Arlegui included frogs and worms (Arlegui 1851: 168; Pérez de Ribas III 1944: 273, 281; BL 1600-1602; BL 1604; BL 1748).

Pérez de Ribas stated that possibly the ground or powdered bones of animals were also utilized as food (III 1944: 281). The latter was also referred to by Alonso de León, who gave a rather good account of Nuevo León foods and food processing techniques. Bones, he said, were ground up and mixed with *mesquitamal* (García 1909: 37-40, 42). Rabbits, deer, and birds – including herons (*garzas*), geese (*ánsares*), and ducks (*patos*) – were in great abundance in the Parras-Laguna district (Alegre II 1956: 107; Arlegui 1851: 168; Mota y Escobar 1940: 169; Pérez de Ribas III 1944: 247; BL 1600-1602; BL 1604). These same people, as well as the Salineros, were said to be voracious meat eaters (DHM 1598; DHM 1645).

The bow and arrow was the main hunting weapon. Arlegui also mentioned the use of the head of a deer with fruit stuck in its eyes as a decoy for hunting deer in the sierra of Durango (Tepehuanes?) (1851: 169), a practice possibly with somewhat wider distribution than this. Ducks were mentioned as important in the Laguna-Parras district and, aside from the methods already cited, were also caught by hand. This ingenious hand technique may also have been employed in some of the other lagoons. The hunter covered his head with half the shell of a large round gourd, with holes cut in it to see through. He then submerged himself in the water, approached the ducks with only the gourd shell showing above water, and from this position caught the birds by their feet (Alegre II 1956: 107; Arlegui 1851: 168; Perez de Ribas III 1944: 247).

Bison or buffalo lived to the north in both Nuevo León and Nueva Vizcaya and were no doubt hunted to some extent (Arlegui 1851: 2, 138; Miller and Kellog 1955: 817-818; Reed 1955). The people of the Coahuila area were reported to hunt both buffalo and deer (DHM ca 1706); one group here was known as the Buffalo People (Cíbolos) as was another north of the Río Grande (see Chapter 3). A number of bands along the Río Grande below La Junta, no doubt including Chisos, were said to participate in buffalo hunts during the winter. Also, when Retana made his campaign in the latter part of 1693, the Suniyoliglas did not accompany him because they had gone off with the Cíbolos of Texas to hunt buffalo (BL 1695a). Boboles were reported to be hunting buffalo on the Río Grande in 1675 (BL 1674).

Wild horses or mustangs were cited as hunted specifically by the Acoclames and Cocoyomes (AHP 1708a; AHP 1716Aa; AHP 1720Aa; AHP 1722A), and wild cattle by the Cocoyomes in 1691 (BL 1693b). In this same year, the Cocoyomes were said to have had a great many wild mustangs in pasture (*repastando*) (BL 1693b). This use of domestic animals gone wild was probably true for other groups as well. Arlegui mentioned that many wild horses and cattle throughout Coahuila were used for food by the Indians (1851: 130, 134). Probably many of these wild animals came from those lost by the Indians after raids as they drove stolen herds back to their camps – losses partly due to the great haste with which they usually traveled (BL 1693b).

Stolen animals from Spanish holdings and settlements, particularly horses and mules but also cattle and sheep, were an important source of food for all groups (Hackett 1926: 220; Portillo 1887: 222; AHP 1653Ad; AHP 1653Ae; AHP 1654Ac; AHP 1654Ca; AHP 1656Aa; AHP 1657Bb; AHP 1669Ba; AHP 1670B; AHP 1673Ab; AHP 1677A; AHP 1699a; AHP 1704Ab; AHP 1715Aa; AHP 1716Aa; AHP 1724Aa; BL 1649-1700; BL 1693-1702; BL 1694-1698; BL 1709-1715; BL 1748). There is evidence of an increasing reliance on these animals as a food supply as the Colonial Period progressed. However, for the time span encompassed in this study, some raiding activity was reported in the earliest years. The *Anua* of 1600-1602 mentioned a place in the Parras district where there were found many bones of the mules and horses (*bestias*) the Indians had stolen and eaten. In another spot there were "small huts (*chosuelas*) in the form of caves from where they endangered (*oseaban*) the roads and valleys and farther ahead at intervals in a wash the graves (*sepulturas*) of those [animals] they had killed in quantity" (BL 1600-1602). The 1604 *Anua* referred to a band that had uprisen and had lived off raiding Spanish cattle and haciendas, until it had been put down by another group (BL 1604). The *Anua* of 1606 also cited raiding by the group at Pelayo a few years previously (BL 1606). The Chiso band captured in 1748 was selective about the animals it stole. During the interrogation Chief Nepomuceno stated that his people tried to steal only fat horses and that they killed or simply left the thin ones behind (BL 1748).

These animals were prepared for eating in several ways. These methods of preparation were probably employed also for game animals, although the majority of references concern the stolen domestic variety. The use of jerky was most commonly cited and was considered one of the more usual of Indian fares. Spaniards sometimes reported having come by surprise upon Indians preparing jerky from the animals they had killed (Arlegui 1851: 130; AHP 1653Ae; AHP 1657Bb; AHP 1658Aa; AHP 1658Ab; AHP 1724Aa). Alonso de León encountered Indians fifteen leagues from the Río Grande, on the Texas side of the river, preparing jerky from buffalo meat (Portillo 1887: 227). This treatment, of course, would make the meat much easier to store and to keep, and it could be more easily used while on the trail (AHP 1724Aa). Sisimbles in 1748 declared that while traveling on foot when they had no horses they carried dried meat reduced to powder, which they mixed in water for use as food (BL 1748). Meat was also cooked or roasted (AHP 1653Ae). Venison was cooked (AHP 1656Aa; AHP 1704Ab), as was beef tripe by Salineros (AHP 1656Ab), and colts were prepared *en barbacoa* (AHP 1644A). Cabezas and Tobosos roasted six oxen (*bueyes*) and a goat when Father Castillo was with them (AGN 1667), and a steer was cooked (*tatemaron*) by El Tecolote's band in the 1690's (BL 1694-1698).

Horses

A few other items representing the horse complex as developed by the Indians have come to light. One of the most notable is the occasional reference to the use of corrals. Out in the Guapagua-Río Angosto region the Spaniards discovered "a corral of large stones where they [the Indians] enclosed all of the horses they had stolen" (AHP 1653Aa). Two others were also mentioned, although they were undescribed as to size and construction materials. One was found at the Cerro de Pelayo in which the enemy had enclosed "a great many animals" (AHP 1652Ab), and another at San Juan de Casta near Mapimí in which stolen mules had been kept (AHP 1656Aa). Horse and mule herds were often discovered at enemy camps (e.g., AHP 1718Ac; AHP 1724Ab; also see elsewhere). Wild mustangs were not only hunted for food but also caught and broken (*domarlos*) (BL

1693b) and consequently, no doubt, used for mounts.

Two more items may throw some light upon practices Indians used with horses. A Mexican muleteer, who was attacked by two Indians whom he judged to be Salineros, partly from their accents when they spoke the Mexican tongue, described a halter (*freno*) they were using as a *barbiquejo* (mat-like affair?) of *palmilla*, apparently tied around the head in some fashion (?). These two "Salineros" were wearing a type of colored blanket (*frasadas coloradas*) used only at Minas Nuevas; there is no way to determine if these were stolen or not, or if these were hacienda or other Indians (AHP 1657Bb). One vague reference may indicate the use of skins on the hooves of animals either for muffling sound or blotting out tracks (*y de buelta la parte q les Cabia* (?) *de bestias las llevaban En gamuzas por no ser descubiertos en case de llevar Ropa o Caballos a la buelta a su pueblo*). This was cited as the practice of two Coahuileño Indians who on several occasions had joined the Acoclames to raid (AHP 1704Ab). Some stirrups (*dos pares de estriberas y un estribo suelto*) once were found at the water hole of Acatita — no description was given, and they probably were Spanish (AHP 1715Aa).

General Social Organization

Bands

The largest social unit of the Greater Bolsón peoples seems to have been the "nation" or band. Unfortunately, practically no information is available regarding the specific features of these units, although some of their general characteristics were noted by the early writers. Father Francisco de Arista noted how divided and scattered (*tan divididos y esparcidos*) the Indians (apparently meaning bands or rancherias) were (Pérez de Ribas III 1944: 255). Many rancherias were reported in the surrounding mountains of the Parras-Laguna district, and many were located in quite inaccessible places as far as the Spaniards were concerned. Pérez de Ribas, discussing the many "nations" in and around this area, stated that, "these, although of few people, I call nations because they themselves treated and named each other with as much difference as do those that are very different in Europe, and I do not know how to designate this difference, except with the term different nations" (Pérez de Ribas III 1944: 255-256, 264-265).

Alegre (1956 II: 42, 56-58, 106, 108, 150) and Arlegui (1851: 136-137) also referred to the numerous nations in and about the Laguna region. Arlegui went on to say, somewhat exaggeratedly, that the major part of the bands "have no abode (asiento) anyplace — they continually go about naked, live in the open (en los campos), sheltering themselves in the winters in the ravines and caves in the most austere mountains, and in the summers they live in the same fashion, and they are so accustomed to the rigors of the climate that they seem [to be] insensitive" (1851: 137). However, each band had its territory, as "they have divided among themselves the mountains, fields, rivers, and plains, such that each nation hunts, fishes, and makes use of that which it has marked out (senalado)" (1851: 150).

The Anua of 1596 described the Laguna peoples as "half fish, half men, part live in the water, part on the land; but in no place do they have a stable dwelling (habitacion fuerte)." They never remained in any definite place "except where they think they can find food, today here, tomorrow over there, wandering all the year" (DHM 1596). The 1607 Anua, speaking of the difficulty of bringing the surrounding groups into the missions, stated that "they are divided into rancherias that have their abode (asiento) in their mountain tops and hills" (AGN 1607c).

In 1654, Spaniards again noted the territoriality of the "Toboso" groups. They recognized the traditional enmity among many of the bands who would not dare trespass upon each others' territories. At the same time, the Spaniards were aware that alliances often were cemented among the bands (AHP 1654Ad). Governor Pardiñas wrote in 1693 that the Toboso bands had "no fixed place in which to reside." Furthermore, they needed "no passes" for their entradas, which they made where least expected, as they traveled easiest over the roughest mountain ranges (BL 1694-1698). The Bishop of Guadalajara in 1676, apparently aware of the breakdown of the tribal territories of some groups, stated that the Coahuileños — including the Cabezas, Salineros, Babozarigames, and Mayos — although they were wanderers, each had their own territory to which they would return sometime during the year (BL1676).

Alonso de León's description of the Nuevo León peoples seems to fit quite well the area of concern here, for which reason it is quoted at this time. He stated that the type of government the natives had was "anarchy" (apparently struggling for terminology as was Pérez de Ribas), and that "they inhabit brushy areas in flat lands (por montes en bajios), moving from one place to another, the families splitting up or coming together by whim as they are accustomed to . . . . The greatest group (congregacion) [which is called a rancheria (which is apparently inserted by the editor, Genaro García)] which they form, usually comprises fifteen huts (chozas) in the form of bells (campanas); these they place in rows (hileras) or in half-moons, fortifying the ends (puntas) with another two huts, and this is particularly when they have wars, and when not, each family or rancho, or two together, travel around the hills, living two days here and four there; however, not because of this should it be understood that they go out of their boundaries and territory which they have marked off with another rancheria, if it is not with their consent and permission, in each rancho or bajío, and eight or ten, or more persons, men, women and children come" (García 1909: 34-35).

Only a few hints have come to light concerning the nature of these bands. There seems to have been a primary or minimal named group that was quite small. There is little information on the size of these groups; however, one of the best indications comes from the report on twelve bands that arrived in Atotonilco in January of 1646. The Nonojes consisted of some fifty-nine persons and the Ocomes forty-three. The other ten nations comprised 396 individuals, making an average of about forty persons per band (CD 1650a). Information from other sources (see Chapter 3) indicates that the named groups ran from about twenty-five to seventy-five persons.

These figures are, of course, only approximate and are derived partly from estimates based on the number of warriors reported. The best calculation seems to be to add roughly three to four persons per warrior (because the latter were not necessarily family heads, adding four or five as was usually done for settled Indians seems to result in too high a figure, as not all warriors were married). Therefore, a fifteen-warrior band would probably contain fifty to sixty persons. Utilizing the figures from the various reports is made more difficult, however, by vague or generic use of "nation" names, which often possibly included allies. This becomes even more true with progress of time, as the native groups disappeared or were decimated and/or permanently joined to other bands.

Most of the data indicate that the exogamous social unit was this small, named band or "nation," as the Spaniards generally called them. Particularly in the early years these seem to have been the groups most often referred to in the documents. Later (see Appendix 1), the tendency was to use more generic terms, although for some groups, such as the Salineros, and probably the Cabezas, generic usage was common from the 1640's on. On the other hand, this increasing general use of terms, and the converse dropping of specific terms, appears to reflect that these groups did in fact become more and more composite, not only because they took refuge with each other as they diminished in numbers but also because larger groups of people could remain together for longer periods of time as the native economy became reoriented.

The church records of the "band" of Cabezas that settled in Parras in the 1690's definitely show the composite nature of this group. They also seem to indicate that the specific named groups were the exogamous units, as in the overwhelming majority of cases there was no marriage between persons of the same band affiliation. A few exceptions do exist, but most of these involve a known generic term such as "Cabeza" (see Appendices 2 and 3).

Other cases of band intermarriage tend to support this. A Batayoligla declarant (in a somewhat ambiguous passage) stated that three Suniyoligla men were related to him and were married to Sisimble women (BL 1709-1715). More "distant" bands sometimes also intermarried. In one instance twelve Chisos went to the Acoclames with their families, taking along four girls who were to marry Acoclames. These marriages did not materialize, however, and unfortunately it was not stated if the girls were to remain with the Acoclames after marriage (AHP 1704Ab). Blood relationship was reported elsewhere between Cocoyomes and Cabezas (BL 1693b) and between Acoclames and Coahuilenos (AHP 1704Ab). Chisos intermarried with some of the La Junta nations (BL 1695a).

Such matrimonial ties between bands were reported to cement alliances. One long-time captive of the desert Indians indicated that around 1686 this

had been the case between the Cabezas and Cocoyomes. The Cabezas had been allied with the Cocoyomes because a Cabeza named Gáspar had been married to a Cocoyome woman, "because the said Indian Gáspar owing to his marriage had made the alliance that only lasted until at Pozo Hediondo about two and a half years ago [before August, 1691] in an encounter the Spaniards killed, among others, the said Gáspar, and afterwards the Cocoyomes began to lose confidence in the Cabezas." It had been understood that because of the marriage there had been peace, and soon afterward the two groups became enemies (BL 1693b).

If the foregoing regarding exogamy is correct, then these bands would have represented, at one time at least, small lineages. In 1653, a Toboso (Antón) was questioned regarding the number of his people left. He stated that only his father remained and, "that although it is said that among the Nonojes there were four Indians of his nation, naturally they are not because they are the sons of the women of the said Nonojes." This contradicted the statement at the beginning of the declaration, that "he said he is named Antón, son of Cristóbal Zapata, Indian of the Toboso nation, and this declarant is of the said nation." If the first statement actually does evince matriliny, then it may be that the second is a supposition of the scribe or of some other patrilineally oriented Spaniard. Later, in his testimony, Antón reported that one Santiago, a Nonoje, had been killed together with the Tobosos and, "that his being with the latter was because he was married to a Toboso woman" (AHP 1653Ad).

While this evidence is very weak, and the last statement may refer only to Santiago visiting his wife's kinfolk, Gonzalo de las Casas reported in the sixteenth century that among (some of?) the Chichimecas to the south there was matrilocal residence (Las Casas 1936). In 1694 Captain Martín de Hualde wrote that a captive had declared that the Cocoyome chief "Contrerillas joined the Hijos de las Piedras and had married there" (BL 1695a). There is also slight evidence that the Chisos may have been matrilocal. In 1713, a Suniyoligla, telling of the ill feeling between his group and the Sisimbles, declared that three warriors from his band "were with the Sisimbles because of having married into the latter (alla) and that these three are brothers (hermanos) and are the ones who defended Antonio and his two companions so they [the Sisimbles] would not kill them, and he [the declarant] is certain that because of this they are probably distrusted (*malmirados*) by the Sisimbles, and he imagines that they have now gone to join the Suniyoliglas" (BL 1709-1715).

Evidence from church records is also confusing. In only a few instances did priests note the band or "nation" affiliation of both a person and his parents. The following cases are taken mostly from the Parras Parish Archives (unless otherwise stated).

Matriliny

(1) A baptism in 1609 states that Lucía Paianboa was the daughter of Perico Leguaquin (Bautismos, 1605 . . . .).

(2) Baptism, 1658: ". . . Angelina Yndia de nacion Tusar hija legitima de Nicolas Tooca y de Beatris Tusar . . . ." (Libro 2b, Bautismos).

(3) Baptism, 1659: ". . . Andres infante hijo lejitimo de Nicolas Tooca y de Luisa Su muger quaaguapaia . . . ." On the margin Andres is listed as "Andres Quaaguapaia" (Libro 2b, Bautismos).

Patriliny

(1) In 1694 occurs the baptism of Micaela, a Cabeza, whose parents are said to be Juan Baca and Juana. From several entries these two are a Cabeza and Toboso, respectively (Libro de Bautismos, Ranchería de los Cabezas).

(2) Baptism, 1695: ". . . P.o Agustin yndio de Nazion quesal, yJO + [legitimo] de gaspar Yndio de dicha nasion Y de Marta yndia de Nazon [sic] Cabeza . . . ." (Libro de Bautismos, Ranchería de los Cabezas).

(3) Marriage, 1706, of a Contotore ". . . ijo legitimo de Sebastian indio de la nacion Contotores, y de Margarita india de la nacion manos prietas . . . ." (Libro de Matrimonios, Ranchería de los Cabezas).

(4) Marriage, 1706 (from the same entry above), of ". . . Magdalena india de la nacion Cocoyome Yja ligitima de fran.co indio de nacion Cocoyome, y de Magdalena de nacion Cabeza . . . ." (Libro de Matrimonios, Ranchería de los Cabezas).

(5) Marriage, 1708: ". . . a Joseph Gonzales Indio de la Nacion Maya hijo legitimo de Domingo Mayo, Y de Catalina con Michaela hija lejitima de Juan Baca Indio de Nacion Cabeza, y de Juana . . . ." (Libro de Matrimonios, Ranchería de los Cabezas).

(6) Marriage, 1719: an Alazapa is said to be the son of an Alazapa man and a Tetecora woman (Libro de Matrimonios, Ranchería de los Cabezas).

(7) Burial, 1719, of a Maya woman, ". . . hija de Magdalena de Nacion Cabeza y de Fran.co . . . ," apparently Mayo (Libro de Entierros, Ranchería de los Cabezas).

(8) Baptism, 1672, of a Toboso, son of Antón Zapata, who possibly is the Toboso, Antón Zapata, who testified in 1653. (Libro: Bautismos 1662-1678, Archivo de la Parroquia de Allende (Valle de San Bartolomé)).

One doubtful case, that is, whether it might be evidence of matriliny or patriliny, depends on whether the Pies de Venado can be identified with the Babozarigames or not (see Appendix 1). In 1717, the burial of an old Pies de Venado man said to be the ". . . hijo de Margarita de la Cruz, de su P.e [padre] no se sabe el nom.e [nombre] ni nacion de los dhos, aunq.e dice es su M.e [madre] de la Nacion Bozeregamui [Babozarigami] . . . ." (Libro de Entierros, Ranchería de los Cabezas).

There is no way to carry this analysis further or to resolve the contradictions until more data are uncovered. It is possible that both matriliny and patriliny existed, although this assumption does not solve the ethnographic problem. It is also possible that the earlier information is correct and that the entries of the Cabeza Rancheria of Parras reflect either the ignorance or the bias of the priests and/or breakdown or switch in the lineage or naming system.

Marriage

Very little information has come to light regarding specific marriage practices. Arlegui mentioned both monogamy and polygyny (as well as group marriage?) but does not specify the groups or localities where these customs prevailed. He also stated that some kind of bride price, either in goods or in work by the groom for his father-in-law, was common among the central Mexican plateau people — the most usual was for the man to deposit a deer he had hunted at the house of his prospective bride. Separation or "divorce" was also common (1851: 142-143). The 1598 *Anua* referred to the premarital freedom of women and the brittleness of liaisons (DHM 1598). One case of sororal polygyny among the desert Tepehuán of the Mapimí area was cited in the 1606 *Anua* (BL 1606). Possibly a statement by the Spanish governor in 1674 to the Salineros and Cabezas, who had gone to make peace, indicated some polygyny for these groups. He admonished them that those men who had more than one wife would have to give up the extra women and remain with only the one to whom they were legitimately married (BL 1649-1700). The case of Don Pedrote and the two sisters he was living with before his Catholic marriage indicates the possibility of sororal polygyny in this instance (see Appendix 1).

Arlegui noted the berdache among the Tejas (Texas) Indians (Arlegui 1851: 144), but there is no evidence that this custom existed among the Nueva Vizcayan and Coahuilan peoples.

Chieftains

The people of the general area were reported to be governed by captains or chiefs (Arlegui 1851: 142; Pérez de Ribas III 1944: 259). Arlegui stated that these were the men who had the greatest reputation for valor among them; at each rancheria some obedience was given to the bravest (1851: 142). There is some evidence of patrilineal aspect or inheritance of chieftainship. Toboso women testifying in 1653 tended to rank chiefs according to their fame, but one stated that the captain of the Gavilanes, the man of greatest reputation among them who had died during the Río Angosto battle, had been replaced by his brother. Since this woman had been captured during this fracas, this seems to have been somewhat of a foregone conclusion (AHP 1653Ad).

Another declarant, Antón, stated that Francisco Casa Zavala and his sons, now all deceased, had been "captains" of the Nonojes, who were now led by Casa Zavala's grandson; and, the deceased Ocome chief had been succeeded by El Zurdo, "his son" or "his nephew" — Antón's two statements as reported being rather confused (AHP 1653Ad). In one series of declarations the Cocoyome chief was said to have been called "captain" since he had been a small boy because his father had also been chief (AHP 1715Aa). Likewise, a Chiso, Ventura, was stated to be a chief, as his father had been before him (AHP 1704Ab). During the absence of the Cabeza chief, Santiago, his brother, Bartolomé, had taken over (AHP 1673Ab), and these may have been the same Bartolomé and Santiago who were cited as Cabeza chiefs some fourteen years later (BL 1693b). Alegre told of a chief at Parras who had referred to his right of birth and deeds of war (Alegre II 1956: 149-150).

One ex-captive indicated the importance of kinship in leadership as well as the role of age. He told of a gentile chief called El Julime (said elsewhere to be a Chiso or Julime) who was "married to an Indian woman relative of El Tecolote and that because of this he is the one who virtually governs (manda) all and who is obeyed more because now not so much attention is given to El Tecolote since as an old man he cannot govern so strongly (tan resio)." El Tecolote was judged to be about fifty years old at this time. (Possibly, El Julime was Lorenzo). Another ex-captive also noted the decline of El Tecolote's authority because the people "no longer pay attention to him because he is only a talker (tatolero) and a coward" (BL 1693b).

In 1692, Lorenzo, the then head chief of the Cocoyomes, recounted how he had come to hold this position. "He said that it is true that Don Francisco Tecolote was always the governor of the said Cocoyome nation and as such he commanded all of those belonging to it and later as soon as the declarant was at a competent age the said Don Francisco Tecolote made him his assistant in the governing (govierno) and in recognition that the said Don Francisco is a man of many years (mayor de edad) all of those of the said nation began to obey him [Lorenzo] and he held them under his charge up until now, and on attempting to make peace and the declarant having worked for this and done everything possible on his part the said Don Francisco, seeing that he had his people reduced, retired saying that now everyone obeyed him [Lorenzo] and he should come as governor to make the peace." Later, "he told the declarant that he was [now] the governor of the Cocoyomes and that he should come with them because he [Francisco] was now an old man" (BL 1693b).

In an earlier testimony of a mestizo ex-captive of the Jojocomes, it was stated that "although Don Francisco Tecolote is named [as governor] he does not have as much influence as the two Lorenzös [one the chief of the Jojocomes], as these men have it with much prestige (credito) with these nations [Cocoyomes and Jojocomes]" and regarding difficulties of coming to an agreement concerning peace among these peoples, "not withstanding that everyday they are admonished by Don Lorenzo [which one?] not to do any damage or to steal horses" (BL 1693b).

Arlegui stated, possibly somewhat exaggeratedly, that the people would treacherously kill their chiefs in order to get out from under their yoke (1851: 142). Another ex-captive of the Cocoyomes said that he had heard during discussions about making peace with the Spaniards that El Tecolote had said that the rest could surrender but that he would not (BL 1693b). This and Arlegui's statement may be indications of the limited authority of the chiefs; Arlegui's comment may also point to a certain amount of "fear" that chiefs may have instilled in their followers. Some chiefs, at least, possessed supernatural power, as noted subsequently for the Cocoyome chiefs; Juan de Lomas. Governor Castillo wrote the Viceroy of the reputation of "El Tecolote [who] because of the great fear and in order to carry out his wizardry (*hechiserias*) with which he took advantage (*se aventajava*) a great deal of all of the others, always went off from the others in order to sleep alone" (BL 1693b). One chief of the Yrbipias was reported to have been a witch (*echisero*) (Portillo 1887: 86).

Warfare

Warfare-and-raiding was one of the major activities of the Tobosos and other desert tribes during Colonial contact times. The early writers characterized some of the aspects of warfare for the people of the general region. In precontact or early post-contact times wars were said to have been endemic, although they took place particularly in the dry season when fighting would occur over water and other resources (e.g., the fish the lakes might contain). Alegre noted that these wars were somehow connected with the practice of cannibalism, attributing the latter to the lack of food at these periods (Alegre II 1956: 235; Pérez de Ribas II 1944: 289). Seasonality was also noted for the raiding activities of later times.

Arlegui described the central plateau tribes in the same way — each nation lived in a continual state of war with its neighbors and they would kill anyone, Indian or Spaniard, who did not belong to their tribe. He noted also, however, that alliances took place frequently among "some" bands for particular battles, but that they would quickly disintegrate for the slightest cause and the former hostilities would re-emerge. Trespassing into a neighboring territory to gather, hunt, or fish was sufficient cause for war (Arlegui 1851: 138, 147-148, 150; AHP 1654Ad). A more succinct description, made of the peoples around the Río Grande, probably Coahuileños and possibly including some Chiso speakers, noted that

there was much discord among these groups and they had the custom of killing and eating each other and of capturing each others' children (BL 1674). Even under missionization deaths between bands caused enmity (AGN 1607c). Mota y Escobar described the Laguna peoples as very skillful in the art of war, which they practiced with more order and better stratagems than other nations in the area (1940: 169).

Revenge was an important immediate cause in maintaining hostile relations with neighbors (BL 1676). In one case it was reported that after the Salineros and associated Spanish Indian allies had defeated and killed many of the "Tobosos," four of these bands joined together. Of two Salineros who had been living (married?) among them for years, they killed one in revenge. The other escaped to the Cíbolas. Then the "Tobosos" pooled their efforts "to make munitions in order to make their last effort in [wreaking] their vengeance," planning first to attack the Cíbolas, and later the Salineros and Spaniards (AHP 1653Ad). In another instance a Gavilán leader (El Mapochi?) refused to return to Atotonilco until he had revenged the deaths of his relatives, for which he claimed he would die fighting (AHP 1654Ac). The Salineros and Cabezas were reported to have said in 1673 that they were fighting to avenge deaths the Spaniards had inflicted on them (BL 1649-1700).

Analytically, besides the revenge motive, killing the enemy for prestige and ceremonial reasons was no doubt important (e.g., AHP 1715a; AHP 1722Ab; BL 1709-1715). The Acoclames fought with the Sisimbles and Chisos over a woman, although they soon became friends again (AHP 1704Ab). In one instance a note of collective responsibility for killings emerges. This occurred in the testimony of Sisimbles in Durango in 1748 when it was stated that no particular individual was to be blamed for any of the specific killings committed but that all were responsible. At the same time, however, they said that they had killed two women — one because she was old and the other because she had refused to accompany them. Other killings were carried out by members of the same group in order to steal the clothing worn by their victims. Their own descriptions indicate that specific murders were committed because the victims had become angry (*enojados*), that is, they had put up resistance. In one case the attackers had not killed because the people had given their clothing without becoming "angry." The killing of some Apaches, however, had been in vengeance (BL 1748).

The Spanish military and administrators recognized and used this actual and potential enmity in dealing with the various Indian groups. This practice was largely responsible for their success in employing Indians as auxiliary troops. The Europeans knew that latent hostile relations could be fomented into open conflict by getting one group to attack and kill members of another. Although this method often worked, it was not completely foolproof (Arlegui 1851: 138, 166-167; AHP 1716Aa).

Reports from the period concerned here are replete with accounts of raids and attacks by the desert Indians. No attempt has been made to summarize the events of the individual skirmishes, except some of the principal characteristics of the warfare-raiding complex and the results of the general culture contact in this sphere of activity. The size of raiding parties ranged from small groups of six to twelve men to large forces of well over one hundred warriors for mass attacks (e.g., AHP 1652Da; AHP 1655Ab; AHP 1656Aa; AHP 1715Aa).

War party organization was somewhat more complex than this, however. Informants in 1654 stated that only some of the warriors of a band would go out at any one time and that often such parties would then later be divided into smaller squads (AHP 1654Ac). Some raiding parties that stayed out for considerable periods of time were accompanied by women who helped the men keep camp (AHP 1655Ab). One unidentified group, operating in the general Cuencamé region, had the women and children along to make arrows for the warriors (AHP 1669Ba). On one occasion it was reported that a large composite group (of El Mapochi and others) had planned to stay in an area for a rather long period — until the rainy season began — and had taken the women and children with them (AHP 1655Ab).

For attacks, large war parties would often be divided into two or more squads, and both mounted and unmounted warriors (cavalry and infantry) were reported. It is not certain when these groups began using the horse, but it was no doubt very early. Enemy Tobosos, Nonojes, and "other nations" in the spring of 1643 were said to be all mounted (CD 1643a; also see Forbes 1959b). The adoption of certain Spanish forms seems to have occurred over a period of time, a trend that began farther south in the sixteenth century when the Spaniards started their penetration northward (see Powell 1952: 40, 45-47, 49ff, 174). This is not surprising since not only could the Indians see how the Spaniards organized large groups of men when they were in battle, but many individual Indians, if not groups, at one time or another fought as auxiliaries on the Spanish side. Furthermore, Spaniards were favorably impressed when their allies demonstrated good military discipline. On one occasion Salineros and Cabezas arrived in Parral with "a great deal of order," carrying a red (colorada) banner with a cross on it and a pole with the Toboso scalps they had taken in battle (AHP 1653Ad).

Occasionally information on the organization of attacking Indian parties occurs in the sources. One group, poorly identified, but with men nude and painted, divided into two squads to carry out its assault, and each squad carried poles with scalps attached (AHP 1654Ca). Father Castillo reported that on one occasion the group of Tobosos and Salineros he was with divided their squad into six lines (hileras) of twenty-five men each (AGN 1667). Another time, Tobosos and Chisos attacked a wagon train in three squads (AHP 1684Aa). The Cocoyomes and Coahuileños made a raid on El Charco in the Parras district divided into four squads, two mounted and two on foot (AHP 1722Aa). Banners (banderas) were often reported carried by the raiders. Sixty Indians operating near Cerro Gordo flew five banners (AHP 1715Aa).

The most Spanish-sounding attack (largely described elsewhere but repeated here) was one that occurred at the presidio of San Francisco de Conchos. A large force, later judged by witnesses to have consisted of over 100 men on horseback plus those on foot, attacked some twenty-five soldiers guarding the presidio's horses. The enemy came in carrying three different banners, sounding both fifes (pifanos) and drums (tambores). The tactics employed in this case apparently were effective, as, in the midst of the shouting and the dust, the Spanish soldiers never had a chance to regroup themselves for a counterattack and the entire herd was lost. Several of the soldiers later stated that this attack procedure was something never seen in this area before. However, somewhat previous to this, some fifty to sixty Indians had made an assault in the vicinity of Cerro Gordo with three banners, a fife, and much war whooping (AHP 1715Aa; AHP 1718Ac).

One of the main defensive tactics of the Indians when surrounded by Spaniards was flight under the cover of night, often under truce, when negotiation for some kind of a peace settlement was being begun (e.g., BL 1649-1700; BL 1694-1698; BL 1709-1715). One ex-captive stated that he had heard the Indians say a number of times that they often agreed to peace in the battlefield in order to get out of tight situations, such as when the Spaniards had them corraled on the top of a hill or mountain (BL 1693b). Defensively, at least, rocks were of some importance. During the Nonolat battle it was stated that there had been danger from the showers of arrows (*flecheria*) and stones (*galgas*) (BL 1649-1700). In such defensive situations the women also participated by throwing stones.

Offensively, when the Indians were attacking Spanish holdings, their express purpose of fighting was to steal animals (usually "*caballada*") and clothing (*ropa*) and to kill Spaniards (e.g., AHP 1715Aa; AHP 1722Ab; BL 1709-1715). Of course, many other material goods were stolen and many nonrebel Indians were killed during offensive operations. Animals that could not be run off efficiently (e.g., cattle and sheep) were often killed on the spot. One Concho leader was overheard telling his men to kill all the mules so that the Spaniards would have no mounts to ride on.

The Spaniards felt that there was much wanton killing and cruelty, and destruction — such as the burning of buildings that destroyed the supplies and sometimes the people inside. A number of atrocities were reported. During the 1644 Revolt, the Tobosos cut off the head and other parts of the body of a man near Parral, and they beheaded another Indian near the Florido River (DHM 1645). The arms and heads of victims were amputated in an attack in the Parras area (AHP 1662C). In the Santa Bárbara mountains it was reported that "there was found the dead body of a woman between two rocks with many arrow wounds, the stomach opened up, the intestines taken out and the stomach filled with stones, the scalp removed, and many other atrocities committed" (AHP 1655Aa). Chisos were reported to have cut the genitals off of their victims (AHP 1684a). In the flight after one raid, a woman captive was tied to the tail of a horse when Spanish troops began to gain on the enemy. The Indians then shot an arrow at the horse so it would start up with a leap, but the animal was hit in such a fashion that it died immediately. The woman was picked up by the pursuers (BL 1709-1715).

A number of other examples exist of the raiders'

offensive behavior. Bodies discovered after raids often had been mutilated in some form — heads and bodies smashed, mangled by rocks, and chopped to pieces. An Indian woman and two children at Atotonilco were burned alive inside a hut, and another child was literally cremated in a box. A mixed band of Salinero and Concho (?) holed up some other Salineros in a cave, piled up wood and grass at the entrance, and set fire to it to burn them out. In one instance the Acoclames and Cocoyomes cut the ear off of one dead soldier and the genitals from another (AHP 1651A; AHP 1652Ba; AHP 1653Ab; AHP 1653Ad; AHP 1653Ae; AHP 1654Aa; AHP 1654Ab; AHP 1655Aa; AHP 1655Ab; AHP 1656Aa; AHP 1657Bb; AHP 1667Aa; AHP 1673Ab; AHP 1715Aa). Atrocities were not committed in every case, however, as when the Acoclames and Cocoyomes denuded some women without harming them (BL 1709-1715). As a note of interest, Father Rodrigo del Castillo reported that the Cabezas and Tobosos who had captured him washed the scalp and another trophy (*pedaso de aldilla*) they had taken from their victims after battle, as well as washing the blood from themselves (AGN 1667).

There was a rhythmic character to the Indian raiding pattern. Attacks were particularly frequent around the time of the full moon each lunar period. A Spaniard testifying in 1710 stated that for many years not a single full moon had gone by without the Indians committing a number of murders and robberies (BL 1709-1715). Coupled with this was seasonality, noted by the earlier writers. The Tobosos were reported to retire to the most inaccessible parts of their territory during the rainy season. This was the time when local natural resources were the most plentiful, and raiding activities would noticeably diminish. As soon as the dry season set in, the Indians would come forth again to plunder and murder. Berroterán, after the extinction of the "Tobosos," wrote that campaigns had been made regularly into their country during the months of September and October, the beginning of the dry season, for many years (DHM 1748). This dry season activity, however, was of particular detriment to the Spaniards who had great difficulty in campaigning when water was scarce, largely because of their horses (it is unknown to what extent the Spaniards utilized plant resources for moisture as the Indians did). The problem of water for the animals may have been much less of a drawback to the wild Indians who probably often ran their stolen animals to death, or killed them for food at camp (AHP 1654Ac; AHP 1656Aa; AHP 1709Ab; AHP 1708b; AHP 1724Ab; DHM 1645). Indeed, the Spaniards probably would not have been as successful as they were had it not been for their Indian allies. These knew the land and could get along better in it than could the non-Indians in the Spanish forces, and consequently they were greatly valued as scouts and trackers, as well as soldiers (see also Arlegui 1851: 166).

Captives were frequently taken by the Indians during raids and taken back to camp. Young children were often adopted into the group, and there were several references to non-Indians raiding with and speaking the language of the Indians (e.g., Ventura, the mestizo, and the mulatto and Negro, all with the Cocoyomes). Female declarants toward the end of the period (1715) stated explicitly that they captured and kept young children because these could be educated in the ways of the Indians (a practice that possibly intensified as their population declined but that no doubt existed in precontact times). Older captives, however, were generally killed, particularly at ceremonies, since the Indians realized they could not re-educate them. Nevertheless, not all older people taken as captives were killed. Some were put to work (at least until they were killed) doing menial chores such as fetching water and firewood and getting mescal. Some were traded or ransomed (AHP 1651A; AHP 1653Ad; AHP 1704Ab; AHP 1715Aa; AHP 1716Aa; AHP 1718Ab; AHP 1720Aa; AHP 1720Ab; BL 1709-1715). A few were reported simply living with the natives in the back country (AHP 1724Aa).

In 1692, one ex-captive of about 17 years of age said that when very young he had been taken prisoner by the Cabezas. Later when these people made peace (apparently at Parras) he had been given to a Jojocome "who had kept him with him and treated him well, calling him 'brother' and treating him as a son, not even letting him walk on foot nor that any other person mistreat him" (BL 1693b). Most captives seem to have "belonged" to men. One, however, definitely "belonged" to a Cocoyome woman, and when her Cabeza husband left her permanently to settle with his band at Parras, the captive, because he was a boy, remained with the woman and the Cocoyomes, although the Cabezas had wanted to take him with them (BL 1694-1698). This evidence, of course,

indicates that these young captives probably tended to be treated as any other "adopted children," although this is merely a guess. One other case suggests adoption, but there is a lack of supporting information that might disclose what it actually was an example of. One Acoclame testified that he was not the son of the person he lived with (El Ratón), as the Spaniards had thought. It was true, he confessed, that he lived with El Ratón as if the latter were his father, and El Ratón had raised and educated him. However, he admitted that on one occasion he had told the Spaniards that El Ratón was his father (AHP 1704Ab).

Religious and Ceremonial Life

Some of the characteristics of the ceremonialism of the peoples of the Greater Bolsón area were dancing, ceremonial killing and cannibalism, self-sacrifice or blood-letting, and the use of the narcotic peyote. This ceremonial behavior was associated with a number of different activities, including warfare, hunting, sickness, and the formalization of interband peace and alliance pacts. Although not specifically mentioned, "ceremonialism" could reasonably be assumed to have taken place at the annual meeting mentioned by "Toboso" deponents in 1715 (AHP 1715Aa). The Toboso governor of Conchos stated once that it was the Toboso custom to have dances (*mitotes*) during conferences and talks (BL 1693b), and the same was noted for the Cabezas and other "Coahuileños" around Nadadores in 1688 (Portillo 1887: 208). For the people of Nuevo León, Alonso de León stated that dances and *mitotes* were carried out on all occasions of war, peace, and general celebrations. These occurred at any time of the year but particularly in the summer when food was more plentiful, which concords with the 1600-1602 *Anua* for the Parras area (García 1909: 43; BL 1600-1602).

Dances

Dances at Parras, according to the *Anua* of 1604, were held for war and as celebrations for happiness or sadness. Such a dance "lasts at times eight consecutive days and nights, some entering and others leaving, and occasionally it occurs that some dance night and day without stopping" (BL 1604). Pérez de Ribas gave one description of the dances of the Parras missions. These were generally at night, performed by a large group of people in a circle around a fire. There was "some division between men and women but [the dances] were not free from abuses," including drunkenness. These dances usually lasted until sunup the following day (Pérez de Ribas III 1944: 248). Other sources confirm this description and include other features; singing or chanting, cannibalism, and the use of peyote, often ground and mixed with water and sometimes with the powdered bones of a victim, were common throughout the north Mexican area (García 1909: 42-46; Pérez de Ribas III 1944: 248, 252, 263; AHP 1652Ab; AHP 1653Aa; see also Arlegui 1851: 146, 154, who adds some details — including snake dances, beliefs about owls, a reverential attitude toward fire, and the like — but it is uncertain to what group(s) these pertained). The *Anua* of 1598 recorded that dances in the Laguna district were ordered by the devil, and included drunkenness, peyote taking, and child sacrifice (DHM 1598).

At the missions, native dancing was continued but reoriented toward the divine (*a lo divino*) (Pérez de Ribas III 1944: 255-256). In 1607 it was reported, however, that the Indians would dance all night on Saturday night, and would be so tired the following day that they were unable to attend Mass (DHM 1607). By 1614, the *Anua* of this year stated that the dances, during which many offensive things occurred, had now been eradicated. Nevertheless, after one had been prohibited at a certain rancheria, the old people (*viejos*) managed to carry it out in the dead of night, including a very "solemn" inebriation with peyote (BL 1614).

The *Anua* of 1600-1602 reported that in the days of "*vendimia y agosto*" "for these people which is the time of the most copious and famous harvest that they have [during] the year, the Lord grants it in this desert of mezquite and *tuna*." Everyone would go to this harvest, from which cakes (*panes*) and wine would be made in abundance. Many bands (*rancherias*) would get together, each inviting the other by sending bows and arrows as a sign of peace and alliance. They would drink peyote, paint themselves in their own style, and carry out great dances and drunks, as well as go fishing, as the lagoon was close by. Hardly a single person would remain in the valley (of Parras?) who would not attend these *fiestas*, to which they would go as happy as if they were going to a wedding (BL 1600-1602).

Some Tobosos and Coahuileños — specifically Cabezas and Conianes were mentioned, although this no doubt referred to other groups of the Nadadores area — also held dances at the time of the tuna harvest. In 1688 it was learned that ". . . after the tuna was finished they would try to cement friendships during the *mitotes* that they hold when they are harvesting it" (Portillo 1887: 202). Possibly the annual meeting of the Cocoyomes, Acoclames, Chisos, and Sisimbles mentioned by women declarants in 1715 was also a ceremony for the harvest of desert fruits, although it was said to be held during the dry season (possibly at the end of the summer rains) (AHP 1715Aa).

In another place, with regard to the Irritilas and other peoples around Parras, it was reported that from 100 to over 200 persons would dance at a time, adorned with the variegated feathers of parrots (*guacamayos*) and other birds, with arrows in their hands. They would sing their songs, no longer barbarous (i.e., after missionization). The verses (? — *motetes*) were sung "with the tone and pause which they use, the way that with organ music (? — *canto de órgano*) the song is stopped and repeated [with] short verses" (Pérez de Ribas III 1944: 265; DHM 1598).

A ceremonial dance that took place in the area of Mapimí appears to contain a good many facets of the dance ceremonialism. Reference to it occurs in the *Anua* of 1607, Alegre, and Pérez de Ribas, although the description here is taken mainly from the latter, which is the most detailed. The occasion concerned the appearance of a comet, which the natives considered a source of danger. A plague also occurred about this time, and such astronomical phenomena were definitely associated with sickness and disease.

Several "rancherias" participated. The people came out to dance in pairs, and included males and females from 7 to 100 years of age. Each person carried a little basket in his right hand while holding an arrow with the obsidian (*pedernal*) head placed against his heart with his left. Bringing up the rear were four or five old men who were painted. Each one had a hide whip (*azote de cuero*) in his hand (the letter of Father Pangua in Alegre stated "little fans" or type of *aventador*). The baskets were filled with dates (*dátiles*), *tunas*, and mescal or mesquitamal fruit, and dead mice, *tuzas*, rabbits, fish, and snakes. Some people wore feathers; others wore mountain lion, wolf, or coyote tails, because they believed that the tail of the comet was similar to either bird plumage or animals' tails, and each person mimicked the animal that to him the comet seemed to resemble.

In the center of the dance ground (*plaza*) in the middle of the pueblo was a large fire into which all of the baskets and their contents were thrown as a burnt sacrifice. This was done so that the smoke would rise to the comet, which would then have something to eat and would therefore do the people no harm. As the smoke rose the old men began to lash out with their whips (*cimbrar*) or fans, in rhythm on the four sides of the fire, ordering the smoke to go directly to the comet. It so occurred, however, at this time that a breeze came up and diverted the smoke. Apparently (from Alegre), with this the participants set up a noisy crying. The old men, that is, the shamans, took this breeze as indicating a bad omen to the effect that the comet was angry. In order to handle this contingency, the hair of six maidens (*doncellas*) (in Alegre only one girl is mentioned, around nine or ten years old) was cut off at the roots. The old men then began to scratch themselves with combs (*peines*) or spines (*espinas*) so that blood began to flow. The rest of the people followed suit, even the newborn infants being subjected to this sacrifice. The blood was collected by the oldest shaman in some large jugs (*jícaras*) or platters (*plato o escudilla*) (and from Alegre, was mixed with an equal part of water; or with some water, according to the 1607 *Anua*). The old men (or man), using the girls' hair as a wand (*hisopo*) sprayed (*rociaban*) the blood in the air — at the same time giving forth with horrendous cries (*bufidos; bramidos*) — three times in each of the four directions. Finally, they threw the remaining blood into the fire and again began to beat the smoke from the fire, which now, because the breeze had died down, went straight into the air. Thus ended the ceremony (Alegre II 1956: 151-152; Pérez de Ribas III 1944: 273-275; DHM 1607).

The gentile Indians of the hinterland of the Parras area during the plague of 1624 were said to have carried out "great dances and *mitotes*" in order to placate the pestilence. These were held for three or four days and nights without the participants eating a thing. This was done before an idol from which the devil would appear to the Indians. At the end of the period they would fall to the ground "some dead and others fainted" from exhaustion (AGN 1624).

Alonso de León described a Coahuiltecan ceremony in which both sexes danced in one or two circles around a fire. The words to the songs they sang had no meaning, only harmony, but so much in unison it seemed like a single voice. Sometimes there would be over 100 persons in the group. In this particular ceremony, peyote, ground and dissolved in water, was drunk until the Indians lost their senses and fell on the ground as if dead. They also drew large quantities of blood by scratching themselves with the "beaks of a fish called *abuja* (*aguja*)" and smeared it over their bodies (García 1909: 44-45). Arlegui cited the scratching technique — with sharp pieces of obsidian or ground-up maguey leaves — as a cure for tiredness (*pencas*) (Arlegui 1851: 140).

War Ceremonies

Most references to ceremonies associated with war cite celebrations occurring after battles, although there were also pre-battle ceremonies. Arlegui describes a general pre-war, pre-hunting ceremony in which an all-night circle dance was performed around a deer skull with the antlers still intact. At the end of the ceremony the skull would jump and immediately the Indians would sally forth in the direction in which the cranium had indicated (Arlegui 1851: 146-147). Deerheads, with the antlers attached, were believed to have special power, such as to grant good hunting, and for curing (Pérez de Ribas III 1944: 248, 262-263; BL 1604).

During the ceremony, when the people were drunk, an old woman who was held as an oracle would get up and remind them of their ancient liberties and of the evil the Spaniards had wrought upon them. She would exhort them to join in squads and to go forth and destroy everything they could. She would also send them against their neighbors to avenge deaths committed on their own group and would incite them by calling them cowards (Arlegui 1851: 146-147).

A Spaniard, held captive for five years by the Cocoyomes, testified that Cocoyome women, especially the old women, had the worst character (*mal natural*) regarding peace and war. Once they had said, when many of their own people had died, that it would be a good idea to make peace until their children had grown so that they would have more people — presumably to fight the Spaniards (BL 1694-1698). Another ex-captive of the Cocoyomes (1691) stated that the old women contradicted any word (*vos*) suggesting peace "and that the indignation that the women have against the Spaniards is so great that when they [the men] sally forth to kill and rob, some women go in their company desirous of killings" (BL 1693b). The *Anua* of 1600-1602 noted that the older the women, the worse they were (BL 1600-1602).

Shamans were often involved in armed resistance to the Spaniards, and there exists one more interesting reference to a female concerned with this. During the Tepehuán Revolt, it was reported that among the old people (*viejos*) at Parras an undercurrent of talk concerned a certain old mountain lady who was held in great veneration. The lady was angry because her people had accepted the Spanish priests. Attempts to pacify her with clothing and other gifts did not mitigate her ire (BL 1616).

Post-battle ceremonies seemed to have included dancing with the head, scalps, or other "items" belonging to the enemy, as well as the eating of captives. It is less certain what the pre-battle ceremonies involved. Both types of ceremonies did occur, however, and one Diego de Estrada, who had been a captive of the Acoclames and Cocoyomes for fourteen years, recounted a number of dances connected with hostilities. After a raid near Indé "the said Indians went to Poso Hediondo and divided up all of the theft among the Acoclames and Cocoyomes, and they danced their *mitote*, they split up, some in the direction of Mobana and others toward Sierra Mojada in the Sierra of Tagualiloncate [Tagualilo], and having danced their *mitote*, they sallied to commit deaths and robberies." Again on "another occasion they convoked the Chisos who were at the Sierra de Chocamueca, and they came, and all having danced — Cocoyomes, Acoclames, and Chisos — they came to attack San Antonio," and after another raid "they went and came together and danced and they divided up the theft, and the Chisos left them and they returned to Chocamueca" (BL 1709-1715).

Another witness, also an ex-captive, testified that on one occasion the Acoclames and Cocoyomes met at "Sierra Mojada and they carried out their dances and decided to go out and kill and rob" (BL 1709-1715). On one occasion when the Gavilanes received word that a Spanish force was on the march to meet them in battle, they "celebrated" the news by dancing (AHP 1688Cb). Again, Cocoyomes, Acoclames, Sisimbles, and Suniyoliglas "after their

dances (*bailes*) and merry-making (*guelgas*) that they carried out, they divided up into squads for different areas" (BL 1709-1715). Another time, after a number of "Toboso" women had escaped from prison at one of the presidios, their arrival was celebrated, and then "challenged" squads (that is, the men had been exhorted to go out and fight their enemies) went off to raid (BL 1694-1698).

Some of the post-battle celebrations were more detailed. On one occasion the Chisos and Tobosos got together and danced with the head and clothing of a Spaniard they had killed (AHP 1655Ab), and at a later date the Chisos threatened one person with cutting off his head and dancing with it (AHP 1684Aa). Once the Spanish military located and attacked a large gathering of Indians after the latter had just held a great, all-night dance (*mitote*) celebrating the arrival of a raiding party that had brought back to camp a number of horses and mules (AHP 1653Ad). A Sisimble woman in 1748 recounted that after killing Spaniards the warriors brought their *cueras* (Spanish leather military jackets) and then held a *mitote* (BL 1748).

Another time the Cocoyomes took an adult captive to the place where they danced. "Several Indian men and women [were] dancing, and one woman with a pike wounded him several times and another [woman] beat him with a stick until they had killed him, having many laughs at the sight of the movements he made in order to die." The following day, the witness to this, who had also been held captive at the time, while fetching water found the head of the victim but did not learn what had been done with the body (AHP 1716Aa). This appears to be a fairly good example of the role of women in the warfare ceremonial pattern, which seemingly began when the prisoners first arrived at the Indian camp. A Sonora Indian, taken captive by some Cocoyomes, was beaten with clubs and sticks by the women when he and his captors arrived at the camp at Sierra del Diablo (AHP 1686Bc). Another time, at the arrival of two prisoners, the women came out and beat them with clubs (*garrotes de quiote*) (AHP 1724Aa).

On another occasion, Chiso women (*viejas*) killed a little captive Spanish girl, who was later eaten. This was the group of Santiago's at the Peñol de Santa Marta, and it is possible that the event is the same as noted in another place (BL 1695a) where a captive Spanish girl was killed and eaten by the women of a combined Chichitame and Sisimble, and possibly Guesecpayolicla, group (Hackett 1926: 332 — apparently also referred to by Marín, p. 396). The circumstances of the next reference are not clear, but the Cabezas and other groups once killed, roasted (*en barbacoa*), and ate the children of a Spanish woman — all captives (AHP 1652Dc). The Cabezas of Don Pedrote would get together with the Quechales of the mission of Nadadores and dance with the scalps of those they had killed (Portillo 1887: 195).

The torture, killing, and eating of one's enemies — although not captured in actual battle — was also practiced and supports Arlegui's statement of the perpetual state of war in which these people lived. When Dieguillo, the son of El Ratón, was at the Suniyoligla camp, according to the Suniyoligla testifying in 1713, the people of the latter place "did not let him leave for any place, and the whole day and night he spent crying and also he became ill from the mistreatment that his relatives [of the Suniyoligla testifying] had given him" (BL 1709-1715). The *Anua* of 1604 told of a messenger sent to the hinterland who was simply killed and eaten by one of the nations he encountered (BL 1604). Don Baltazar, the Chiso, who was killed by the Sisimbles when he went to persuade them to make peace, was knocked down by one Indian with a pike, and the others there finished him off. Then, "they cut off his head, legs, and arms, and they cut off pieces of meat, they roasted them and they ate them up" (BL 1709-1715).

The same Suniyoligla told of another incident where an "outsider" (?) (that is, there is no information on kinship or other ties here) was killed apparently for reasons of "social solidarity." A certain Pedro Gabriel, some kind of "Chiso," fled the Conchos pueblo and joined a group of Sisimbles. The Indians then stole some horses, but the soldiers from Conchos took them back, and "as soon as they arrived back at the [Sisimble] camp, the said Pedro Gabriel was accused of evil disposition (*mala disposicion*) with which he had taken the horse herd for which reason they immediately took his life" (BL 1709-1715).

All the foregoing references concern "enemy" or "rebel" Indians. However, the Spaniards permitted their Indian allies to carry out their war ceremonies and actually fostered the taking of scalps, heads, and hands (AHP 1653Ad; AHP 1654Ac; AHP 1657Bb; AHP 1658Aa). Two instances were reported of the enemy picking up its dead and taking them off. It was felt that this had been done in order that the Spanish auxiliaries could not dance and perform their own rites with them (AHP 1655Ab; AHP 1657Bb). Arlegui also noted similar practices by the Spaniards' Indian allies (1851: 167), and he stated in his general description of warfare practices that the Indians committed unbelievable atrocities upon the bodies of those they killed. They pulled out the intestines and hung them in trees (possibly referring here to the murder of a Franciscan that occurred sometime before 1715 near Durango, when the Indians draped his intestines over a mesquite tree; BL 1709-1715). They would eat the meat, "human bodies being for them the tastiest of morsels, removing the skin from the skull in order to drink from it with joy and as a sign of victory" (Arlegui 1851: 138, 167).

Petroglyphs

Pictures or petroglyphs were no doubt connected with several facets of the native religion, but because two of three references to them mention warfare they are noted at this point. They were reported by one of the early missionaries in the general Laguna district as "characters and letters made in blood in a place and location so high that only the devil could have drawn them" (Pérez de Ribas III 1944: 263; BL 1604). In 1715, the Spaniards, while inspecting a camp of over seventy huts (*jacales*) at the water hole of Acatita, found on a rock (*peñasco*) nearby "many and various pictures, very lively done (*a lo vivo*) of the deaths that they had committed " when they had murdered an ensign in one attack on the Spanish military as well as when they had killed the captain and some others at Mapimí, "showing in them the person of the said captain and that of the priest Don Carlos on his mount" (AHP 1715Aa). Berroterán was apparently referring to petroglyphs of some type at Acatita La Grande which depicted an attack on a party of which the Bishop of Durango, Don Pedro Tapis, had been a member (DHM 1748).

Other Ceremonies

Some kind of "ceremonialism" often took place at intergroup meetings, although the evidence is sketchy, and some of the references given herein perhaps better fit with pre-battle ceremonies.

Once the Ocomes invited the Tobosos to dance. The latter went to Río Angosto where they met and danced with the Ocomes, Gavilanes, and Nonojes (AHP 1653Ad). A meeting between "Tobosos" (generic or specific?) and Cabezas was celebrated by a great *combite* at the camp of the Tobosos, who had many cattle with them. Afterward they went off to raid together. A great dance was also held when "Chisos" and "Tobosos" were contracting a war alliance (BL 1693b).

Another time, the Cocoyomes and Coahuileños spent a night dancing together (AHP 1722Da). Sometimes the back-country people were said to have danced with settled Indians. Three Cocoyome messengers spent three days with the Babozarigames and Coahuileños at the presidio of El Pasaje dancing *mitotes* (AHP 1716Ab). Another time the Cocoyomes and others danced *mitotes* with the Indians living at Parras (AHP 1722Aa).

Less complicated customs were also reported when people of different groups met. Bows and arrows were exchanged (AHP 1654Aa). In one instance, two Coahuileños gave the Acoclames a pinch (*manojo*) of tobacco when they visited the latters' camp (AHP 1704Ab). Arlegui stated that messengers would take an arrow and lay it at the feet of the chief of the host group. If an alliance was cemented, the instigating group would get together an abundance of food and drink (alcoholic) to receive their new friends (Arlegui 1851: 148).

A more elaborate ritual was once reported, involving some kind of interband peace pact. One group, apparently Tobosos and Salineros, exchanged a boy (*muchacho* – apparently prepubertal) with another group composed of Babozarigames and Baborimamas. Each group killed the boy it had received and then cooked and ate him. Afterward the bones of the boys were ground into powder, mixed with peyote, and the potion was drunk. Those present then "embraced" each other and departed on their separate ways (AHP 1652Ab; AHP 1653Aa).

One description from the 1690's indicates a certain amount of fusion of Colonial and native elements in ritual behavior. One mestizo ex-captive who had been with the Jojocomes (Ocomes) a number of years reported the ceremonialism he had witnessed among these people and the Cocoyomes. This was centered on a banner (*bandera*) the Spanish governor had sent them as part of peace negotiations. He stated that "before setting it [the banner] up (*enarbolarla*), word was sent to all of the nations that they meet together

to see it and to kiss it as the insignia of the King, Our Lord, and that when all had come together it was put up and that the governors and captains went first passing underneath the said banner kissing it consecutively. After them, all the men and women, young and old, did the same, and they carried out dances (*mitotes*) with great pleasure, saying that that sign (*señal*) was true peace and that by means of it they had the assurance of the promise of pardon, and that against this [the peace] he did not hear a single thing." Later, when two Franciscans went out to visit them, the Indians "lined up in the style of war with their banner which they waved (*la batieron*) to the priests and then one by one they went to kiss their habits and hands" (BL 1693b).

Shamans, Curing, and Supernatural Power

Shamans, or curers, were reported to attend the sick in the Parras district, although there is little information on specific curing procedures. A fire was "usually" kept burning at this time, and apparently more than one medicine man could attend at one time. One report stated that the patient was surrounded by the heads of deer with the antlers still intact. Various items, such as large obsidian knives (*navajas de pedernales*), dead hawks (*gavilanes*), or their claws, were hung on the doors of huts to keep sickness out. This was done after the shamans had seen visions of various supernatural figures (Alegre II 1956: 151; Pérez de Ribas III 1944: 261-262, 269-271, 291; BL 1600-1602). One sick person was said to have hung a snake (*víbora*) at his head (*a su cabezera*) (BL 1605).

The sacrifice of a newborn infant presumably prevented the death of, and would cure, a sick person. One case that occurred soon after the beginning of missionization was that of a woman who had dreamt that her relatives were going to die. When she awoke, she strangled (*ahogó*) a child who had just been born, thus preventing the deaths of the others. Infanticide for this reason was said to be common.

Large dances were held to turn the tide of plagues. Visions of supernatural beings at this time – in the form of fire, deer, serpents, or a figure armed to the teeth (*de punta en blanco*) – would threaten the natives with illness because they had become Christians. The way to placate such spirits (i.e., the "devil," according to the missionaries) was to dance, the dances lasting three or four days and nights, the participants performing before an idol without eating until they would fall to the ground. Alegre stated that the old men involved in these ceremonies were both the sacrificial priests and doctors (Alegre II 1956: 151; Pérez de Ribas III 1944: 261-262, 269-271, 291; DHM 1598; DHM 1607). For Nuevo León, Alonzo de León mentioned old men as curers and the practice of child sacrifice to avert disaster (García 1909: 47, 49).

Specific characteristics of diseases were not mentioned, although deaths due to smallpox (*viruelas*), measles (*sarampion*), and *cocolixtli* (probably usually smallpox) were often referred to. In one instance some Chisos at Ocotán were reported to be afflicted with *mal de ojos* (evil eye?) (BL 1695a).

Once in the Mapimí country when disease struck (and despite the previously described performance of the ceremony regarding the comet), an attempt at child sacrifice was also made. When one of the chiefs became ill, his relatives tried to obtain a newborn infant. They went to the mother with deer skins, jugs (*jícaras*), gourds (*tecomates*), strings of beads and bones (*sartas de cuentas y huesos*) to exchange for the child. The woman, at night, fled some three leagues from the pueblo. The others armed themselves and followed her but encountered resistance from her relatives, and a skirmish ensued. The mother then escaped to Mapimí. Meanwhile her now-frustrated enemies burned alive one of her child's (and hers?) elderly relatives who was sick in a hut. They then threw his ashes to the winds, saying that the plague would now cease (Pérez de Ribas III 1944: 275).

Another reason for child sacrifice was given in the *Anua* of 1606. Two children (*niños*) were strangled (*ahogados*) upon birth because the old men had dreamt of wars and disturbances and had persuaded themselves that these children were going to grow up and be troublesome and the cause of much harm. The chief told also that a son had been born to him a few days before and that afterward he had some very vivid dreams that convinced him that he should listen to the old people, although he did not carry the sacrifice through (BL 1606). The sacrifice of the firstborn was also reported (DHM 1598). The *Anua* of 1596 noted that the "superstitious" killing of children left the Indians less encumbered in their rovings (DHM 1596).

Shamans were involved in resistance to the Spaniards. During the Tepehuán Revolt, a medicine man at Parras tried to whip the people there into rebellion

(BL 1616). Just prior to this, the 1615 *Anua* reported a medicine man some twenty leagues from Parras (direction unstated) who had a vision in which he apparently received a message, connected with the Tepehuán Revolt, for the people of the Parras-Laguna district. It is uncertain if he was a Tepehuán or not, although he had a relative living at Parras who had learned of this "plot" at a dance. The vision involved a great lord (*Señor*) who had appeared to him several times in the form of a human being, a deer, or other wild animals (*fieras*). These supernatural manifestations seemingly had told the medicine man that this "lord" was coming from the east to kill all of the Spaniards, Tlaxcaltecos, and (Indian and other) laborers (*gente laboria*), thus freeing the Indians from them. However, for this, the natives would have to take his message westward in order that all of the nations living in this region (*en esta derecera*) would recognize and obey him. The old medicine man gave his Parras relative a bow, which he claimed belonged to this great lord. All of the old Indians (*viejos*) of the Parras area revered this bow, and they kept it with much veneration in a house, because, they said, he who did not venerate it would die. A Tlaxcalteco learned of this, went to the house, took the bow and stamped on it with his feet, causing a great deal of wonder among the elders when he did not perish immediately (BL 1615a).

Some years earlier, a medicine man from the Nuevo León area — as reported in the 1600-1602 *Anua* — managed to incite the people at Parras. He sent some bows with a message "in which he said that everyone should be prepared (*se apercibiessen*) because those bows spoke in such a way that hearing them caused fright and astonishment, and that smoky (*fumosos*) winds were going to arise that would cause great evil so that a time would come in which the men would turn into women and vice versa, and other things of lesser consideration (? *partonas*)." One priest went out to stop this, and "coming óne day along one of the streets of the town, he met an old Indian medicine man ... who was carrying in his hand some bows and arrows of a very large size with some rattlesnake rattles (*caxcaueles*) and feathers and a piece of deer fat (*unto de venado*) and a hunk of half-burnt wood (*tizón*), and he was going from house to house boasting (*haciendo alarde*) of these insignias" (BL 1600-1602).

As previously noted, at least some chiefs presumably possessed supernatural power, and some may also have been shamans. On one occasion Indian declarants reported that during a *mitote* the Cocoyome leader, Juan de Lomas, performed a ritual in order to communicate with the supernatural. He filled a gourd container (*calavazo*) with water and covered it with a large piece of cloth (*paño*). Holding this in one hand, he took a cross with the other and announced to the rest that God had just come down from the "most high" and spoken with him. The message was for the Cocoyomes and Coahuileños not to surrender to the Spaniards at this time but to flee, as the latter were planning to kill them (AHP 1722Da). One instance of rebel Indian war magic was recounted by a Spaniard, who took it as an example of how the master of the underworld assisted the Indians. On an occasion when the Indians were being pursued, they invoked the devil, repeating the word "fog" (*neblina*). Immediately, a bank of fog had come up between them and the pursuing Spaniards (BL 1709-1715). Alegre cited a chief who communicated with a supernatural in the form of a woman (Alegre II 1956: 149).

The early missionaries reported many occurrences of visits by, and visions of, supernatural beings, which they considered to be manifestations of the devil. Some of these beings let themselves be seen in daylight. They were said to be "horrible" figures – sometimes a black man who shot fire from his eyes or expelled blood from his mouth and ears, or other times a wild beast that caused dread, terror, and fright. One figure was in the image of a woman who would talk to people. The commands of these beings were backed up by the threat of sickness or death (Pérez de Ribas III 1944: 248, 286; BL 1605; BL 1614; BL 1616). On one occasion at La Laguna "two horrible black men with small, sunken eyes" preached to the natives that they should not let themselves be baptized because they would die of *cocolixtli* Dreams among the Laguneros and Zacatecos were considered by them to be caused by the "devil," according to the missionaries (DHM 1598; DHM 1607). One sick woman was reported to have dreamt of a fierce and misshapen figure (BL 1606).

During the 1624 plague when many dances were performed to stem the tide of illness, the devil appeared in several forms – as fire, in the figure of a deer, in the shape of a snake (*serpiente*), or "armed to the teeth" (*armado de punta en blanco*) with an angry and enraged face. He threatened the natives that he would send another pestilence if they did not

dance (AGN 1624). Tobosos, who sent messages to the Cabezas at Tizonazo around 1666 in an attempt to get the latter to uprise, had had a repeated vision that sanctioned their hostilities. This was "in the figure of a Spaniard, spewing flames from his mouth, and he would assure them in his exhortations that they would succeed in everything that they attempted" (BL 1649-1700). One Mataraje was disturbed by the devil in the figure of a black man who, however, was dispelled when the Indian was baptized (AGN 1622). Alegre told of Indians from the valley of Coahuila who arrived in Parras in 1669 saying they had had visions of "wonderful things" which included a figure suspended in the air who taught them to cross themselves and pray (Alegre III 1956: 298). For Nuevo León, Alonso de León mentioned that the people there had previously, but no longer at the time of his writing, experienced visions during dances (Garcia 1909: 46).

One holy place or shrine was discovered by one of the missionaries when he followed a native, said to be possessed by the devil (*energúmeno*), to a place where supernaturals dwelled. These had the forms of a snake (*serpiente*) and of a priest of small stature so fierce and frightful that with his glance (*vista*) he had killed many people. Here the supernatural beings seemingly often made their appearances and spoke to the Indians. The location was full of human skulls and bones over which the natives had thrown rocks in order that – so it was reported – the deceased, who had killed so many people simply by looking at them, would not come out and appear before the natives. There were many petroglyphs on the higher rocks at this place. The aforementioned native who was followed to this place was said to be a shaman (Pérez de Ribas III 1944: 263-264; BL 1604).

The 1606 *Anua* recounted that the chief of the De la Peña group took a missionary to a large rock (*peña*) and removed a stone that covered a hole. This he showed to the Father, stating that before he and his people had become Christians the devil had destroyed (*despeasaba* – *sic*) many people at this place, disappearing later down this hole (BL 1606).

Pérez de Ribas reported one story of a supernatural appearance in particular which is strongly suggestive of a guardian spirit or *nagual*. This concerned a youth whom a supernatural being (*demonio familiar*) constantly accompanied. The being seemingly would appear to the boy (*mozo*) in various forms and would help him in many ways (Pérez de

Ribas III 1944: 284). The *Anua* of 1624 speaks of a similar case (very likely the same one, judging from the language of the description). This being would sometimes appear in the form of a calf (*vecerro*); he would give the Indian everything he needed and could inform him of events in distant places.

A certain Indian woman was reported to have been accompanied by a demon who for six years had kept her terrified "day and night" in such a manner that she would lose consciousness because of his terror and threats (AGN 1624).

Arlegui mentioned the *nagual* specifically; he said that possession by a guardian spirit was customary among the people of the south in the mountains — apparently meaning the Tepehuán or their neighbors (Arlegui 1851: 145). An old woman in the Laguna district reportedly kept a lizard (*lagarto*) in a cage (*enjaulado*). When asked why she watched over it with such care, she answered "that it was her God whom she adored and feared a great deal." The priest attempted to demonstrate to her that this was not true, when he threw the lizard into the fire and it was consumed by the flames (DHM 1596). Another woman from the same mission was gravely tormented by the "devil," who every day would raise her from the ground over an *estado* in height, whirl her around in the air, make her froth at the mouth, and also make her face become twisted (AGN 1626).

Death and Burial

Some instances of death and burial exhibit a certain amount of religious syncretism of native and Christian elements. The dead were usually buried, although Gonzalo de las Casas reported cremation for the Chichimecas to the south (Las Casas 1935). Alonso de León reported both cremation and burial for the people of Nuevo León, as well as endocannibalism and the pulling out and cutting of hair in mourning (García 1909: 42, 57). Aside from burial, hair cutting and the destruction of property seem to have been customary features. Tobosos were reported to have killed a Spanish woman captive they were holding just before they went to the Spaniards to make peace. They buried her and put a cross on her grave (AHP 1652Dc).

In another case, nine enemy graves of Cocoyomes and their associates were discovered at Pozo Hediondo. The deaths were thought to have been caused by sickness (AHP 1716Aa). On one occasion a Salinero discovered many dead and rotting bodies of the enemy, apparently Tobosos, in a cave at a *peñol* near the scene of a battle, assumed to have died there of their wounds (AHP 1653Ad). With regard to hair cutting, many locks of hair (*melenas*) were discovered at a rancheria that had been abandoned because of sickness (AHP 1716Aa). Another time Acoclames and Cocoyomes cut off locks of their own hair (*un poco de cabello*) because of grief resulting from the death of their comrades (AHP 1704Ab).

In 1652 Indian scouts discovered an abandoned camp, apparently belonging to the Salineros and Cabezas, out in the Acatita area. They recounted that "they found many utensils (*trastes*) with which they [the enemy] served themselves, and very scattered, and many locks of hair that, it seemed, belonged to women, which they had cut (*tusado*) and with that demonstration they let their great sorrow be known of the many people [killed] and the loss that they had suffered in the battle of Acatita" (AHP 1652Ab). An Indian camp, apparently abandoned because of plague, revealed many locks of hair thrown about, many *guacales*, "and many broken ollas and there was [also] found destroyed in the said place arms, quivers, deer skin bags (*costales de gamuza*), *lienzos de cria* and others, Cholulan and Mexican cloth (*paño*), cloaks (*capotes*), overcoats (*gabanes*) and *almellas*, and the said dead bodies which were recognized to be of both sexes, were wrapped (*amortajados*) with the above-mentioned items, some with crosses placed [on them] and others without them and at the heads (*cabezeras*) *reales* and other things were piled (*agregados*)" (AHP 1716Aa).

A mourning wail was also reported. Following a skirmish with the Cocoyomes in which eight of the latter had died, the women at the top of the mountain at Sierra Mojada were heard crying (AHP 1715Aa). After another battle at Sierra Mojada, the women were heard wailing (AHP 1716Aa). After the Gavilán band was decimated, when the Cocoyome camp heard the news, the women put up a great wailing (1693b). Another time Spanish troops burned alive some of the enemy when they fired the brush (*monte*), and the mourning wail was later heard (AHP 1656Aa).

Indian scouts reported after they had visited the Peñol de Nonolat that "they saw a large number of enemy Indians who were all crying over the dead at the said *peñol* and they had broken the crosses and disinterred Don Gerónimo and [had] chopped him (*echolo*) into pieces and [they had] buried many of their own" (AHP 1653Aa).

Other sources refer to the extraordinary wailing of the Laguneros. Friends and relatives of the deceased would get together at the grave, with their faces painted or blackened, and then the men and the women would wail their sorrowful tune. Singing and dancing were part of mourning activities, and women friends and neighbors acted as mourners (cryers, *lloraderas*). The qualities of the deceased — his deeds, bravery in war, prowess in hunting, ability as a provider for his children, as well as the hardships his absence was going to cause them — would be sung (Pérez de Ribas III 1944; 262, 282; BL 1614 DHM 1598). Wailing was also practiced by the Nuevo León peoples (García 1909: 57). The Chisos settled at San Francisco de Conchos in 1713 were reported to have held a dance because of the sentiment they felt over the death of a Batayolicla (BL 1709-1715).

A rite involving deerheads, often with the antlers still attached, seems to have had some kind of mourning significance. This may have been one of the exceptional (*celebres*) ceremonies that were performed at various times of the year. The heads were reverently kept in memory of the hunter who had killed the animal. A head would be taken out for the ceremony. After the dancing had begun one of the old men who presided over the affair would throw some pieces of deer bones and antlers into the fire. When the flame grew larger with this new fuel, he would "persuade" the people that this was the spirit of the deceased which was coming at this call to communicate to them the skill and prowess he had had during his lifetime as a hunter. His sons and relatives would be given some of these bones powdered in drink which would transfer to them the swiftness of the deer so that they could better pursue them while hunting. When one of the missionaries went to burn the deer heads employed during a curing ceremony the shamans said they would die if the smoke should reach them (Pérez de Ribas III 1944: 262-263; DHM 1598; DHM 1607).

Alegre gave a description of the same or a similar rite. The kinsmen of the deceased would keep the deer heads, and at the end of a year all would leave the house of the deceased at dusk, singing a sad and mournful song. An old woman would follow them with the head of the principal deer in her hands. She

would put it in a fire on top of some arrows, but apparently out of reach of the flames, and around this the entire group would remain the night — she would cry and the rest would sing and dance. At dawn, the head would be thrown into the fire and when it had turned into ashes "the memory of the deceased would remain buried" (Alegre II 1956: 108; BL 1694-1698).

Little information is available about attitudes toward the dead. With regard to kinsmen, a Salinero woman declared that her people were happy to surrender and to return to Tizonazo because they had all their relatives buried at the church there (AHP 1652Dc). Attitudes toward the dead enemy can be inferred only from the ceremonial behavior. In one case, however, the Acoclames and Cocoyomes were said to have deposited the clothing of some priests, two of whom they had killed, in a cave on top of a framework (*tapeste*). They were afraid to wear these clothes lest they die, and a previous case in which this had occurred was reported (AHP 1704Ab).

One group or band (*parcialidad*), the Pachos of the Laguna district, believed that all of those who were present at the time a death occurred would also die. Therefore, anyone whom they considered to be in the last throes would be taken to the grave (*sepultura*) to die there or be buried alive so that the rest would not be present when it happened.

In another place is related the case of a boy who was kicked in the head by a horse. His relatives quickly assumed that he was dead and set up a wail that lasted all night. This premature beginning of mourning may be an example of the above-mentioned belief. However the boy was much recovered by the following day. His relatives killed the horse in retaliation (Pérez de Ribas III 1944: 262, 282; BL 1614; DHM 1598).

The *Anua* of 1600-1602 describes the burial and mourning of an Indian woman in the Parras area. The old men and women were seen "to throw themselves forcefully upon the ground, to beat themselves, to dance and sing together, bewailing and crying over the deceased, and coming to the burial to inter with her all of the things (*trastos*) and trifles (*baratijas*) she possessed, and the old mother of this deceased woman buried herself alive with her dead daughter and she was covered up with earth with her, and she remained buried thus all day until the afternoon, when coming back to finish [the ceremony? — *bolviendo acabar*] she was found alive, which is a thing of admiration that she was not accidentally suffocated" (BL 1600-1602).

Other Beliefs and Customs

Other customs relating to the supernatural are reported mainly in the published literature. In the Laguna district, birth involved a five or six (Alegre) or six or seven (Pérez de Ribas) day abstention from eating meat or fish. This was on the part of the father who remained indoors, according to the *Anua* of 1604, for five to six days. This abstention was to prevent the game animals from becoming "contaminated," in which case they would retire to the mountains or to the deepest part of the rivers and the lagoon. At the end of the period an old man, a shaman, would come and lead the father out of the hut (Alegre II 1956: 107; Pérez de Ribas III 1944: 247-248; BL 1604).

Arlegui described a ceremony for the firstborn son of a father. This description is not repeated here with any detail, as there is no way of determining for which group it applies, although Arlegui leads one to believe that it was common throughout "Zacatecas" (that is, the Franciscan province). It should be noted that the ceremony involved a one-day fast for the father, after which he was given peyote to drink. Kinsmen and others would seat him on some deer antlers out away from camp (*en el campo*) where with sharp bones and teeth they would scratch him. The amount of suffering the father could withstand would indicate the bravery the son would enjoy (Arlegui 1851: 144-145). The same author cited a rite involved in the formation of fictitious kin (*parentesco*), which contains a number of similar elements (Arlegui 1851: 149).

Whirlwinds (*remolinos*) were also connected with the spirit world. Pérez de Ribas reported that the people who saw these would throw themselves on the ground, saying to each other, *Cachinipa*, "the name which they gave to the devil or to whom they feared and revered in that whirlwind, because they did not know how to explain who it might be" (Pérez de Ribas III 1944: 248). The 1598 *Anua* made reference to whirlwinds, stating that the people believed that the devil, named *Cachiripa* (in another place simply *Chiripa*, and another *Cane*), was inside and that they would prostrate themselves so that they would not die (DHM 1598).

Arlegui stated that spirits were connected with natural phenomena and objects such as rivers, springs, and trees (an instance of the latter is cited for the Sierra de Colotlán) around which rites and beliefs were focused. He also mentioned beliefs about heavenly bodies influencing or controlling sickness and health (the rite performed at Mapimí) (Arlegui 1851: 152-153, 157).

The attitude held toward a deceased priest's clothing in one instance has already been mentioned, apparently a fear of the magic power the clothes might contain. Father Rodrigo del Castillo reported the great reverence Tobosos and Cabezas had for him when they captured him, as well as a request from one of the chiefs for some Holy Earth that Castillo had with him (AGN 1667).

Arlegui characterized some of the food beliefs for the central plateau, some of which may be pertinent here. Horses and mules were favored for consumption because these were swift animals, and some of this characteristic was believed to be transferred to the consumer of their flesh. Conversely, the flesh of cattle was looked upon as a liability. The Indians also ate the flesh of their own people in order to acquire whatever special traits the deceased might have possessed, such as healing powers or hunting skill (Arlegui 1851: 138-139).

It is possible that the bezoar stone (*piedra bezal*) was of generally high estimation in the region. One Simón de Echevarría wrote from Parras to the Indian governor of Santa Rosa de Nadadores, Don Diego de Valdez, a Quechale, in 1692, requesting such a stone (BL 1695a). While it is not certain that the stone was used by the local Indians, Mota y Escobar wrote that in the Saltillo area that the bezoar was found in a certain kind of *ciervos* called *cornicabras*. The local natives constantly hunted them for the stone because of the great demand for them among the Spaniards. They traded these and others they made from a certain kind of earth and *betún* (tar, wax?) to the Europeans (1940: 163).

Games

Slight information has come to light regarding two games played by the Indians. The Acoclames and Cocoyomes specifically were reported to have played *patole* and *pelota* (AHP 1704Ab). Both games were described for the general area by Arlegui.

Patoli (*patole*) consisted of six small sticks of the same size with different marks on them, used as dice.

These were thrown together to the ground, and wins or losses were calculated according to how the sticks landed. When the dice were thrown the player(s) would beat themselves on the chest, the one hitting himself the hardest being considered the strongest.

Pelota, which Arlegui called *hule* (i.e., *pelota de hule*), was played on a large plain, three or four leagues long. Equal sides would be chosen and a final goal line determined. The players had sticks of *encino* with which they would hit the ball. Eventually one side or the other would get the ball to the goal line, although this might take several days, the spot where the ball rested at the end of each day marked so that play could resume there the next. Betting was common, and much drinking and shouting went on during the games (Arlegui 1851: 148-149).

The Spanish captain, Martín de Alday, of El Pasaje Presidio, mentioned both *pelota* and horse racing being played while he was negotiating peace with the Cocoyomes during a campaign in the back country. He wrote, "and to the said Indian Alonso I ordered given a horse from those of my *silla* and they ran (*corrieron*) the game of *pelota*, the Coahuileño Indian auxiliaries with the Cocoyomes, betting clothing, and the said Cocoyomes won." The next day the Babozarigame auxiliaries came out in defense of the Coahuileños, but the Cocoyomes won again. The Cocoyomes immediately made a match with the soldiers for a horse race, the soldiers winning on this occasion. Then horses were traded for cloaks (*capotes*) and *justacores*. On another occasion three Cocoyome messengers footraced with a soldier at the presidio of El Pasaje (AHP 1716Ab). The reference to horses connected with the game of *pelota* seems to evince cultural fusion, but unfortunately no description of the game is given. Betting was probably common. One ex-captive of the Cocoyomes reported (1710) that Ceja Blanca's band went to the camp of the Cocoyomes, taking some spoils "which they went to gamble (*jugar*) at the said rancheria" (BL 1709-1715). Again, there is no description of the game.

Counting

Small stones or grains of corn were employed as an aid in counting when fairly large numbers were involved, at least in front of Spaniards during interrogations, and one Sisimble counted on his fingers (AHP 1653Ad; AHP 1704Ab; BL 1748; CD 1650a). Years were reckoned as *aguas* (rainy seasons) and

months as "moons" (*lunas*) (AHP 1704Ab; AHP 1716Ab; AHP 1720Aa; AHP 1724Aa). Notched sticks may have been common for sending certain types of messages. The Salineros showed the Spaniards such a stick which recorded the number of enemy they had killed (AHP 1653Ad), and the Chisos did the same with a notched bow (*arco rayado*) (AHP 1655Ab). Smoke signals were also used for communication (AHP 1716Aa; AHP 1722Aa).

Language

Information regarding the various languages and dialects of the Greater Bolsón area is extremely limited, and broader linguistic relationships and individual language boundaries for the most part remain obscure. Much of the documentary evidence is inconclusive and confusing, although some of it does suggest a few rather definite conclusions. However, some of the problems that contribute to the inconclusiveness and ambiguousness of the evidence should first be mentioned.

Real progress will not be made in unraveling the linguistic complexities of this area until adequate, substantial data can be compiled in the form of vocabularies and grammars. The information offered here is believed to be the best available at present. For the purpose of this discussion, it is assumed that negative evidence — that is, statements referring to dissimilarities between languages — carries more weight than does information indicating likeness.

One of the principle problems stems from the fact that considerable bi- or multi-lingualism existed on the north Mexican frontier in the sixteenth, seventeenth, and eighteenth centuries, although no doubt it diminished as time progressed. Some bi-lingualism must have existed even in precontact times, owing to the practices of intermarriage with and the capturing of children of neighboring bands. With the Spanish conquest of the area and the greater movement of peoples and contact among different groups, multilingualism probably increased, and a considerable amount of dialect leveling undoubtedly occurred.

Early observers of the general region noted a great number of languages, although it may have been that some of the differences assumed to be on the "language" level were merely dialectal. Alonso de León wrote that there were a great number of languages in the neighboring area of Nuevo León

(García 1909:32). The 1607 *Anua*, speaking of the Parras-Laguna district, referred to the "very great variety of tongues that there are among them and none of the tongues so general that it was used among all, of which their ministers might make use" (DHM 1607). Mota y Escobar about this same time contradicted this somewhat, stating for the people of Parras that although they comprised distinct nations and languages, the Irritila tongue was understood by all (Mota y Escobar 1940: 164). While no statements have been found that refer specifically to Tobosos, Chisos, and Coahuileños, it is reasonable to assume that some dialectal variation may have existed in the languages of these groups also.

At the same time, the use of the Mexican (Nahuatl) language was widespread in the region; it was employed as the daily operating language on many haciendas and other Spanish holdings, and it was also used as a *lingua franca* where Indians of different tongues got together. Its use was noted by the Jesuits in the earliest days of their penetration into the Parras-Laguna area. Arnaya in 1601, and the 1600-1602 *Anua*, stated that the Mexican language had been learned by the Indians when many had been away working for Spaniards (BL 1600-1602; DHM 1601). In 1598, the *Anua* noted that *mexicano* was of general use in this district, and the most *ladino* of the people prided themselves in speaking some, although they did so "barbarously" (DHM 1598). Mota y Escobar made virtually the same observation (1940: 164), and Tello noted the common use of Mexican among the Chichimecas farther south, although they also spoke their own languages (Tello 1891: 776).

The use of Nahuatl was so extensive, especially in the seventeenth century, that many Spaniards knew the language. Although no attempt has been made here to document its use thoroughly, a few examples are cited. In one attack the enemy was reported to have spoken Concho and Salinero, as well as fluent Mexican (*ladinamente*) (AHP 1657Bb). Two Indians speaking Mexican were judged by a native speaker of the latter to be Salineros because of their accents (AHP 1657Bb). In an attack upon some Tarahumaras, Conchos spoke to them in Mexican (AHP 1653Ae). A *borrada* Indian woman, fluent in the Mexican tongue and who also knew Salinero, stated that while a prisoner she had overheard the enemy (unidentified), who did not speak Salinero, to the effect that, "by

some words that she heard from the said three Indian women in Mexican, she learned that . . ." (AHP 1654Aa). A number of hacienda workers were said at one time or another to speak *mexicano* (e.g., AHP 1685Da).

One interesting statement exists regarding the quality of this Mexican spoken in the north. An edict was published in Nahuatl in 1684 at the time of the *residencia* of an official. One recipient of this edict at San Juan y la Concepción stated in his acknowledgement of receipt that "el lenguaxe mexicano que por aca se estila esta tan adulterado quanto basta para no entender la perfecta lengua mexicana q es la del Edicto" (AHP 1684Ab).

Interrogations of Indians were carried on either in Spanish (more frequently as time went on) or in Mexican, although the native tongue of the questioned was not Nahuatl, or an interpreter in Mexican was appointed along with one in the native language, in which case three languages – Spanish, Mexican, and the native – were employed (e.g., AHP 1658Aa). This use of *mexicano* also shows up in a number of places, bands, and personal names – for example, Ocotán (Ocotlán), Acatita (Acatitlán; Martínez del Río 1954), Cocoyome, and El Tecolote.

It is for these reasons, as well as because most native terms that occur in the sources do so with no stated meaning, that the aboriginal words and names collected during the course of this study are of little value. Moreover, it is dangerous and fallacious to rely to any degree upon the tribal or band identity of persons who interpreted for natives during interrogations, because usually, after the interpreters were appointed, it was not stated in what language the questioning actually was carried out. Sometimes this questioning was entirely in Mexican and Spanish, as a number of the back-country Indians knew some of one or both of these languages, learned during the short periods they were under mission control or while working for Spaniards. Nevertheless, in lieu of better evidence, a few instances of the kinds of interpreters employed are given for what little value they contain. At the same time, statements about language made by Spaniards should be held highly suspect, as usually it is not clear if and when they possessed any real knowledge about the Indians.

There seems to be little doubt that the Tobosos, Nonojes, Acoclames, Ocomes, Cocoyomes, and other "Toboso" groups spoke basically the same language. In 1654 it was stated that "the Tobosos . . . had joined with Casa Zavala and with the Nonojes and Acoclames because of being companions and of the same language." Prisoners who belonged to the Tucumuraga, Mamorimama, Ocomite (Ocome), Coyote (Cocoyome?) nations were questioned apparently by the same interpreter on one occasion, but the language employed was unstated (AHP 1654Ac). In 1645 it was reported that one Cristóbal "served as interpreter because he understands the tongue of the said Tobosos and other said nations and Castillian" — the other said nations here being Nonojes, Acoclames, and Ocomes (AHP 1645Aa). In 1692 three Tobosos were chosen as interpreters for the "Toboso, Cocoyome, and Gavilan language" (BL 1693b). A year later Governor Pardiñas wrote that the Gavilanes, Cocoyomes, and Jococomes (Ocomes) spoke a single language (BL 1694-1698). In 1715 and in 1720 that language was explicitly noted as "the Acoclame and Cocoyome language" (AHP 1715Aa; AHP 1720Aa).

The Chisos apparently spoke the Concho language. In 1684, when Conchos and Chisos were interrogated, the same person interpreted for both groups. This interpreter was said to use "la lengua chisa y Concha," and this was later referred to "En el dho Ydioma" (AHP 1684Aa). One witness, in support of his identification of attackers while testifying in 1710, stated that "he knows the Acoclames very well, ever since they were settled in peace at Atotonilco . . . and that also he recognized that there were Chisos because these speak the Concho language which the Cocoyomes and Acoclames do not speak and he heard them [speak] the Concho language which the witness understands very well" (BL 1709-1715). (See also: Kroeber 1934; Sauer 1934.)

Chiso and Toboso seem definitely to have been distinct languages. Moreover, interpreters interrogating some supposedly Toboso children, who were actually Chisos, stated that the declarants could not understand "Toboso" (AHP 1655Ab). Another instance, quoted here at some length, indicates the difference between Cocoyome (Toboso) and Sisimble (Chiso). For the interrogation in the case against the Sisimbles in Durango in 1748, a Spaniard, Francisco Páez, who had been a captive of and virtually raised by the Cocoyomes, was chosen as interpreter. With the first confessant, the Sisimble leader Juan Nepomuceno, it was reported that "having spoken in a language that the said interpreter stated was that of the Cocoyomes, the said Indian became astonished

(suspenso), without answering him, and having questioned him again, he continued in this uncertainty . . ." still with no answer. With this, "the said Indian was made to understand by signs and words if he was a Cocoyome, to which he responded with only this word, 'Sisimble,' indicating with his head that he was not a Cocoyome, with which demonstration and other words that he uttered in his language the interpreter said that what the Indian was speaking was not the language of the Cocoyomes which he understood, because he had understood nothing of what was spoken to him" (BL 1748).

However, this evidence does not necessarily mean that Toboso and Chiso belonged to entirely different linguistic stocks. One statement made by an Indian of unstated ethnic affiliation may indicate that the two languages were related and somewhat similar, and that a person with a certain amount of linguistic sophistication or experience who spoke one of the languages could perceive similarities and fairly readily learn at least to understand the other. During the interrogation proceedings of this ex-captive of the Cocoyomes, it was stated that "since the confessant knows the Concho language and it is somewhat similar to that which the Tobosos speak, he understood very well what they said" (BL 1693b). Also, the governor, Francisco Bautista, of the settled Tobosos at San Francisco de Conchos, often interpreted for Chisos together with another Toboso (BL 1693b), but again this constitutes extremely flimsy evidence.

On the basis of nonlinguistic evidence the Cabezas, Salineros, Mayos, and Babozarigames were Coahuileños (BL 1674; BL 1676; BL 1722). This probably also included the Matarajes, Baborimamas, and even the Cíbolas from Coahuila. However, most of the information that might hint that the Salinero-Cabeza language was similar or different from others of the area is quite vague and inconclusive.

"Salinero" was apparently definitely different from Tepehuán and Concho alike. In 1650 it was stated that the Salinero language spoken at the missions of Tizonazo and El Zape was distinct from Tepehuán (AGN 1648-1649), and earlier Tepehuán was said to be different from both Zacateco and the language of Mapimí (Irritila and/or "Salinero"?) (AGN 1607c). With regard to Concho, it was stated on one occasion that "the Cabezas spoke to the enemy according to the Concho who did not understand them because their language is different from his" (AHP 1654Ac). Witnesses, testifying about another attack, distinguished between the Salinero and Concho languages that were used by the enemy (AHP 1657Bb).

The evidence is somewhat more confusing with regard to Toboso and Salinero, although apparently these were distinct (mutually unintelligible) languages. Once, when Salineros and Tobosos were being questioned, when it came the Toboso's turn, a new interpreter had to be chosen. His name was Juan Concho, although no tribal affiliation was given, and it is questionable how much his "surname" can be taken to indicate this (although from another source it appears he might have been a Salinero or Cabeza; AHP 1653Bb). At this time it was stated that "inasmuch as there is no one in the camp who understands the Toboso language, and there is no other except Juan Concho friendly Indian who [can] declare to the interpreter of the government in Mexican" (AHP 1652Dc). Again, a woman who had been held by rebels at Acatita claimed she could not understand the language they spoke as they were *not* of the Salinero tongue, which she apparently understood; her husband was a Salinero. Apparently, the group she referred to was "Toboso," but this is a pure guess (AHP 1654Aa). Another time, some Salineros indentified a group as speaking both Toboso and Concho, and one of these enemies had spoken to the Salineros in Mexican. This might indicate a difference between Salinero and both Concho and Toboso, although it is not stated whether the Salineros were spoken to in any other language (AHP 1655Ab).

There is some evidence that contraverts this, however. A Tarahumar was reported to have declared that "during the time of the battle he recognized that they were speaking the language that is common to Tobosos, Gavilanes, and Salineros" (AHP 1657Bb). Once, for the interrogation of a Toboso prisoner, two interpreters were appointed, one for the Mexican language and the other, Francisco Mama the Salinero "for his own native tongue" *(para la suya natural)* (AHP 1653Ad). In both of these cases there is no assurance that either the Tarahumar or the Spaniards could actually recognize the difference between Salinero and Toboso, if there were any. At later dates, a Cabeza acted as interpreter for the Cocoyomes (AHP 1704Ac) as did a Babozarigame (AHP 1722Ab; BL 1722); the language of the interrogation was not stated.

One shred of evidence indicates that "Lagunero" (Irritila?) was distinct from "Salinero." A

"Lagunero" telling of a meeting between Coahuileños and Cabezas in Parras stated that he did not understand the language they spoke (AHP 1722Ab). Presumably a Lagunero would at least recognize, if not understand, Spanish, his own language, and Mexican — the latter owing to the Tlaxcaltecan population resident at Parras. It is also possible, of course, that the language of this "Lagunero" was Zacateco or Cuachichil.

For the greater Parras-Laguna district, early missionaries reported that they employed the Zacateco language up close to the district itself. Father Ahumada claimed that the major portion of the Nazas River was Zacateco-speaking, and he added that the language had the widest use in "all of this mission" (of Parras?) (AGN 1607c). The Jesuit Arista states that the catechism at Parras had been put into two languages, but he gives no hint as to what these were. The 1598 *Anua* said that one language was Irritila, which belonged "to this valley" (apparently of La Laguna), and the other was Mexican (Pérez de Ribas III 1944: 251-253, 256; DHM 1598). Ahumada also stated that the language of a great many of the Indians of Mapimí was Tepehuán; but, unfortunately, he does not say what the language of the remaining people was (AGN 1607c). Decorme divides the general area into three languages: Zacateco along the Nazas River and southwestward; Irritila at Parras, Patos, La Laguna, and Mapimí; and, Toboso north of the latter region — but it is not clear on what this classification is based (Decorme II 1941: 17).

The Cocoyome language apparently was different from Tepehuán. A Tepehuán woman stated that she could not understand the language of the Cocoyomes (BL 1693b).

Only six native terms with meaning have been located during the course of this investigation. Two are Chiso, one is Toboso, one is Salinero, and the other two are from an unidentified language or languages from the Parras-Laguna district — this may have been Irritila, if in effect it was a distinct language.

(1) *Chiso: sibalba,* "agua del zorrillo" or "skunk water," and *bayacabam,* "donde se acaba la corriente," or "the place the stream terminates." These were names for two water holes picked up by General Juan de Retana in a campaign of 1693 into Chiso country. The route went roughly eastward from the town of Julimes (BL 1695b).

(2) *Toboso: cable cable*, "soy sacerdote" or "I am a priest." This is apparently "Toboso," although it could be "Cabeza." The writer of this letter, Father Rodrigo del Castillo, while a prisoner of a combined group of Tobosos and Cabezas, stated that he went toward the Capitan General who led them, ". . . fuime para el diciendole, *Cable Cable* que en su lengua quiere decir Soy Sacerdote . . . vino luego otro Toboco . . ." (AGN 1667).

(3) *Salinero: Baturi, Baluzi, Baluri*, "Pies de Liebre" or "rabbit's feet" (Alegre III 1959: 37, 40; DHM 1645).

(4) *San Pedro de la Laguna: naboya*, said to be the name for the *balsas* used at San Pedro de la Laguna (BL 1605).

(5) *Parras: noas*, a kind of mescal described for the Parras district (Mota y Escobar 1940: 170).

5. SUMMARY OF BAND DISTRIBUTION AND HISTORY

This chapter is presented as a summary of the evidence given in previous chapters (principally Chapter 3) of the history of the several groups of people of the Greater Bolsón. Tentative conclusions are drawn regarding tribal distribution. Since ethnic distribution changed over time, in any discussion of the placement of the various bands it is necessary to keep different time levels separate. While the information here is not adequate for a conclusive distributional picture, there is enough to show the outlines of the history of tribal distribution and to indicate the many factual problems still in need of solution.

In early contact times the people of central northern Mexico were basically hunters and gatherers organized into a great number of small bands, apparently exogamous lineages (see Chapter 4).

On the basis of the rather scanty historical and linguistic data, it is possible tentatively to group these bands into larger units that, for convenience, can be termed "tribes."* The three major tribes that have emerged in this study are the "Coahuileños" in the south and east, the "Chisos" in the north along the Río Grande drainage, and the "Tobosos" occupying the middle region.

One of the major problems in determining the territorial distribution of aboriginal groups, as already noted, is the lack in many instances of adequate historical documentation that might afford a fairly concrete notion of time depth. It should be emphasized again that the earliest available cultural data on the region of the Greater Bolsón — that is, data at the time of the founding of the Jesuit missions in the Parras-Laguna district — are in some ways quite late (aside from being incomplete). There is no way at this time, except by inference, to appraise the changes that may have taken place on this southern periphery before the arrival of the Jesuits. Yet some kind of changes most probably did occur owing to the great activity, including a considerable amount of warfare,

that went on to the south during the last half of the sixteenth century. Aside from whatever transformations in cultural features might have taken place, population reduction owing to disease and armed hostilities probably affected to some extent the tribal distributions farther northward.

If the introduction of the Jesuit missions in the Parras-Laguna district in the 1590's did not begin the breakdown of tribal territories, it certainly sped up the process, judging from the band movement and resettlement as evidenced in the early Jesuit records. Moreover, even though events south of Zacatecas previous to the 1590's had no noticeable effect on the Parras and San Pedro de la Laguna region, the Spanish settlements in and around the Greater Bolsón in the area of Saltillo as well as those in the Santa Bárbara-San Bartolomé district probably did. By the 1640's, when more abundant information on a number of groups north of Parras and San Pedro de la Laguna is available, tribal or band territories may well have begun to change rather significantly.

It is uncertain how much of a general process can be inferred for this early period from the movement of peoples southward during the last half of the seventeenth century and the eighteenth century until the arrival of the Apaches. In effect, there may not have been any significant southward movement until well into the 1600's. This problem is unsolvable at present, but it should be noted that the Jesuits did transport bands living north of Parras and San Pedro southward, as well as people from other directions, into their missions. One process that seems to have taken place was that, although aboriginal groups did not markedly change the general locations óf their territories (i.e., areas with more or less well-delimited boundaries recognized by the various groups living within the vicinity) as these existed at the beginning of the sixteenth century, they did, however, extend their zones of sustenance or ranges (the total areas that they traveled over and utilized in one way or another) to include larger geographical regions. This extension of range was the result of the introduction of new animals, such as the horse, the pressure for new, wider (in a geographical sense) and perhaps

---

* "Tribe" is not to be taken here to imply any characteristics of social organization, as the term is employed by Service (1962), because the documentary sources simply have not yielded adequate data to enable any kind of classification in a social structural sense.

slightly more enduring alliances owing to the different kind of warfare brought to them by the Spaniards, as well as the necessity for traveling longer distances for subsistence goods when groups went out to raid Spanish holdings.

In later years, during the latter part of the 1600's and in the 1700's, bands did move southward, attracted in part by Spanish settlements while filling in a "vacuum" left by the previous inhabitants as these vanished. One very general and obvious rule with regard to the disappearance of Indian groups is that those bands closest to Spanish settlements disappeared first and, conversely, those located farther away persisted longer. Of course, there are exceptions to this because the crucial factor was not geographical distance itself but rather a group's accessibility to the Spaniards either for warfare, missionization, or labor. However, such groups as the Cocoyomes and Sisimbles apparently persisted longer because in effect they were located originally a considerable distance from Spanish holdings.

Finally, tribal and band movement under contact pressure remains one of the fundamental problems in the unraveling of some of the ethnic complexities of the central north Mexican area. This point is, for example, particularly pertinent with regard to the "Salineros" and "Cabezas," although it concerns all groups. In 1676, a rather late date, the Bishop of Guadalajara wrote that the territory of the Salineros, Cabezas, Mayos, and Babozarigames was in the vicinity of Cuatro Ciénegas, and that these groups were called "Coahuileños" (BL 1676). Whether or not this statement accurately reflects the territorial locations of these bands of, say, around 1600 cannot be determined at present, although, from other information, it appears that these people may have dwelt to the south of Cuatro Ciénegas.

The "Salineros" by name from the earliest references were located somewhat farther south of Cuatro Ciénegas. There seems to be little doubt that the "Salineros" and "Cabezas" both were "Coahuileño" peoples in later times, although during the early years it is likely that some Tepehuán people were dubbed "Salineros" by the Spaniards.

However, specific connections among the several groups involved cannot be made with any degree of assurance, except for the "Cabezas" settled at Parras during the 1690's. In view of the southern and western range of the "Salineros" in Colonial times, as well as their settlement at the mission of Tizonazo and at

the towns reported founded for them around 1626 at Agua de Pelayo and La Mimbrera, it seems probable, although tentative, that they occupied a territory that extended westward to and around Mapimí. This area apparently included a portion of the desert north and possibly northwest of Mapimí at the time missionization was begun in the 1590's.

If this interpretation is accurate, then, in this early period there existed a belt of Coahuileños from around Mapimí, eastward and north of the Parras-Laguna district (very possibly they included part of the latter), into the actual areas of old Coahuila (i.e., around the town of Monclova — Jiménez Moreno 1958: 106) and Cuatro Ciénegas northward. North of the western part of this belt and west of the Coahuileño territory on the east were the Tobosos. While these people may also have been "Coahuileños," it seems best to assume on the basis of the meager linguistic data that has come to light that they were not. If they were Coahuileños, they seem to have formed pretty much of a separate group. Although no definite information is available, the boundary between the "Salineros" and "Tobosos" can tentatively be placed around the area south of Las Cañas, leaving the boundary between the two tribes as a general northeast-southwest line running between the Sierra Mojada and the Sierra de Tlahualilo.

The southern boundary of the Salineros still remains in considerable doubt, particularly since their "original" involvement in the Parras and Laguna missions is not clear. It was hoped at one point that investigation in the church archives of Parras would throw some light on this question as well as on the disappearance of the other groups reported in the region by the early Jesuits. Unfortunately, however, this has only shown the replacement of groups by names, the latter usually different from the designations employed in administrative reports in the early 1600's through the 1640's. Nevertheless, some "Coahuileño" bands were part of the early missions, and Jesuits reported bringing in people from a place called "Cuaguila" (around Monclova) some thirty leagues away from Parras. It would almost seem likely that a few "Tobosos" may have been brought into these missions, but no direct evidence exists for this — except perhaps the one occurrence, in 1617, of the name Toboco.

Aside from "Coahuileños," at least three other linguistic groups were represented in the general Laguna district, the speakers of which made up part of the mission population — Tepehuán around the Mapimí area, and possibly in parts of the Nazas River country; Zacateco along the Nazas River; and, Cuachichil to the south and east of Parras. The Irritila language reported spoken in the region by some early writers (Pérez de Ribas III 1944: 251-253, 256; DHM 1598) does not emerge in any clear-cut fashion from other data consulted, and the Irritila as a specific group does not appear to have had any conspicuous importance, despite the fact that in one place they were reported to be one of the two original groups at Parras. At present, there is no way to determine if "Irritila" was a separate language or linguistic stock spoken in this region or if actually it was only a dialectal variation of the "Coahuileño" tongue spoken by the Salineros and Cabezas, or of the languages of the Zacatecos, Tepehuanes, or Cuachichiles.

The problem is further complicated by the fact that many of these named groups disappeared soon from the record. In many cases the earlier sources contain indigenous names that occur a few times never to be repeated again. In the Parras records several general terms such as Chibicano and Bahanero, which become common after the 1640's for groups around San Pedro de la Laguna, do not occur in the earlier years. At the same time "Coahuileño" band names become more and more frequent, no doubt in part because of the decline in the original Parras and Laguna mission population and because "Cuaguilas" were brought or induced in as replacements. However, there still remains the possibility of more actual continuity in the population of this area than the recorded terminology indicates. This possibility is borne out to some degree in the trend toward dropping of specific terms as time went by and the application of some early specific terms in a generic sense (e.g. Toboso and Cocoyome) or the occurrence of a new general term (e.g., Lagunero).

Despite name changes, which are no doubt quite indicative, it has also been noted that many of the people from the Parras-Laguna region had joined the rebels in the 1640's, and later. However, it is difficult to tie these people — that is, those mentioned in the Parras mission records — by name with those who appear in the administrative reports. It is possible that many of the earlier recorded bands later (i.e., ca 1640 and after) came to be designated as Salineros and Cabezas (the latter which at a still much later date in the 1690's was quite composite — see Appendices 2 and 3). Some later writers (AGD n.d.; DHM 1653) stated that either the Salineros and Cabezas were

rebels from the Parras-Laguna district or that groups from the latter were in the back country in revolt which, from administrative reports, would make them part of the Salineros and Cabezas.

If attempts to delineate the "tribal" territories are rather inconclusive, it is even more difficult to determine the locations of specific bands. However, from the documents consulted, and it must be kept in mind that these have a bias since the majority emanated from Parral, it is possible to make a few inferences regarding the relative locations of some bands after 1640. There were apparently several groups of "Salineros," and guessing from the fact that at least some of these were settled at the Tizonazo mission and their raiding activities were in the southwestern portion of the territory, these "Salineros" probably occupied the most southwestern part of "Coahuileño" country. The Matarajes may have been one of these western bands. The "Cabezas" were farther east, closer to the Parras district. This term, however — like "Salinero" and "Toboso" — had rather general usage, and it is possible that it (as well as "Salinero") included various named groups in the 1640's as it did in the 1690's. However, it must be kept in mind that the internal makeup of the "Cabezas" with regard to specific named bands was perhaps rather different at these two dates, owing to general population reduction and the amalgamation of bands as a result of warfare and disease during the intervening fifty years.

Around Parras were the Mayos and/or Tusares. To the north of the Parras-Laguna area were the Baborimamas and Pies de Venado, and possibly a little farther away the Babozarigames in the direction of Cuatro Ciénegas. To the north of these groups were the Colorados, and possibly to the east of these were the so-called Cíbolos or Siboporame. Others, such as the Corcobados, Tetecos, Tocas, and Quaaguapayas, dwelled — roughly — in this area. These are the principal groups for which it appears at all reasonable to attempt even an impressionistic placement.

The boundary of "Toboso" country, although vague in the south where Toboso bands bordered the "Salineros," is much better delineated in the west and north. The western edge was apparently fairly close to the Florido River, or at least in this area. In the north, the Jaque-Encinillas region (assuming that the present-day range of mountains north of the Laguna de Jaque is the same Las Encinillas as that referred to in the seventeenth century) was said on several occasions to be "Toboso" country. A later reference (1715) said that Las Encinillas and Agua de Mayo were where "Chisos" camped, which possibly is an indication of the "Chisos" extending their territory southward.

Where the borderline ran westward from around Las Encinillas to the Conchos River is unknown, but one possibility suggested by the general picture obtrudes itself with regard to general Chiso-Toboso habitation. Very possibly the Chisos, being an extension of the river-dwelling Conchos, lived in the desert area drained by the Río Grande and Conchos rivers, while the "Tobosos" occupied principally the region of internal drainage to the south, and possibly in places to the east of some of the "Chiso" bands along the Conchos River. This may have been the case in the west, although how it would hold up in the eastern "Coahuileño" area is not clear at present. It is always possible, in terms of the prehistory of the area, that this type of "Chiso"-"Toboso" border situation was actually of rather recent date, a problem that in part will have to wait for archaeological investigation. At least in historical times the evidence indicates that the "Chisos" and "Tobosos" were quite distinct linguistically, although not necessarily unrelated.

Where the eastern border of "Toboso" country was is unknown, but it seems to have been somewhere east of Sierra Mojada and west of Cuatro Ciénegas. Aside from the problem of not having any definite statement from Colonial documentation regarding where this boundary might have been, it is also unknown how many bands that are mentioned in the sources actually were "Tobosos." Certainly, the Toboso proper, the Acoclames, Cocoyomes, Gavilanes, Ocomes, and Nonojes were, and apparently so were the Hijos de las Piedras, Hijos de la Tierra, and Hijos de los Palos. Some of the other groups, such as the Tatalcoyomes, may also have been, but this is not at all certain. A number of the names that appear in the early sources (ca 1640's and 1650's) may actually refer to very small groups who were quickly absorbed into larger bands, or at least their separate identities were obscured or overshadowed in Spanish reports owing to the fact that they were either generally under the wing of a larger group or that they resided somewhat further away from Spanish settlements and were less well-known to the Europeans.

Of the groups that seem to have been definitely "Toboso," it seems reasonable that the Toboso proper were one of the bands originally closest to Spanish settlement, that is, to the San Bartolomé Valley (Allende) district. This is given somewhat

further probability because Tobosos were settled at the Atotonilco mission apparently as early as 1612, although it is not clear what bands actually were involved in this reduction. Bands close by and apparently living to the northeast were the Nonojes and the Acoclames, an interpretation based in large part on the close association of these three groups during the 1640's and 1650's, and the fact that the Tobosos and Nonojes disappeared rather early.

The Ocomes and Gavilanes probably occupied a region somewhat to the south of these bands, judging from the fact that their raiding territory seems to have had a much more southern extent to it. It would appear from a few of the earlier statements that the Cocoyomes dwelt somewhere in the northeastern portion of "Toboso" territory, as on several occasions they were reported to be the "Toboso" group located farthest away from Spanish settlements and to have had the least contact with Spanish civilization. Moreover, they were said to have had the most contact with "Chisos" to the north. This more interior location of the Cocoyomes probably was one of the prime reasons that they lasted longest as a group, absorbing remnants and refugees from other bands such as the Xexet and the Acoclames.

The "Chisos," while desert dwellers, also lived along the Río Grande southeast of La Junta or the confluence of the Conchos and Río Grande rivers, and apparently north of the latter river in the Big Bend country (Sauer 1934). How many bands they actually comprised and how far they extended eastward is unknown. Cacuitataomes were one of the river-dwelling Chiso groups (AHP 1684Aa) and also one of the least troublesome, according to the historical references. The Batayoliclas seem also to have been in a somewhat similar category, perhaps also river dwelling (if the etymology given in Appendix 1 is at all correct). A reasonable guess would seem to be that these groups lived fairly close to the La Junta settlements.

The Osataba, Chichitame, Osatayolicla, Osataba, Guesecpayolicla, and Suniyolicla bands lived somewhat farther away (the first two on the far side of the Río Grande) and, particularly the last, were more troublesome. At least the Suniyoliclas were closely associated with Cocoyomes at a later time, which may be an indication of a more eastern location for them, although they might also have been close to the Batayoliclas. Even more distant dwelling, and possibly one of the most northeastern groups, were the Sisimbles. By analogy with the Cocoyome case, the factor of distance probably is the reason that the Sisimbles persisted so long, being the last of the "original" inhabitants of the desert of the central north Mexican region considered here.

While, in general, information on the "Chiso" bands is the most meager, possibly documentation from archives still extant in the present-day state of Coahuila will eventually throw more light on their eastern extension, as well as on the eastern extension of the "Tobosos" and on a more exact demarcation of the band boundaries of all groups.*

One other matter particularly concerning the Tobosos should be mentioned. On occasion some writers have stated that the Tobosos were either Apaches or Athabaskan-speaking forerunners of the Apaches. In the last century Orozco y Berra wrote that, "The Tobosos are of the Apache family, and they prepared the way for them into our lands, serving as a vanguard for them, since while they existed the Apaches did not frequent the missions south of the Río Grande. The Cocoyomes and the Cabezas are of the same family" (1864: 309).

While the present evidence is highly circumstantial, there seems to be nothing in it to indicate that the Tobosos, or any of the other central northern Mexican groups for that matter, were Athabaskans. Nor is there any definite information that would lead to placing the Cocoyomes with the Cabezas in any kind of relationship other than that of an occasional mili-

tary alliance. The identification of Apaches with Tobosos and other Greater Bolsón inhabitants seems to have been based upon the fact that these peoples occupied part of the same territory, albeit at different times, and that they possessed similar raiding-type ways of life, developed probably under similar Colonial conditions. The answer, of course, must await further historical evidence, especially the kind that will be amenable to linguistic analysis.

The history of the disappearance of the aboriginal peoples of the Greater Bolsón area can be summarized in a few lines. At the time of first contact by the Spaniards, the region was inhabited by a number of small bands of people who for the most part disappeared within some two hundred years after European penetration into the area. Thus, many of the original "nations" encountered around the Parras mission district were pretty well extinct by the 1650's. By the 1690's most of the Salineros and Cabezas and their allies were no longer active, and by 1730 the Tobosos had virtually vanished. The core of the original inhabitants left in the region were Chisos, although with survivors and stragglers from other groups, until these too became extinct by 1750, being replaced by invaders from across the Río Grande, the Apaches.

The general process ran more or less as follows. Groups closest to Spanish settlements tended to disappear sooner than those more distantly located; once a group had been extinguished, all or part of its territory was occupied, at least as a zone of sustenance, by the closest surviving bands. This occupation was not a matter of the neighboring nations moving lock, stock, and barrel into the territory of their extinct neighbors; rather, it was that at least some of the remaining bands would extend their ranges into this now-vacant territory. As time progressed there took place an expansion of territories and ranges of the remaining bands of people as well as, apparently, a greater spacing out of these groups. Finally, this process continued to the point at which the groups originally encountered by the Spaniards when they first settled in the region had vanished. Peoples from farther north, in turn, moved across the Río Grande and took over the Greater Bolsón (as well as other parts of Northern Mexico), at least utilizing the region as part of their own territories and ranges for the acquisition of economic goods and other benefits.

---

* One of the problems is that although Chisos are referred to as (apparently) a general group from early in the seventeenth century, specific "Chiso" band names seemingly do not appear until the 1684 Revolt. After this date there are only scanty references to them. One somewhat perplexing problem and an example of the terminological confusion that reigns in the historical sources in this area occurs in a 1684 document. In 1653, a Mamite (Concho) Indian, Don Hernando de Obregón, was appointed governor of the Eastern Concho Indians and of the Jumano speaking towns of La Junta. In his title it is expressly stated that the Chisos were to be under his jurisdiction. However, thirty-one years later, in 1684, during an investigation, Obregón recited the names of twenty-nine "nations" over which he was governor but mentioned neither the Chisos as such nor any of the specific Chiso bands – the names of which occur in the same document (AHP 1652Ab; AHP 1652Ba; AHP 1684Aa). It is always possible that some of the band names that Obregón gave in this testimony were alternates for these other names, but at present there is no way of determining this. The groups cited by Obregón were the Guamichicuama, Baopapa, Obomes, Yacchicava, Yaochane, Topacolmes, Aycalmes, Guitates, Poricas, Culebras, Oposmes, Polacmes, Posalmes, Cacalotitos, Mesquites, Conejos, Yeguacat, Guelapijipicmi, Guiaguita, Abasopaeme, Olobayapuame, Bachichilmi, another Obome nation, Yaculsari, Sucayi, and Coyamit (not included in Appendix I) (AHP 1684Aa).

6. GREATER BOLSÓN CULTURE CHANGE: ANALYSIS AND INTERPRETATION

Many aspects of the ways of life of the desert tribes of the Greater Bolsón de Mapimí remain unknown or quite obscure. However, enough of the basic outlines of these cultures and of the modifications they underwent in interaction with the Spanish Colonial system seem to exist to warrant an attempt at explanation in general theoretical terms. Such an interpretation should serve to organize and to summarize the data presented and to suggest problems, factual and theoretical, for future research. Of necessity this kind of summary can be carried out only in a general way, because historical data are not for the most part precise or complete enough for specific formulations.

The general framework is one of the ecology of cultural or social systems and the processes by which these modify and adapt as their total external environment changes. To be more explicit, it is necessary to state a minimum view of the nature of a social system adequate for the present purposes, that is, a framework to serve as the simplest, or the most "economical," way to describe the phenomena at hand. This framework is taken mainly from the writings of Frake (1962), Nadel (1957), Parsons (1959), Pike (1954, 1955, 1960), Radcliffe-Brown (1952), and Sahlins and Service (1960).

A social system is viewed here as a set of cultural elements organized with respect to each other by sequences of behavior. The actors who participate in a system carry out these behavioral sequences to execute tasks they consider necessary to keep the system viable. These tasks and the ways to effectuate and to consummate them are prescribed mainly by tradition. The behavioral sequences or patterns, which include various cultural items, material and otherwise, employed in certain ordered or patterned ways, often with a number of alternatives, are grouped into larger sequences or clusters. Different clusters of behavioral sequences go to make up roles, that is, groups of sequences that go together as units, which people enact at different times for task performances. Such compound sequences and the elements that go to make them up must be isolated and considered within the system of which they are a part, not on

the basis of some outside system or set of criteria. This parallels the linguist's method of analyzing a language in its own terms, not in those of another language.

The concept of "role" here helps establish an empirically definable upper limit to a cluster of behavioral patterns. Because such clusters are often recognized and named by the people of a society, the notion of "role" is a convenient conceptual level in considering a social system as sets of sequences of behavior. It must be emphasized that such a system is "open" and "productive" in that combinations of old forms from within the system and new elements from outside the system can be utilized to create new sequences of behavior and clusters of these for dealing with new problems and handling new tasks.

Roles or clusters of behavior patterns are related to each other in different ways. For the present purpose it is enough to state only two of the more obvious. One kind of relationship exists when actors occupying complementary roles carry out expected and generally approved behavior in direct or face-to-face interaction. Another occurs when one role implies another for the same actor (e.g., "father" implies "husband"), rather than for a different actor. Inter-role relationships and proper associated behavior are recognized by other members of the society, and this recognition is one aspect of a system of operating roles. For example, in a specific society everyone will know when a man is acting like a "father" vis-a-vis a "son" or like a "hunter." He may be a "hunter" before a "father," and usually is, but generally not the reverse, and the fact of his being a "father" may make him become even more of a "hunter."

A social system, then, consists of a number of cultural items, bits of learned behavior or custom and associated material accoutrements, put together in longer behavioral sequences. Some of the latter are linked to other sequences as segments within roles and to still others by virtue of the fact that roles are related to each other in some complementary or reciprocal form of task execution. Roles also, of course, embody certain kinds of knowledge, sets of

[143]

values, duties and rights (including those for the application of social sanctions) regarding other roles, into which for present purposes it is not necessary to go since the data are not complete enough to warrant it. Naturally, of course, all behavioral sequences within roles and all roles in a society are not enacted (that is, they are not actually played) all of the time or at the same time. Some are triggered off periodically (e.g., annually or monthly) and others aperiodically by special circumstances, such as external threat.

It is essentially this kind of system, transmitted by learning, that human beings have built as a survival mechanism during the course of evolution. Men usually meet and cope with new conditions and contingencies mainly on the basis of the tradition of their particular way of life, discounting, for the present, differences in individual response due to idiosyncratic factors. Such cultural tradition includes acceptable — actual and expected — ranges of behavior, or as Pike has put it, emic patterns, that are associated with the traditional roles.

Under conditions of change new roles may be created, although old roles may be merely restructured internally. A change in the circumstances or conditions in which role behavior is carried out is likely to cause a reorientation to some extent of the behavior, material items, knowledge, expectations, and the like, associated with the role — a reorientation that is necessary to cope with the new situation or situations. Conditions that remain more or less stable will probably induce a rather stable range of expected behavior; new conditions will evoke a new response. The latter may be rather slight, and people will still recognize the role, possibly being scarcely aware that there has been some change; the role will still be called by the old name. However, some new things, new sequences of behavior, or new material items will have been added and possibly some of the old lost, although a good share of the older pattern may still remain. The result is a reorganization to some degree of the elements internal to the role.

At the same time, roles may be reorganized externally; that is, the network of relationships among them becomes altered. In this case the systemic links, as well as the channels for the communication of ideas, transfer of goods, and so forth, have also changed. Such restructuring may lead to some new, unprecedented cultural or social change or to a

reaffirmation of older values and goals, such as prestige from warfare, because the new conditions have intensified these aspects. Also, the new conditions may change the "function" (contributions to the survival of the society) or functional emphases of the roles.

In the present case, one function of the role of warrior was to adapt or adjust the society to external conditions through the maintenance of external boundaries; another was to assist in maintaining the social integration and solidarity of the society through revenge and by the connection of warfare with the ceremonial portion of the way of life. With the advent of Spanish society in the north Mexican area another activity was added to (or much increased with respect to) the external adaptive aspect of the warrior role. This was within the area of the "productive" activity of the society, in the sense of the acquisition of subsistence goods. Such "production" was complementary to, but also probably actually replaced to some extent, the activities of the "hunter" and "gatherer" (only perhaps in the sense that less time was devoted to them). For example, if squash planting ceased or diminished in frequency, as seems to have been the case, this would be an example of sociocultural change within the formulation employed here. Unfortunately, not enough information is available in the present case to afford any notion of what specific changes occurred, internally or externally, with such roles as "shaman" or "kinsman," among others. Nevertheless, this framework seems to facilitate interpreting the several changes, no matter how minor, that took place in the ways of life of the desert Indians of central northern Mexico.

In general review, these peoples at the time of first European contact existed as a number of small, kin-based bands, each living within its own territory and gaining its livelihood by hunting, gathering, and possibly occasional agriculture. These bands, denominated during the Spanish period by some kind of name, tended to form somewhat larger groupings or clusters. However, except for alliances at times against the common Spanish enemy, the internal nature of these larger groupings is unknown.

The native social systems were not self-sufficient or independent, and fairly definite patterns of relationships were maintained with neighboring bands. These relationships consisted of two principal alternating types — on the one hand, hostility, mainly in the form of warfare, and, on the other, friendship in the form of alliance, intermarriage, and trade. Some kind of ceremonial exchange occurred in both. It may have been that for the most part, in aboriginal times, hostile relations tended to occur outside the clusters and more of the non-hostile within them. The smaller, or possibly smallest, named (in the Colonial period) group at least in some areas seems to have been an exogamous unit. A so-called band cluster, then, would have consisted of several exogamous groups.

While the existence of band-clusters may be doubted for the pre-contact period without the pressure of the Spanish military forcing native inter-band alliances, it seems reasonable that such a phenomenon also occurred before conquest, because some bands would be thrown into closer relations to each other owing to an uneven distribution of food and water resources throughout the area. Such clusters would themselves be ecological groups and the boundaries between them would also be natural ecological boundaries. The human beings composing such groups could build upon local geographical features in order to delimit their respective territories.

However, as conditions of the *total* environment were modified, within a few years the social systems existing within the ecological setting were presented with a number of new factors; the people "living in" these systems were obliged to make some decisions that were unprecedented in the traditions which had been developed under the previous environmental conditions. Some of these factors were new diseases, new food resources, new methods of transportation, and new ideas.

New diseases introduced during the Colonial period changed, in this case increased, the frequency and distribution of the occurrence of sickness and death. This increase led to an intensification of part of the traditional ceremonial and ideological life, the mechanism by which the natives dealt with these biological phenomena. One would guess that at the same time a noticeable increase in sickness and death would cause a reappraisal to some extent of these practices when they appeared not to yield expected results. The borrowing of elements from another social system which covered the same class of phenomena in order to obtain better results could be expected and could explain the appearance of crosses, for example, on the graves of essentially non-Christian Indians, although possibly they had been baptized at some time or another. In general acculturation terms, this would be the borrowing of new, specific forms of elements and practices, which were no doubt reinterpreted within the native system of meanings. The fear of priests' clothing, cited in one place, could be interpreted on this basis.

The novel conditions that occurred in the general environment of the natives during the Colonial period offered a number of physical items, the transfer of which to, and their integration in, the native social systems would have been impeded because the Indians themselves could determine no worthwhile use for them. The first step of such transfer, initial acceptance, would be relatively simple because no agent, such as is required in the transfer of intangibles, would have been needed. However, ex-captives, auxiliary troops, workers of the Spaniards returning home, and short periods of missionization of some groups would have supplied agents in many instances. The second step, the working of these new elements into the native systems so that they actually become part of the shared, expectable behavior (emic) patterns of these systems would, however, be thwarted if the natives could not perceive or determine a use for them.

This was no doubt the case with many items of material culture the Indians acquired, either through theft or for the short periods when they had more intensive contact with Spaniards at missions and haciendas, and during battles. This material culture probably included agricultural tools, wagons, and the like. Other goods, which would be merely functional replacements for things the native cultures already possessed, might be accepted and used on a regular basis only if their acquisition from outside sources or by alien techniques was easier then that by traditional native methods, and, of course, there was no ideological predisposition against or adverse meaning associated with the item. Arquebuses seem to be a case in point. These firearms were accepted and used by the natives occasionally, but the Indians were restricted at the source and could obtain the guns, as well as the necessary powder (which required considerable care if it were to remain useable) and balls, only by theft. This mode of supply for these three functionally interrelated items — guns, powder and balls — was too irregular for the spread of their use. (See Secoy for a similar situation in the general Plains area; Secoy 1953). At the same time, the native bow was not much less efficient than the arquebus, and it

was simply not worthwhile to try to replace it under the circumstances.

One new feature, however, which did have far-reaching consequences, was the domestic animals of the Spaniards, particularly horses and mules. All of the animals of the Spaniards were a potential new source of food for the Indians, but horses and mules were by far the most important single additions, especially since they supplied a new mode of transportation as well as sustenance. The Spaniards raised many animals both for food and for use in wagon and mule trains, and for hacienda and mine work. To the Indians, these beasts existed in their environment merely for the plucking. At the same time, a number of these animals eventually escaped from the Spaniards, became wild and adapted to living in the desert back country; while they increased the food supply to some degree, they also may have replaced wild grazing animals, such as deer. Nevertheless, these novel creatures in the environment probably made for a more readily available food supply, for they would be concentrated more often in one location in a herd.

The new, more efficient mode of transportation meant a much wider range of movement. Small bands roving on foot could exploit only a certain restricted territory; a larger but more mobile band could exhaust the resources at one spot with the knowledge that it was equipped to move to another more distant area and do the same. An additional factor was that the item that afforded this greater mobility was also a potential and actual movable food supply. These two factors, greater mobility and a change in the nature of the food supply (possibly including an increase), may account in considerable degree for changes in the pattern of band distribution. The decimation of the native population through disease and war, the latter of a different style and somewhat more intense than the aboriginal type, no doubt also played a large part in the modification of the size and distribution of bands.

The modifications that can be inferred to have occurred in warfare and hunting are particularly significant here. In the precontact situation these two activities were rather distinct, although they probably shared some common general elements. Any activity can and usually does contribute in some measure to the maintenance of a social system in more than one way; this seems to have been so in the cases of hunting and warfare. From the data presented here as well as from general ethnographic information, a few differences in the "function" of these two activities can be outlined.

Hunting was one of the principle activities that contributed to the adaptation of the social system to the external environment. Whether it was carried out singly or in groups is not of great importance here. What is of significance is that it was a "production" technique in the economy of these Indian societies. There was also, of course, a complex of beliefs or ideology and ceremonial behavior, as well as the network of social relations which supplied "meaning," "purpose," and rewards, to hunting for the participants — all of which are needed to some extent as positive reinforcement for the successful operation of any activity in human society over a period of time. No doubt the operation of the total hunting complex — the activity itself plus its associated ideology and ritual — functionally contributed to the social integration of the society. However, its principal function was that of external adaptation.

Warfare also contributed to the external adaptation of the native social systems, but apparently it was more important as a mechanism of internal integration. Externally it functioned to maintain the territorial boundaries of the society, and it served at times, at least, in a minor way in the acquisition of resources. This would occur when battles were fought over waterholes, hunting grounds, and the like, and when some pillage actually took place. However, as an economic enterprise the contribution of warfare was probably almost nonexistent. The type of social system native to central north Mexico did not include the storage of quantities of foodstuffs and other material goods as part of the associated cultural practices, and a predatory kind of warfare simply could not yield any profitable result as a tool of economic exploitation.

On the other hand, war activities were one of the main mechanisms for fomenting social solidarity. Associated with warfare was a complex of ceremonial behavior in which all the members of a band would participate actually or vicariously. Warfare was one form of crisis rite — a rite that dealt with the crises of external threat that would bring into play some of the principal aspects of the religious system such as the torture and eating of captives, and dancing and chanting around a fire. Such behavior would engender and renew feelings of unity in the members of the society and reaffirm traditional religious values. And, when several bands were joined together, the warfare complex would serve as a group-wide solidarity rite that would not necessarily be focused, as other crises rites concerned with the life cycle, upon any particular kinship group or groups.

With the changed conditions of the external environment that afforded a new source of food supply, the war parties began to bring back booty that contributed much more directly to the economic life of the band. The raiding party then became more of a part of that segment of the social system directly concerned with economic "production." Hunting in its older form was not given up, but its frequency may have become less, as the raiding party organized around the warfare complex brought in a large percentage of basic economic goods. The same, although slight, reduction in importance may have been true with the other subsistence activities of gathering and fishing, where the latter was practiced. The now economically oriented raiding party, which apparently sallied forth with more frequency than the older raiding party, also afforded an increased opportunity for the reinforcement of the traditional values of the warrior, involving prestige from the exploits of battle, as well as giving greater opportunity for the segment of the religious system connected with war to operate.

At the same time, a certain amount of new behavior was also instigated by the change in "function" of the warfare complex. Since horses and mules began to be kept at camp at least until eaten, new behavior was required for their maintenance. They had to be watered and fed and at least occasionally corraled. With the greater supplies of meat now available, the structure of work groups probably also changed to some extent at the times when a number of animals were processed on a single occasion for jerky and other items. It is quite likely that more people would be involved in this activity at any one work session than in the similar processing of a single or a few game animals.

The make-up of the raiding party also seems to have changed. With more mobility and a greater food supply on the hoof, the maximum possible size for such a group increased. Some organizational changes may also have taken place — a few references indicate the adoption of some Spanish form, including larger squads, division into infantry and cavalry, the use of banners, drums, and fifes, and some other items of Spanish military equipment. Raiding parties ap-

parently also stayed in the field for longer periods of time than they could or would when on foot and merely fighting with neighboring bands. A change in the internal organization of raiding parties may also be indicated by references to the fact that women sometimes were taken along to assist the men by maintaining camp and making arrows.

Furthermore, the network of interrelations among the native societies in the area changed. Under precontact conditions the aboriginal bands were economically self-sufficient except for a small amount of trade in "luxury" goods that probably took place. Native groups, however, were dependent in other ways upon their neighbors, including a ceremonial dependency for the operation of the warfare complex. With the new ecological conditions the total network of relationships changed. Ceremonial dependency upon neighbors continued to exist, but now it included more distant-dwelling peoples, not the least important being Spaniards. Moreover, in the economic sphere the high degree of self-sufficiency changed to one of a fair degree of dependency upon the Spanish empire, while political independence was maintained. From a viewpoint internal to the Indian social systems, the war raiding party became a "production" unit. However, from the standpoint of total economic relations, the raiding party became a link in a chain of economic distribution, and the Indian societies were now connected to the economic system of the Spanish empire. The Indians had no part in the actual "production" of many of the items which they used for one purpose or another, and often, no doubt, they had little or no notion of the functioning of elements such as the production unit or technique of manufacture.

One other new feature also comes to mind. This was the new "role" of spy — of someone actually staying in the enemy camp (i.e., among the Spaniards) who would act as an informer. Often the persons involved as spies would be left behind when their group departed for its home territory in the desert, although sometimes people already settled would be used for this purpose. At any rate, the total picture appears to indicate that this was essentially a new type of linkage with the social system of a neighboring group, in this case the Spanish empire, that developed under the new ecological conditions.

The principal roles that may not have been based entirely upon kinship were those of "chief" and "shaman." Kinship may have played a part in the recruitment of both, but they are, in Service's terms, basically sociocentric, and other criteria were no doubt involved (Service 1960; 1962). Unfortunately, only the early published material refers to shamans, and no more about them can be said here. Chieftainship may have been slightly hereditary, although from the data one of the conditions was probably a "necessary" amount of fame in warfare (if this were not sufficient) in order for a man to be acceptable as a leader — a coward or a weakling would simply be bypassed, and some other arrangement for obtaining a leader would be found. It is possible that a certain amount of supernatural power was also involved, although the information concerning this is very scanty. There are no data concerning how much talking ability a chief should possess.

Either as bands tended to become larger or as smaller bands tended to associate with each other for longer periods of time in conjunction with the increased raiding, it appears that the native systems developed more intermediately ranked chiefs who were mainly raiding party leaders. Unfortunately, no information is available on changes in the position of "chief." With an increase in band size or at least in the numbers of persons associated together during the latter part of the period, however, it might be inferred that later chiefs were "bigger," that is, they wielded influence over more people.

This discussion has been couched in the terms of sociocultural adaptation. That is, an attempt has been made to show what happened to a group of social systems when the environment in which they existed and to which they were adapted was modified. Traditional sequences of behavior and their component elements were reorganized, replaced, and added to as new decisions were made by the natives concerning how to cope with and to take advantage of a changing environment, as new forms, material and otherwise, were adopted. Many new elements appeared in the external environment which the participants in these systems attempted to utilize in varying ways. The acceptance of these new items into the Indians' own ways of life immediately changed the cultural inventories of these systems, although the new features could be or were employed only in certain, and possibly quite restricted, contexts. However, as the new elements were integrated into the native social systems, at least some reorganization of these systems took place. The relationships of people to people and of people to material items within the systems were modified as change took place in tra-

ditional sequences of behavior for accomplishing tasks necessary for the maintenance of the societies. New behavioral sequences, that is, new ways of doing things, were added. Sometimes this would be an almost entirely new addition, such as minimal care of horses (which would be somewhat different from "caring for" a dog, although some kind of analogic creation probably took place considering this activity *in toto*), including the making of bridles and corrals. Again, the new behavioral sequences might involve only minor additions or reorientations to the traditional ways of carrying out tasks.

In the somewhat narrower terms of the Interuniversity Summer Research Seminar (Spicer 1961), the principle culture-contact context in north central Mexico was one of nondirected culture change, and the dominant process of acculturation was "incorporation." Nondirected change occurs in those situations in which the members of a society receiving cultural elements from another way of life make their own decisions without outside interference regarding what elements will be borrowed and how they will be used and integrated into their own social system. In this case, the culture of the borrowing society furnishes the determinants for the acceptance and rejection of the new cultural features (Spicer 1961; Vogt 1961).

The acculturation process of incorporation that occurs mainly in nondirected contact situations refers to the transfer of cultural elements and their integration into a recipient system, in Spicer's terms, "in such a way that they conform to the meaningful and functional relationships within the latter." These new forms only enhance the basic organization of the recipient social system (Spicer 1961; Vogt 1961).

Nondirected culture change is contrasted to directed change. In the directed variety, decisions concerning the acceptance and integration of cultural elements are based partly upon the interests and culture of a dominant society that holds power to enforce its decisions. Several processes of acculturation (i.e., replacive, fusional, and isolative) occur in directed change situations (Spicer 1961).

While the over-all picture of the Greater Bolsón region was one of nondirected change, some directed change also took place. However, the dominant acculturation process seems in any event to have been one of incorporation. In the southern part of the area, in the Parras-Laguna district, directed change conditions were set up and lasted for a period of some fifty years. Nevertheless, considering the rather constant replacement of native population in this area, for the most part any one group was seemingly under these directed conditions for actually only a rather short period of time. While the data for this area are not by any means complete, it appears that in this mission system, aside from the fact that many natives perished, some were assimilated, and some, after short contacts, returned to the hinterland.

Haciendas, mines, and a few other units of the dominant Spanish society also furnished directed culture change contexts. No doubt some individuals were either assimilated or perished in these places. However, for the continuing back-country groups, these social units seem to have served for the most part as points of contact for the natives with the Spanish empire where the transfer of cultural elements took place. Much the same can be said of the missions at Parras and San Pedro de la Laguna.

In a summary of the acculturation history of the Greater Bolsón, for the purposes of discussion, several stages may be isolated. There is little information for the first stage which lasted approximately from 1550 to 1600. During these years there was some direct, but apparently largely indirect, contact with the Spanish Empire; however, there was some adoption of a few new items, including the horse. A second stage, lasting from 1598 to 1646 for the peoples at the Parras-Laguna mission district on the southern periphery of the area, was one of directed culture change. As previously noted, actual direct contact for many of these people was short-lived. Outside of the Parras-Laguna region, it can probably best be said that stage I lasted until the 1640's. However stages I and II are viewed, the predominant acculturation process, except for those groups that remained for some time at the missions, was the same as that noted by the previously cited Seminar for the initial contact of a number of other Indian groups. This was what was termed by the Seminar as "additive integration" in which there takes place an extensive acceptance of a number of material and some nonmaterial items, although none of the native elements of importance are replaced (Spicer 1961). Such an initial period is, apparently, one of "experimentation" on the part of the native societies with fitting the novel elements into their own organization. It appears that in the Greater Bolsón area the major outlines of the modification in native culture took place during this early formative period.

The third stage began in the 1640's and (at least from the available documentation) was characterized

by much more intensive contact with Spaniards, mainly in the military sphere. While this type of military contact continued to the extinction of the native desert population, at least a substage was entered when the Spaniards modified their own policy in the direction of the extermination of the aborigines around the 1690's.

Through these several stages various additional processes can be noted. One was an apparently steady decrease in native population and the number of bands in the area; a second, a slight growth in the size and an increase in compositeness of membership of the remaining bands; a third, a gradual extension of the range (not necessarily the specific territory) of bands, particularly southward as the more southern of the native groups disappeared; and, a fourth, an increase in the specialization of the native ways-of-life in raiding. While many individual groups perished, these general processes did not stop until the latter part of the nineteenth century when the intruder Apaches in the general Bolsón and Chihuahua areas were defeated and deported.

After the initial additive stage, when presumably no native cultural elements of importance were replaced, the incorporative period took over, differing from the first stage in that, as the groups specialized more and more as desert raiders, some of the native elements, such as squash agriculture, were lost. The important point here is that not only were Spanish cultural elements either rejected or accepted and integrated into the existing system but that this integration and reorganization took place in the context of the total native social system that was adjusting to generally changed environmental conditions, including neighboring native social systems that were also undergoing adaptive changes. Furthermore, from what can be inferred from the available information, all aspects of native culture did not change at the same rate or in the same direction. And, merely because these social systems were in contact with the Spanish system, they did not become more and more like the Spanish system in any general sense. Instead, they adopted some Spanish forms that principally assisted them in maintaining their own ways of life and independence. The native social systems, then, changed in some ways as they adapted to a new ecological situation, and in such a manner that they could achieve some new degree of stabilization.

Harding (1960: 45-68) suggests a principle of stabilization which, in summary, states that the more a cultural or social system is adapted to its total environment, to that extent it will tend "to remain at rest." Since a social system is an "open" system, it reacts to changes in the environment in order to re-adapt to new conditions and to achieve again a new stability. Harding also notes, as a corollary to the principle of stabilization, that "when acted upon by external forces, a culture will, if necessary, undergo specific changes only to the extent of and with the effect of *preserving* unchanged its fundamental structure and character" (1960: 54). This is in effect "Romer's Rule," as cited by Hockett and Ascher in their effort to interpret early hominid data, as "the initial survival value of a favorable innovation is conservative, in that it renders possible the maintenance of a traditional way of life in the face of changed circumstances" (1964).

Harding's corollary and Romer's Rule seem to "explain" reasonably the phenomena of the largely nondirected culture contact the Bolsón peoples had with Spaniards during the Colonial period. The cultural changes that can be noted from the evidence seem to have been specific, adaptive modifications directly related to the survival of the individuals who identified themselves with the native social systems. The decisions of such individuals regarding the acceptance and rejection of new items and the ways to cope with new situations that arose out of the new environmental conditions were made on the basis of their traditional ideology with the aim, albeit unconscious, of preserving the system that they knew and with which they identified themselves. Consequently, a number of changes did take place but only those which would increase the survival value of the culture although not its basic "character." The same can be noted for the Spanish system. Certain modifications took place in response to the changing (i.e., adapting) Indian societies — for example, changes in the number of military personnel and in the number of presidios and in policy toward the desert Indians — modifications that were principally aimed at maintaining the Spanish system as Spaniards felt by tradition it should be.

Hypotheses that seem formulable from the present data and analysis appear to have been summed up by Harding's and Romer's principles: A social system adapted to one kind of total environment will, when that environment undergoes modification, adapt itself to the new conditions by internal reorganization and the borrowing of elements from the outside, only to

the extent that it has to in order to maintain its traditional nature. From the present data it can be added that those cultural aspects of a social system upon which "selective" pressure is exerted most strongly will tend to be the most modified as the participants in the social system make decisions about its change in an attempt to maintain the integrity of the system.

These hypotheses (roughly) fit the present data on a situation of nondirected culture change when there is no rapid and thorough disruption of the native system. Under different kinds of conditions, particularly those of directed culture change where a social system is more completely and in different ways disrupted, the adaptive modification will be at different rates and in different ways, with possibly quicker pulsations in the form of revitalization movements (Wallace 1956, 1960) and the like. For these different conditions, additions and corollaries must be made to the preceding hypotheses.

One other matter of a general sociological nature should be mentioned regarding the "new environment" created by the Spaniards during the implantation of their own social system in the region here considered. Under the "frontier" conditions created by Spanish society there existed what can be considered as a "social-ecological niche" that led to the development of frontier banditry. The Spanish frontier system left many items, which it itself supplied, in a semiguarded or unguarded position. In the absence of more efficient enculturation and social control mechanisms these items were there for the taking. Some of the personnel participating in the Spanish system, for whatever reason, did not compete "successfully," or did not feel they did so, in that system. And, instead of using "legitimate" recourses to action to satisfy their wants and needs, they passed beyond the bounds of "legitimate" society and set up social units that operated outside these bounds. These were the several groups of bandits frequently referred to in the documentary record.

These groups of "bandits" (any group of raiders that did not belong to a continuing, self-recruiting native sociocultural system, regardless of the actual ethnic identity of the individual participants) were still tied to the Spanish system, economically and probably in other ways, and operated for varying periods of time. Many of the hacienda Indians, probably in different stages of acculturation, were at one time or another involved in this kind of activity, although many of the bandits were also Spaniards, mestizos, mulattos, and Negroes. In summary, it appears that it was the Spanish social system itself, in a sociological sense, that created these groups by offering a "niche" which the bandit type of subsocial structure could, and frequently did, fill. While the social structure of the natives in the hinterland was different in specific type and in genesis, it also in part moved in to fill this socioecological niche.

7. SUMMARY AND CONCLUSIONS

The expansion of Spanish Colonial society into the general region of central northern Mexico set into motion several varied and complex processes of change on the social and cultural level, as well as the biological processes of race intermixture and modifications in degrees of tolerance for disease.

Before European contact the human beings in the area lived in a number of social systems, each virtually a replica of the other, which were fairly well stabilized within the local environment. These native social systems were "politically" and, by and large, "economically" independent, although they possessed ties with one another through intermarriage, through a small amount of trade in what were in effect "luxury" goods, and in ceremonial behavior through such activities as the warfare complex.

Into this situation in which each native system was fairly well adjusted in its relationship to the others and to the natural environment, bearers of the ways of Spanish Colonial society penetrated. In the broadest terms, the entrance into and conquest of the area by the Europeans constituted the "adaptive radiation" of the Spanish social system into a new ecological "niche." The bearers of Spanish culture were drawn into the area for several reasons, but essentially permanent penetration and settlement rested upon the knowledge and power embodied in the Spanish sociocultural system to exploit and to utilize resources of the region, partly in ways that the native systems were incapable of doing. The Indians also exploited the region but in less varied ways than did members of Spanish society. Certainly the Spaniards knew how to exploit the region through what were essentially the gathering techniques (including hunting and fishing) of the natives. Over and above this, however, the members of Spanish Colonial society brought with them, among other things, plow agriculture and animal husbandry, as well as a number of new methods for manufacturing and other tasks as part of their more complex way of life and, specifically for present purposes, more differentiated economy. Spanish and native society did not occupy exactly the same niches, but their overlap in occupancy was great enough in many realms that the two types of systems came into conflict at a number of points.

The implantation of Spanish society in the north Mexican region brought about a number of new conditions to which the aboriginal ways of life were forced to accomodate because the stability of the natives' adjustment to precontact conditions had been disturbed. As the Indians' social systems were modified to meet the new conditions created by the influx of Spaniards and their institutions, several processes were begun. Ultimately these processes led to several different results. One result was a decline both in the native population and in the number of native societies, even though the people who remained were grouped into slightly larger social units, each of which had a somewhat wider geographical range of activities than the precontact societies had. Concomitantly, there occurred a reorientation, to some extent, of the native systems in several spheres of activity. This reorientation included the development of a certain amount of economic and ceremonial dependency upon Spanish society, although the native societies remained politically outside of Spanish domination.

As part of the same over-all set of processes, Spanish society was obliged in turn to adjust to the now-modified native societies, the changes in which the Spaniards themselves had been largely instrumental in effecting in the first place. Thus, each step in the adjustment process of native and Spanish ways of life to each other was the result of decisions on the part of the participants of each social system to maintain their own societies as these were traditionally conceived.

The development was, then, one of a few undominated native groups becoming more specialized in living in the new environmental conditions. Furthermore, these Indians who maintained their "political" freedom for the most part became more difficult for the Spaniards to deal with in their usual mode of contact, that is, militarily. It must be emphasized that this is the over-all picture. Actually, there were many ups and downs in the domination of Spanish society and way of life in the north Mexican Greater Bolsón region. During some periods, such as in the latter part of the eighteenth century, which lies outside the scope of this monograph, Spaniards and natives were virtually at a standstill in their relationship to one another regarding domination in the area.

In the long run, however, Spanish society, as a sociocultural system, contained more "information" and was more diversified and flexible than the native societies, owing to its greater social and cultural complexity, including the fact that it was a literate society that could draw upon the experiences of persons widely separated in space and time. Eventually, in its adjustment to the conditions of its *total* north Mexican environment, Spanish society became by and large more "efficient" than the native societies, and this efficiency led to the extinction of many or most of the native ways of life. The Indian societies that survived after two centuries or so of contact were in geographically and socially marginal positions and quite highly adjusted to the new ecological situation.

APPENDIX 1
TRIBAL AND BAND GROUPS

An alphabetical listing of band and tribal names is given here, as the easiest way to summarize and present the great number of names that have appeared during the course of research. Little can be said about most of these names, except to give a rough indication of the geographical location of the group, the dates the names occur, and variant terms.

Many of these names, particularly those from the parish archive of Parras, do not occur in the text. For these names, all the scant data gathered have been included in the Appendix entry. For prominent names — such as Cocoyome and Nonoje — only the barest outline of collected data is given in the Appendix entry. Sources are usually not cited in the Appendix except when they do not occur in the text. A number of the Coahuileño or "Coahuiltecan" bands on the eastern border have been given little analysis due to limited availability of significant new data (other than that from Orozco y Berra (1864), Rouecking (1955), and a few others). A more thorough analysis of these bands will be possible when new information from local and other archives can be utilized.

It seems unprofitable at this time to attempt to push an analysis of these names very far, although suggestions of duplications and overlaps have been indicated, with the hope that the information may afford leads for other researchers.

A few general comments should be made concerning the multitude of "group" names that occur historically in central and eastern northern Mexico. Among other things, language aside, Indian groups were designated at different times in different ways — by some "actual" name for the band, by a chief's name, or by the name of a geographical point or camp site. At the same time, the recorders of these names (Spaniards) usually knew little or nothing of the languages they were transcribing, which in itself has been one of the major sources of the great number of variants that show up. Syllables, no doubt, often were omitted from longer indigenous names, further adding to the confusion (see Del Hoyo n.d.: 490-500, for similar problems in transcription of names from northeast Mexico). A few names that appear to be Spanish may actually have been a Spanish word suggested by the "form" of an indigenous one.

Some names occur a number of times in the sources and consequently appear to be "stable" names. Others occur only once or a few times, which makes it likely that they are merely variants of one of the more stable terms. Some of these alternates may be the same name in another language — for example, Coyotes (Spanish form of the Nahuatl *coyotl*) and Cocoyome (Nahuatl plural, *cocoyomeh*). Because the use of Nahuatl was widespread during this period, some groups may have been designated in as many as three languages, and possibly more — Spanish, Nahuatl, and one or more local languages. The same group probably also called itself by more than one term in its own language at times.

Terms were used in both a general and a specific sense. Some names refer to a single band, some refer to a group of bands, and some were used both generically and specifically. In a few instances (for example, Cocoyome) some specific names apparently came to have generic usage over time, possibly because of an increasing compositeness of the band make-up itself. In addition, Spaniards tended to use generic terms for groups located at some distance from them, while they often employed more specific names for proximate groups. Consequently, "Coahuileño" was commonly used by Spaniards living in Parral for Indians dwelling in the direction of Coahuila, while Spaniards from the latter place designated the same Indians by their specific band names.

Many of the listed names, particularly those from Parras, occur usually as surnames. In some cases it is impossible to determine whether a surname is also a band name, although many of them were so used at times (where the term "nación" was added by the priest in parish records, this has been noted in the Appendix entries). Because of this usage as both surname and band name, and from the scant information from marriage and other records, these names do seem to refer to an exogamous lineage of some type (see section on ethnography and Appendix 2).

Most of the names encountered during the present investigation have been listed in Appendix 1. A major source from which names have *not* been included is

Marín's 1693 list, as it involves certain problems and does not seem to contribute materially to the compilation here (see Appendix 4).

Some names that appear to be Spanish are quite possibly native names — for example, in one entry in Parras the name Porras, which occurs a great number of times and appears to be a Spanish surname (and very possibly is), is listed as "de nación Porras" (Bautismos, 1615-1616, Parras Parish Archive). Porras, here, may have been an early Spanish appellation used as a variant alongside the native name; however this is pure guesswork, and there is no way to investigate the problem further at this time. No doubt in the future, with careful linguistic analysis and with additional historical information, it will be possible to reduce many of these names to variants of each other.

NOTE: In the list that follows, the parish archives of the town of Parras, Coahuila, have been cited as (psa), because a great number of names come from this source. Other parish archives are identified completely when reference is made to them. In general, the most frequently occurring term is given first and italicized.

BAND AND GROUP NAMES

Achome. 1671, nation at the hacienda of Agustín Echeverz, Parras area (psa).

Acoclames ("Tobosos"), Ococlames, Coclames, Achacomes, Achaclames, Ajocames (?). First cited in 1621 and practically nonexistent as a separate band in 1723 when the "Tobosos" were deported. Closely associated with the Nonojes and Tobosos in the early years and with the Cocoyomes during the latter part of the period. Some Acoclames are listed in the Parral Parish Archives between the years 1706 and 1730.

Ahomamas (Alamamas?). The Ahomamas, with the Vasapalles, were said to be one of the four nations from La Laguna in the *Anua* of 1598.

Ajocames (see Acoclames).

Alalaca, Alasaca, Lalaca. Parras, 1605 to 1640 (psa).

Alamama. In the Parras-Laguna area and consisted of seven bands (*parcialidades*) according to the 1604 *Anua.* Parras, 1605 to 1632 (psa).

Alasapas (see Xalazapas). 1671; Cabeza band, 1719, Parras (psa).

Alauza. 1642, Parras (psa).

Alayuyo, Alayuio, Alaiuio, Alilluyo. Parras, 1615 to 1641 (psa).

Alegocha, Alegoche. Parras, 1605-06 (psa).

Ancha (Spanish?, "broad"). Parras, 1657 (psa).

Añimama. Parras, 1605-06 (psa).

Aomania (Ahomama or alamama?). Given as a personal name in La Laguna in the *Anua* of 1598.

Apache. Parras, 1658 (psa).

Apes (see Xapoz). 1674 and 1675 associated with the Catujanes. At the mission of Coahuila in 1766 (Portillo 1887: 80-81, 124).

Aquitadotdacam. (Coahuila). 1674, associated with the Hueyquetzales (Gueiquesales).

Atapo (nación). 1698 and 1699, Cabeza band, Parras (psa).

Auxigual. 1629, Parras (psa).

Ayaiula (nación) (probably an orthographic error for Alayuyo). 1644, Parras (psa).

Baba. 1610, Parras (psa).

Babani. 1671, Parras (psa).

Babias, (nación) (Bauiamamares, Babiamares?) 1657, Parras (psa).

Babijomama (Baborimama?). 1680, Laguna area (psa).

Babimamar (Bauiamamares, Babiamares?). 1693, general Río Grande area.

Babinamama (Baborimama?). 1651, apparently in the Patos area (psa).

Babol, Babola, Babora (Bobol, Baborimama?). 1630, 1638, and 1643, Parras (psa); 1673, Coahuila, with the Tetecoras and Cuaguilas.

Baborimamas Boborimamaras, Mamorimamas, Mamorimamaras, Baburimamas, Bamoribama, Bamorimamas, Mamarimamari (?), Mamisa (??). 1652 to 1673 associated with "Tobosos" and "Salineros," apparently "close" to the "Salineros" and "Cabezas."

Babosarigames, Babuzarigames, Babucaligamas, Babosaricas, Babozaligamen, Bobonizanigames,

Bobozarigames, Bauzarigames, Bozeregamui (1717), Babozarigas. From 1646 to latter part of seventeenth century, closely associated with "Salineros"-"Cabezas" and "Tobosos," and later with Colorados, Itocas, Contotores, and Pies de Venado. Some settled and living at the town of Cinco Señores during the early eighteenth century. Apparently a southern Coahuileño group, close to and/or part of the Salineros and Cabezas.

Babury (Babol, Baborimamas?). 1674, associated with the Hueyquetzales (Gueiquesales).

Bacacuyo. Given as a personal name at La Laguna in the *Anua* of 1598.

Bacaranan (Coahuila). 1674, associated with the Boboles.

Bacorame, Bacoram. (Coahuila). 1674, associated with the Hueyquetzales (Gueiquesales), and at Nadadores in 1704.

Bahaneros, Baganeros, Bajaneros (see Vahaneros). 1674, associated with the Catujanes (same as the "Bahaneros" at San Pedro de la Laguna?).

Bahari, Vahares. 1649 to 1671, Parras. 1659: "quaguila de nación Bahari" (psa).

Baiamamar (Maymamara; Bajamares? — See Appendix 3; Bauiamamares?). 1694, Cabeza band, Parras (psa).

Baja (nación), (Bajaramares?). 1642 and 1644, Parras (psa).

Bajamares (Baiamamaras? — see Appendix 3). (Coahuila). 1687, Cabezas. (Listed together with the Bidamamara.)

Bajares, Baxares (Bajamares or Bahari?). (Coahuila?). 1670, raiding the Saltillo and Monterrey areas (AHP 1670A), and in 1675 with the Pachaques, Jumees, and apparently the Catjuanos (Portillo 1887: 96).

Bamarimamares (see Baborimama and Mamarimamari). (Coahuila). 1674, associated with Mayos and Hueyquetzales (Gueiquesales).

Bamichicoame (possibly a Concho or Jumano group). 1693, in the general Río Grande area.

Bapacolani (possibly a Concho or Jumano group). 1693, general Río Grande area.

Bapacorapinanacas (see Bapocares). (Coahuila). 1675, with the Hueyquetzales (Gueiquesales) (Portillo 1887: 85).

Bapocares. (Coahuila). 1675. (Apparently a group distinct from the Bapacorapinanacas

since the two groups are supposed to have fought each other) (Portillo 1887: 85).

Batayolicla, Batayogligla, Batayolicua, Vatayocua, Batayulica, Batlaboylas, Batayolicuas. 1684 to 1713, a Chiso group (accepting that the Chisos spoke the Concho language [see section on Language and Sauer 1934: 63] and the correctness of two of the Concho words reported by Kroeber [1934: 13-14], this name possibly has the following etymology: *bate* "water," and *yolli* "people," plus locative?).

Bauanes. (Coahuila). 1674, associated with the Boboles.

Bauiamamares, Babiamares. (Coahuila). 1674, associated with Mayos and Hueyquetzales (Gueiquesales), and 1675 with Gueiquesales (Portillo 1887: 77).

Beyocho. 1618, Parras (psa).

Biamomama, Biamoma (Baborimama?). 1610, Parras (psa).

Biay. 1670, inland (*tierra adentro*) from Monterrey, possibly from Coahuila.

Bibit. (Coahuila). 1675, apparently with the Jumee.

Bichuia, Bichoya, Bichoio (Bichuyegua?). 1605-06, 1608, and 1618, Parras (psa).

Bichuyegua (Bichuia?). 1615-1616, Parras (psa).

Bidamamara. (Coahuila). 1687, with the Cabezas, and listed with the Bajamares (Portillo 1887: 195).

Bimama. 1605-06, Parras (psa).

Boayo, Bohayo (Bohain?). 1605-06 to 1615-16, Parras (psa).

Bobamari (Baborimama?). 1638, Parras (psa).

Boboac. 1630, Parras (psa).

Boboles. 1670, with the Catujanos (AHP 1670A); 1674 and 1688, north Coahuila (Portillo 1887: 11, 63, 124-125, 218).

Bocoras. (Coahuila). 1675, with Hueyquetzales (Gueiquesales) and Pinanaca, and 1687-1688 with Cabezas (Portillo 1887: 77, 126, 195).

Bohain, Bohaym, Vohain, Boayn, Vaoy (Boayo?). 1605-06 to 1615-16 Parras (psa).

Boquillurimamara. (Coahuila). 1687, with the Cabezas (Portillo 1887: 195).

Borrado (Spanish?). 1605-06 to 1693-94 at Parras (psa), 1715 at Parras (AHP 1715Aa), Cabeza band 1717, Parras (psa), and at a Coahuila mission in 1766.

Brieiatiolyagua. 1652, (probably an alternate

for a better known "Toboso" or possibly "Salinero" group).

Cabacbitac or Cabacbitae. 1646, with "Tobosos" and "Salineros."

Cabezas (Spanish: "The Chiefs"). 1644 to the 1720's. At the Cuatro Ciénegas mission and Parras, and some in the service of Isabel de Urdiñola, 1644 (Portillo 1887: 11, 32-36). The name occurs in the Parras Parish Archive in 1657, 1680, and 1681, and band was finally settled at this place in the early 1690's; the Jesuit baptismal, marriage, and burial records for them run from 1693 to 1722. Previous to this, ca 1680, they had also been settled near Parras at the 'puesto of San Sebastián, six leagues, said to contain Cabezas, Salineros, and Colorados (psa). Apparently, a Coahuileño group: ". . . Yndios Cavesas de la dicha Nasión Coaguileña que Residen en el Referido Pueblo de Parras . . ." (BL 1722).

Cabezas Blancas (Spanish: "White Heads" or "White Chiefs"). 1693, in general Río Grande area.

Cabezas de Huacal (Huacal – Nahuatl: "carrying crate"). 1693, in general Río Grande area.

Cacafes. (see Jacafes). (Coahuila). 1688, settled at the town of La Caldera (Portillo 1887: 205).

Cacalote (Nahuatl: "crow"). Cabeza band, Parras, 1718 and 1719 (psa). (Possibly from the Río Grande.)

Cacaxtes (Nahuatl: 'baskets"). (Coahuila). 1674 and 1675 with the Hueyquetzales (Gueiquesales) (Portillo 1887: 77).

Cacoin. (Coahuila). 1670, associated with groups raiding the Monterrey and Saltillo areas (AHP 1670A).

Cacuitataome, Quaquithatome, Cacuitatahumet, Taquitatomes, Otaquitatomes, "La Nacion de San Lucas" (AHP 1723A). "Chisos" 1684 into the 1720's – said to live on the Río Grande (AHP 1684Aa), and in the 1690's in the town of San Lucas near San Pedro (de Conchos) (BL 1693-1702; BL 1694-1698.)

Calaraque (see Colazaque), (a Zacateco group?). 1605-06 to 1617, Parras (psa).

Caliani (?). 1630, Parras (psa).

Camiseta (nación) (Spanish: "undershirt"). 1654, Parras (psa).

Canamara. 1615-1616, Parras (psa).

Canos. 1766, at a Coahuila mission.

Capiquamara (see Hapiquamara). 1607 and 1609, Parras (psa).

Carajos (Spanish?). (Coahuila). 1670, associated with groups raiding the Saltillo and Monterrey areas (AHP 1670A).

Carray, Carrai, Caray, Saray. 1605-06, 1609, 1615-1616, Parras (psa).

Carrizos. 1766, at a Coahuila mission.

Catujanos, Catuxanos, Catuxanes. 1670, associated with the Cuahuijos and a number of others in the general Saltillo area (AHP 1670A); 1671, a Catuxane was reported at the Patos hacienda (psa). Territory northeast of Ciudad Guadalupe, associated with the Tilijaes, Apes, Pachaques, and others.

Cauisera, Cauicera, Caguicera, Caguiçera, Cavisera. Cavisera is given as a personal name in La Laguna in the 1598 *Anua*; this group and the Paogas were said to make up one of the four nations at this place. 1605-06 to 1630, Parras (psa). Possibly was later corrupted to Cabeza.

Chacahuales (see Chaquales). 1674, associated with the Mayos and Hueyquetzales (Gueiquesales).

Chachatiolyagua. 1652 (probably an alternate for a better known "Toboso" or possibly "Salinero" group).

Chacuiyacua. 1684. A "Chiso" group.

Chamancas. 1670, associated with groups raiding Saltillo and Monterrey. (Occurs in the same declaration as Xaamnacanes and is therefore apparently distinct from it) (AHP 1670A).

Chaquales (see Chacahuales). 1670, Saltillo area.

Cheva (?). 1653, Parras (psa).

Chibicano, Chivicano. 1627 to 1657, Laguna area (psa).

Chicanimama, Chicanima (Chuanimama). 1607 and 1609, Parras (psa).

Chichitames, Chichitamen, Chuchitamen. 1684 to 1693. A "Chiso" group.

Chilchihuiscan (?). 1635, Parras (psa).

Chiles. 1655, a Toboso band name given once by a Chiso declarant (AHP 1655Ab). (May be a key to a native Toboso band name.)

Chiso, Chizo, Chiço (generic and apparently specific application). 1624 to at least 1720's. Lived east of the Conchos river and south of the Río Grande in Chihuahua, and north of Río Grande into the Big Bend country. Name occurs in 1677, 1679, 1697 to 1713 in the church records in Allende (San Bartolomé) and 1681 to 1725 in those of the Parral church.

Cholomes (probably a Jumano group, Sauer 1934: 67). Lived among the lower Conchos River. 1692, with Chisos, 1693.

Chuanimama (Chicanimama?). 1605-06, Parras (psa).

Churi. 1637, Parras (psa).

Cíbolos, Cíbolas ("buffalo") Come Cíbolas ("buffalo eaters") (see Siboporame). Two groups, one from Coahuila said to be a different group from that in Texas in the area of the confluence of the Conchos and Río Grande rivers. The Coahuila people (apparently the Siboporame) lived in the area of Cuatro Ciénegas and bordered the Contotores. 1652 to 1675; 1717; 1766, at a Coahuila mission.

Cien Orejas (Spanish: "one hundred ears"?) (nación). 1720, Cabeza band, Parras (psa).

Cocobiptas (Curuipicas?). 1675, with Hueyquetzales (Gueiquesales). (Coahuila) (Portillo 1887: 77).

Cococomesno. 1693, general Rio Grande area.

Cocohua. 1631 and 1635, Parras (psa).

Cocojitas. 1655, Parras (psa).

Cocoma. 1701-1705 (Parral Parish Archive).

Cocomaque. (Coahuila). 1675, with the Hueyquetzales (Gueiquesales) (Portillo 1887: 77).

Cocomuliam. 1670, associated with groups raiding the Saltillo and Monterrey areas.

Cocoraboroquiaya, Coroboroquiaya. 1670, inland (*tierra adentro*) from Monterrey (Coahuila?).

Cocotiolyaguas. 1652, apparently an alternate for a better known "Toboso" or "Salinero" name.

Cocoxibo (nación) (Cocoxiua, Cocoxima?). 1629 to 1658, Parras (psa).

Cocoxima (Cocoxibo?). 1629, Parras (psa).

Cocoxiua (Cocoxibo?). (nación). 1655, Parras (psa).

Cocoyome, Coyomes, Cocoiome, Cocoyolme, Cocotome (once only in Hackett). 1644 to 1720's, and virtually extinct with deportation in 1723. Name occurs in the parish archives of Parral between 1721 and 1730, and in Parras, 1706, Cabeza band (psa). (This seems to be most probably a Nahuatl term meaning Coyotes. There is some confusion between these people and the Coyotes, although most of the time the terms seem to be reducible to a single people. Linguistically, the term can be broken down as follows: *coyotl* (Nahuatl) "Coyote," with the plural forms of *coyomeh* or (reduplicated) *cocoyomeh* (Olmos 1875: 31-34; Molina 1944: 24). In the early years this was one of the "Toboso" groups farthest from Parral.

Cocuytzam. (Coahuila). 1674, associated with the Hueyquetazales (Gueiquesales).

Codam. (Coahuila). 1674, associated with the Hueyquetzales (Gueiquesales).

Cohumeros. (Coahuila). 1766, at the Coahuila mission of San Miguel de Aguayo.

Coinama, Coinam, Cuinama, Cuiname. 1610 to 1628, Parras (psa).

Coioapa, Coioapaes, Cuayapa (see Cuabapae and Quaaguapaya). 1643 and 1654, Parras (psa).

Colazaque Zacateco (see Calaraque). Occurs as a personal name in the *Anua* of 1598 for Parras; Colazaque is possibly the same as Calaraque.

Colimote. 1630, Parras (psa).

Colorados (Spanish: "The reddish colored"). 1629, 1680 (Laguna area), 1717, Cabeza band, Parras (psa). 1644, in the general Río Grande area in 1693, at a Coahuila mission, 1766. Said to be located between Parras and Coahuila and in the Sierra de Coahuila (1645).

Coma. 1618, Parras (psa).

Comales (Nahuatl?) (nación). 1722, Parras (AHP 1722Aa).

Comaroya. 1605-06, Parras (psa).

Comeajeme. 1687, with the Cabezas (Portillo 1887: 195).

Comibopo. 1618, Parras (psa).

Conapomama. 1617, Parras (psa).

Concho (Spanish: "shell"). 1575 through eighteenth century. Lived along Conchos river. 1719 and 1720, Cabeza band, Parras (psa).

Coniani, Coniane, Coñani (18th). (see Coinama?). 1674, with Hueyquetzales (Gueiquesales) 1687, with Cabezas; 1688, with Quechales. 1694 to 1719, Cabeza band, Parras (psa).

Contotores, Contotol, Contotoli. 1661 into eighteenth century. Bordered Cíbolas. Cuatro Ciénegas, mission of San Buenaventura. 1698 to 1721, Cabeza band, Parras (psa).

Coopabo. 1617, Parras (psa).

Corcobados (Spanish: "The hunchbacks"). 1653, with "Salineros." From area of Cuatro Ciénegas.

Cosau (nación). 1657, Parras (psa).

Cotomamar, Cotohomamar. 1693, general Río Grande area, in Coahuila, and near or bordering the Sisimbles.

Cototoholome, Cototoolome, probably also Totoholomes. 1684. "Chiso" group.

Cotzales (Hueyquetzales?). At Santa Rosa (de Nadadores) mission with the Manos Prietas (Portillo 1887: 11).

Covaya (Obaya?). 1723, Parras (psa).

Coyotes, Cocoyotes (possibly two groups; one the Cocoyomes, another from the Mapimí area). 1644, Revolt; 1645, operating with the Negritos in the Mapimí area.

Cuabapae, Cuabaae (see Quaaguapaya). 1655, Parras (psa).

Cuachichil, Guachichila. 1617, 1618, Parras (psa).

Cuaguila, Quahuila, Cauila, Cuaguilla. General term used for Indians from the Coahuila area. People from this area were in Parras in the earliest years. Names occur in the extant records of this archive from 1605-06 to 1657, 1671, and 1693-94, and as part of the Cabezas band in 1717 and 1721 (psa). Cuaguilas also show up in the parish records of Parral between the years 1701 and 1725. (This name is said to mean "Lowland" — Spanish, *Bajío* ; Nahuatl *Tazinta*, or *Tlazintla* in Classical Nahuatl — Jiménez Moreno 1958: 106).

Cuahuijo (nación) (Cuaguila?). 1670, in the area of Coahuila, Saltillo and Monterrey (AHP 1670A). 1671, Parras (psa).

Cuautomanas. 1714, from Coahuila.

Cucubipi (see Cocobiptas). 1693, general Río Grande area.

Cuecuapay (Quaaguapaya). 1630, Parras (psa).

Cui. Given as a surname in the *Anua* of 1598 for Parras.

Curias (Spanish?). 1628, Parras (psa).

Curuipicas (see Cocobiptas?). 1693, general Río Grande area.

Daparabopo, Daparavapos. The first is given as a personal name for La Laguna in the *Anua* of 1598, and it is later said to be one of the four nations of the Laguna. 1606 *Anua* states the Daparavapos are from Parras. 1605-06 to 1610, Parras (psa).

Decafez. 1670, associated with groups raiding Saltillo and Monterrey areas (AHP 1670A).

Dedepos (see Idedepos).

Ditehagopob. 1605-06, Parras (psa).

Doaquioydacam. (Coahuila). 1674, associated with the Hueyquetzales (Gueiquesales).

Dohobopo, Dotobopo. 1607 to 1609, Parras (psa).

Domaxames. 1670, inland (*tierra adentro*) from Monterrey (Coahuila?).

Dopobahopob. 1605-06, Parras (psa).

Egope (Eguapit?). 1628 and 1634, Parras (psa).

Eguapit (Egope?). (Coahuila). 1674, associated with the Hueyquetzales (Gueiquesales).

Emomama, Emoma (see Yamomama).

Enabopo (see Inabopo).

Enemigos del Cerro (Spanish: "Enemies of the hill"). 1693, general Río Grande area.

Epimama (see Hipimamal).

Epiquamara (see Epiquiomar). 1605-06, Parras (psa).

Epiquiomar (see Epiquamara). 1605-06, Parras (psa).

Escabaca. (Coahuila). 1675, associated with Hueyquetzales (Gueiquesales).

Escomiagamos. (Apparently Coahuila). 1717.

Espopolames (Siboporame, etc.?). (Coahuila). 1675, with Hueyquetzales (Gueiquesales).

Etapai, Etapa, Ytapay, Etaiu. 1608, 1615-16, 1619, and 1630, Parras (psa).

Euacan(?). 1627, Parras (psa).

Futaanames. 1670, associated with groups raiding the Saltillo and Monterrey areas. Apparently from Coahuila (AHP 1670A).

Gabilachos (Gavilanes?). 1606, *Anua*, located at Mapimí.

Gamplam. 1670, associated with groups raiding Saltillo and Monterrey areas (AHP 1670A).

Garafes. (Coahuila). 1674, associated with Catujanos.

Gauchan. 1660, Parras (psa).

Gavilanes. (Spanish: "Sparrow-hawks"). There were possibly two groups of Gavilanes: one very closely associated with the "Toboso" Ocomes, and said in one place (1653) to be the same as the Ocomes; the other from the Coahuila area. "Toboso" Gavilanes first are mentioned in 1644 and were virtually wiped out by Spanish forces in 1691. Only individuals appear after this, but

Gavilanes are cited again in 1717 together with a number of Coahuila groups. 1661-1665, Parral Parish Archives.

Gicocoges. (Coahuila). 1674, at the Río de las Sabinas with Boboles and Yoricas (Portillo 1887: 71).

Girigaias. 1697, Cabeza band, Parras (psa).

Gordos (Spanish: "The fat ones"). 1654 and 1655. "Tobosos" or "Salineros"?

Govossos, also Jogosos. 1652 and 1653. (Apparently distinct from the Toboso proper, as it occurs in the same sentence with "Toboso.")

Guacales (Nahuatl: "Carrying crate") (see Guaquales). 1693, in the general Río Grande area.

Guadiamanar. 1720, Cabeza band, Parras (psa).

Guamaroa, Guamarua. 1605-06, Parras (psa).

Guaquales (see Guacales). 1670, associated with groups raiding the Saltillo and Monterrey areas (AHP 1670A).

Guaquimamara (see Quaquimama; Guimutiquimamara?). 1696, Cabeza band, Parras (psa).

Guasapayoligla (see Guesecpayolicla).

Guayaboa (Gueyapaes?). 1638, Parras (psa).

Guazahuayos, Guasahayo, Guasahaio, Uazahayo, Vazahayo, Guaçaayo, Guasaayo, Huaçayo, Huaçahaio, Gusayo, Usario(?). Reported at Parras by Mota y Escobar ca 1605; 1605-06 to 1629, Parras (psa).

Gucara. 1638, Parras (psa).

Guechales (see Gueiquesales, Hueyquetzales).

Gueimama. 1627, Parras (psa).

Gueiquesales (Hueyquetzales). Coahuila). Territory northeast of Ciudad Guadalupe (Portillo 1887: 124). 1675, with Manos Prietas, Colorados, Contotores, Oodame, Babiamares, and others 1887: 77).

Guejolotes (Nahuatl: "Turkeys"). (Coahuila?). 1717.

Gueripiamos (see Yeripiamos).

Guesecpayolicla, Guesecpayoliglao, Guesecpamot, Guesapame, Guazapayoligla, Guasipayoles, Guesipayoles, Guasapagoligla. A "Chiso" group. 1684 to 1693. Said to be from the "Land of Las Auras" (AHP 1684Aa).

Gueyapaes (apparently, Quaaguapaias). 1652, with "Salineros."

Guicales (see Guicasales, Gueiquesales, etc.). 1675. (Coahuila).

Guiguigoa. (Coahuila). 1674, associated with Hueyquetzales (Gueiquesales).

Guijacales. (see Guisacales, Quequesales). (Coahuila). 1673.

Guilime. 1638, Parras (psa).

Guimutiquimamara (see Guaguiguamara). 1687, with Cabezas (Portillo 1887: 195).

Guisacales. (see Guijacales, Gueiquesales, Hueyquetzales?). (Coahuila).

Guitola, Guitolos, Guilolas (see Guitalos). 1636 and 1638, Parras (psa).

Gusiquesales (see Gueiquesales, Hueyquetzales). 1674, at the puesto de Castaño (Portillo 1887: 63).

Haicos. 1606, *Anua,* at Mapimí.

Hanimama. 1609, Parras (psa).

Hapiquamara (see Capiquamara). 1605-1606, Parras (psa).

Hazpipina. 1605-06, Parras (psa).

Heguan (Yegual?). 1636, Parras (psa).

Herbipiamos, Hiervipames, Yerbiapames. (Coahuila). 1688, with Terocodamos and Jumanes and Tejas (Portillo 1887: 126); 1717. 1670 (AHP 1670A).

Hijos de la Pared (Spanish: "Sons or children of the wall" – Palisade?). Apparently an eastern or northeastern "Toboso" group. 1653, only occurrence and group is said to be with the Hijos de las Piedras and Cocoyomes. (Hijos de los Palos?).

Hijos de las Piedras (Spanish: "Sons or children of stones"). 1653 to 1705. "Toboso"?

Hijos de la Tierra (Spanish: "Sons or children of the Earth"). 1677 to 1705. "Toboso"?

Hijos de Lodo (Spanish: "Sons or children of mud"). Apparently an eastern or northeastern "Toboso" group. 1692.

Hijos de los Palos (Spanish: "Sons or children of trees, sticks, or stakes"). Apparently a "Toboso" group. 1653 and 1677.

Hioricas (see Yoricas).

Hipalabo. 1618, Parras (psa).

Hipimamal, Hipomamal, Hypimamal, Ypimama, Ypomama, Ypimam, Ipimama, Hypimama, Hypomama (see Epimama). 1605-06 to 1623.

Hobe. 1628, Parras (psa).

Hoera (see Yoera and Loera). Said to be from Parras in the 1598 *Anua.*

Horames (see Orames, and Hurabama?).

Hores (Orames?, Hoera?). 1669, Parras (psa).

Huatamama. 1605-06, Parras (psa). (Cuautomanas?)

Hueyquetzal (Nahuatl: "Large Quetzal" or "green Feather") (see Gueiquesal). 1674.

Huhuygam. (Coahuila). 1674, associated with the Hueyquetzales.

Huitaaco (Huitaro?). 1607, Parras (psa).

Huitaro, Huitero, Huitala, Huitalo, Guitalo (Huitaaco?). 1654 to 1674, Parras (psa). 1662, rancheria at the hacienda of Francisco Gutiérrez Barrientos, one and a half leagues from Parras (AHP 1662C).

Hurabama, Urabamo, Horabam (Orames?). 1605-06 to 1609, Parras (psa).

Hyamara. 1605-06, Parras (psa).

Iboquiba (Igoquib). 1687, associated with the Cabezas (Portillo 1887: 194).

Idedepos, Dedepos. 1674, associated with the Hueyquetzales; 1687, associated with Babozarigames, Colorados, Odames, Itocas, and Cabezas (Portillo 1887: 194-195).

Igoguib (see Iboquiba).

Iguanolaxtac (Nahuatl?). 1629, Parras (psa).

Ileepo. 1605-06, 1608, 1635, 1638, Parras (psa). Pérez de Ribas cites a Cacique named Ilepo in the Parras-Laguna district in the early years (III 1944: 279).

Imarina. 1642, Parras (psa).

Imudagas. 1654, with Gavilanes, Ocomes, Gordos, and Tucumuragas.

Inabopo, Ynabopo, Inibopo, Enabopo (probably Yanabopo). Inabopo occurs as a surname at the Laguna in the 1598 *Anua*. 1605-06 to 1635, Parras (psa), and 1630 "Ynabopo Lagunero."

Iracancatecuamana. 1605-06, Parras (psa).

Iritila, Yritila, Irritila. First recorded in the Parras area in 1595 as the original inhabitants, together with the Mayranos (AGN 1619), given as surname in the 1598 *Anua* in which the group is said to be from Parras. Mota y Escobar mentioned them at Parras about 1605, and Pérez de Ribas stated they inhabited the general Laguna area (III 1944: 265). 1605-06 to 1617, Parras Parish Archives (psa). Later variants are Airitilas (Morfi) and Arritilas (DHM ca 1706).

Isale (Gueiquesal or Quesal?). 1718 and 1720, Cabeza band, Parras (psa).

Itocas (see Toocas). 1687, associated with Babozarigames, Colorados, and others (Portillo 1887: 194).

Jacafes (Cacafes?). (Coahuila?). 1674, at the puesto de Castaño (Portillo 1887: 63).

Jajames (Xexet?). 1706, with Cocoyomes and Acoclames.

Jaloma. 1638, Parras (psa).

Jaquue or Jaqueie. 1645, only occurrence and closely associated with the Toboso band. Possibly refers to the place of Jacue (Jaque, today Jaco?).

Jeapes (see Xeapoz). 1675, with the Yoricas some four leagues from the Río Grande (Portillo 1887: 113).

Jigualli, Jigualis. 1638, Parras (psa).

Jogoso (see Gobossos, another version). This "Toboso" band was apparently distinct from the Toboso proper, as the name occurs in the same sentence with "Toboso." "Jogoso"/ "Gobosso" as a distinct band may account for the name "Jobosos" instead of "Tobosos" in one of the Espejo transcripts (Bolton 1916: 171).

Jojocomes (see Ocomes). 1691 and 1692, a variant of "Ocome."

Julimeños. 1766, at one of the Coahuila missions; originally from the town of Julimes in Nueva Vizcaya.

Jumanes. 1674, associated with the Boboles. 1688 (Portillo 1887).

Jumees (see Xumees). 1675, with Catujanos, Bajares, and Pachaques (Coahuila) (Portillo 1887: 80-81, 96, 116).

Junia, Hunia, Honia (nación). 1627 to 1657, Parras (psa).

Jurive. 1706, at the hacienda de Barrientos, married to a Conian woman.

Jusquiopoion. 1636, Parras (psa).

Lagunero (generic term apparently used for only some groups of the Laguna de San Pedro area). Term occurs in the Parras Parish Records from 1629 to 1694, and specifically in the Cabeza band from 1698 to 1719. 1655, at Puesto de las Habas, said to be where all the Laguneros resided; 1657, at the rancho of Baycuco; and, 1670-1678 at the puesto de Xocononotoca (psa). Laguneros are generally distinguished from some other groups such as the Chivicanos in the same area. The name also shows up in the baptismal records of the Parral parish between the years 1681 to 1685.

Laomama (Ahomama or Alamama?). 1605-06, Parras (psa).

Largos (Spanish?). ". . . . la Casta de los Largos q estan aggreg.^{dos} a los lagun.^{os} . . . ") 1669-1671, Parras (psa).

Legua (Yegual?). 1605-06, 1607, 1608, Parras (psa).

Leguaquin. 1609, Parras (psa).

Loera (yoera, Hoera?). 1605-06, 1607, 1609, 1615-16, Parras (psa).

Mabibit (see Bibit). 1674, associated with the Catujanes.

Maçaltipilguas, Maçalypilguas (Mazatichigua?). 1646, with the "Tobosos" and "Salineros."

Maçarabopo,   Maçayabopo,   Macarabopo. 1605-06 to 1609, Parras (psa).

Macarue. Given as some kind of alternate personal name for Mainara in the *Anua* of 1598 for Parras.

Macho. 1608, Parras (two occurrences) (psa).

Macobenamama. 1630, Parras (psa).

Madmedas. (Coahuila). 1674, associated with the Catujanes.

Mainara. Given as some kind of alternate personal name for Macarue in the 1598 *Anua.*

Mairana, Mayranos. 1605-06 to 1629, Parras (psa). "Mayranos," together with the Irritilas, were said to be the original inhabitants of the valley of Parras in 1695 (AGN 1619).

Malas Flechas (Spanish: "Bad Arrows"). 1693, in the general Río Grande area.

Malinero (see Molinero). 1609, Parras (psa).

Mamaçorra, Mamacorra, Mamacora, Mamaceras. 1605-06 to 1617, Parras, (psa). The Mamaceras are reported to have been recently settled in Parras, in the 1605 *Anua*, and were said to be from a place some thirty leagues from Parras. (Cuachichiles?).

Mamarimamari (see Baborimama?). 1680, Laguna area, Parras (psa).

Mamaura. 1605-06, Parras (psa).

Mamaya. 1615-16, Parras (psa).

Mamisa (see Baborimamas).

Mamoquana, Mamoquan. 1643, 1644, 1646 (the last two dates at Patos), Parras (psa).

Mamorimamas, Mamorimas (apparently Baborimamas). Mamorimamas are called "Salineros" in one place.

Mamuasen. 1670, associated with groups raiding the Saltillo and Monterrey areas (from Coahuila?).

Manahues,   Manaue,   Manave,   Manague, Manahua, Managua, Managui. 1605-06 to 1635, Parras (psa). The Managues, according to the 1606 *Anua*, settled in Parras after a fight with another nation.

Manguara (Manhues?). 1683, Parras (psa).

Manos de Perro (Spanish: "Dog Hands"). 1766, at a Coahuila mission.

Manos Prietas (Spanish: "Black or Dark Hands"). 1674, associated with the Hueyquetzales; 1687 with the Cabezas; 1688 with the Quechales (Gueiquesales) (Portillo 1887: 11, 77, 85, 195). Said in one place to be "de la asistencia del río del norte y su comarca. . . " (Portillo 1887: 106). 1698 to 1707, Cabeza band, Parras (psa).

Manqui. 1629 and 1638, Parras (psa).

Mapoch (Nahuatl? – "Left Handed"). 1634 and 1635, Parras (psa).

Maqualistaca (see Mazatichigua and Appendix 3). 1687, with the Cabezas (Portillo 1887: 195).

Martaja Mesquite (Spanish). 1693, in the general Río Grande area.

Masames. (Nahuatl? – "The Deer People"). A "Toboso" group. 1644, 1652, and 1653. In 1671 a Spaniard testified that the Masames revolted in 1632.

Masiabes. 1674, associated with the Catujanes.

Matarajes. "Salineros" or "Cuaguilas." 1644, 1652, and 1653.

Mauitovi. 1615-1616, Parras (psa).

Maxiconera. 1595, Parras area (AGN 1619). 1605-06, 1607, 1615-1616, Parras (psa).

Mayconera, Maiconera (probably Maxiconera). Given as a surname in the 1598 *Anua* and said to be from Parras.

Maymamamara (Mamarimamari?) (nación). 1696, Cabeza band, Parras (psa). Almost certainly the same person is cited as a Baiamamar (psa) (see Appendix 3).

Mayo (plural occurs in one place as *Mayoes*, which possibly indicates that the stress fell on the *o*). Said in one place to be an alternate name for the Tusares of Parras (AHP 1654Ac). "Cuaguilas." 1653, 1673, 1675; 1674, associated with the Hueyquetzales; 1687, with the Cabezas

(Portillo 1887: 195). 1694 to 1717, Cabeza band, Parras (psa).

Mayoco(?) (Mayo?). 1638, Parras (psa).

Mayrana (see Mairana).

Mazatichigua (nación). (see Maçaltipilguas, Maqualistaca — see Appendix 3). 1696, Cabeza band, Parras (psa).

Meguira, Meuira, Mehuira, Hehuera, Mevira. Said to be from Parras in the 1598 *Anua*. 1605-06 to 1630, Parras (psa).

Meriano. Given as a surname in the 1598 *Anua* at the Laguna.

Mesa (Spanish?) (nación). 1642, Parras (psa).

Mescales, Mexcales (Nahuatl: Mexcalli; Spanish Mescal?). 1670, with the Catujanos (AHP 1670A); 1674, also with the Catujanos. 1721, Cabeza band, Parras (psa). 1766, at a Coahuila mission.

Mexues. Said to be at both Parras and La Laguna ca 1605.

Milijais Milixayes. 1674, associated with the Catujanes; 1670, with groups raiding the Saltillo and Monterrey areas (AHP 1670A). Portillo cited them as at the mission of San Bernardo de la Candela (n.d.) with Catujanos and Tilijais (1887: 11).

Miopacoa, Miopacoba (once). Said to be from Parras in the 1598 *Anua*. 1605-06 to 1628, Parras (psa).

Mischales (nación) (see Mescales?). 1670, Parras (psa).

Misquiti, Misquit (nación). 1671, Parras (psa).

Moçanamara. 1605-06, Parras (psa).

Moiote (Nahuatl?: Mosquito). 1635, Parras (psa).

Molineros (Spanish: "Millers") (see Malineros). Reported by an anonymous Jesuit about 1706 to be one of the four nations — including Salineros, Vaqueros, and Cabezas — settled in the Parras-Laguna district.

Muliam. 1670, associated with groups raiding Saltillo and Monterrey (AHP 1670A).

Nacababal, Nacababa, Nacabatlas. 1609, 1615-16, 1633, 1639, Parras (psa). Possibly this name is connected to the place of Nacababit, located apparently somewhere between Parral and Mobana: ". . . Y que haviendo Juntado Cavallada y Mulas hacia detras del Parral hacia Santa Barvara la llebaban y les Salieron los Soldados en Nacababit hacia San Blas y se la

quitaron y ellos fueron huyendo a dho Mobana a la Rancheria . . ." (from the declaration of an Acoclame, 1705: AHP 1704Ab).

Nacacavora (??) (Nacababal?). 1607, Parras (psa).

Nacatzatza (Nacababa?). 1639, Parras (psa).

Namar (??). 1626, Parras (psa).

Negritos (Spanish). 1644 to 1670's(?). A Tepehuán group from around Mapimí, named after its governor Juan Negrito of the early 1600's (*Anua* of 1606). 1665 and 1672-74, Parras (psa).

Nonoje, Nonoxe, Nonox (singular used in 1640's especially); plus three variants given by Hackett but which occur nowhere else: Noñojet, Noñoques, and Nonoties (1926: 124, 126). 1618, 1621, 1624, 1625, and important, usually as allies of the Tobosos and Acoclames, into the 1660's when they seem to disappear as a separate group of any importance. Probably associated with the place of Nonolat. Cne "Toboso" envoy of 1692 was said to be a Nonoje.

Nostligueguei, Nostigueguei. 1670, associated with groups raiding the Saltillo and Monterrey areas (AHP 1670A).

Oba (Obaya?). 1643, Parras (psa).

Obaides (Obayas). 1661, raiding in the general Parras area.

Obayas, Ovayas. 1670, from the Coahuila area, associated with the Sipopolames and Orames (AHP 1670A); 1674, with the Hueyquetzales; 1675, in rebellion in Coahuila. 1766, at a Coahuila mission. 1671, at Patos, and in 1694, 1697, and 1719 with the Cabezas at Parras (psa).

Obebopo, Obebo. 1605-06, 1615-1616, Parras (psa).

Ocames, Ocanes? 1670, associated with groups raiding the Saltillo and Monterrey areas (from Coahuila. Portillo 1887: 114).

Ocanes, Ocames? 1670, associated with groups raiding Saltillo and Monterrey (AHP 1670A). 1675, Coahuila (Portillo 1887: 114). 1766, at a Coahuila mission.

Ocolas. Reported at both Parras and La Laguna about 1605.

Ococlame (see Acoclame).

Ocomes, Ocomites (occasionally), and Jojocomes (1690's). (Possibly the plural form, *ocomeh*, of the Nahuatl, *ocotl*, "resinous pine"). 1644 to 1690's, when they became for the most part extinct as a separate group.

Odame, Odaame, Oodame, Hodahame. 1675, with the Gueiquesales; 1687, with the Babozarigames, Colorados, Cabezas, and others. 1643 to 1671, Parras (psa).

Ohoes, Oho, Oha, Ohe (?), Hoa. 1615-1616 to 1630, Parras (psa). The *Anua* of 1604 states that the Ohoes were from the general Parras-Laguna area, and that the name meant "enemies."

Ojahue (Ohoe?). 1618, Parras (psa).

Omomones (Omoomas?). 1654, Parras (psa).

Omoomas (Omomones?). 1661, raiding around Parras; lived fifty leagues from Saltillo.

Onat. 1653. Possibly a "Salinero" band.

Ooche, O,oche, 'ooche, oche, (and one each for) odre and oodre. 1605-06 to 1639, Parras (psa).

Opaguico. 1632, Parras (psa).

Orames (see Horames, Hores, Hoera?). 1644 to 1657 (1644 and 1646 at Patos). 1670, with the Catujanos (AHP 1670A).

Osataba, Osatabay, Osatapa, Osatame. "Chisos." 1684. Said to inhabit the mountains around the confluence of the Río Grande and Conchos rivers. (Apparently distinct from the Osatayoliclas, since the two names are given for separate bands by Indian informants while listing various "Chiso" groups.)

Osatayolicla, Ostayolic, Osatayoligla, Osatayogligla, and occasionally Osatayolida (see Osataba). 1684, 1693.

Osicame. 1638, Parras (psa).

Ostujanes. 1766, at one of the Coahuila missions.

Otauay (Osataba?). "Chisos."

Otecamegue. 1655, Parras (psa).

Otocame. 1662, 1671, Parras (psa).

Otolcoclomes, Otolcoclames. "Tobosos." 1644, 1646.

Oxao (see Ojahues, Ohoes?) (nación). 1671, Parras (psa).

Oyaa. 1615-1616, Parras (psa).

Oymama, Oimama, Oymana. 1605-06 to 1629, Parras (psa). Given as a personal name in the 1598 *Anua* for La Laguna.

Paboris. Coahuila. 1714, at Nadadores mission with the Terocodames.

Pachales, Patchales, Patzales, Patzhales. 1670, Saltillo area (AHP 1670A).

Pachaques (see Parchaques). 1674, associated with the Catujanes; 1675 with the Catujanes, Apes, Bajares, Tilijaes, and Jumees (Portillo 1887: 80-81, 96, 124).

Pachoches (Pachos, Pachaques??). 1766, at a Coahuila mission.

Pachos. Given as a surname in Parras in the 1598 *Anua*, and reported again at Parras by Mota y Escobar about 1605. They were said to be originally from around the Saltillo area. 1605-06 to 1671, Parras (psa); one shows up in the baptismal records of the Parral parish for the 1645-1648 period.

Pacpoles. 1766, at a Coahuila mission.

Pacuafin. 1766, at a Coahuila mission.

Pajalatames. 1766, at a Coahuila mission.

Pampopas. 1766, at a Coahuila mission.

Pamuliam, Pamoliam, Ypamuliam. 1670, associated with groups raiding in the Saltillo and Monterrey areas (AHP 1670A).

Panague. 1670, inland (*tierra adentro*) from Monterrey (Coahuila?) (AHP 1670A).

Paoga, Pahoga, Pahogua. Classified together with the Caviseras as one of the four nations of La Laguna in the 1598 *Anua*. 1605-06 to 1630, Parras (psa).

Parchaques, Parchales (Pachales?). 1670, Saltillo area (AHP 1670A).

Pataguac, Pataguaques. 1670, inland (*tierra adentro*) from Monterrey (Coahuila?) (AHP 1670A); 1675, Coahuila (Portillo 1887: 114).

Pausanes. 1766, at a Coahuila mission.

Payaboa, Paiaboa, Paiamboa, Paianboa, Payaboan. 1605-06 to 1618, Parras (psa).

Payaguales (Payaguames?). 1670, associated with groups raiding the Saltillo and Monterrey areas (AHP 1670A).

Payaguames (Payoanes, Payaquales?). 1766, at a Coahuila mission.

Payoanes (Payaguames, Payaboas?). 1670, associated with groups raiding around Saltillo and Monterrey (from Coahuila?) (AHP 1670A).

Pazaguantes or *Pazaguates*. 1582, a nation encountered by Espejo between the Conchos and the Jobosos (Tobosos).

El Pellejo Blanco, the people of (Spanish: "White Hide"). 1693, in the general Río Grande area.

Perros (Spanish: "Dogs"). A Toboso band name given once by a Chiso declarant (AHP 1655Ab). (May be a key to a native "Toboso" band name.)

El Pescado, the nation of (Spanish: "The Fish"). (Possibly a Jumano group; Sauer 1934). 1693, in the general Río Grande area.

Pies de Venado (Spanish: "Deer Feet"). 1653; 1674, associated with the Mayos and Hueyquetzales; 1675, with the Babozarigames; 1687, with the Cabezas; 1688, with the Quechales (Gueiguesales). 1693 to 1719, Cabeza band, Parras (psa).

Piguiques. 1766, at a Coahuila mission.

Pimotologas, Pimotocologas. 1644.

Pinanaca, Pinanacama, Pinanacam. 1674, associated with the Hueyquetzales; 1675, with the Gueiquesales and Bocora; 1687, with the Cabezas (Portillo 1887: 77, 117, 126, 195).

Piquamara (see Hapiquamara). 1605-06, Parras (psa).

Pitarday (nación). 1718, Cabeza band, Parras (psa).

Pitas. 1766, at a Coahuila mission.

Popora (see Siboporas?). 1671, near Patos? (psa).

Popoyehua, Popoiegua, Popoyihua, Popoyeua, Popoiehua, Poponiua, Popaega, Popoigua. 1605-06 to 1639, Parras (psa).

Porras, Poras (infrequent) (1615-1616: "de nación Porras"). 1605-06 to 1630, Parras (psa). Given as a personal name in La Laguna in the *Anua* of 1598.

Prejos(?) or *Presos*(?). 1670, Parras (psa).

Puapo (nación). 1722, one person at Patos, another at Nadadores (AHP 1722Da).

Quaaguapaias, Quaaguapaya, Quaguapaias, Quaguapayas, Quaguapaes, Quaapayas, Coaguapai, Cuaguapai (see Cuabapae). "Cuaguilas": "indios cuaguilas de nación quaguapaias." 1651 to 1671, Parras (psa).

Quaguimama (see Guaguimamara).

Quailos. 1669, Parras (psa).

Quamamara (Guaguimamara?). 1609, Parras (psa).

Quamoquanes. 1607, lived on the Nadadores River; after a punitive expedition of this year many moved down and settled at San Francisco de Patos (Alessio Robles 1938: 146).

Quautic, Quactic (Nahuatl?). 1605-06, Parras (psa).

Quechales (see Hueyquetzales, Gueiquechales). 1687, with Cabezas (Portillo 1887: 195).

Quenxames. 1670, associated with groups raiding Saltillo and Monterrey (AHP 1670A).

Quequesales, Quesal (see Hueyquetzales, Gueiquesales). 1694 to 1717, Cabeza band, Parras (psa).

Quimichi. 1636, Parras (psa).

Rana (Spanish: 'Frog"?). 1606, Parras (psa).

Rayado (Spanish: "Painted"). 1630, Parras (psa).

Saaquel, 1644, Patos. (nación). *Sasqueles* (nación) 1654(?) (psa).

Sadujanes. 1766, at a Coahuila mission.

Saesse (see Xaeser, Siaexer?). 1674, associated with the Hueyquetzales.

Saguach(?). 1655, Parras (psa).

Saguales, Saguala (Saaquel?). 1644, east of Parras with the Cabezas, and at the Urdiñola hacienda (Portillo 1887: 34-36).

De la Salina (apparently "Salinero"). 1605-06, Parras (psa).

Salineros (Spanish: "from the Salt Flats"). 1624 and 1625, considered as the usual allies of the Tobosos, Acoclames, and Nonojes; name seems to have dropped out of usage pretty much by the 1690's. 1654 to 1680, name occurs in the Parras parish archives, twice with reference to the Laguna area; 1695 to 1704, Cabeza band, Parras (psa). 1634 to 1705, term shows up in the Parral parish archives, in 1675 and 1676 in the Allende (San Bartolomé) parish records. Name seems to have been used generically to a good extent from the earliest years, or at least from the 1644 Revolt on.

Salineros of Don Cebrián. One of several "Salinero" groups. 1644 Revolt. 1652 and 1653.

Samay. 1670, associated with groups raiding in the Saltillo and Monterrey areas (AHP 1670A).

Sanague. 1670, inland (*tierra adentro*) from Monterrey (Coahuila?) (AHP 1670A).

Sarames. (Seems to be distinguished from Xarames.) 1670, inland (*tierra adentro*) from Monterrey (Coahuila?) (AHP 1670A).

Satapayogliglas, Satayolila (see Osatayoliclas?). "Chisos" ("la Nación Satayolila de los Chisos" — BL 1693b). 1691.

Satzpanal. 1670, associated with groups raiding

the Saltillo and Monterrey areas (AHP 1670A).

Seoporami, Seoporan (nación) (see Sibopora-me). 1643 and 1646, Parras (psa).

Seromet. 1674, associated with the Hueyquet-zales.

Seuliyolicla (Sunigugliglas?). "Chisos." 1684.

Siaexer (see Saesse). (Coahuila). 1675, with the Gueiquesales (Portillo 1887: 77).

Siboporame, Sipopolas, Sibopora, Sipopolame, Sivoporame, Sibopolame, Sibapora, Sibapo-lame, Sibopola, Sibopolo, Sopolame, Soporame, Sibaporame. This nation is most likely the one the Spaniards from the Parral called the "Cíbolas" or "Cíbolos" from Coahuila; one en-try in the Parras records cites "de nación síbola Porame" (almost all of these variants come from the Parras archives). 1642 to 1671, in the Parras records; 1643, 1644, 1646, specifically at Patos; 1670, at La Castañuela (psa). 1652, with the "Salineros;" 1670, confederated with Oba-yas, Orames, and others of Coahuila.

Sicpam. 1670, associated with groups raiding the Monterrey and Saltillo areas (AHP 1670A).

Siguares. 1766, at a Coahuila mission.

Silangayas. 1766, at a Coahuila mission.

Sisimbles, Zizimbles, Xiximbles (1640's) Sisimbres, Sinsimbles, Asisimbres, Simbles, Sinibles(?). This group was said to be called "Toidas" in Coahuila (AHP 1704Ab), which is the only reference to "Toidas" encountered. 1644 to 1748. 1730 to 1735, name occurs in the Parral parish records.

Sisituemeto. 1638, Parras (psa).

Sitiminich. 1638, Parras (psa).

Sodomamara. 1687, with the Cabezas (Portillo 1887: 195).

Suçaze (nación). 1671, Parras (psa).

Sumee (see Xumee, Jumee).

Sunigugliglas, Suninolilas, Sunilolilas, Sonolo-lila, Suninoligla, Suniloligla, Solinolicua, Sinilo-lila, Sinayoligla, Simplolilas, Siniyoliglas, Senayoligla (see Seuliyolicla). "Chisos." 1692 to 1713.

Taamnan. (Occurs in the same declaration as Xaamnacanes and Chamancas, separate group?). 1670, associated with groups raiding Saltillo and Monterrey (AHP 1670A).

Tacquites. 1766, at a Coahuila mission.

Taimamares. 1675, with the Gueiquesales (Portillo 1887: 77).

Talcoyotes, Talcoyomes, Tatalcoyomes. (Apparently, Nahuatl from *tlalli* "earth," and *coyotl* "coyote;" reduplicated plural: *tlatla-lcoyomeh*. Nahuatl: "Prairie Dog"?). 1646, with "Tobosos" and "Salineros;" 1652, 1653, with the Ygoquiba and Yguitoros.

Taparabopo (Daparabopo). 1617, Parras (psa).

Tapohoamama. 1607, Parras (psa).

Taquarabopo (Daparabopo?). 1615-16, 1617, 1618, 1635, Parras (psa).

Tatalcoyomes (see Talcoyotes).

Tatamulis. 1653, possibly a "Salinero" band.

Tauanbo. 1608, Parras (psa).

Teaname. 1675, at San Isidro Labrador (Portillo 1887: 118).

Tegas (apparently, "Tejas"). 1705, Cabeza band, Parras (psa).

Teguanes (apparently, "Tepehuanes"). The 1606 *Anua* stated that these people were at Mapimí, La Cadama (some five leagues from Mapimí), and in the Pelayo area. Three bands are mentioned at this time — those of Tibulena (Tobulina), Serofaunu, and of El Negrito (the latter apparently the same as the Tepehuán group "Los Negritos" under chief "El Negrito").

Tejuane (Teguanes?). 1609, Parras (psa).

Teneimamar (see Teymamar). 1675, with the Gueiquesales at San Vicente Ferrer (Portillo 1887: 117).

Teneymama. 1674, associated with the Huey-quetzales.

Tensasame (nación) (see Teusasame). 1655, Parras (psa).

Tepehuanes (see Teguanes and Negritos). 1605-06, Parras (psa).

Tepolgueguei. 1670, associated with groups raiding the Saltillo and Monterrey areas (from Coahuila area?) (AHP 1670A).

Tereodan (Terocodames?). 1675, at San Isidro Labrador (Portillo 1887: 118).

Terocodames, Terococodames, Teodocodamos. 1688 to 1717; 1766, at a Coahuila mission. They lived somewhere north of Parras and San Pedro de la Laguna and were said to be relatives of the Cabezas (AGN n.d.).

Tetecoras, Tetecore. 1655 and 1671 (at La Castañuela) in the Parras parish archives; 1694 to 1719, Cabeza band, Parras (psa). 1661, raid-ing around Parras; 1674, associated with the

Hueyquetzales.

Tetecos (apparently, the same as Tetecoras). 1652, with "Salineros."

Tetenagua(?). 1638, Parras (psa).

Tetenobapar. 1638, Parras (psa).

Teterxames(?) (Texuyames?). 1670, Parras (psa).

Tetexon, Tejon. 1618 and 1630, Parras (psa).

Tetonbopoca. 1636, Parras (psa).

Teusasame (see Tensasame). 1654, Parras (psa).

Texuyames, (this apparently should read Teruyames, the Spanish orthographic *r* is sometimes written as *x*). 1662, said to be related by blood (*parientes*) to the Totonocas (AHP 1662C).

Teymamar (apparently, the same as the Teneimamar). 1674, associated with the Hueyquetzales.

Tibocabopo. 1615-16, Parras (psa).

Tilijais. 1674 and 1675, with the Catujanos (Portillo 1887: 80-81, 124). 1766, at a Coahuila mission.

Timamares (Teymamares?). 1766, at the Coahuila mission of San Miguel de Aguayo.

Titioyo, Teteoyo. 1605-06 to 1617, Parras (psa).

Titipora, Titepore, Tetepora. 1645 to 1671, Parras; 1670 and 1671 at La Castañuela (psa).

Tlalcoyome (see Talcoyote). 1656, Parras (psa).

Tlenamama. 1609, Parras (psa).

Toa. 1670, associated with groups raiding the Saltillo and Monterrey areas (AHP 1670A).

Toamares. 1675, with the Catujanos (Portillo 1887: 80-81).

Toarames (listed separately from the Orames in the same declaration). 1670, inland (*tierra adentro*) from Monterrey (from Coahuila?).

Toarmas (see Toarames, Toamares). 1674, associated with the Catujanos.

Toboco (possibly should read Toboço, i.e., "Toboso"). 1617, Parras (psa).

Tobosos, Tobossos, Tovosos, Tovossos. (Used both specifically for the Toboso band and generically for the nations "that are allied and that commonly [*vulgarmente*] have the name Tobosos . . ." (BL 1693b). First encountered by the Espejo expedition in 1582; at the Atotonilco (Villa López, Chihuahua) mission about 1612; cited later in 1618, 1621,1625, 1644 Revolt on into the 1650's when, in 1653, the Toboso as a separate band was virtually wiped out, although what appear to be individual Tobosos show up in the later 1650's, 1666, and 1673. Tobosos, the term probably being used in a generic sense, are cited in the Allende archives in 1662, 1672, and 1677; the Parral Parish archives forty-seven "Tobosos" occur in the baptismal records between the years 1649 and 1730, twelve after 1706 are either Acoclames or Cocoyomes. 1694 to 1702, Cabezas band, Parras (psa). 1766, at a Coahuila mission.

Tocamomom. 1674, associated with the Hueyquetzales.

Tocaymamares. 1674, associated with the Hueyquetzales.

Tocho, Toche. 1630, 1637, 1638, Parras (psa). Four are cited in the baptismal books of the Parral parish between the years 1640 and 1660.

Tohobapojo (see Tohobopo?). 1608, Parras (psa).

Tohobopo, Toobopo. 1609 to 1618, Parras (psa).

Toidas. 1705, said to be the name for the Sisimbles in Coahuila (this is the only occurrence of "Toida").

Tomahuac (1605-06) and apparently Jomaguas (1630). Parras (psa).

Tomaxpuecpe, Tomayxpucpe. 1670, inland (*tierra adentro*) from Monterrey (from Coahuila?).

Tonmamal, Tunmamar. (Possibly the Cotomamar, Tuimamar, or even the Teimamar of the Marin Report of 1693.) (The Cotomamar were said to live in a sierra in the area of the confluence of the Río Grande and Concho rivers — Hackett 1926: 393).

Tooca, Toca, Tuca, Toques (see Itoca; Tucumamara, Tucumuragas? — see Appendix 3). (The majority of entries in the Parras records write "Tooca" with one instance of "Toooca," certainly an orthographic error but possibly an indication of vowel length; other sources cite "Toca.") 1643 to 1680, Parras (psa). 1652, with "Salineros." 1674, Toques are associated with Mayos and Hueyquetzales. Portillo states that they were at the Nadadores mission (n.d.) with Colorados, and were or had been allied with Mazapes and Cenizos from Nuevo León (1887: 11, 194).

Torquimamara. 1696 and 1697, Cabeza band, Parras (psa).

Tosimoras. Area unknown but cited together with several Coahuila tribes as extinct in 1746.

Totohame. 1654, Parras (psa).

Totoholomes, Totoolomes (see Cototoholome). "Chisos." 1684, and 1693 in the general Río Grande area. Said to inhabit the mountains in the region of the confluence of the Río Grande and Concho rivers (Hackett 1926: 392).

Totolcoyome. (Occurs apart from Talcoyome and apparently is distinct.) 1645, with "Tobosos" and "Salineros."

Totonoca. 1636, 1638, 1668(?), and 1678-79, Parras (psa). Said to be blood relations (*parientes*) of the Texuyames (AHP 1662C).

Tripas Blancas (Spanish: "White Bellys or Intestines"). 1717, and said to be extinct by 1746. Apparently a Coahuila group.

Tubaymamar. 1646, with "Tobosos" and "Salineros."

Tucumamara, Tucumama (Toocas? — see Appendix 3). 1701 and 1702, Cabeza band (psa).

Tucumuragas (Tucumamara?; Toocas?). Possibly a "Salinero" group. 1654, with the Gordos, Imudagas, and Gavilanes.

Tucurames. 1670, inland (*tierra adentro*) from Monterrey (from Coahuila area?) (AHP 1670A).

Tuimamar. 1693, in the general Río Grande area. (See Tonmamal.)

Tumamar (see Tonmamal?; Tuimamar?). 1675, at San Isidro Labrador (Portillo 1887: 118).

Tusares, Tusaras (see Mayo). 1618 to 1671, Parras (psa). 1652, with "Salineros."

Upiquamara (see Hapiquamara?). 1609, Parras (psa).

Uquiqualuo. 1636, Parras (psa).

Vahanero, Vaanero, Vajanero, Vanero, Baanero, Bahanero, Vaganero. 1654 to 1684, Parras; 1712 and 1719, Cabeza band, Parras (psa).

Vaiaja, Vaiatsa. 1608, Parras (psa).

Vaqueros. Reported by an anonymous Jesuit ca 1706 as one of the four nations settled in the Parras-Laguna district — the other three being the Salineros, Cabezas, and Molineros.

Vasapalles. The *Anua* of 1598 stated that they, together with the Ahomamas, constituted one of the four nations from La Laguna de San Pedro.

Vichilgua. 1615-1616, Parras (psa).

Vivoras (Spanish: "Snake," "Viper"). 1693, in the general Río Grande area.

Xaamnacanes (see Xanamacam). 1670, associated with groups raiding the Saltillo and Monterrey areas (AHP 1670A).

Xacactic. 1634, Parras (psa).

Xaeser (see Saesser and Siaexer). 1675, with the Gueiquesales (Portillo 1887: 117).

Xalazapas, Jalazapas (see Alasapas). 1722, one from the hacienda of San Miguel de Aguayo (AHP 1722Aa).

Xalepa. 1605-06 to 1627, Parras (psa).

Xanamacam (see Xaamnacanes). 1670, associated with groups raiding Saltillo and Monterrey areas (AHP 1670A).

Xanaque. 1670, associated with groups raiding the Saltillo and Monterrey areas (AHP 1670A).

Xanimama. 1615-1616, Parras (psa).

Xapoz, Apex, Xape, Xeapes, Xiapez, Xoapez, Xiapoz (possibly this deals with more than one group). 1670, in the general Saltillo area (AHP 1670A).

Xaqueban (Xaquibama?). 1607, Parras (psa).

Xaquibama (Xaqueban?). 1609 and 1610, Parras (psa).

Xaranames, Xarames. 1670, inland (*tierra adentro*) from Monterrey (AHP 1670A).

Xexet, Jeget, Xexetes (pl), (see Jajames). A small group closely associated with the Cocoyomes ca 1704.

Xiabanes (see Xoabanes). 1670, associated with groups raiding the Saltillo and Monterrey areas (AHP 1670A).

Xiancocadam . 1674, associated with the Boboles.

Xicocales (Gicocoges, Xicocosses?). 1674, puesto de Castaño (Portillo 1887: 63).

Xicocosses (see Gicocoges and Xicocoxes). 1674, associated with the Boboles.

Xicocoxes (see Gicocoges, Xicocosses). 1653, a camp in the general Parras area (AHP 1653Aa).

Xicocuage (see Xicocoxes). 1655, Parras (psa).

Xinicares. 1670, associated with groups around Saltillo and Monterrey; inland (*tierra adentro*) from Monterrey (AHP 1670A).

Xipocales (Xicocales?). 1624, only occurrence, a group associated with the Acoclames and Nonojes.

Xixames (Jajames?). 1766, at a Coahuila mission.

Xoabanes, Xoames(?), (Xiabanes?). 1670, inland (*tierra adentro*) from Monterrey (from Coahuila area?).

Xoman (Xumee?). 1675, at San Isidro Labrador (Portillo 1887: 118).

Xomi (Xumee?). 1671, Parras (psa).

Xonaqui. 1609 and 1627, Parras (psa).

Xoxame (Jajame, Xixame?). 1671, Parras, (psa).

Xuman (Xumee?). 1636, Parras (psa).

Xumee (see Jumee). 1670, associated with groups raiding around Monterrey and Saltillo (AHP 1670A), 1671, Parras (psa).

Xupulames (Sipolames, Sibopora ?). 1674, associated with Boboles.

Yamomama, Iamomama, Yamomaroa, Ymomama, Imomama, Emomama, Emoma. 1605-06 to 1627, Parras (psa).

Yanabopo (see Inabopo). 1605-06 to 1630, Parras (psa). Said to be one of the four nations at La Laguna in the 1598 *Anua*.

Yaoymama (Oymama). 1630, Parras (psa).

Yaquabuzmama. 1617, Parras (psa).

Yataioio. 1627, Parras (psa).

Ychuimama. 1610, Parras (psa).

Ydabiri. 1618, Parras (psa).

Yegual, Iegual, Yogual, Sugual(?). 1642 to 1670, Parras (psa).

Yerbiapames (see Herbipiamos).

Yerbuibas. 1674, associated with the Boboles.

Yeyeraura (nación). 1670, at the Echeverz hacienda (psa).

Ygoquibas, Igoquib. 1653, from around Cuatro Ciénegas, with Cíbolos, Mayos, Babozarigames, and Yguitoros. 1674, associated with the Mayos and Gueiquesales.

Yguabo. 1617, Parras (psa).

Yguamira, Yhuamira, Iguamira, Yyguamira, Guamira. 1605-06 to 1631, Parras (psa). Guamira is given as a personal name in the Laguna in the 1598 *Anua*.

Yguitoros. 1653, with Cíbolos, Mayos, Babosarigames, Tatalcoyomes, Tusares and Ygoquibas.

Ylasaio. 1644, Parras (psa).

Ylaura. 1671, Parras (psa).

Ylauraquasivaha. 1671, Parras (psa).

Yoera, Yohera, Iohera, Yohere. 1605-06 to 1609, Parras (psa).

Yoguocomes. 1652, with Tobosos.

Yome (originally "Home" but written over in the manuscript) (nación) (see Xumee?). 1671, Parras (psa).

Yoricas, 1670, 1674, 1675 associated with the Boboles, Gicocoges, Jeapes. At Sabinas river and some four leagues from the Río Grande (Portillo 1887: 63, 71, 113; AHP 1670A).

Yrbipias (Herbipiames).

Ytocame (see Otocame). 1671, Parras (psa).

Yurbipames (see Herbipiames).

Yxdaroc. 1670, inland (*tierra adentro*) from Monterrey (from Coahuila area?).

Yyuguimi, Yuyguimes. 1654 and 1658, Parras (psa).

Zacateco, Çacateco. 1598 *Anua* gives the name of one individual as Colazaque Zacateco. Mota y Escobar mentioned Zacatecos at Parras around 1605. Zacatecos were said to live along the Nazas River and to border the Laguna and Parras. 1627 and 1657 Zacateco is cited in the Parras parish records (psa).

Zamoi. 1655, a Toboso band name given by a Chiso declarant (AHP 1655Ab).

Zuchil. 1670, at La Castañuela (psa).

It has been possible in one case to follow the life-histories of a pair of individuals with some degree of certainty, although for the most part this is exceedingly difficult or impossible to do, owing to duplications in names and the lack of completeness of the records. This particular case is taken from the church archives in Parras and seems to demonstrate the use of multiple terms for the same persons or bands and also possibly the change in the use of terms over time. The case concerns the "Cabeza" chief Don Pedrote and his wife Leonor.

In January of 1680 at Parras the natural daughter of a woman named Helena was baptized — the father was said to be Don Pedrote of the Mamarimamari nation, and Helena a Cabeza (Parras, Libro 2, Bautismos). This Helena was apparently the sister of Leonor, the future legal wife of Don Pedrote. In a marriage dispensation of May 31, 1683, granted to Don Pedrote, it is stated that the latter had been having relations with two sisters (sororal polygyny?) — Leonor and Elena. The dispensation granted permission for Don Pedrote, now said to be a Cabeza, to marry the former, a Babozarigame (PSA 1683a). In support of the evidence in the dispensation, a month after the baptism of Helena's child, a child born to one Leonor (no nation cited) was baptized; the father was reportedly Don Pedrote, a Mamarimamari (Parras, Libro 2, Bautismos). After the dispensation, the marriage of one Don Pedro of the Cabeza nation with Leonora, a Babozarigame, is recorded on June 20, 1683 (Parras, Libro 3, Bautismos, Casamientos, Entierros). There would seem to be little doubt that this is the same couple.

Don Pedrote and Leonor are not heard of again in the church records consulted until the 1690's, after the Cabeza band went to Parras to settle. In the books of baptisms and burials for the Cabeza rancheria, the baptism and death of a daughter belonging to Don Pedrote and Leonor is recorded for 1695, the parents being listed in both instances as "Cabezas." In 1696, another entry notes the death of a daughter of Don Pedrote "Indian of the Salinero nation and of Leonor Indian of the Pies de Venado nation," although the baptism of this child does not seem to be listed in the records. Two years later, on August 15, 1698, an entry notes the burial of Don Pedrote "Yndio de Nazion Salinero, marido que fue de leonora Yndia de Nazion Pies de benado." In the year 1704, entries in the baptismal and burial records refer to the child of a widow named Leonor of the Pies de Venado nation; this may or may not have been the same Leonor, although it seems likely that it was (Parras, Libros de Bautismos y Entierros de la Ranchería de los Cabezas).

From the preceding information, several conclusions may be tentatively drawn — aside from the one that utter confusion reigned in the priests' minds regarding the ethnic identity of their Indian flock. One is that the term "Cabeza" was used in a generic sense to refer to a group or cluster of "bands" — a conclusion also noted elsewhere. Secondly, it is possible that "Salinero" and "Cabeza" were used interchangeably at times — a possibility also noted elsewhere (see specifically the 1644 Rebellion). A third is that perhaps the terms "Babozarigame" and "Pies de Venado" were used to designate the same group, although it is always possible that Leonor's parents were a Babozarigame and a Pies de Venado and that the Fathers were uncertain what to call her. Another source stated that the Babozarigames and Pies de Venado were closely associated — a Babozarigame testifying stated that the Pies de Venado were *agregados* to his group (Portillo 1887: 94-95). The last possible conclusion is that the occurrence of "Mamarimamari" (possibly the same as the Baborimama, etc.) is another instance of the dropping of the usage of a specific term by the Spaniards for a more general one, in this case for "Cabeza" and "Salinero."

APPENDIX 2
HINTS ON BAND COMPOSITION FROM THE PARRAS ARCHIVES

This list of band (by surname) affiliations of married couples has been extracted, by year, from baptismal, burial, and marriage records in the Parras Parish Archives. The marriage records are by far the most complete in this respect; the majority of entries in other records fail to record one or both of the individuals' band affiliations (but where they are stated they have been included here). The records of the Cabezas are summarized completely in this Appendix, but those from the remainder of the Parras Archives are not, and are merely cited here as further examples. However, the latter bear out the picture given by the Cabeza records in that in the overwhelming majority of cases people of different "surname" or band name married — not those with the same name. In the cases where the same name occurs for both spouses, such as with the name "Cabeza," there is evidence that the name was sometimes used loosely or generically (see Appendices 1 and 3). Consequently, it seems that in many instances what the Spaniards called *naciones* in a specific sense were named, lineal bands.

Baptisms:

1605:	Comaroya/Hazpipina
	Pacho/Piquamara
	Mamaçorra/Legua
1606:	Inabopo/Daparabopo
	Yamama/Daparabopo
	*Porras Tlatuani/Porras
	Hapiquamara/Ditehagopob
	Manague/Ileepo
	Manague/Ileepo
	Manague/Bichoya
	Porras/Popoyeh
	Yoera/Maxiconera
	Jalepa/Huatamama
	Mehuera/Mairana
	Hyguamira/Rana
	Lalaca/Hiraca
1607:	Chicanima/Hurabama
1608:	*Yamomama/Yamomama
1609:	Bohayo/Hanimama
1615:	*parents of the "Nacababal" nation

The slant symbol (/) in the following list indicates marriage. Some of the entries in the different record books are no doubt duplications of each other — that is, they refer to the same persons. In the few cases where these could be checked against each other with any degree of certainty, this has been done. However, in the majority of cases it is not certain whether the persons involved are the same couple, even though the names are the same. Consequently, any absolute count of persons from these records has little or no value, but for the present purpose of demonstrating interband marriage, this duplication merely strengthens the evidence.

NOTE: In the following list, asterisks are used to call attention to those instances in which marriages involved couples of the same band name or surname.

From the early Parras Archive records (males are listed on the left, females on the right):

1616:	Calaraque/Mauitovi
	Mayran/Quahuila
	Saray/Mamayga
1617:	Taparaboco/Alamama
	Toboco/Conapomama
	Xalepa/Oymama
	Manahue/Yguabo
	Taquarabopo/Epimama
	Iritila/Pacho
	Taquarabopo/Payaboan
	Yanabopo/Yamomama
	Yamomama/Taquarabopo
	Meguira/Miopacoa
	Tlaxcalteco/O,oche
1618:	Xalepa/Popoiehua
	Porras/Yamomama
	*"Alayuios de nacion"
	Yanabopo/Ydabiri

Marriages:

1626:	de Cuaguilla/Alayuyo
	Alamama/Alaiuio
1627:	Çacateco/Alayuyo

Marriages, 1627 (cont.)

        Alamama/Zonia [or Honia]
        Alaiuyo/Euancan
        Paoga/Meguira
        Gueimama/Barrigueta
        Tonalteco/Alalaca
        Borrado/Cuaguilla
        Ytaioio/Oha
        Epimama/Enabopo
        Chabarria/Chibicano
        Corma/Alaiuyo

1628:   Hobe/Cuiname
        Mançanares/Junia
        *Cojo/Coja
        Egope/Alaiuio
        Alalaca/Alalyuo
        Yguamira/de la Laguna

1629:   Alalaca/Cuaguilla
        Alamama/Cuaguilla
        Alalaca/Cocoxima
        *Junia/Junia
        *Lagunero/Lagunera

1630:   Etaiui/Bopoac
        Oha/Icsotl
        Tlaxcalteco/Alalaca
        Toche/Tlaxcalteca

1633:   *Junia/Junia
        Nacababa/Tusara

1634:   Mapoch/Lagunera

1635:   Xuman/Cocoxibo
        Epimama/Ileepo
        Cocoime/Borrada
        Alayuyo/Cuaguilla

1636:   Teton Bopoca/Jusquiopoion
        Totonoca/Heguan
        Cocoxibo/Guitola
        Hep.e(?)/Quimichi
        Cocoxibo/Heguan
        Uquigualuo/Heguan
        Alayuyo/Alalaca

1637:   *Cuaguilla/Cuaguilla

1638:   Tusara/Babora
        *two couples "de nacion Quahuilas"
        Guilime/Laguna
        Jigualli/Sisituemeto
        Cocoxibo/Osicame
        Totonoca/Osicame
        Cocoxibo/Guitolos
        Tetenagua/Quaguila

1642:   nacion Mesa/nacion Baja
        Titipora/Siboporame
        *Cuaguila/Cuaguila
        *Yegual/Yegual

1655:   Cuabapae/Cocoxiua

1662:   Coaguapai/Otocame

"Cabezas" Indians (1693 - 1722; Ranchería at Santa María de las Parras)

1694:   Cabeza/Coniani
        Cabeza/Tobosa
        Coniani/Tobosa
        Cabeza/Coniani
        Cabeza/Mayo
        Cabeza/Tobosa
        Coniani/Mayo
        Baiamamar/Pies de Venado
        Mayo/Cabeza
        Quequ.esal/Coniani
        Mayo/Tetecora
        Obaia/Cabeza

1695:   Coniane/Maya
        Coniane/Cabeza
        Mayo/Salinera
        Quesal/Cabeza
        Coniane/Torquimamara
        *Cabeza/Cabeza (per baptismal entry; Cabeza/Coniani per marriage entry).
        *Cabeza/Cabeza (per two baptismal entries — one that cannot be further checked, and one that refers to Pedrote and Leonora [see Appendix 1]; Coniani/Coniani per third baptismal record)
        *Cabeza/Cabeza (per burial record; Cabeza/Coniani per marriage record)

1696:   Salinero/Cabeza
        "de Nazion Mazatichigua"/Contotore
        Coniane/Mazatichigua
        Coniane/Contotore
        Coniane/Guaguimamara
        Tetecora/Salinera
        Cabeza/Tobosa
        Salinero/Pies de Venado
        Maymamara/Pies de Venado
        Coniani/Tobosa
        Coniane/Quaguimama
        Coniane/Mayo
        Cabeza/Tobosa
        Coniane/Cabeza
        Coniane/Maya
        Cabeza/Coniane
        *Cabeza/Cabeza (per baptismal record; Obaya/Cabeza per marriage record)

1697:   Girigaias/Salinera
        Obaya/Cabeza
        Mayo/Tetecora
        Mayo/Salinera
        Quesal/Cabeza
        Coniane/Cabeza
        Cabeza/Coniani
        Coniani/Torquimamara
        Coniane/Toboza
        Coniane/Cabeza
        Coniani/Torquimamara
        Mayo/Tetecora
        Cabeza/Toboza

1698: Manos Prietas/Lagunera
Cabeza/Contotore
Cabeza/Mayo
Mayo/Tetecora
Quesal/Coniane
Coniane/Contotore
*Cabeza/Cabeza (cannot be checked against other records)
Salinero/Pies de Venado
Coniane/Contotore
Salinero/Atapo

1699: Cabeza/Coniane
Coniane/Cabeza
Mayo/Salinera
Salinero/Atapo
Cabeza/Tobosa

1700: Quesal/Cabeza
Manos Prietas/Lagunera
Coniane/Cabeza
Cabeza/Tobosa

1701: Tucumama/Coniane
Cabeza/Contotore
Cabeza/Lagunera
Cabeza/Babozarigame
Quesal/Cabeza (Quequesal/Coniani per marriage records)

1702: Cabeza/Pies de Venado
Quesal/Cabeza
Cabeza/Coniane
Maio/Tectecora
Coniane/Mayo
Tucumamara/Coniane
*Cabeza/Cabeza (apparently Coniani/Mayo from marriage records)
Coniani/Tobosa

1703: *Cabeza/Cabeza (no way to check further)
Manos Prietas/Lagunera

1704: Coniane/Salinera
Manos Prietas/Lagunera
Coniane/Lagunera
Contotore/Tobosa
Contotore/Coniane
*Cabeza/Cabeza (no way to check further)
Coniane/Mayo
*Cabeza/Cabeza (no way to check further)
Coniani/Salinera
Coniani/Mayo

1705: Tegas/Quesale
*Cabeza/Cabeza (Cabeza/Tobosa per baptismal records)

1706: Contotore/Cocoyome
Contotore/Manos Prietas
Cocoyome/Cabeza

*Cabeza/Cabeza
*Cabeza/Cabeza
Parras/Cabeza (One baptismal entry reads: the child "de Juan de Parras, y de Marta lagunera Yndios todos de la nacion cabeza.")

1707: Manos Prietas/Contotore
Cabeza/Coniane

1708: *Cabeza/Cabeza (four baptismal entries)
*Cabeza/Cabeza (one burial entry)

1709: *Cabeza/Cabeza
*Cabeza/Cabeza

1710: *Contotolis/Contotolis (parents of a woman)
*Cabeza/Cabeza (parents of another person)

1711: (no band affiliation mentioned)

1712: Vaganero/Cabeza

1713: (no band affiliation mentioned)

1714: (no band affiliation mentioned)

1715: (no band affiliation mentioned)

1716: (no band affiliation mentioned)

1717: *Cabeza/Cabeza (Both parents of person are said to be Cabezas)
Cabeza/Quesal
Contotol/Conani
Conani/Cabeza
Pies de Venado/Borrada

1718: Pitarday/Babozarigame
Contotol/Cacalote
Cabeza/Pies de Venado
Contotol/Cacalote
Cabeza/Coniani
Contotol/Conani

1719: Ovaya/Contotol
Cabeza/Concha
Conani/Maya
Alazapas/Tetecora
Pies de Venado/Tetecora
Cabeza/Pies de Venado
Mescale/Contotol
Bahanero/Conani
Contotol/Maya
Contotol/Cacalote
Cacalote/Quezal
Contotol/Cabeza

1720: Cien Orejas/Guadiamanar
Cabeza/Concha

1721: *Cabeza/Cabeza
Mexcale/Contotol

1722: (no band affiliation mentioned)

APPENDIX 3

ETHNIC COMPOSITION OF THE CABEZA "NATION" AT PARRAS, 1693 - 1722

Appendix 3 .is a rough summary of the ethnic composition of the Cabeza Indians who were settled at Santa María de las Parras at the end of the seventeenth century. This has been done by listing and counting the number of times each band name occurs in the baptismal, marriage, and burial records kept by the Jesuits who administered them.

The absolute figures of such a count, however, signify little. In the first place the records are not complete with respect to band names. A great many individuals are mentioned with no band affiliation, partly because different priests recorded differently in this regard. Furthermore, there is much duplication; the same person's name may appear a number of times in the records — for example, once each for his own baptism, marriage, and death, and again when his children are baptized. Because complete names are often not given and there is much duplication in given names, it is usually impossible, except in a few cases, to determine whether the same individual is being dealt with in various entries. Still, the number of occurrences of these names probably gives a rough indication of the percentage of the various bands. For these reasons, the figures are not given for the band names counted, except in a few instances when they seem to contribute to the overall picture.

The term "Cabeza" occurs almost three times more frequently than any other name, but this is to be expected because it had generic application, aside from whatever specific one it might have had. In a few determinable instances persons listed as "Cabezas" are also called by another term in another entry (see Appendix 2). The specific name with the greatest frequency is "Coniani" (50), followed by "Mayo" and "Contotore" with over half (26). "Pies de Venado," "Quequesal," "Tetecora," and "Toboso" follow (11-13). The remaining names occur fewer than eight times, most between one and five. The total list of band names for the Cabezas follows.

Alazapas	Isale
Atapo	Lagunero
Babozarigame	Manos Prietas
Bahanero	Maymamara
Borrado	Baiamamar
Cabeza	Mayo
Cacalote	Mazatichigua
Cien Orejas	Mescale
Cocoyome	Obaya
Colorado	Pies de Venado
Concho	Pitarday
Coniani	Quequesal
Contotore	Quesal
Cosiguirachic	Salinero
Cuaguila	Tegas (probably
del Reyno de Leon	phonetically *tejas*)
Girigaias	Tetecora
Guadiamanar	Toboso
Guaguimamara	Torquimamara
Quaguimama	Tucumama
	Tucumamara

NOTE: The four indented names in the preceding list are variants that occur in the documents.

Portillo (1887: 194-195) gives a list of allied nations under Don Pedrote, chief of the Cabezas during the year 1687:

Bajamares	Iboquiba
Bidamamara	*Manos Prietas
Bocoras	Maqualistaca
Boquillurimamara	*Mayos
*Cabezas	Odames
*Colorados	*Pies de Venado
Comeajeme	Pinanacama
*Conianes	*Quechales
Dedepos	Sodomamara
Guimutiquimamara	Tocas

Comment: The direct overlap of only seven (marked by an asterisk in the preceding list) of the twenty names of this list with the various groups that formed part of the "Cabezas" at Parras suggests that perhaps in effect there was a much greater overlap, disguised here by variant terms. Possibly "Bajamares" is equivalent to "Baiamamar" or "Maymamara," the "Guimutiquimamara" to the "Guaquimamara," the "Maqualistaca" to the "Mazatichigua," and the "Tocas" (Toocas) to the "Tucumamara."

APPENDIX 4

THE MARIN 1693 REPORT OF NUEVA VIZCAYA INDIANS AND COMPARISON WITH RETANA'S 1693 LIST

In 1693 the *Maestre de Campo* Joseph Francisco Marín submitted a report on the Indians of Nueva Vizcaya to the Viceroy, Conde de Galve, dated in Parral on September 30. The portion of the report that is pertinent here lists the "nations" that dwelled from "Durango to the confluence of the Conchos and Río Grande Rivers." From this statement and from other sources there appears to be some order to Marín's listing, running from south to north. However, some things are confusing or apparently in error, and the problem is to determine to what point his list is reliable.

For regions where more definite information is available, Marín gives place, band, or tribal, and even provincial names, all as the names of "nations." For example, he lists the Taos, the Moquinos (Hopi), and the people of New Mexico as three separate nations, and no other New Mexicans are cited except Apaches. Likewise, in the Sonora area he includes Pimas, Sobal (Sobas? — also Pimas), Seris, Tepocas (also Seris), Sonoras(!) (Opatas?), Yaquis, the Rau (apparently referring to the Yaqui village of Raum), and so forth. In an over-all sense, then, there is some geographical order to Marín's list, but any particular "nation" name may not fall within this order, and it may be duplicated or overlapped somewhere else in the list by a chief's or a place name.

One gets the impression that Marín included in his list every band or group name that he had ever heard or could recall. Furthermore, it is not certain that all of these "nations" were actually in existence at the time of this report — for example, Tovossos and Salineros. However, this may be the best single report to afford a notion of the number of "peoples" that inhabited central northern Mexico about the 1690's.

The only additional comments here are taken from General Retana's list, since Marín explicitly refers to Retana's *entrada* in his report. A more general comparison is made in Appendix 1, where all band or "nation" names encountered in the course of this study have been cited, except those of Marín's list.

However, a number of the names in Marín's list do not appear in other sources, and there is no way to place them relative to general groupings. Marín's list is taken from Hackett 1926: 390-394, and Retana's from BL 1695a. What slight geographical order there is to Retana's list seems to be from west to east. The full list is reproduced in the section on Band History.

The Marín Report is as follows:

The Tepeguanes; the people of Parras; the Tovossos; the Cocoiomes; the Gavilanes, cited 27th and next to last by Retana; the people of El Sombrero Prieto; the Cocoyomes of Thecolote, cited 26th by Retana; the Babosarigames; the Hijos de la Tierra, 5th by Retana; the Hijos de las Piedras, 6th by Retana; the Hijos del Lodo; the Negritos; the Salineros; the Jojocomes; other Gavilanes; the people of Coahuila; . . .

Following this, Marín states that the next seven names are those of Chiso nations, although this is clearly in error, since from other sources (see Band History) the two names following these seven are also "Chisos."

Marín's list continues:

. . . the Chisos; the Chichitames, the first group in Retana's list; the Satapayogliglas; the Guazapayogliglas, 3rd by Retana; the Osatayogliglas, 4th by Retana; the Cacuitaomes; the Otauay; the Batayogliglas; the Sunigogliglas; the Cacucoat; the Cuamichiquat; the Bajopapay; the Boomes; the Cocosut; the Colorados, 16th in Retana's report; the Ajames; the Tuimamare, 8th by Retana; the Teimamar; the Oymamare; the Sinibles, apparently the Sisimbles reported 2nd by Retana; the Mo;mututur; the Totomonos called Cabezas Blancas, cited 12th and by the last name by Retana; the Cocomoguacales (there is a slight possibility that this is the Guacales group cited 14th by Retana); the Salineros; the Bacopo; the Pobas; the Estoytto; the Subuitutilca; the Esauqui; the Cuicuiguas; the Trimomomos (ttrimomomos); the Cuurbipicas, cited as Curuipicas 20th by Retana; the people of El Pescado, 23rd on Retana's list; the Pinanacas, called the Desorejados; the Pinanuas called the

Apagados, the Bobori called the Cometunas; the Tuidamoydan called Hijos de la Sierra; the Mascagua called the Duros; the Utacas; the Parugan called Hedor Fiero; the Tuigare, called the stick with which they crush (*martajan*) the *Opoli*; the Tuicuigan, called *por aqui* (*sic*?); the Popos Pocodomen called Comesacate; the Guascadome called people of the nuts (*nueces*); . . .

The next eighteen, beginning with *Acoclame* through *Malas Flechas*, Marín states were "discovered" only in July of this year (1693) by Captain Juan de Retana on his expedition to the Río Grande-Conchos rivers confluence. They were said to inhabit the mountains around this area. Whatever "discovered" means, it hardly applies to groups such as the Acoclames, Cholomes, and Totolomes, among others. Furthermore, the last six names of these eighteen do not appear on Retana's list consulted here. These eighteen are: the Acoclames, 7th by Retana; the Cholomes, 9th by Retana; the people of Pellejo Blanco, 13th on Retana's list; the Cabezas de Guacale, 15th by Retana; the Enemigos del Cerro, 17th by Retana; the Papacolani, 18th by Retana; the Cucubipi, 19th by Retana; the Mastajamesquite, cited as Martaja Mesquite and 21st by Retana; the Malas Flechas, 22nd by Retana; the Babimamar, 24th by Retana; the Cotomamar, 25th by Retana; the Totolomes, 28th by Retana; the Osatames; the Cocomas; the Parucan; the Tuigar; the Opulas; the Manos Prietas.

On the other side of La Junta, between Texas and New Mexico, Marín claimed fifty-four nations. These were the Salchomis; the people of Pie de Recacalote (*sic*, Tecacalote); the Guacali, possibly the Guacales cited 14th by Retana; the Sinorejas; the people of Cabellos Blancos; the Salcocolomes; the Bapacores; the Sallas; the Borrados; the Siniples (possibly another reference to the Sisimbles); the people of Los Dientes Alazanes; the people of Cassas Moradas which are four nations of the same name; the Cabezas; the Conejos; the Alzados; the Pajaritos; the Humanas (Jumanas); the Come Síbolos; the Arcos Tirados; the Sívolos; the Apaches; the Mesquites; the Cacalotes; the Posalmes; the Polacmes; the Oposmes; the Pulicas; the Topacolmes (Tapacolmes); those of the Long Limbs (*miembros largos*); those who eat all food made into pinole (*que comen todo manjar hecho pinole*); the Gaapa; the Paiaias Cuchite; the Canaq; the Tuques; the Cruiamos; the Ymittes; the Rayados; the Ysuguarios; the Mamuyas; the Satatu; the Yaguat; the Comeviejos; the Chauares; the Mapoch; those of Silent Hands (*manos sordas*); those of the Rotten Bows (*arcos podridos*); those of Good Bows (*arcos buenos*); other Borrados; those of Long Tails; the Texas.

The only group cited by Retana and not by Marín is the Cococomesno, tenth on Retana's list. Marín may have known, and probably did, of Retana's other list, but a number of things, either by comparison with the latter or with information from other sources, are erroneous.

APPENDIX 5

CHIEFS' NAMES

In this Appendix are listed the names of the chiefs of the several tribes and nations that occur in the text. These are cited alphabetically under the general name for the group or geographical area from which the chief came. The specific band name that occurs in the sources is listed in parentheses.

San Pedro de la Laguna

Aomania (1595)
Bacacuyo (1595)
Bartolomé (1595)
Gaspar Cavisera (1595)
Daparabopo (1595)
Guamira (1595)
Juan Inabopo (1595)
Mateo (1595)
Oymana (1595)
Pedro Meriano (1595)
Porras (1595)

Parras

Antonio Martín Irritila (1595)
Colazaque Zacateco (1595)
Francisco Cui (1595)
Juan Mayconera (1595)
Mainara or Macarue (1595)
Martín Pacho (1595)

Teguanes or Tepehuanes

Naytra Iclotre Quimarato (Teguán) (1606)
El Negrito (Tepehuán and Teguán) (1606) and
Don Juan Negrito (Tepehuán) (1622)
Serofaunu (Teguán) (1606)
Tibulena or Tobulina (Teguán) (1606)

Tobosos

Acoclames:

Alarcón (apparently Acoclame) (1693)
Brazos Chicos (1655)
El Chapetón (head chief) (1705)
Dieguillo (apparently Acoclame) (1716)
Espinazo de Culebra (1653)
Juan Cola de Coyote (apparently Acoclame) (1693)
Jaunaljipil or Jaunalpipil (1653)
Nicolás (1705)
Panzacola (1705)
El Ratón (1705)

Cocoyomes:

Bartolo or Taribiquic (Coyote, i.e., Cocoyome) (1653)
Ceja Blanca (1705)
Contreras (1691; 1692) (head chief: 1705)
El Gallo (1720)
Francisco el Tecolote (1687; 1691)
Joseph (1720)
Juan de Ibarra, also called Sombrero Prieto? (1692)
Juan de Lomas (1716-1723)
Lorenzo (1692; 1705)
Mutat (1653)
Pedro (1720)
Simón (1646)
Ventura (1720)

Gavilanes:

Chapsani (1653)
El Gavilán (prior to 1653)
Felipe el Tuerto (1691; appointed governor of the Gavilanes and Jojocomes by the Spaniards, 1692).
Joxocomi (1652)
Juan (1646)
El Mapochi (seems to have been known as both a Gavilán and an Ocome; 1658)

Jaquue of Jaqueie:

Cristóbal Zapata (1645)

Nonojes:

Cristóbal (1652; 1653)
Francisco Hauchuli or Hauchile (1646)
Juan Casa Zavala (occasionally Casavala) (1645; 1652; 1653; 1654; 1655; 1656)
Pupuye (1653)

Ocomes:

Alarconsillo (Jojocome) (1692: under Lorenzo)
Andrés (1654)
Juan Mapochi or El Zurdo (1653; 1654, 1655; 1677, 1686, 1687)

Juan Sombrero Prieto (1692: under Lorenzo)
(Jojocome)
Lorenzo Delgado or Lorencillo Sau Muyaget
(1692) (Jojocomes)
Miguel (1646)

Tobosos:
Cristóbal (1645; 1653)
Cristóbal Zapata (1645; 1653; 1658)
Don Agustín (1624)
Don Francisco (1674)
Don Jusephe (1621; 1624)
Juan Campos (1674)

Cabezas-Salineros:
Alvaro de Moranta (1644; 1646) (Salinero)
Baltazar (Cabeza) (1646)
Baltazar (Salinero) (1646)
El Baquero (1688)
Don Bartolo Sinarvee (1688)
Don Cebrián (Salinero) (1644; 1652)
Don Fiscal or Felipe el Tuerto (Gavilan?)
(1688)
Don Francisco Sunori or Sunora (1688)
Don Pablo (1688)
Don Pedro (Salinero governor) (1645)
Don Pedrote (Cabeza, and allies) (1687; 1688;
1690's)
Francisco Mama (Salinero) (1644)
Francisco el Tuerto (Salinero) (1645)
Gabriel Pacho (Salinero) (1645)
Juan Bonifacio (Salinero) (1645)
Juanillo (1688)
Nicolas Baturi (Salinero) (1645)
Santiaguillo (Salinero) (1652) (Santiago: head
of a Cabeza group settled at El Canutillo,
1658)

"Coahuileños" and Other Bands

Baborimamas:
Baltazar (1652)
Don Pedro (1673)

Babosarigames:
Baibiadaga (Babosarigas) (1646)
Salvador (1675)

Boboles:
Juan de la Cruz (1674-75)

Cabacbitac or Cababitae:
Nicolás (1646)

Concho:
Frasquillo (leader of small group associated with
the Tobosos and their allies, 1654)

Catujano:
Don Miguel (1674-75)

Coahuileños:
Isidro (1724)
Don Pablo (Terocodame?) (1714; 1716)

Hueyquetzales:
Don Esteban (1674-75)

Maçaltipilguas or Maçalypilguas:
Martín (1646)

Manos Prietas:
Don Pablo (1675)

Matarajes:
Cahico (1646)

Mayo:
Don Fabián (1673; 1674-75)

Talcoyomes:
Pedro (1646)

Tubaymamares:
Hicabiaca (1646)

Chisos

Sisimbles:
Bartolomé (1693)
Juan Nepomuceno (1748)

Chisos:
Santiago (Conulayaca) (1692)

Satayoliclas:
Don Santiago (1691)

Others

El Julime (1691)
Marcos (1726: leader of a mixed band consisting mostly of Sisimbles and Coahuileños)
Ymuticari (1653) (apparently a "Toboso" but
no nation listed)

BIBLIOGRAPHY

Documents

Archive of the Cathedral of the City of Parral, Chihuahua.
   Baptismal Records.

Archive of the Jesuit Church of the City of Parras de la Fuente, Coahuila.

PSA 1682 — Santa Maria de las Parras, 7 y 8 de octubre de 1682.

1683a — Despensa de matrimonio, Durango, 31 de maio, 1683, Fray Bartolome, Obispo de Durango (plus certification).

1683b — Fray Bartolome Garcia de Escanuela al alcalde mayor o su teniente de Santa Maria de las Parras [the auto that follows this letter is dated, Durango, ca 31 de agosto, 1683].

   Baptism, Burial, and Marriage Records.

Archivo General de la Nación, México, D.F.

AGN 1607a — Diego Diaz de Pongua al Pe Illefonso de Castro Provincial de la Compa de Jesus de nueva espana, Mapimi 7 de mayo de 607.

1607b — Diego Larios, Guadiana y mayo 12 de 1607.

1607c — Pe Luis de Ahumada al Pe Proal Illefonso de Castro, Mapimi 7 . Mayo . 607.

1617 — Historia Vol. 308. Francisco de Arista, Relacion de La guerra de los Tepehuanes este mes de dic.e de *1617*.

1618 — Historia, Tomo 308. Francisco de Arista, Relacion delo succedido en la guerra de tepehuanes este mes de febrero de 1618.

1619 — Certificacion q dio el Pe franco de Arista Ror de la

AGN

1622 — casa de Guadiana y visitador de las missiones de Parras y Tepehuanes de la Compa de jhs sobre el assiento del pueblo de Parras y discurso, q ha tenido sobre la poblacion de el de 22 anos a esta parte. Misiones 25. Carta Annua de la Provincia de la conpania de Jesus de la Nueva Espana del Ano de 1622, Mexico, Maio 15 de 1623.

1624 — Misiones 25. Carta Annua de la Prova de la nueva Espana de 1624, Juan Lorenco, mayo 20 de 1625.

1626 — Misiones 25. Carta annua de la provincia de la nueva espana del ano de 1626, Juan Lorenco, Mexico, mayo 20 de 1627.

1640 — Misiones Leg. III-7. Autos, 4 y 5 de enero, 1640, gobernador Francisco Bravo de la Serna, Parral.

ca 1640 — Misiones Leg. III-7. Guadiana; Pareseres q el sr G.1 Don franco bravo de la serna govor y cappan General deste Reino de la nueva Viscaya ymbia al exmo sr Marqs de Cadereita Virrey de la Nueva espana el uno sobre la entrada de los Padres de La compania de Jesus a la nueva Comberssion de los yndios de la nacio'n Taraumar, Y el otro del descubrimiento que se a echo de una laguna de sal Muy Considerable a su Mag.d y a sus Rs quintos en las Naciones Tepeguanes y Tobosos.

1645-1647a — Misiones 25. Anua del pueblo del Tiçonaço desde el ano de 1645 . 46 . y 47.

AGN 1645-1647b   Misiones 25. Diego Ossorio and Gmo Rosario, Partido del Tiçonaço [accompanies AGN 1645-1647a].

1648-1649   Misiones 26. Carta Anua de la Provincia de Mexico, 1648-1649, Mexico, Julio 10, 1650, Andres de Rada.

1662   Misiones 26. Letter from Pe Franco de Mendoza, Zape 6 de junio de 1662, to visitador grl Hernando Cavero.

1667   Misiones 26. [Letter, 1667, Rodrigo del Castillo, S. J.].

1672   Misiones Leg. III-7. Vigilio Maes al Provincial, P Andres de Obian, Guadalajara, 4 de febrero de 1672.

1678   Misiones 26. Relacion de las Missiones que la Compania tiene en el Reyno y Provincias de la Nueva Viscaya en la Nueva Espana echa el ano de 1678 con ocasion de la Visita General dellas que por orden del Pe Provincial Thomas Altamirano hizo el P. Visitador Juan Hortiz Zapata de la misma Compania.

Bartolome de Estrada al Pro-

1683   Bartolome de Estrada al Provincial Bernardo Pardo, Parral y febrero 13 de 1683.

1725   Juo de Guendulain, Cocorin, Dicieme 22 de 1725. Pe Provincal Gaspar Roder.

1751-1757   Estados de las missiones q adentro se espresan, sus familias, Casamtos Baupmos y entierros desde el ano de 1751 a 57, Dionysio Murillo, Sta Anna de los Chinarras y Febrero 23 de 1758.

✓ 1793   Historia Tomo 42. 27 de diciembre de 1793, Mexico, Exmos.r — El Conde de Revilla gig — do Exmos s.r D.n Pedro de Acuna [includes a report of the missions of Nueva Vizcaya].

AGN n.d.   Historia, Vol. 308. Relacion y Sucesos acaecidos con los Yndios de la Laguna de Sn Pedro sin rason de ano. Yasimismo la promocion de los Pes Jesuitas de los dos Partidos. Parras, y la Laguna.

Archivo de Hidalgo del Parral, Parral, Chihuahua.

AHP 1641A*   34.** Expediente sobre las doctrinas mandadas observar en este Real de San Jose de Parral.

1644A   No. 13. Ynformacion que rinde Fernando Gardea [sic-Garcia] para que se vea que su Hda esta muy immediata alas naciones de los indios rebeldes.

1645Aa   No. 104. Expediente formado con motivo de la paz de los yndios Tobosos por el Maestre Francisco Montano de la Cueva.

1645Ab   102. Autos para acordar lo conveniente a la seguridad y al recibimiento de los Yndios que se mandaron traer de tierra adentro para la cosecha detrigo.

1646Aa   G-20. Testimonio de las diligencias que se practicaron con motivo de la reforma de las doctrinas de Atotonilco.

1646Ab   G-48. Informacion mandada practicar por el Sr Govr del Reyno pa Saber el estado en q se halla el mismo.

1646B   G-30. En averign de los fundamentos q tuvieron los Indios Salineros para alzarse.

1647   1. Mandamientos para averiguar el robo de unas limosnas y una imajen que quitaron a unos indios.

* Capital letters A, B, C, and D following the date indicate the microfilm reel designation of that particular year.

** The first number in the citation refers to the document number on the reel.

AHP 1651A   No. 104. Testimonio de los fundamentos que tubieron los Yndios para alsarse y como el Gobernador dio el correspondiente asiento de paz.

1652Aa   Manuscritos incompletos de un Solo legajo.

1652Ab   No. 33. Expediente sobre la guerra que se hizo contra las naciones indias alzadas.

1652Ac   N 9. Autos, sobre la recepcion de la Yndia Felipa de nacion Tobosa.

1652Ba   G-75. Expediente pa q se hagan unos pagos y continue la guerra contra los Indios Tobosos.

1652Bb   G-104. de Guerra; Diferentes declaraciones y papeles tocantes al levantamiento de los Indios rebelados contra la Real Corona.

1652Da   G-12. Criminal Contra Juan yndio en averiguacion de si fue de los indios sublevados.

1652Db   No. 113. Criminal contra Pablo Yndio de Sinaloa por haber tomado participio en el alzamiento de los indios tobosos.

1652Dc   No. 77. Criminal, contra Francisco, Antonio y Juan Naturales del Pueblo del Tizonaso por haberse alzado contra la Real Corona.

1653Aa   G-101. Administrativo y de Guerra, Autos de guerra hechos por el gobernador Diego Guajardo Fajardo sobre la campana contra los Tarahumares.

1653Ab   No. 25. Autos de guerra sobre la paz de los indios retirados de los Tobosos.

1653Ac   No. 25. Autos de Guerra contra los Yndios formados por Enrique de Avila.

1653Ad   No. 10. Autos sobre la paz de los Yndios Salineros.

AHP 1653Ae   No. 5. Autos de Guerra contra los Yndios Tobosos por Diego Guajardo Fajardo.

1653Ba   No. 22. Autos sobre la paz que se otorgo a varios Yndios.

1653Bb   No. 4. Autos sobre la venida de los Yndios Tarahumares para la guerra de los Tobosos.

1653Bc   No. 3. Autos de guerra contra los Yndios alzados seguidos por Cristoval Nevares en el pueblo de San Felipe.

1653Bd   No. 1. Autos formados con motivo de la venida de Hernando Obregon y de la Junta de Guerra contra los Yndios.

1654Aa   No. 2. Autos De Guerra hechos por el Gobernador General don Enrique Davila y Pacheco contra los indios Conchos y Tobosos que roban y matan a un carbonero de Santiago de Minas Nuevas 28 de Enero.

1654Ab   No. 4. Autos hechos por el Justicia Mayor del Pueblo de las Bocas (Villa Ocampo, Dgo.) Sobre la averiguacion de las muertes que los indios enemigos hicieron en el camino real en el parage que llaman de los Sauces hallando en el Cuatro cuerpos muertos y entre ellos a Juan de Oses.

1654Ac   No. 5. Expediente relativo a la paz que se hizo con los Yndios Tobosos.

1654Ad   No. 72. Informacion Original hecha en este Reyno de la nueva Vizcaya de las muertes, robos, y danos que los Yndios naturales de ella hacen.

1654Ca   N 41. Criminal en averiguacion de las muertes que hicieron los indios en el Paraje de la Sierra.

1654Cb   No. 46. Criminal Contra un indio Tarahumar y Pablo

AHP

1655Aa   Indio, Salinero, por muerte, en la persona de Marcos Perez–.

43. Autos que practico el General Enrique de avila y Pacheco Gobernador de las Probincias de la nueva Viscaya con motivo de la persecucion de los indios que mataron a Miguel de Arrieta.

1655Ab   No. 5. Autos de guerra con motivo de las frecuentes abusos que cometen los indios enemigos de la Real Corona.

1655Ba   No. 48. Criminal querella de Felipe de la Cruz mulato esclavo de Domingo de Apresa contra dos indios salineros por lesiones inferidas al querellante.

1655Bb   Num. 109. Criminal en averiguacion de la muerte que cometieron los indios en la persona de Miguel Arrieta y demas diligencias practicadas con motivo de sus bienes.

1655Bc   N. 44. Criminal, averiguacion con motivo del robo de ganado contra un indio llamado Geronimo y complices.

1656Aa   No. 3. Autos y Diligencias originales practicadas con motivo de la guerra que hacen los indios enemigos de la Real Corona.

1656Ab   N 16. Autos y diligencias practicados con motivo de haber intentado los indios quemar la Hacienda del Capitan Juan Leal.

1657Ba   G-109. Criminal Contra Juan Andres Indio por espia.

1657Bb   N 113. Criminal iniciado en Durango por el Gobernador Davila Pacheco sobre asalto q en el paraje de cerrillos serca del rio de Nazas cometieron los indios al tres de carros/?/

AHP

de matiasde Hinojosa q resulto herido.

1658Aa   N 6. Diligencias practicadas con motivo dela guerra que hacen a la Real Corona por los indios alzados.

1658Ab   No. 9. Autos de Guerra contra los indios rebelados.

1662C   N 44. Criminal, querella de Rafael y Cristobal Ramos contra Juan Boyero y Diego indios por espias de los enemigos por lo cual fueron condenados a muerte.

1667Aa   N. 4. Autos sobre la guerra que hacen los Yndios rebelados contra la Real Corona.

1667Ab   N g-101. Autos sobre la guerra que se hace a los yndios enemigos de la Real Corona.

1667B   N 68. Criminal Contra Lorenzo Yndio de la Nacion tovosa por sospechas de que fuera espia de los rebelados.

1669Ba   N 39. Criminal contra Gregorio Yndio por indicios de que puede ser espia.

1669Bb   N 44. Criminal contra unos Yndios apaches por homicidio perpetuado en la persona de Antonia Yndia.

1669Bc   103. Autos practicados con motivo de dar paz a los indios enemigos.

1670A   G-25. Autos de guerra contra los Yndios Revelados por el Gral Juan Antonio de Garcia.

1670B   G-34. Criminal en averiguacion de los delitoš que cometen los Yndios Conejos y negros.

1673Aa   No. 103. Expediente de Consultas, autos, y ordenes practicados con motivo de la Guerra que hacen los indios a la Real Corona.

1673Ab   No. 107. Autos relativos a las guerras con los indios

AHP

1673Ac

1674Aa

1674Ab

1676Aa

1676Ab

1677A

1684Aa

1684Ab

1685Da

1685Db

1686Ba

enemigos de la real Corona para evitar los danos y robos que estos hacen.

No. 152. Expediente sobre la Poblacion y misiones de los alsados de Don Pablo Yndio Tarumar en la tierra adentro.

N 104. Diligencias practicadas por el Maestre de Campo Jose Garcia relativas a la paz en el Real de Mapimi.

N 105. Autos de guerra contra los indios rebelados.

N 13. Testimonio delexpediente que se remitio al Virrey relativo a los indios sublevados.

G-100. Despacho Militar con Referencia a los indios Tobosos y Sus Aliados El Testimonio fue Mandado al Valle de Mexico.

132. Administracion y de Guerra, autos de guerra contra los indios Salineros, ocomes, Cocoyomes, acoclames, y gavilanes.

No. 106. Expediente formado con motivo de la guerra que hacen los indios alzados a la Real Corona.

No. 113. Autos de guerra contra los Yndios alzados en Conchos.

No. 46. Criminal contra un Indio de nacion Concho por presunciones de ser uno de los que asaltaron los Carros de Diego de Andavaso.

N 45. Criminal contra Domingo Indio por presuncion de ser de los alsados.

N 24. Criminal, Orden de Gobernador don Jose Felipe de Neira y Quiroga para que el alcalde mayor de San Juan de la Concepcion remita el proceso contra Felipe de Nacion Tiguas aquien se

AHP

1686Bb

1686Bc

1687Aa

1687Ab

1688Ca

1688Cb

1697Aa

1697Ab

1697Ac

remitia por a los morteros de las minas de este Real.

N-23. Criminal, En averiguacion del asalto y muerte que dieron los indios en los Sauces cerca de Santiago Papasquiaro en ese asalto mataron 7 personas y se llevaron 350 mulas de una recua que se dirigia a Durango.

N-26. Criminal, Sobre la muerte de unos indios en la hacienda de Sta Cruz.

N 11. Guerra, Informacion hecha a peticion de Bartolome Vazquez sobre el asalto que a una recua y carros que Venian de Mexico para este Real dieron los indios en la Boquilla del Gallo e informacion del Gov de Neira y Quiroga, para ver si cumplieron con su deber los jefes de los presidios.

Num. 8. Autos, Acordados por el Gobernador referentes a la guerra con los Yndios rebelados contra la Real Corona.

N 129. Criminal en averiguacion de si cuatro Yndios que aprehendieron son o no de los enemigos—.

128. Criminal contra un Yndio llamado Alonso, por traicion a la Real Corona.

34. Informes de Guerra levantados por el Gral Juan Fernandez Retana, sobre sublevacion de los Tarahumaras.

No. 35. Testimonio de los autos que se practicaron con motivo del alzamiento de los Yndios de la nacion Taraumar seguido por el Gral Juan Fernandez.

G-33. Autos practicados con motivo de la Sublevacion de los Yndios Seguidos por Don Andrez de Rezabal.

AHP 1699a   N 123. Criminal en averiguacion si tiene o no culpa Nicolas Castaneda por encontrarse entre los indios enemigos.

1699b   103. Autos practicados con motivo de dar la paz a los indios enemigos.

1700a   n 122. Criminal contra Juan Antonio indio por haberse puesto de acuerdo con los indios rebelados contra la Real Corona.

1700b   G-142. Queja de los indios de Babonayaba.

1703   N 32. Autos practicados para hacer la guerra a los indios rebelados contra la Real Corona.

1704Aa   no. 104. Diligencias practicadas con motivo de la paz que piden los indios de las Naciones acoclames y cocoyomes.

1704Ab   # 103. Autos practicados con motivo de la guerra que hacen a los enemigos de la Real Corona.

1704Ac   N 136. Guerra, Autos de la campana que hizo el Gral. Martin de Alday por orden del Gobernador Maestre de Campo don Juan Fernandez de Cordova contra la Real Corona.

1704Ad   No. 105. Autos de guerra contra los enemigos de la Real Corona.

1704Ba   G-142. Criminal, Sublevacion contra la real corona.

1704Bb   No. 133. Criminal en averiguacion de la fuga de unos indios.

1708a   N 5. Diligencias practicadas con motivo de la paz que piden los Yndios de Nacion Acoclames.

1708b   N 34. Administrativo y de Guerra, Autos de Guerra y

AHP   diligencias practicadas contra los enemigos de la Real Corona.

1710a   G-2. Informe que rinde el Alferez Andres de Mendoza sobre persecucion de los indios Cocollomes en el Real de Guanacevi.

1710b   N-7. Decreto por el que se impone una contribucion a los vecinos de Durango para mantener a los indios acoclames prisioneros en guerra.

1710c   G-26. Criminal que se sigue contra los indios rebedes /sic/ a la real Corona.

1710d   N G-24. Criminal contra el indio Diego Rafael por falsedad.

1711A   N 102. Provicion para que se instruya en la fe Catolica a los indios cocoyomes acoclames y demas naciones y se saquen de la Carcel publica de este Real.

1712   G-1. Administrativa, Instancia que ante el governador don Juan Felipe de Orozco y Medina hacen los caciques de la nacion Baborigames para que se les den tierras para fundar un pueblo.

1715Aa   N 106. Guerra, Expediente relativo a la campana hecha por el governador don manuel san juan de santa crus contra los indios Cocoyomes y Acoclames.

1715Ab   N 108. Informacion sobre las muertes y robos que han cometido los enemigos de la Real Corona.

1715Ac   G 134. Administrativo, Diligencias practicadas con motivo de la orden para que vuelvan los indios que estaban en el Valle de San Bartolome a sus pueblos de la junta del

AHP

1716Aa G-104. Guerra, Documentos relativos a la rebelion de los indios Acoclames Cocoyomes, y sus aliados.

1716Ab G-107. Guerra, Orden del general y gob. Manuel de San Juan y Santa Cruz, para hacer la guerra a las naciones Cacoclames, Cocoyomes y sus aliados, con fecha 10 de Septiembre de 1716, y diligencias que con tal motivo se practicaron y correspondencia de los capitanes de Presidio que en ella participaron.

1716Ac G-101. Autos Sobre la Reduccion de los Yndios Janos a la Mission de Sn Antonio de Cassas Grandes, y Administracion de Unos y Otros — Siendo Govor y Capn Grl el sr Dn Manuel sn Juan de sta Cruz, Cav [   ] del Orden de sntiago.

1718Aa No. 7. Comunicaciones y autos de guerra contra los enemigos de la real Corona.

1718Ab No. 9. Guerra, Testimonio de un Despacho de Virrey Duque de [Alburquerque] de 1656 para hacer la Guerra a los Tobosos.

1718Ac N-7. Comunicaciones y autos de guerra contra los enemigos de la Real Corona.

1718Ad N 5. Autos sobre remision de una Yndia llamada Juana que solicita Antonio Arias Visitador de la tarumara.

1720Aa G-102. Guerra, Diligencias y documentos relativos a la paz que ofrecieron los indios Acoclames, Venidos de Sierra Mojada del Gob Martin de Alday.

1720Ab G-147. Administrativo, Des-

rio del norte, y contradiccion que hicieron los labradores del valle.

AHP

pacho del Virrey Marques de Balero, sobre consultas que hizo el Gob del Parral, dn martin de Alday, sobre Repartimiento de indios para las minas de parral, chihuahua, Cusihuiriachic. Reduccion de indios Cocoyomes — efectos de Paz y Guerra y sublevacion de indios del Rio del Norte — 9 fs.

1721Aa G-1. Administrativo, Autos de guerra de la campana hecha por el Governador Martin de Alday, en la provincia de coahuila.

1721Ab G-147. Administrativo, Investigacion practicada por orden del Gob Don Martin de Alday con motivo de la oposicion del P. Fray Domingo Ortiz de Villasian, de la orden de San Francisco para que salgan a campana los indios de su mision de Julimes, sigue informe del Gral Don Diego de Salgado, Gob. de dicho pueblo y carta del citado misionero, conchos, 8 fs.

1722Aa G-103. Guerra, Diligencias sobre los indios rebeldes de las naciones coahuilena cocoyome, cabezas, acoclames, que el gobernador martin de Alday mando a aprehender y sobre las diligencias de jurisdicion sus citados entre las autoridades eclesiasticas de Santa Maria de Parras.

1722Ab G-106. Autos de Guerra, hechos contra los indios enemigos y paz de los yndios cocoyomes por el governador don martin dealday.

1722Ba G-106. (Continuation of AHP 1722Ab.)

1722Bb G-112. Autos de Guerra, Orden del General Jose lopez

AHP

1722Da

de Carbajal, gobernador de la provincia para perseguir a los indios que robaron en la hacienda de Santa Cruz pertenecientesa los lic Neiras. G 121. Criminal, Instruida por orden del Gobernador Martin de Alday, contra los indios Coahuilenos de pueblo de Santa Rosa de Nadadores, por haberse alzado, apostado y cometido unos robos y muertes.

1722Db
G-123. Criminal contra unos vaqueros de la hacienda de Conchos por haber matado 4 indios de San Francisco.

1723A
G-104. Guerra, Testimonio de los autos que su fulminaron sobre la sublevacion y pacificacion de los indios de nacion Tacuitatomes "alias" Chisos que habitaban en el Pueblo de San Francisco de Conchos por el Gob don Martin deAlday.

1724Aa
G-121. Guerra, Autos de Guerra contra los indios enemigos de quienes se recibieron informes por Cautivos que se les escaparon desde Sierra Mojada y narran los crimines y costumbres de los indios alzados—.

1724Ab
G-104A. Guerra, Autos de la Campana hecha por ordenes del Gob. Lopez de Carbajal a los indios de la region de Mapimi en la que tomo parte el mismo Gob y el Cap Dn Jose de Berroteran Cap. del Presidio de Mapimi.

1725Aa
#107a. Guerra, Orden del Gov Lopez de Carvajal para que los Capitanes de los Presidios imediatos a parral opinen sobre la campana que se iba a hacer a los indios COCOYOMES, ACOCLAMES, SI-

AHP

1725Ab

SIMBLES, TRIPAS BLANCAS, Y CUAGUILENOS, San Felipe el Real, agosto 9 de 1725. G-104. Guerra, Representaciones que ante el Gob Lopez de Carvajal hicieron los soldados de los presidio del gallo, mapimi, pasaje y cerro gordo por el descuente de haberes ordenado por el Brigadier Pedro de Rivera visitador de Presidios y testimonio de diligencias sobre la fuga de los soldados del valle de San Bartolome, cartas del Capn de Janos y del gob de nuevo mexico.

1725B
G-137. Administrativo, Documentos Varios.

1725Ca
G-123 k. Guerra, Despacho del Sargento Mayor d. Jose de Sarmiento con relacion a la orden dada por el Gov. Lopez de Carvajal para hacer campana a los indios enemigos cocoyomes, acloclames, sisimbles, tripas blancas y coahuilenos.

1727Aa
G-6. Administrativo, Testimonio de los autos hechos por el Gov. Lopez de Carvajal sobre la oferta de paz que hicieron los indios Cocoyomes y acoclames en Parral—.

1727Ab
G-11. Administrativo, Iligencia sobre la retirada de los indios del Pueblo de Cinco Senores del Rio de nazas.

1787A
No. G-32. Guerra, noticias que por orden del Gavallero de Croix rendian los Alcaldes de este Real sobre las incursiones de los indios a esta jurisdicion durante los anos de 1778 - 1787.

Bancroft Library, Berkeley, California
BL 1600-1602 Bolton Papers 255, Nueva Vizcaya. Carta Anua, 1600-1602.

BL 1602 Bolton Papers 255, Nueva Vizcaya. Anua de 1602.

1604 Bolton Papers 255, Nueva Vizcaya. Vaulken, Newberry Library. Anua de 1604.

1605 Bolton Papers 255, Nueva Vizcaya. Vaulken, Newberry Library. Anua de 1605.

1606 Bolton Papers 255, Nueva Vizcaya. Vaulken, Newberry Library. Anua de 1606.

1610 Bolton Papers 255, Nueva Vizcaya. Vaulken, Newberry Library. Anua de 1610.

1614 H. H. Bancroft Collection. Mexican Manuscripts, Misiones, 1717. Carta Annua de la Prov.a de la Comp.a de Iesus de Nueva Sp.a del ano de 1614.

1615a H. H. Bancroft Collection. Mexican Manuscripts, Misiones, 1717. Carta Annua de la Compania de Jesus de la Prov.a de Nueva espana de 1615.

1615b Bolton Papers 255, Nueva Vizcaya. Vaulken, Newberry Library. Anua de 1615.

1616 Bolton Papers 255, Nueva Vizcaya. Vaulken, Newberry Library. Anua de 1616.

1649-1700 AGI: Audiencia de Guadalajara 29 (66-6-18). Simancas y Secular, Audiencia de Guadalajara. Cartas y expedientes de los Gobernadores de Durango. Ano de 1649 a 1700.

1674 Bolton Papers 475. Saltillo: Archibo de la Secretaria de Gobierno del estado de coahuila; Legajo No. 1, Anos 1688 a 1736; Ano de 1674 — Coahuila. Autos de la Conquista de la Prov.a de Coahuila.

1676 Bolton Papers 477. Archive

BL
of the secretaria de gobierno of the Bishopric of linares; Legajo 1. 1779. Relacion of Coahuila and the Indians, Bishop of Guadalajara, 10 de abril, 1676.

1693a AGI: audiencia de Guadalajara 152 (67-4-12). Nueva Viscaya Ano de 1693. Ynforme fho por la Prov.a de Sonora Sobre el estado en q se halla Con la guerra que remite a su Mag.d el Sarg.to m.or D. Juo Ysidro de Pardinas Villar de francos gov.r y Cap.n gen.l de este Reino.

1693b AGI: audiencia de Guadalajara 152 (67-4-12). Nueva Viscaya. Ano de 1693. Autos Sobre las Ynvasiones q hasen los Yndios Reveldes en este Reino Y lo q se ha ejecutado sobre la Guerra ofenciva — Tobosos Gavilanes Cocoyomes Hijos de la tierra y de las Piedras, chichitames, y otras etca. Por el Sr Sargto mor Dn Ju Ysidro de Pardinas Villar de francos Cav.o del orden de Sntiago Gov.or Y Capn Genl de la Nueva Viscaya por por su Magd etca.

1693-1702 AGI: audiencia de Guadalajara 151 (67-4-1). Secretaria de Nueva Espana, Secular. Audiencia de Guadalaxara. Expediente sobre la guerra de los Yndios enemigos de Parral: anos de 1693 a 1702.

1694-1698 AGI: Audiencia de Guadalajara (67-4-12) 152. Expediente sobre los Yndios Tobosos y sus aliados. Anos de 1694 - 1698.

1695a AGI: Audiencia de Guadalajara 151 (67-4-1). Govierno. Ano de 1695. Testimonio de

BL   los auttos fhos Sobre las Providencias dadas en tiempo de Dn Gabriel deel Castillo Governador de el Parral Sobre operaciones de Guerra Y otros Puntos.

1695b   AGI: Audiencia de Guadalajara 151 (67-4-1). Govierno. Ano de 1695. Testimonio de autos de Guerra Tocantes al Capitan franco Ramirez de Salazar Con los motivos y Resolucion de Junta para la formacion de la Compania Volante de Sonora Con el numero de Cinquenta Soldados que ay Sirve Dn Domingo Jironza Petris de Cruzati.

1697-1703   AGI: Audiencia de Guadalajara 156 (67-4-16). Secretaria de n.E. Secular. Audiencia de Guadalajara. Testimonio de autos Sobre la pacificacion y castigo de los Yndios Taraumaras, y hostilidades de los Tobosos en la Nueva Vizcaya — ano de 1697 a 1703.

1709-1715   AGI: Audiencia de Guadalajara 164 (67-4-24).

1722   Audiencia de Guadalajara 171 (171-4-31). Supr Govo Ano de 1722. Testim.o de los autos fhos Sobre las Operassiones de los Yndios Coahuilenos, Acoclames, y Cocoyomes de la Nueva Vizcaya y estado de la guerra Y prov.s.

1723-1724   Audiencia de Guadalajara 171 (171-4-31). Secretaria de N.E. Secular. Adu.a de Guadalajara. Expediente sobre la Conquista y reduccion de varias castas de Yndios de la Provincia de la Nueva Vizcaya. anos de 1723 y 1724.

1728   H. H. Bancroft Collection. Mexican Manuscripts, General and Miscellaneous, 1777.

BL   Mexico, 1728. Rivera y Villalon, Pedro de, Informe sobre los Presidios de las Provincias Internas; con documentos suplementarios [incomplete].

1729   AGN: Historia, Tomo 52. Diario de la Campana de 1729 por Jose de Berroteran a la Junta de los Rios.

1746a   AGI: Audiencia de Guadalajara 137 (67-3-31). Joseph de Berroteran, Joseph de Ydoiaga, Juan Antonio de Unanue, y Francisco Joseph Leisaola; San Francisco de Conchos, 21 de octubre de 1746, al virrey Juan Francisco Huemes y Horcasita.

1746b   AGI: Audiencia de Guadalajara 191 (67-3-51). Superior Governo, 1746. testimonio e los auttos fhos a ynstancia del R Pe fr Juan Miguel Menchero, sobre varias providencias que pido Pa el Restablizim, to de las Misiones del Rio de la Junta en el Govierno de el nuebo Mexico y demas q dentro se expresa—.

1748   H. H. Bancroft Collection. Mexican Manuscripts 406:13. Mexico, mayo 3, 1748. Autos Criminales que por comision del senor Governador Y capitan General deste Reyno esta siguiendo don Francisco de Ayala Vrena Contra los Yndios enemigos de la Nacion espanola.

1749-1750   H. H. Bancroft Collection. Mexican Manuscripts, 1784. 1749 - 1750, Nueva Vizcaya. Gobernador (Puerta y Barrera). Expediente sobre la Campana de Jose de Berroteran, y los cargos que le resultaron de ella.

BL   1751a   AGI: Audiencia de Guadala-jara 191 (67-3-51). Capitania gral – 1751. testimonio de las diligencias con que el capitan del prisidio de conchos dio quenta al ex.mo Senor Virrey de este Reino de tres indioz y doz indias que Se presentaron el la Ya del Pueblo immediato de San Franco homisidas y desvastadores que havian quedado de la perniciosa quadrilla de los indios Zimbres–.

1751b   AGI: Audiencia de Guadala-jara 191 (67-3-51). Capitania gral – 1751. Testimonio de los Autos que Se formaron a pedimento de Don Jph de la Sierra Se los Puebloz de los Sumas infieles y Liga que tienen con los Apaches Mes-caleroz, y Salineros y los colomez por el capn y Alcalde Mayor Don Alonzo Victorez Rubin de Zeliz que lo es Vitalicio de este Rl Pre-sidio de nra Senora del Pilar y San Jph del Paso del Rio del Norte y Su Jurisdiccion–.

1786   H.H. Bancroft Collection. Mexican Manuscripts, Misiones, #431. Ano de 1786. Provincia de Coahuila; Estado actual de las Misiones de la Provincia de Coahuila y Rio Grande de la misma Jurisdiccion.

Centro de Documentación, Castillo de Chapultepec, México, D.F.

CD   1643a   Serie Parral, N 38. Autos formados por Don Melchor de Valdez Contra los Yndios tobosos.

1643b   Serie Parral, 1643. En-comienda de indios en la provincia de Santa Barbara, (Conchos) Expedido En Villa Durango (Julio 24, 1606) por

CD   Francisco de Urdinola. N 64. Civil, por Diego del Castillo por reclamo de unos indios contra Diego de Porras.

1644   Serie Parral. 1644, Rebelion de indios tepehuanes.

1645-1650   Serie Parral, 1645 - 1650, Asuntos de Guerra Contra Indios Barbaros.

1646a   Serie Parral, N 48. Ynforma-cion mandada practicar por el Senor Gobernador del Reyno para saber el estado en que se haya el mismo.

1646b   Serie Parral, #20. Testimonio de las diligencias que se practi-caron con el motivo de la reforma de Doctrinas en Ato-tonilco.

1647-1648   Serie Parral, 1647 - 1648. El Maese de campo d. francisco montano y sus campanas con-tra los barbaros.

1650a   Serie Parral. Documentos – Presentados por el Pbtro. Don Felipe de la Cueva Montano, referentes al Gral, Francisco Montano de la Cueva. 1650 [without number].

1650b   Serie Parral. Testimonio de los fundamentos que tuvieron los Yndios para Alzarse y como su asiento de Paz lo dio Luis de Valdez.

1655-1663   Serie Guadalajara. Dispo-siciones sobre los indios barbaros. 1655 - 1663, Legajo 3, Expediente 39.

[1671]   Serie Guadalajara. Expediente #7, Legajo 1, siglo XVII.

Documentos para la Historía de México (published; Vicente García Torres, ed.).

DHM 1596   Del Anua del Año de 1596. Cuarta Serie, Tomo III. México: 1857.

1598   Del Anua del Año de 1598. Cuarta Serie, Tomo III. México: 1857.

1601   Carta del padre Nicolás de

DHM

1607   Arnaya dirigida al padre provincial Francisco Báez el año de 1601. Cuarta Serie, Tomo III. México: 1857.

1607   Del anua del año de 1607. Cuarta Serie, Tomo III. México: 1857.

1645   Jesús. Relación de lo sucedido en este reino de la Vizcaya desde el año de 1644 hasta el de 45 acerca de los alzamientos, daños, robos, hurtos muertes y lugares despoblados de que se saco un traslado para remitir al padre Francisco Calderón, provincial de la provincia de Mexico de la Compañía de Jesús. . . . Nicolás de Zepeda, San Miguel de las Bocas, abril 28 de 1645, más addendum de 11 de septiembre de 1645. Cuarta Serie, Tomo III. México: 1857.

1653   Carta que escribió el padre Gáspar de Contreras al padre provincial Francisco Calderón el año de 1653, Parras, 1 de mayo de 1653. Cuarta Serie, Tomo III. México: 1857.

1667a   Mandamiento del Señor Virey, Marqués de Mancera, sobre las doctrinas de Casas-Grandes que estaban en los Yumas, Jurisdicción de San Felipe del Parral. Plus enclosures: carta de Antonio de Oca Sarmiento, Guadiana, Septiembre 22 de 1667, y carta de Francisco de Gorráez Beaumont, México, Octubre 25 de 1667. Cuarta Serie, Tomo III. México: 1857.

1667b   Otra Carta. Antonio de Oca Sarmiento, Guadiana, septembre 22 de 1667. Cuarta Serie, Tomo III. México: 1857.

1668   Memorial del Padre Procur-

DHM

ador General de la Orden de San Francisco. Fr. Antonio Carrillo. Plus enclosures: decretos, parecer, Auto de Junta, e Informe de Oficiales Reales de Durango con fechas entre setiembre 22 de 1668 y agosto 17 de 1669. Cuarta Serie, Tomo III. México: 1857.

1669   Patrocinio del glorioso apóstol de las indias S. Francisco Javier en el reino de la Nueva Vizcaya, año de 1669. Accompanying Auto dated 4 de Diciembre de 1668, por D. Antonio de Oca Sarmiento. Cuarta Serie, Tomo III. México: 1857.

1704   Escrito a S.E. México, Agosto 4 de 1704. Francisco Cuervo y Valdés, Gregorio de Salinas Baraona, Juan Ignacio de la Vega y Sotomayor, Martín de Sabalza, Juan de Salaises. Cuarta Serie, Tomo IV. México: 1857.

ca 1706   Carta de un Padre Ex-Jesuita [no date, no place, no signature]. Cuarta Serie, Tomo IV. México: 1857.

ca 1720   Petición que contiene importantes noticias del Parral de Manuel San Juan de Santa Cruz. Cuarta Serie, Tomo IV. México: 1857.

1748   Informe acerca de los presidios de la Nueva Vizcaya. José de Berroterán, México, abril 17 de 1748. Segunda serie, Tomo I. México, 1854.

18th.a   Descripción de la Nueva-Vizcaya. Cuarta Serie, Tomo III. México: 1857.

18th.b   Primeras misiones de la Vizcaya. Cuarta Serie, Tomo III. México: 1857.

Documents Division, University of Texas, Austin, Texas.

UTD 1592-1643   1592-1643. Vol. 12. Cunningham Transcripts. AGI 66-6-17, Audiencia de Guadalajara. Comision y conducta de los servisios de Capitan General de la Nueva Galicia por los Senores Virreyes — Junio — 1607.

1648   Vol. 14. Cunningham Transcripts. AGI 66-6-17, Audiencia de Guadalajara. [1648: correspondencia de Nueva Vizcaya.]

1671-1685   1671-1685. Vol. 66. Dunn Transcripts. AGI 58-4-13, Audiencia de Mexico. Durango -- Consultas que hizo el Gobernador de la Nueva Vizcaya al Virrey tocantes a la seguridad y defensa de aquella Provincia. Bino sin Carta. Informe que hizo a Su Magestad el Governador Don Antonio de Oca.

1683-1697   1683-1697. Vol. 16. Nuevo Mexico. AGI 67-4-11, Audiencia de Guadalajara. [1688: correspondencia de Nueva Vizcaya.]

1701-1730   1701-1730. Vol. 22. Cunningham Transcripts. AGI 67-3-29, Audiencia de Guadalajara. Superior Gob.no, 1746, Quaderno 6°. Testimonio de los autos fechos a consulta de Don Joseph Velarde Cosio Theniente de Governador del Reino de la Nueva Viscaya, sobre la visita executada en los veinte y dos Pueblos por Don Joseph de Berroteran Capitan del Presidio de Conchos — Secretario Don Joseph de Gorraez.

1707   1707. Vol. 77. Dunn Transcripts. AGI, 62-2-29, Audiencia de Mexico. [Report on Missions of Nuevo Leon.]

UTD 1710-1738a   1710-1738. Vol. 23. Dunn Transcripts. AGI 67-3-12, Audiencia de Guadalajara. 1726. Testimonio de los Auttos fhos sobre la Sublevacion, y Alzamiento de los Yndios Sumas; de las Misiones de SnTiago de la Zienega de el Coyame, y Junta de el Nortte — Presentado con memorial de fray Francisco Seco, Procurador general de Yndias del orden de San Francisco.

1710-1738b   1710-1738. Vol. 23. Dunn Transcripts. AGI 67-2-2, Audiencia de Guadalajara. Real Cedula, Buen Retiro, Marzo 2 de 1726, al virrey de la Nueva Espana.

1710-1738c   1710-1738. Vol. 23. Dunn Transcripts. AGI 104-6-15, Audiencia de Guadalajara. Copia del Diario de la Campana executada de orden del Exmo Senor Marques de Casafuerte, por Dn Joseph Berroteran Capitan del Presidio de Conchos, para el reconocimiento de las Margenes del Rio del Norte, en el ano de 1729.

1713-1721   1713-1721. Vol. 80. AGI 61-6-35, Audiencia de Mexico. (A) carta de fray Antonio de San Buenaventura Oliuares, al Gobernador Martin de Alarcon, ministro de San Juan Baptista, Junio 5, 1717. (B) Carta de Domingo Ramon, Provincia de Tejas, 22 de julio de 1716. (C) Pagos a los presidios de las cajas reales, Mexico, 30 de diciembre de 1717.

1730-1736   1730-1736. Vol. 82. Dunn Transcripts. AGI 62-1-41, Audiencia de Mexico. [carta e informe sobre indios] Joseph Antonio Fernandez de

UTD

1733-1738
Jauregui Urrutia al Virrey. Mexico, enero 11 de 1735, y Monterrey, 23 de abril, 1735. 1733-1738. Vol. 84. Coahuila. AGI 61-2-18, Audiencia de Mexico. Diario y Derrotero de Blas de la Barza Galcon Governador de Coahuila y Joseph Antonio de Ecay y Musquis, Capitan del Presidio de San Juan Bautista del Rio Grande; [includes] Padron de la Mission de San Juan Bautista, 1734, firmado por Fr. Miguel Sebillano de Paredes, 18 de marzo, 1734.

1749a
AGN, Historia, tomo 52. Nueva Vizcaya, Ano de 1749. Autos fechos sobre la desercion de los tres Indios, Matheo, Gabriel y Aguilar de la Nacion Sisimbres Con Maria Antonia y Francisca de Paula Mugeres de Matheo y Gabriel que desertaron del Pueblo de Conchos, y Cargos que sobre ello se le hicieron al Capitan del Presidio de este nombre Dn Joseph de Berroteran, Por, El Senor Governador y Capitan General de este Reyno—.

1749b
Vol. 20. AGI 89-2-23, Audiencia de Mexico. Sup.or Govierno, 1749. Consultta del Governador de la nueva Vizcaya en que informa el esttado de los Presidios de

UTD

1755-1760
aquella Governacion, y resolucion tomada sobre la extincion de los Presidios de la Cordillera. S.rio Dn Joseph Gorraez. 1755-1760. Vol. 30. AGI 194 (67-5-3), Audiencia de Guadalajara. Testimonio de consulta hecho por Don Alonzo Castessi Governador que fue de este Reyno a el Senor Don Matheo Antonio de Mendoza Cavallero profeso de el orden de Santhiago Coronel de Dragones de los Reales Exercitos Governador y Cappitan General de este Reyno de la nueva Vizcaya sobre el estado en que se halla esta Provincia.

Latin American Collection, University of Texas, Austin, Texas.

UTL 1706...
Janos Collection: Folder 1, Section 1 [beg. 1706].

Parish Archive of Valle de Allende (San Bartolomé), Chihuahua.

Baptismal, Burial, and Marriage Records.

Texas Western College, El Paso, Texas (courtesy of Mr. Rex Gerald).

TWC 1738
El Gobernador Manuel de Urango, San Felipe el Real, 29 de augosto, 1738. [Janos Collection, Reel 1, film 9, frames 12-16; courtesy of Mr. Rex Gerald, Museum of Texas Western College, El Paso].

Published Works

Alegre, S. J., Francisco Javier
1956, *Historia de la Compañia de Jesús*
1959 *en Nueva España.* Tomos I, II, III, Nueva Edición por Ernest J. Burrus, S. J., y Felix Zubiliaga, S. J. (1956-1959). Institutum Historicum S. J., Roma.

Alessio Robles, Vito
1938 *Coahuila y Texas en la época colonial.* Editorial Cultura, México.

Arlegui, Joseph
1851 *Chrónica de la provincia de N.S.P.S. Francisco de Zacatecas.* J. B. de Hogal, México.

Balcarcel, Antonio de
n.d.   La conquista de Coahuila. In *Periódicos Varios,* edited by Manuel Redonvar.

Barra y Valencia
1944   *Raíces etimológicas del idioma náhuatl.* Ediciones "Educación." México, D.F.

Bolton, Herbert Eugene
1916   *Spanish Explorations in the Southwest, 1542-1706.* Charles Scribner's Sons, New York.

Bancroft, Hubert Howe
1884,   *History of Texas and the North Mexican*
1889   *States.* 2 vols. The History Company, San Francisco.

Bosque, Fernando del
1916   The Bosque-Larios Expedition (1675). In *Spanish Explorations in the Southwest,* edited by H. E. Bolton, pp. 281-308. Charles Scribner's Sons, New York.

Decorme, Gerard
1941   *La Obra de los Jesuitas mexicanos durante la época colonial, 1572-1767.* 2 vols. Antigua Libreria Robredo de J. Porrúa e Hijos, Mexico.

Dunne, Peter Masten, S.J.
1944   *Pioneer Jesuits in Northern Mexico.* University of California Press, Berkeley.

1948   *Early Jesuit Missions in the Tarahumara.* University of California Press, Berkeley.

Forbes, Jack D.
1959   The Appearance of the Mounted Indian in Northern Mexico and the Southwest, to 1680. *Southwestern Journal of Anthropology,* Vol. 15, No. 2, pp. 189-212.

Frake, Charles O.
1962   Cultural Ecology and Ethnography. *American Anthropologist,* Vol. 64, No. 1, pp. 53-59.

García, Genaro (editor)
1909   Historia de Nuevo León, con noticias sobre Coahuila, Texas, Nuevo México. Por Alonso de León. En *Documentos inéditos o muy raros para la Historia de Mexico,* Tomo 25. Bouret, Mexico.

Hackett, Charles Wilson (editor and translator).
1926   *Historical Documents Relating to New Mexico, Nueva Vizcaya, and Approaches Thereto, to 1773,* Vol. 2. Carnegie Institution of Washington, Washington, D.C.

Haring, Clarence Henry
1947   *The Spanish Empire in America.* Oxford University Press, London.

Hockett, Charles F., and Robert Ascher
1964   The Human Revolution. *Current Anthropology,* Vol. 5, No. 3, pp. 153-68.

Hoyo, Eugenio del
n.d.   *Vocablos de la Lengua Quinigua de los Indios Borrados del Noreste de México.* (Inédito). [Instituto Technológico de Monterrey, N.L.]

Huerta Preciado, María Teresa
1963   *Rebeliones indígenas en el noreste de México en la época colonial.* Tesis, Universidad Nacional Autónoma de México, Facultad de Filosofía y Letras, México, D.F.

James, Preston
1950   *Latin America* (revised edition). The Odyssey Press, New York.

Jiménez Moreno, Wigberto
1958   *Estudios de historia colonial.* Instituto Nacional de Anthropologia e Historia, México, D.F.

Kroeber, Alfred L.
1934   Uto-Aztecan Languages of Mexico. *Ibero-Americana,* No. 8. University of California Press, Berkeley.

Lafora, Nicolás
1939   *Relación del Viaje que hizo a los Presidios Internos en la Frontera de la América Septentrional, perteneciente al Rey de España.* P. Robredo, México.

1958   Relación del viaje que hizo a los presidios internos situados en la frontera de la América septentrional, perteneciente al rey de España. In *Viajes y viajeros; viajes por Norteamérica.* Aguilar, Madrid.

las Casas, Gonzalo de
   1936   Noticias de los Chichimecas y justicia de la guerra que se les ha hecho por los españoles. In *Trimborn, Hermann, Quellen zur Kulturgeschicte des präkolumbischen America*. Strecker und Schröder, Stuttgart.

Martínez del Río, Pablo
   1954   La comarca lagunera a fines del siglo XVI y principios del XVII según las fuentes escritas. *Publicaciones del Instituto de Historia*, I, 30. Universidad Nacional Autónoma de México, México.

Massey, William C.
   1949   Tribes and Languages of Baja California. *Southwestern Journal of Anthropology*, Vol. 5, No. 3.

Mecham, John Lloyd
   1927   *Francisco de Ibarra and Nueva Vizcaya.* Duke University Press, Durham.

Molina, Alonso de
   1944   *Vocabulario de la lengua castellana y mexicana.* 2 vols. (México 1571). Madrid.

Morfi, Juan Agustín
   1958   Viaje de indios y diario del Nuevo México. In: *Viajes y viajeros; viajes por Northeamérica.* Aguilar, Madrid.

Mota y Escobar, Don Alonso de la
   1940   *Descripción geográfica de los reinos de Nueva Galicia, Nueva Vizcaya y Nuevo León.* Segunda Edición. Editorial Pedro Robredo, México, D.F.

Nadel, S. F.
   1957   *The Theory of Social Structure.* The Free Press, Glencoe.

Newcomb, W. W., Jr.
   1960   Toward an Understanding of War. In *Essays in the Science of Culture, in Honor of Leslie A. White*, edited by Gertrude E. Dole and Robert L. Carneiro. Thomas Y. Crowell Company, New York.

Orozco y Berra, Manuel
   1864   *Geografía de las lenguas y carta etnográfica de México.* Imprenta de J. M. Andrade y F. Escalante, México.

Parsons, Talcott
   1957   General Theory in Sociology. In *Sociology Today, Problems and Prospects*, edited by Robert K. Merton, Leonard Broom, and Leonard S. Cattrell, Jr. Basic Books, Inc., New York.

Pérez de Ribas, Andrés
   1645   *Historia de los triunphos de nuestra santa fee entre gentes las mas bárbaras y fieras del Nuevo Orbe.* A. de Paredes, Madrid.

Pike, Kenneth L.
   1954,   *Language in Relation to a Unified Theory*
   1955,   *of the Structure of Human Behavior*,
   1960   Vols, I, II and III. Summer Institute of Linguistics, Glendale.

Pike, Zebulon M.
   1810   *An Account of Expeditions to the Sources of the Mississippi.* Bonsal, Conrad and Co., Petersburgh.

Portillo, Esteban L.
   1887   *Apuntes para la historia antigua de Coahuila y Texas.* Saltillo.

Powell, Philip Wayne
   1952   *Soldiers, Indians and Silver.* University of California Press, Berkeley.

Radcliffe-Brown, A. R.
   1952   *Structure and Function in Primitive Society.* The Free Press, Glencoe.

Reed, Erik K.
   1955   Bison Beyond the Pecos. *The Texas Journal of Science*, Vol. VII, No. 2.

Riezgo et al.
   1822   *Memoria sobre las proporciones naturales de las Provincias Internas Occidentales, causas de que han provenido sus atrasos, providencias tomadas con el fin de lograr su remedio, y las que por ahora se consideran oportunas para mejorar su estado, e ir proporcionando su futura felicidad.* Formada por los Diputados de dhas Provincias, que la subscriben.

Riezgo (cont.)

Imprenta de D. José María Ramos Palomera. [The date and name that appear on the last page are: México, 1 de julio de 1822; Juan Miguel Riezgo, Salvador Porras, Francisco Velasco, Manuel José de Zuloaga.]

Ruecking, Frederick, Jr.
1954   Bands and Band-Clusters of the Coahuiltlecan Indians. *Student Papers in Anthropology,* Vol. I, No. 2. University of Texas, Austin.

Sahlins, Marshall D., and Elman R. Service (eds.).
1960   *Evolution and Culture.* The University of Michigan Press, Ann Arbor.

Saravia, Atanasio G.
1956   *Apuntes para la historia de la Nueva Vizcaya.* Tomo 3, Las Sublevaciones. Impreso Reveles, México.

Sauer, Carl O.
1934   The Distribution of Aboriginal Tribes and Languages in Northwest Mexico. *Ibero-Americana,* No. 5. University of California Press, Berkeley.

Secoy, Frank Raymond
1953   Changing Military Patterns of the Great Plains. *Monographs of the American Ethnological Society,* XXI. J. J. Augustin, New York.

Service, Elman R.
1962   *Primitive Social Organization.* Random House, New York.

Spicer, Edward H.
1961   Types of Contact and Processes of Change. In *Perspectives in American Indian Culture Change,* edited by Edward H. Spicer. University of Chicago Press.

Tamarón y Romeral, Pedro
1937   *Demostración del vastísimo obispado de la Nueva Vizcaya.* (Biblioteca Mexicana de Obras Inéditas, 7. 1765). Antigua

Librería Robredo, de José Porrúa e Hijos, México.

Tamayo, Jorge L.
1949   *Geografía general de México.* Vols. I and II, plus Atlas. Francisco Cervantes, México.

Tello, Antonio
1866   Fragmentos de una historia de la Nueva Galicia, escrita hacia 1650, por el padre fray Antonio Tello de la orden de San Francisco. *Colección de documentos para la historia de México,* Tomo Segundo, publicada por Joaquín García Icazbalceta. Antigua Librería, México.

1891   *Libro segundo de la crónica miscelánea, en que se trata de la conquista espiritual y temporal de la santa provincia de Xalisco en el Nuevo Reino de la Galicia y Nueva Viscaya.* Guadalajara.

Vivó, Jorge A.
1949   *Geografía de México.* Fondo de Cultura Económica, México.

Vogt, Evon Z.
1961   Navaho. In *Perspectives in American Indian Culture Change,* edited by Edward H. Spicer. University of Chicago Press, Chicago.

Wallace, Anthony F.C.
1956   Revitalization Movements. *American Anthropologist,* Vol. 58, No. 2, pp. 264-81.

1961   *Culture and Personality.* Random House, New York.

Wallén, C. C.
1956   Fluctuations and Variability in Mexican Rainfall. In *The Future of Arid Lands,* edited by Gilbert F. White. American Association for the Advancement of Science, Washington, D.C.

West, Robert C.
1949   The Mining Community in Northern New Spain. *Ibero-Americana,* No. 30. University of California Press, Berkeley.